Trans-Atlantic Passages

The New Urban Atlantic
Edited by Elizabeth A. Fay

The New Urban Atlantic is a new series of monographs, texts, and essay collections focusing on urban, Atlantic, and hemispheric studies. Distinct from the nation-state mentality, the Atlantic world has been from colonial times a fluid international entity, including multiple Atlantic systems such as the triangle trade and cacao trade that extended globally. The series is distinct in three prime ways: First, it offers a multidisciplinary, multicultural, broadly historical, and urban focus. Second, it extends the geographical boundaries from an Old World/New World binary to the entire Atlantic rim, the arctics, and to exchanges between continents other than Europe and North America. Third, it emphasizes the Atlantic World as distinct from the nation-states that participate in it. Ultimately, The New Urban Atlantic series challenges the conventional boundaries of the field by presenting the Atlantic World as an evolving reality.

Creole Testimonies: Slave Narratives from the British West Indies, 1709–1838
Nicole N. Aljoe

Stumbling towards the Constitution: The Economic Consequences of Freedom in the Atlantic World
Jonathan M. Chu

Urban Identity and the Atlantic World
Edited by Elizabeth A. Fay and Leonard von Morzé

The Transatlantic Eco-Romanticism of Gary Snyder
Paige Tovey

Hospitality and the Transatlantic Imagination, 1815–1835
Cynthia Schoolar Williams

Trans-Atlantic Passages: Philip Hale on the Boston Symphony Orchestra, 1889–1933
Jon Ceander Mitchell

Trans-Atlantic Passages

Philip Hale on the Boston Symphony Orchestra 1889–1933

JonCeander Mitchell

TRANS-ATLANTIC PASSAGES
Copyright © Jon Ceander Mitchell, 2014.

All rights reserved.

First published in 2014 by
PALGRAVE MACMILLAN®
in the United States—a division of St. Martin's Press LLC,
175 Fifth Avenue, New York, NY 10010.

Where this book is distributed in the UK, Europe and the rest of the world, this is by Palgrave Macmillan, a division of Macmillan Publishers Limited, registered in England, company number 785998, of Houndmills, Basingstoke, Hampshire RG21 6XS.

Palgrave Macmillan is the global academic imprint of the above companies and has companies and representatives throughout the world.

Palgrave® and Macmillan® are registered trademarks in the United States, the United Kingdom, Europe and other countries.

ISBN: 978–1–137–45349–5

Library of Congress Cataloging-in-Publication Data is available from the Library of Congress.

A catalogue record of the book is available from the British Library.

Design by Newgen Knowledge Works (P) Ltd., Chennai, India.

First edition: December 2014

10 9 8 7 6 5 4 3 2 1

Transferred to Digital Printing in 2015

To Bridget and Barbara

Contents

List of Figures — ix

Acknowledgments — xi

Series Introduction — xiii

Introduction — 1

Part I

1 1854–1889 — 9
   Norwich—Northampton—Exeter—Walt Whitman—Yale—Albany—Studies in Europe—Marriage— Return to Albany

2 1889–1900 — 21
   Musical Life in Boston to 1881—Higginson—The Boston Symphony Orchestra and its Early Influence—Boston in 1889—Hale's Arrival—Boston Critics—*Boston Home Journal*—St. Botolph's Club—*Boston Post*—*Boston Musical Herald*—*Boston Journal*—A False Start—Nikisch—The Dvořák Controversy—Paur—Gericke—*The Musical Record*

3 1900–1903 — 63
   Symphony Hall—The Longy Club—Boston Pops—Entr'acte—Reinstatement as Program Annotator—Correspondence in Periodicals Regarding Hale—*Musical World*

4 1903–1917 — 81
   The Boston Herald—On the Criticism of Music—*Salome*—On Various Conductors—Muck—Fiedler—Mahler—The Tavern Club and the Thursday Evening Club—Boston Opera—Early Recordings

5 1917–1933 — 123
   Muck's Arrest and Fallout—Monteux—The Fradkin Incident—The Strike and Its Aftermath - Burgin—*New York Times* offer—Hayes - Koussevitzky—Guest Conductors—Boston Symphony Orchestra's 50th Anniversary—Henschel's Return—Commissioned Works—Final Reviews

6	Aftermath and Conclusion: 1933–1936 Retirement—Hale's Passing—Testimonials	171

Part II Selected Writings of Philip Hale

Appendix I	Essays in the Boston Symphony Orchestra Program Booklets	183
Appendix II	Essays from Newspapers	193
Appendix III	Concert Reviews and Extracts in Newspapers	213
	A. Composers and Their Works	213
	B. Conductors	238
	C. Soloists	250
Appendix IV	Columns on Sundry Topics	255
Notes		263
Bibliography		277
Index		283

Figures

1. Philip Hale's childhood home, "The Gables," Round Hill, Northampton, MA. Author's private collection.   176
2. Walt Whitman's inscription from *Leaves of Grass* in the cover of *Quarante Mélodies Choises de F. Schubert*, given by him to Philip Hale. Mortimer Rare Book Room, Smith College, Northampton, MA.   176
3. Philip Hale, n.d. [probably 1890s]. Mortimer Rare Book Room, Smith College, Northampton, MA.   177
4. "Tanglewild," Philip Hale's summer home at Osterville, MA. Mortimer Rare Book Room, Smith College, Northampton, MA.   177
5. Philip Hale, Bachrach Studios, 1914. Boston Symphony Orchestra Archives, Boston, MA.   178

Acknowledgments

First and foremost, the author wishes to thank Bridget Carr, Senior Archivist extraordinaire for the Boston Symphony Orchestra, and her assistant Barbara Perkel, the dedicatees of this book, who have offered never-ending help, guidance, and humor—not only for the present book, but for past projects as well. Also to be mentioned are Robert Miller and Richard Fletcher, members of the BSO Archives Thursday "crazies," as well as Brian Bell, for their strong moral support.

The author also wishes to extend his thanks to three people at University of Massachusetts Boston, his home institution: Emily McDermott, Dean of the College of Liberal Arts; Robert Lublin, Chair of the Department of Performing Arts; and Diana Lewis Burgin, Professor of Russian and daughter of Richard Burgin, Boston Symphony Orchestra concertmaster from 1920 to 1962.

Expressions of gratitude also go to Janice Mahinka, herself a Philip Hale scholar, Laura Pruett of Merrimack College, Jane Winton, Curator, Print Department of the Boston Public Library, Diane Ota, Curator of Music at the Boston Public Library, Maria Serpa of Boston University's Mugar Library, Karen Kukil, Associate Curator of Special Collections at the Neilson Library Mortimer Rare Book Room at Smith College, Andrea Cronin, Dan Hinchen, Betsy Boyle and Sabina Beauchard of the Massachusetts Historical Society, Emily Walhout of Harvard University's Houghton Library, Richard Vallone of New England Conservatory of Music's Spaulding Library, as well as to personnel at the New York State Library in Albany, New York and at the Providence, Rhode Island Public Library.

Finally, a big thank you goes to my wife Ester, who has always been there for me during countless conducting and research projects throughout the years.

Series Introduction

"The New Urban Atlantic"

SeriesEd itor: Elizabeth Fay,
University of Massachusetts Boston

Since its inception, the study of the Atlantic World has been premised on the important advances in sixteenth-century technology that made transatlantic voyages possible. Colonization of the North American coast, the establishment of plantations in the Caribbean, European adoption of African slave trade practices, and the subsequent triangle trade network have formed the mainstay of this field. *The New Urban Atlantic* adds to this set of interests by focusing on the cities (both persistent and failed) that have functioned as important nodal points for Atlantic financial, trade, diplomatic, and cultural networks. Attention to Atlantic cities, the frameworks that identify their similarities and connections both synchronically and diachronically, and their divergences from such norms expand research opportunities by allowing new questions to be asked and new problems to be posed.

Methodologically the books in *The New Urban Atlantic* will engage the interdisciplinary fields of literature and cultural history, with the historical framed by the *longue durée* of geophysical realities, the environment, and changes in that environment that have impacted human experience, and the cultural construed as the representational forms and systems that arose out of Atlantic rim interaction. Within this historio-cultural framework, the urban is meant to encompass both coastal and riverine settlements wherever large tributaries provided access to Atlantic commerce in all its senses. Another methodological feature of the series is the attention, wherever possible, to indigenous and Western immigrant cultures in dynamic and multidirectional relations with each other, as well as with preexisting histories of coastal and riverine trade, political, and social networks on all four continents and Caribbean islands, to produce a new cultural arena—the Atlantic World. In consequence of both of these attributes, the historio-cultural framework and attention to multicultural interaction, individual volumes in the series will contribute to its broad purpose of bringing precontact and colonial cultural history in conversation with work on the modern era, and with today's contemporary mediations of sociocultural, environmental, economic, and technological challenges to the Atlantic World.

In addition to an extended historical perimeter of inquiry, *The New Urban Atlantic* is also framed by hemispheric interactivity in cultural networks, trade networks, and global commerce in goods, ideas, and peoples. Of utmost importance to this conception of Atlanticism, as the series' second methodological feature underscores, are interactions and exchanges among indigenous and immigrant peoples in both hemispheres, and the mutual histories these engagements produced. Although contributions of British and Dutch colonizing projects continue to inform understandings of Atlantic systems, these must be seen in relation to Spanish and Portuguese imperial projects, as well as other culturally conditioned contacts and engagements. Moreover, if the Atlantic World is an ongoing yet changeable locus of systems, networks, and identities across and between two hemispheres and four continents, it is furthermore constituted as a system within the larger framework of world systems, and is thus always in dialogue with global networks, especially in terms of trade and technological circuits.

Books in *The New Urban Atlantic* will treat the Atlantic World as a still-ongoing reality that distinguishes the Atlantic rim by its shared concerns and maritime-oriented identity. Cities such as Halifax, Montreal, Albany, Boston, New Bedford, New York, Cahokia, Charleston, Mexico City, Santo Domingo, Rio de Janeiro, Dakar, Lisbon, Amsterdam, Liverpool, or Copenhagen may be defined according to many local, regional, and national factors, but are also conditioned by their geographic location on the edge of a great ocean or with riverine access to it. Whatever other economic, social, or cultural patterns of exchange in which they are hubs, such cities are also characterized by particular relationships that are best understood as part of Atlantic systems. In this sense, through a focus on cities *The New Urban Atlantic* can also foreground urban effects on the environment for both land and ocean ecologies. The transplantation of botanical specimens, importation of livestock, changes in agricultural techniques on city perimeters, and fouling of waterways are just some of the ways in which the Old World–New World interactions have had profound and continuing effects on the Atlantic World. These continued effects influence global environmental activity just as the Atlantic World has been and continues to be conditioned by that activity.

Introduction

Philip Hale was one of the world's greatest arts critics. A citation accompanying his Scholarship Award from the Sigma Delti Chi professional journalistic society in 1932 identified him as:

> ...The Most Learned of American Music Critics, whose authoritative critiques and historical commentaries have been for a generation source material for students and writers in his field; a splendid influence alike upon the musical and journalistic world and upon the stage, as a result of his scholarship and the catholicity of his taste, neither of which has been dulled by time.[1]

Hale considered himself a newspaper man, but he was much more than that. Though he never wrote a book, he was one of the most frequently read American writers of the late nineteenth and early twentieth centuries. His influence was far reaching, affecting people from all walks of life on both sides of the Atlantic. He wrote what he thought, supporting his opinions with research. When it came to making recommendations—from suggesting additional reading material to his clientele, to advising the Harvard University board on prospective music professors, to advocating certain conductors for the Boston Symphony Orchestra—he did not waffle, though over the course of time he occasionally changed his mind.

To say that Hale produced an enormous quantity of work would be shortchanging the reality of the situation. The numbers are staggering: 795 program books (more than thirty-three years' worth) of 2,000 to 4,000 words each for Boston Symphony Orchestra concerts, 1056 weekly Boston Symphony Orchestra concert newspaper reviews (forty-four years' worth) of approximately 1,200 words each, reviews of similar length of the performances of other professional musical organizations in Boston (such as the Longy Club and the Boston Opera Company), reviews of visiting professional organizations (such as Paul Whiteman's Concert Orchestra or the New York Philharmonic), weekly musical essays for the Sunday editions of newspapers, theatre reviews, as well as weekly (and, for a while, daily) columns on sundry topics, from humorous discussions about prohibition to the historical use of the napkin. With a journalistic career spanning fifty-five years—sixty, if articles written during his student days at Yale are counted—his eloquent, erudite, and witty style of writing left its mark on millions of readers throughout the English-speaking world.

Yet Hale himself was not confined to English. He was fluent in German and French, and had at least a reading comprehension of Spanish and Italian. In 1882, after four years of employment at the *Albany Times* (the last two during which he was simultaneously practicing law), Hale went to Europe and spent the next five years doing advanced musical study there, for opportunities to do so in America were extremely limited at that time. This firsthand exposure to societies with refined artistic culture allowed Hale to import and apply a vast amount of knowledge and experience to his writings. His own trans-Atlantic connections, then, fed the artistic cravings of Americans willing to partake of the literary morsels from his pen.

Hale's career spanned parts of seven decades and the transformation of society during those years was phenomenal. The world of 1878 was one of relative simplicity; the United States had fewer than 50,000,000 people and only thirty-nine states. Travel was either by horse-and-carriage or by rail; streets were lit by lanterns. There was the telegraph, but telephones and phonographs were extremely rare (having just been invented). There was photography, but no motion pictures. For the most part, the only way that one could find out what was happening in the world was by reading the newspaper. Brahms, Tchaikovsky, and Wagner were in their heyday, but Schönberg was only a child, and Bartok, Stravinsky, and Shostakovitch had not yet been born.

By the time Hale retired in 1933 the country boasted forty-eight states with 125,000,000 people. Most families owned automobiles, telephones, and phonographs. Electronic recordings, sound motion pictures, and radio broadcasts of symphony concerts (often featuring the works of twentieth-century composers) were now commonplace. The world as a whole, however, was in a difficult state, in the throngs of a deep depression and with the rise of the Nazi party in Germany. Social Security was still a year or two away, though Hale's late retirement at seventy-nine was due to health issues, not monetary need. His personality drove him to continue working almost until the very end of his life.

Over the course of his long career, Hale was music critic for a number of newspapers on or near the Atlantic seaboard, including the *Albany Times* (1878–1882 and 1887–1889), *Albany Union* (1887–1889), *Boston Home Journal* (1889–1890), *Boston Post* (1890–1891), *Boston Journal* (1891–1903), and finally the *Boston Herald* (1903–1933) where, from 1908, he doubled as drama critic. For a brief period he also edited two music journals, *Musical Record* (1897–1901) and *Musical World* (1901–1902), served as an associate editor for the *Boston Musical Herald* (1891–1893) and provided articles for New York's *Musical Courier* and the *Looker-on*.

Hale's longest tenure at writing about music, however, was not as a newspaper critic, but as programme essayist for the Boston Symphony Orchestra, briefly in 1891, and then uninterruptedly from 1901 to 1933. Hale reviewed every concert that the orchestra had played since 1889, but his real clout as a critic, both internal and external, stemmed from this literary association with the orchestra.

From his gallery seat Hale observed eight of the Boston Symphony Orchestra's principal conductors during their tenures: Arthur Nikisch, Emil Paur, Wilhelm Gericke, Karl Muck, Max Fiedler, Henri Rabaud, Pierre Monteux, and Serge Koussevitzky. He also saw their first conductor Georg Henschel on at least two return engagements. There were other conductors as well, including Richard Burgin (the orchestra's concertmaster from 1920 to 1962), Thomas Beecham, Henry Hadley, Gustav Holst, Richard Strauss, Bruno Walter, and Felix

Weingartner. In addition, Hale observed some of the world's finest soloists. This almost endless string included such virtuosi as Bela Bartok, Amy Beach, Nadia Boulanger, Ferrucio Busoni, Teresa Carreño, George Gershwin, Walter Gieseking, Percy Grainger, Lady Halle, Roland Hayes, Ignatz Paderewski, Gregor Piatagorsky, Maud Powell, Sergei Rachmaninoff, Artur Rubinstein, Jesus Maria Sanromá, Xaver Scharwenka, Artur Schnabel, and Lionel Tertis.

Hale actually met many of these musicians, as well as other famous international arts figures from both sides of the Atlantic, at one of the three social clubs to which he belonged. At the turn of the twentieth century the Boston arts scene was dominated by the Boston Brahmins, a close-knit group of upper class families with roots extending back to Colonial days—a type of upscale British diaspora. Membership in their clubs was by invitation only, yet they offered Boston a sense of cultural refinement that the city otherwise may not have had. Though born in Vermont, Hale became a Boston Brahmin via these club associations. As a result, some writers have accused Hale of being a snob, but this was not the case. Olin Downes commented:

> The sense of human fellowship and adventure was strong in him. He felt the truth of art from the same source which made him so shrewd an appraiser of books and fellow beings. If a man or woman were real, that was enough and to spare for him. When he talked at the Tavern Club, the choicest spirits paused to listen, but he was fond of recalling his experiences as a police reporter and he liked to get away from his desk and go down to the wharves on Atlantic Avenue and swap yarns with the longshoremen. He knew that Mozart was a man pulsing with all the human weaknesses, impulses and needs, not only the glorious boy who wrote the Jupiter Symphony. His reading ranged all the way from Mark Twain and Artemus Ward, whom he adored, to Verlaine and Maliarmé, with their reveries of the antique world and their strange and haunting overtones of the subconscious existence. The man was even more than the writing. You'd go far to read Philip Hale, and farther still to chat with him on the way to the office on the back end of a street-car.[2]

It is said that, to a point, music critics determine the repertoire. Hale was always advocating its expansion and during his years as an active critic, the repertoire of the Boston Symphony Orchestra metamorphosed from the severely Germanic programming of Nikisch into the more eclectic mix offered by Monteux and Koussevitzky. It was often a challenge for him to find something new to say about works that were frequently performed (e.g., he heard Beethoven's Fifth Symphony played over thirty times) and, as time went by, he devoted more and more space in his columns either to works receiving their Boston premieres or to particulars concerning the featured soloists' performances.

Sometimes Hale would change his mind about a composition. On December 6, 1894 a concert was given in memory of the legendary pianist and composer Anton Rubinstein (1829–1894). Mrs Ernest Lent was the featured soloist in a performance of the composer's *Piano Concerto No. 4 in D minor*, Op. 70. Hale had the following to say:

> There was a peculiar fitness in giving the D minor concerto at a concert in memory of the great Russian, for the concerto is the most sustained, the noblest of his compositions of long breath. Here is no decrescendo of interest, as there is in so many

of his other works. Indeed this concerto for beauty of themes and ingeniousness of treatment stands among the great pieces for piano and orchestra. It is a heroic concerto and it demands a heroic performance.[3]

Fifteen years later, the same concerto was performed by Mme. Olga Samaroff (the stage name of Texas-born Lucy Mary Agnes Hickenlooper):

> Mme. Samaroff by her performance made the dry bones of the concerto to live for a night, and by the simplicity of her reading of the second movement almost succeeded in removing the reproach of sentimentalism. The concerto, alas, is now to be numbered with the music that was once thought to be "advanced," that once gave hearty pleasure. Its themes now seem commonplace, or sugary, or rowdy.[4]

Of interest is the fact that this concerto was performed at Boston Symphony Orchestra concerts no fewer than thirty-eight times before 1922, but has not appeared on any of the orchestra's programs since. It would be presumptuous to think that Hale had anything to do with this, but such a complete turnaround in appraisal was quite uncommon, especially for him.

From time to time critics have also had a large though indirect say in determining conductors. In his *Memoirs* Georg Solti addressed the abuse that Claudia Cassidy, chief music critic of the *Chicago Tribune*, heaped upon Rafael Kubelik, forcing him to resign the conductorship of the Chicago Symphony Orchestra after only three years. Solti himself also felt her wrath; she kept him from being hired by the Chicago Lyric Opera and, when he was approached by members of the Chicago Symphony board about succeeding Fritz Reiner in 1963, he declined at that time, at least partially because of her.[5] The critic's clout was not to be underestimated. Years later, after Cassidy had given up most of her reviewing, Solti established himself as perhaps the most successful conductor that the Chicago Symphony ever had.

Unlike Cassidy, Hale was not vicious; he was much more supportive. He was very critical, however, about what he considered to be poor choices of repertoire, insincerity on the part of self-promoting second-rate performers, cults, coteries, and the occasional lack of sufficient professional preparation. Hale had his own high standards to maintain, yet he was never abusive; he was not out to get anyone.

Hale's reviews often made you wish you were there. Occasionally there would be a performing artist, such as Teresa Carreño, who would connect with all around her through a thoroughly visceral and passionate performance. In instances like this, Hale made sure that his readers felt a connection with his own listening experience. He supported the work of women musicians, whether they were performers, composers or both. He also championed American music of all sorts—if it was good—regardless of the medium of expression. The Sousa Band and the Paul Whiteman Concert Orchestra stood just as much a chance of securing a positive review from him as did the Boston Symphony.

Hale was not without his quirks. His general dislike for the music of Brahms, though readily apparent, has been overstated. The same could be said for his Francophile tendencies. Then there were two ideas of his that, while making sense at the time, would not find favor in today's programming: his advocacy of placing symphonies first and overtures last in the concert order (so as not to wear out the listener's ability to focus) and his recommendation of cutting movements from symphonies or concertos in order to shorten the length of concerts. Whatever the case, Hale always stood by his convictions even though these continued to evolve over time.

Hale's wit was legendary, though the two most famous accounts of it are through secondary sources. According to Nicolas Slonimsky, when Symphony Hall was built in 1900 Hale was credited with suggesting that the new hall's signs reading "Exit in Case of Fire" be changed to "Exit in Case of Brahms."[6] And E. R. Warren commented about Hale hearing a pianist who had contributed nothing of importance to a long program. Not wanting to destroy a career on account of a single performance, Hale wrote a paragraph summarizing the program itself, followed by only four words: "She consumed valuable time."[7] His two general newspaper columns, "Talk of the Day" and "As the World Wags," often displayed the comedic side of his personality. Letters written to him were regular features in these columns and his responses to them foreshadow the style of any number of late-night radio and television personalities.

Hale continued writing reviews and Boston Symphony Orchestra program notes through the spring of 1933, when his eyesight and the use of his right arm failed him. He passed away due to a cerebral hemorrhage on November 30, 1934 at the age of eighty. Though often seen as a controversial figure, Hale was revered during his own lifetime. Perhaps Mark N. Grant said it best:

> To be hailed by Hale into the Boston Symphony Orchestra annals was to be incorporated by other annotators and professional music appreciationists ever after into the composer pantheon.[8]

Thus it could be said that Hale's writings put Boston on the Trans-Atlantic map in terms of the music world and its circuitry of exchange.

In 1935, shortly after Hale's death, his progamme essayist successor John Nagley Burk assembled many of Hale's programme notes and newspaper reviews into his highly respected and oft-consulted volume, *Philip Hale's Boston Symphony Program Notes*.[9] While capturing many of Hale's finest chestnuts, very few complete columns are included within it and therefore many of the entries appear out of context. Also, none of the entries are documented, leaving no indication of when or where in the continuum of Hale's lengthy career they were written.

It was the original intent of the author to write a book that would supplement Burk's, covering Hale's notes and reviews of important works that Burk left out, such as Beethoven's *Piano Concerto No. 3* or Mozart's *Clarinet Concerto*. Also, since 1939, when the second printing came out, other works reviewed by Hale but not included by Burk, such as Gustav Holst's *The Planets* or the Moussorgsky-Ravel *Pictures at an Exhibition*, have gained significantly in reputation and esteem. To simply supplement Burk, however, would have shortchanged Hale both as a person and for his myriad accomplishments; his was truly a creative and productive life. It also would have left out important events in his life—being hired as a music critic, being fired as Boston Symphony programme essayist (only to be rehired a decade later)— as well as significant incidents that impacted it (i.e., the opening of Symphony Hall, the arrest of Boston

Symphony Orchestra conductor Karl Muck, the orchestra strike, and the fiftieth anniversary commissions).

In order to best serve the subject, this book is divided into two parts. The first is a chronological narrative of Hale's life. It is not so much a biography as an account of his life as it affected—and in turn was affected by—events on both sides of the Atlantic. Effort has been made, even in this first part, to allow Hale to say things in his own words, for his command of the English language was second to none. The second part of the book features a selection of Hale's critiques and notes on a variety of topics, including composers and their works, conductors, soloists, and non-musical matters. It is through reading these passages and others by him that one can fully appreciate and experience one of the greatest arts critics the world has ever known.

Part I

1

1854–1889

Though others preceded him, Philip Hale is considered to have been one of the first great American arts critics. He came into the world on March 5, 1854 in Norwich, Vermont, the first-born son of William Bainbridge Hale (1826–1892) and Harriet Amelia Porter Hale (ca. 1826–1872[1]). The family's roots in this country ran very deep; Philip himself was an eighth-generation descendent of one Thomas Hale, who had landed at Salem, Massachusetts in 1634 and settled in nearby Newbury the following year.

William Bainbridge Hale never went to college, but was a self-educated person, possessing a fine business acumen as well as an exceptional command over the English language. The *Springfield Republican* said of him, "Mr. Hale was a man of more than ordinary ability, of wide reading, and possessed an extraordinary gift of language, which at times amounted to eloquence."[2]

Sometime around February 1858, when Philip's younger brother Edward[3] was born, William became president of the First National Bank of Northampton, Massachusetts and the family relocated there. Northampton, a utopian community of about 6,000, had much to offer. Within a short period of time, William had a home of significant proportions constructed for the family:

> In 1860 he hired [Northampton architect William Fenno] Pratt to design a large, ten-gabled, brick home (described by local architect Karl Putnam as a "Gothic Revival in the Tudor Manner" and known locally as "The Gables"). Hale built for his gardener a small Carpenter Gothic cottage, a structure based on one of [Andrew Jackson] Downing's simplest designs, across the street at 38.[4]

"The Gables," located on Round Hill Road, was built only a few hundred yards from the then-future site of Smith College. It is still standing.

In a speech given to the Massachusetts Historical Society in 1923 titled "Musical and Theatrical Life in a New England Village in the Sixties," Philip Hale reflected on the religious, social, and artistic life of Northampton:

> ...It was an industrious, matter-of-fact, temperate, God-fearing community, with parents endeavoring to bring up their children in the nurture and the admonition of the Lord; a reasonably intelligent if somewhat poker-backed and narrow community, with a sprinkling of the more liberal and more cultured; an old-fashioned community—would that there were more of them in New England of today![5]

It was in Northampton that Philip began studying the organ and the piano. This first phase of his music education came to fruition early, for at the age of 14 he began duties as organist of the local Unitarian church.

In the meantime William continued to improve his position in the community. He was instrumental in the founding of Northampton's public library and in 1871 became president and manager of the Florence Sewing Machine Company. His wealth and status in the world he knew meant that he was able to ensure that Philip's schooling would be of the highest caliber. Indeed, starting in 1870 Philip attended the exclusive Phillips Exeter Academy in Exeter, New Hampshire for two years. While there he developed an interest in poetry and literature, particularly in the writings of Walt Whitman.

He wrote to the poet:

> Exeter N-H.
> Sep 14 1871
>
> DearS ir
>
> I have just got your complete works—Ed 1871 and would like to ask you why you did not reprint the preface to the first edition? I have only read extracts from that preface and should like to have seen the whole reprint. I suppose I can not get the old one now at the stores.
>
> I saw the other day that Mr. Swinburne[6] said he enjoyed your "Song from the Sea" more than any of your other works. Did he mean Sea Shore Memories No. 1 – ? The poem of yours that I read over with the most satisfaction is your Burial Hymn of Lincoln—But as my opinion is not worth anything, being a boy I should not have entrusted it upon you—
>
> If you are pressed with time even then I should like to hear from you—just a word.
>
> Yours most respectfully,
> Philip Hale
>
> P.S. Do you know where I could get a 1st Ed with preface?[7]

Thus, even as a teenager, the future program essayist was concerned with having a sense of completeness with the sources that he read and consulted, and Whitman's extensive 30-page preface to *Leaves of Grass* would serve as a source of inspiration to him for years to come.

Following Exeter, Hale studied law at Yale College (later University). During his years there he was involved in a variety of musical activities, including a stint as pianist for the Yale Glee Club; he also received awards in composition. Away from music, Hale was one of the editors of the nascent *Yale Record*, and he contributed four articles—probably his earliest publications—to *The Yale Literary Magazine*. One of these, "Walt Whitman," appeared in the November 1874 issue. After writing some introductory comments, Hale penned the following passage, some of it nearly self-prophetic:

> Fifty-five years ago Walt Whitman was born. Brought up in out-door life, strong, healthy, now a carpenter, now an editor, always one of the people, he became disgusted with our nature literature, and thought that no poet had come forth to sing the praises of true democracy. With sublime egotism

he said to himself, I will be the poet of this land. To fit himself for the task he travelled much, noting the customs of our States. He studied carefully on politics and government. He read the literature of all lands, giving especial attention to the Greek drama, Homer, and the Bible. In 1855 the fruit of his work appeared, a thin book set in type and published by himself. "Leaves of Grass" was for a time thought to be the ravings of a madman. It was called, at once, gross, yet mystical, superficial and deep, as though a New York fireman had absorbed the transcendentalism of the Dial and had expressed it in his own brawny language....

In the author's preface to the 1955 edition, he says:

"To speak in literature with the perfect rectitude and insouciance of the movements of animals. And the unimpeachableness of the sentiment of trees in the woods and grass by the roadside, is the flawless triumph of art. What I tell, I tell for precisely what it is. Let who may exalt or startle, or fascinate, or soothe; I will have purposes, as health, or heat, or snow has, and be as regardless of observation." And Nature found her long-lost poet.[8]

The following year, Hale once again wrote to him:

>9 South College
>New Haven CT
>Oct 7th 1875

Dear Sir: –

I send you a copy of <u>Yale Lit</u> for Nov 74 containing an article "WW." You will see at a glance that it is simply a condensed rehash of Mr. Burrough's "notes"—a Westminster Review article[9] and your Democratic Vistas.[10]

I have not sent it to you before because somehow or other I have not had the courage. I feared lest you have said in "Calamus"[11]—your cautions to would be pupils of yours—might be true.

I hope that you will not be offended at the imperfect way in which I have tried to express my faith in you. I first became acquainted with your books some four or five years ago and from them I have not only learned faith and courage but have become desirous of seeing you yourself. This last pleasure has been denied me; but one of the pleasantest memories of my life is the recollection of an hour passed with your mother in the summer of '72.

The passage marked } is disjointed—for the false delicacy of the Ed's of *Lit* kept out some remarks upon the physical degeneracy of our women.

>Very respectfully,
>Philip Hale

To
Walt Whitman
Camden
N.J.[12]

Early the following summer Hale ordered copies of new editions of Whitman's books.

Thea uthorw rote to him:

> 431 Stevens St.
> Camden, N Jersey
> July 11 [1876?]
>
> My dear Philip Hale,
>
> I have rec'd your PO order for $10 for my books—for which hearty thanks. I send by same mail with this, One Vol. <u>Leaves of Grass</u>—the other Vol. *Two Rivulets*[13] I will send soon as some copies of a new batch are ready (the old ones being all exhausted).
>
> Please inform me (by postal card will do) if this Vol. comes safe.
>
> Walt Whitman[14]

Throughout his life Hale would maintain an appreciation of Whitman's writings, often quoting him in concert reviews. Among the items that he kept until his death was another of Whitman's self-published pamphlets, *After All, Not to Create Only*, a speech given by the poet on September 7, 1871. Whitman also respected Hale's writings. The following inscription in Whitman's hand appears in the cover of what was undoubtedly a gift copy of *Quarante Mélodies Choises de F. Schubert*:[15]

> Phil: Hale
>
> "All music is what awake[n]s from you when you are reminded by the instruments."
>
> Walt Whitman[16]

Following his graduation from Yale (A. B., 1876), Hale turned his attention toward New York City, contributing articles to *New York World* while receiving private lessons from then well-known composer Dudley Buck (1839–1909), organist at Holy Trinity Church in Brooklyn. Shortly thereafter Hale moved to Albany, New York, where he served as an apprentice in the law office of his uncle, Robert L. Hale. This was fortuitous; it culminated in his being admitted to the New York Bar in 1880. As a result, Hale practiced law in Albany for two years.

Located about eighty miles west of Northampton, Albany had about 90,000 residents during Hale's first period of residency there. This population figure is somewhat misleading, for the city was (and remains) the state capitol and the center of the tri-city metropolitan area consisting of Albany, Schenectady, and Troy. There was already a significant tradition of music making in Albany. At midcentury, Ferdinand Ingersoll Ilsley, owner of F. I. Ilsley & Co., an Albany firm which made square concert pianos for over a decade, conducted performances of Haydn's oratorios *The Creation* and *The Seasons*. The latter was presented by the Harmonia Society, a singing organization founded in 1849. Within two decades a number of other Albany singing societies were established. Among them were The Union Musical Association (1858), The Singing Society Caecilia (1866), The Albany Music Association (1867), and the Gesang-Verein Eintracht Singing Society (1868), which, as its name suggests, cultivated German music, both instrumental and vocal. Sometimes orchestras accompanied these singing societies in their concerts, although, in order to ensure a sufficient caliber of performance, professional musicians—both vocal and instrumental—had to be brought in from New York or Boston. The Germania Orchestra of Boston, for example, was imported for the 1881 performance of Mendelssohn's *Elijah.* Chamber music was also starting to gain a foothold in the city at this time. Among such groups was The Mozart Society (1875).[17]

Performance venues were relatively few and therefore in high demand. Tweddle Hall, located at 81 State Street, was built in 1860. This four-story structure was the principal location for oratorio performances before it burned down in 1883.[18] The building also housed the McCammon Music Store. Nearby was the Perry Building, which also had a performance hall. Also downtown was the Leland Opera House, at 43 S. Pearl St., which opened its doors on November 24, 1873. It was later converted into a venue for vaudeville and movies before its demise in the mid-twentieth century.

Hale, of course, was drawn to Albany's musical offerings. He studied piano and organ there with John Kautz (1850–1918) and from 1879 to 1882 served as organist at St. Peter's (Episcopal) Church on State Street. One year earlier, starting in 1878, Hale began serving as music critic for the *Albany Times.*[19] This marked the beginning of his work in what would become his true profession, even though Hale's position with that paper often entailed writing about nonmusical events, doing telegraph copy editing, or chasing down police reports. Though nearly all of his articles for the *Albany Times* were published anonymously, the identity of the author isn't much in doubt, for stylistic mannerisms associated with his later work did surface. The following anonymous anecdote bears Hale's sense of style and humor:

An Operatic Row

At an operatic rehearsal in Rome the other day, the rehearsal being the last before the presentation of his new work, the composer made a neat little speech to the members of the chorus before they began their work, expressing his gratification at the manner in which they had performed their part, and announcing his intention of treating them to sixty litres of wine (something over thirteen gallons). All went well till after the second act, when the gentlemen of the chorus clamored for part of the wine; the composer urged the advantage of having it all after the rehearsal was over; an angry altercation took place, ending with a partial surrender on the composer's part. Some of the semi-treated chorus returned a little worse for the wine, and the third act suffered accordingly in execution, and when it was over a demand was made for more wine or there would be no chorus. Half the chorus were drunk by this time; the composer scolded them with Italian vehemence; the members of the chorus responded with a torrent of abuse; the *prima donna* indignantly reminded them that the composer had mounted the opera for nothing, and that she had given her services gratuitously, simply to enable the musicians, chorus-singers and other artists to have a chance to earn something during the dull season; the chorus-singers called her all the names in their vocabulary; she fainted, and her husband bounded on the stage and challenged everybody to fight; the orchestra sided with the composer and upbraided the chorus-singers, and a frightful squabble began, which lasted till 3 a.m.[20]

It did not take long before Hale jettisoned his law career for one in music criticism and performance. In order to take up such a career change, Hale did what every serious nineteenth-century American musician had to do—study in Europe.

Starting in 1882, Hale spent five years on the other side of the Atlantic. The first country visited was Germany. He made the most of his time in Berlin, studying organ with Carl August Haupt (1810–1891), director of the Royal Institute for Church Music, and with Albert Heintz (1822–1911), organist at St. Peter's. In addition, he took lessons from the Russian-born concert pianist Xaver Scharwenka (1850–1924). He also studied at that city's prestigious Hochschule für Musik—keyboard technique with the famous piano pedagogue Oscar Raif (1847–1899) and composition with two musicians of stature: violinist Heinrich Urban (1837–1901) and Clara Schumann's half brother, Woldemar Bargiel (1828–1897). The latter helped him with counterpoint and in acquiring a significant amount of score-reading expertise.

It was during this Berlin stay, on June 10, 1884,[21] that Hale wed the Syracuse-born pianist and composer Irene Baumgras. She was the daughter of two artists: German-American portrait painter Peter Baumgras (1827–1903) and American floral painter Mary Brainerd Thomson Baumgras (1840–1928). Irene was a pianist of significant repute; she had studied at the Cincinnati Conservatory of Music and received the Springer Gold Medal there in 1881. She had continued her studies in Europe, with Raif and with Moritz Moszkowski (1854–1925). Irene later wrote music under the pseudonym of Victor Rene and is best known as a composer for her *Morceaux de Genre*, Op. 15, and the four-movement *Pensees Poetiques*, Op. 16.[22]

Following their wedding, Philip Hale became somewhat of an itinerant scholar, studying composition with Josef Rheinberger (1839–1901) from July through December 1884 in Munich, and organ with Immanuel Gottlob Friedrich Faisst (1823–1894) from January through October 1885 in Stuttgart.

Hale ended his European stay not in Germany, but in France, studying organ and composition in Paris with Alexandre Guilmant (1837–1911) for the next two years. He may also have studied with Théodore Salomé (1834–1895), organist at Sainte-Trinité. The second of Salomé's *Dix Pièces pour Orgue*, Vol. III, Op. 48, "Prière," bears the dedication "à Monsieur Philip Hale."[23]

Hale's time spent in Paris, though shorter than that in Germany, had a more lasting effect on him. In Paris there was a certain *joie de vivre* in the musical scene that offset the rather severe academic approach toward music common in Germany at that time. Many of France's best-known composers had joined the Société Nationale de Musique. The society was founded in 1871 by Romain Bussine and Camille Saint-Saëns in order to counteract two prevailing perceptions: (1) the favoring of France's vocal music over its instrumental music and (2) the dominance of German musical tradition. The society's aims were manifested in a number of concert series. The gifted conductor Charles Lamoureux (1834–1899) was presenting his weekly Société des Nouveaux-Concerts at Theatre Château d'Eau. These were very successful and often cited by Hale in his later writings. Lameroux was not alone; a rival, Eduard Colonne (1838–1910), conducted L'Association Artistique du Châtelet at the Theatre du Châtelet, and Jules Pasdeloup (1819–1887) was attempting to restart his Concerts Pasdeloup through a César Franck Festival. All of this French musical nationalism was hard to escape and Hale was taken in by it to the extent that he essentially became a Francophile in his music criticism, generally favoring the Franco-Russian timbre-oriented approaches to orchestral composition over the more Germanic logical development of themes.

After being exposed to the cutting edge of late-nineteenth-century musical activity in France, it must have been with some reluctance that Hale returned to Albany in 1887, even though the musical scene in that city had improved slightly during his absence. Two new choral societies had been founded in 1884: the Apollo Singing Society (an offshoot from the Gesang-Verein Eintract) and the New Harmonia Singing Society.[24] During the autumn of that same year, the Albany Philharmonic Society was founded under the auspices of George Hornell Thacher, Jr. It originally featured only chamber music but by the following year had an orchestra of twenty-nine members.[25] Although amateur based, this was the first orchestra in Albany to have any sense of permanence.[26]

New opportunities awaited Hale, though on the surface they appear to have been on much the same plane as what had been available to him before his European sojourn. He assumed the conductorship of the Schubert Club male chorus, and became organist/choir director at St. John's Episcopal Church in nearby Troy. He supplemented the income gained from these sources by giving organ lessons and teaching theory. In addition, he became music and drama critic for the *Albany Express* and the *Albany Union*, where he also wrote editorials and edited telegraph copy. Meager though these opportunities might have been, Hale made the best of them. His own column, "Amusement," in the *Albany Evening Union*, afforded him ample opportunity to further nurture his own writing style. The column covered everything imaginable, from animal shows to serious opera.

AMUSEMENT.

The Campanini Opera Concert at the Leland

The feature of the concert of the Campanini concert of last evening was the singing of Signorina de Vere. She fully deserved the high praises given her last week by such New York critics as Henderson and Krehbiel. Her voice is of agreeable quality and good compass; and careful study has given her great execution. Her intonation, phrasing and comprehension of the composer's ideas are all alike admirable. Let it be added that she has a very pleasing face and handsome figure. It is seldom that we have a chance to hear such an artist; and what a relief to hear her after the caterwaulings of so many German prima donnas.

Campanini's voice was heard to best advantage in the great romance from Hallevy's "Jewess," where the broken hearted and fanatical Jew Eleazer has decided to send his adopted daughter to the horrible death of boiling oil rather than save her by telling the truth of her birth; for Rachel was really the natural child of the cardinal. It is a haunting melody, full of pathos; and Campanini sang it with full appreciation of its wondrous somber beauty. It was a noble interpretation of one of the most heartrending scenes in the operatic repertoire.

Del Puente did not do justice to the lament of Hoel over the body of Dinorah. His mannerisms seemed exaggerated, particularly his abuse of the tremolo; his phrasing lacked breadth and dignity. In the Toreador's song, which he has made peculiarly his own, and in Valentine's song from Faust, he did better work.

The other members of the company ranged only from "fair to middling." The buffo and the bass had agreeable and well trained voices, but Mlle. Fabbri and Sig. Stehle were of a lower order and provoked feelings of surprise and pain. The latter has a singularly nasal quality of tone. Miss Groebel, to whom nature has given a rich voice, sang with sublime indifference and sluggishness.

The program, which was much too long, included for its final number the garden scene from "Faust." It is the purpose of Sig. Campanini in each concert to give one act from some opera. This is a doubtful experiment. No matter how well the scenes may be sung, in the absence of an orchestra and chorus and fitting scenery there is a total lack of what the French call the dramatic perspective; and the performance inevitably suggests the appearance of "barn-stormers" in a country town. Of course it is a great and unmixed pleasure to hear such a tenor and soprano together, no matter how unfavorable the surroundings may be; but last night the quartet was top heavy, for Sig. Bologna, who was a most estimable little Mephistopheles, was heard with difficulty and the alto, Miss Groebel, sang and acted like an "English Miss."

The company as a whole does not compare with other artists who surrounded Sig. Campanini last yeat. But who can replace the loss of Scalchi, Nanneti, Galassi and Toricelli?

Sig. Ferrari, who had a most thankless task, went through it well, hampered as he was in the act from Faust with a most wretched piano.

The audience was large and enthusiastic. They insisted on many recalls from a desire, no doubt, to "get their money's worth."

There were several features of last night's performance which call for more extended comment, but as there is a press upon the columns of this evening's UNION this comment must be put off until Saturday night.

NOTES.

Next week Edwin A. Arden will appear at Jacob's and Proctor's theatre in a new drama "Barred Out."

This evening the engagement of Mr. Arthur Rehan's company begins at the Leland with the comedy "7–20–8," which will be repeated at the Saturday matinee.[27]

The above column of 595 words, about half the length of most of his future Boston Symphony Orchestra reviews, shows that Hale had arrived at a "first maturity" in his critiquing during this second period of residency in Albany. A number of his stylistic characteristics are now apparent: giving credit to his peers, placing the positive reviews of the performers before the negative ones, and commenting on such nonmusical items as program length, performance conditions (in this case dealing with the "wretched" piano), audience deportment, and deadline constraints. With Hale's commentary, one received a review of all aspects of a performance, not just a superficial account confined to the immediate action of what was happening on stage.

Indeed, there was a reasonable amount of musical activity happening in the Albany–Schenectady–Troy area, but the quality was not sufficient enough to prevent Hale from having higher aspirations. After all, he had experienced the musical life of Dresden, Berlin, Munich, Stuttgart, and Paris, and was now having difficulty in finding personal satisfaction within the musical life of upstate New York. So, Hale began seeking personal fulfillment elsewhere.

On January 28, 1889, possibly as part of an interview process, he performed an organ recital at the First Religious Society (Unitarian) Church in Roxbury, on the south side of Boston. The recital paid homage to Bach as well as to his teachers and acquaintances abroad. The following synopsis appeared in *The Musical Courier*:

—Mr. Philip Hale of Albany gave an organ recital last Monday evening at Roxbury, Mass., and played compositions by Bach, Borgault-Ducoudray, Charret, Dubois, Salomé, Rheinberger, and Guilmant, a fugue in G major by the latter being dedicated to Mr. Hale.[28]

Albany took notice; the following appeared in the *Albany Times*:

It will be a distinct loss to Albany should Mr. Hale decide to leave the city, but sooner or later he is likely to do so. His talent is such that [he] must naturally gravitate to the larger cities, and nowhere would it be better appreciated than in Boston.[29]

From this point forward Hale's Albany reviews began to take a more sarcastic turn. This is manifested in the following reviews concerning performances by two traveling companies: the "Starlight" company, performing musical comedy, and The Boston Ideal Opera Company, also known as The Bostonians, which enjoyed a twenty-six-year existence (1879–1905)[30]:

AMUSEMENT
Vernona Jarbeau in "Starlight" at the Leland.

What sad fate compelled pretty Bessie Cleveland to join the "Starlight" company? What has she in common with the inane drivel and vulgar horse play of that "musical comedy?" Why should she be forced to appear upon sizeable terms with such miserable comedians as the men who last night went through their pranks for the enjoyment of the gallery in return for a weekly salary?

As for Miss Jarbeau—her kick was there, the leg shrouded, as usual, in mysterious black. "Now you see it and now you don't," as a white-haired man in row B nervously remarked. The kick is evidently Miss Jarbeau's stock-in-trade and as such it deserves a separate article.

There was, of course, a topical song which descended fathoms deep into the abyss of stupidity; an alleged comic Irishman was allowed to go through his lines undisturbed by a good natured audience and there were one or two very bad imitations of popular actors.

The singing was fair, but why did Mr. F. Potter Brown, if that be the name of the gentleman who directed, force the singers to take Meyer Helmund's Marguerita at such a pace as to ruin it?[31]

AMUSEMENT.

The Bostonians in English Opera at the Leland
The company known as "The Bostonians"
appeared last evening at the Leland
in a musical arrangement dubbed
"PYGMALION AND GALATEA"

This company might with justice borrow the title of a famous Boston organization and travel as the "Ancients and Honorables," for Messrs. Tom Karl and Barnabee and Miss Stone are chiefly interesting from an historical standpoint. It is true they also serve as pegs upon which can be hung pleasant memories of days long past when Adelaide Phillips was alive and Mary Beabe charmed the eye and ear. Now as singers and players they smell of mortality.

Out of Mr. Gilbert's well known comedy is wrought the text of a so-called opera of last night, and the music has been arranged from one of the works from Ambroise Thomas which bears another name and illustrates another subject. Some of the numbers are of exquisite beauty and it is a pity they cannot be heard with the original instrumentation of Thomas who is a master of that art; who depends often upon brilliant and cunning orchestral effects to conceal poverty of thought. One or two of the choruses were thoroughly delightful and were sung with appreciation, though the Grecian costumes were badly adapted to the peculiar style and beauty of the women of the chorus, whose order of architecture was the Gothic and not the Grecian. The men suffered too from the enforced dress, the general effect upon a careful observer being to give him the impression that the Dime Museums and Freak Exhibitions in the neighborhood of Boston had been heavily levied upon; while to any one suffering slightly from the free use of alcohol stimulants, the spectacle must have seemed like the connecting dream between the appearance of plain, ordinary snakes and the awful vision of the Blue Monkey.

There cannot be much said in praise of the solo work. Mr. Karl, although his efforts are sincere and praiseworthy, has always suffered from two disadvantages: he cannot sing and he cannot act. The voice of Miss Stone is much worn and her execution is faulty. Mr. Barnabee amused the audience with his facial contortions and down-east dialect.

Mr. Cowless, the bass, has a sonorous, manly voice and Miss Davis, as the wife of Pygmalion, showed considerable intelligence, while her voice had an agreeable freshness and fullness, though apparently untrained in the lower register. She has it in her power to do better work. Physically she is comely and robust. It is a pity that she can not breathe her vitality into her poor sisters of the chorus, who are sadly in need of tonics and a nourishing diet. As for that, three or four of the men might lend them a few pounds of their superfluous flesh.

The chorus and orchestra had been carefully drilled by Mr. Studley, who showed himself, as ever, an efficient conductor.

As a whole the opera moved along slowly. Although the audience (which, as a morning paper informed us in advance was "cultivated and refined") applauded freely several members, it was left for Mr. Barnabee to arouse genuine enthusiasm by singing a quasi-topical song. Many were, no doubt, a little disappointed because Galatea did not indulge in a statue-clog.

How true to life is the end of the piece. Pygmalion prays that the stone-woman may be endowed with life. He makes love to her and she responds with her whole heart. Her innocence and his guilt bring trouble upon him. Restored to sight by her means, has he even one word of sympathy or pity for her? He will not look upon her. As though she were a leaper he says, "Depart, depart—thou art unclean." And he returns to his jealous wife, to placid joys of domesticity. Was Galatea in after years revenged? Did not the sculptor ever long for the touch of her snow white arm, the pressure of her warm lips? Did he not often when his arms were about Cynisca dream of the other one? Who can tell? Surely not Galatea for she again became stone.[32]

Hale had outgrown Albany. Knowingly or not, he had set himself up for future success. His development as a critic during this second period of residency in Albany was remarkable and undeniable; his columns had now become harbingers of those that lay just beyond the horizon. Boston was beckoning. The position of organist at the First Religious Society, the prestigious position he had auditioned for, was now offered to him. It was an opportunity that he could not turn down. Taking the job meant relocation to Boston, something that both he and the city accepted with open arms. It was a good fit; Hale would serve in that post for the next sixteen years.

2

1889–1900

By the time of Philip Hale's 1889 arrival, Boston was already the beneficiary of a rich musical tradition. Despite its Puritanical beginnings, the city very early had become known as an educational and cultural center, somewhat deserving of its over-inflated nickname, the "Hub of the Universe," at least in the eyes of New Englanders. Its musical history deserves a glance.

Even before the start of the American Revolution, there existed a school of composers—men of various occupations and professions—who wrote music in their own unique quasi-European style. The compositions of this First New England School featured open fifths, parallel fifths, and four-part harmony with the third (tenor) voice carrying the melody. The primary form of composition was the fuguing tune, a binary form work featuring a chorale first part followed by a mostly polyphonic second part. Notable among the First New England School composers were Francis Hopkinson (1731–1798), a signer of the Declaration of Independence and composer of the first song to be written in the colonies, "My Days Have Been So Wondrous Free" (1759), William Billings (1746–1800), a tanner by trade best known for his Revolutionary war song "Chester;" Daniel Read (1757–1836), and Supply Belcher (1751–1836). A number of these composers also served as itinerant teachers in the Singing Schools, the only places where commoners could learn to read music. The first such school had opened its doors in 1717, on Brattle Street in Cambridge.

As the population of the greater Boston area grew and as more people became educated in singing, a number of choral societies were formed. Chief among them was the Handel and Haydn Society, which became the region's musical flagship. Founded in 1815, it remains the country's oldest continuous nonmilitary performing arts organization.[1] Handel's *Messiah* and Haydn's *Creation* were mainstays though other works, including patchwork abominations, were also programmed. Perhaps the most notorious was *Beethoven's Oratorio of Engedi, or David in the Wilderness* (1853), a pasting by Henry Hudson (a London physician) of Old Testament English text onto Beethoven's music for *Christ on the Mount of Olives*, Op. 85. Thirty years earlier the society had tried to commission Beethoven to write for them, but to no avail.[2]

Boston music-making was given an additional boost through the incorporation of vocal music into the Boston Public Schools in 1838. Lowell Mason (1792–1872), the charismatic banker-turned-music educator and a former conductor-president of the Handel and Haydn Society, was the driving force behind this. It was a seminal moment in music education, not only for Boston, but also for the entire country. Partially as a result of Mason's efforts, more choral organizations sprang up in Boston, including the Mendelssohn Choral Society (1853), the Apollo Club (1871), the Boylston Club (1873), and two choruses that would appear regularly with the Boston Symphony Orchestra: the Harvard Glee Club (1858) and the Cecilia Society (1874). While singing societies flourished, attempts at establishing a permanent opera company in Boston during the nineteenth century failed. There was one traveling repertory company, however, the Boston Ideal Opera Co. (aka The Bostonians), which lasted more than a quarter century, from 1879 to 1905; Hale saw them perform in Albany during the spring of 1889.

Much of Boston's early instrumental music was either imported or performed with the assistance of outsiders. In 1769 the jeweler and engraver Josiah Flagg (1737–1794) organized his first band concert using members of the Band of the 64th Regiment and others;[3] over the next four years, organist W. S. Morgan conducted many of their concerts. About a half century later, in 1821, the Boston Brigade Band was founded. This band, of mixed woodwind, brass, and percussion instrumentation, would continue until the early 1860s, when the Civil War took its toll. Ned Kendall (1808–1861), wizard of the keyed bugle, conducted this band in 1849; he had previously conducted the Boston Brass Band. In 1848, Kendall's rival, Irish-born cornetist Patrick Sarsfield Gilmore (1829–1892), arrived in Boston and made quite a career for himself, conducting the Suffolk, Boston Brigade, and Salem Bands before organizing "Gilmore's Band" in 1857. Much of the classical and romantic orchestral repertoire was introduced to the public by these bands via transcriptions.

In 1869 Gilmore also organized the Grand National Peace Jubilee, held in an immense coliseum not far from the present site of Symphony Hall, with bands, choruses, and orchestras that featured thousands of performers. He followed that up three years later with the World Peace Jubilee, with the numbers of the performers doubled. In 1873 Gilmore left Boston for New York to become conductor of the Band of the 22nd Regiment.

A succession of orchestras played major roles in Boston's musical life, though there was no truly professional orchestra before the founding of the Boston Symphony. The Pierian Sodality, the oldest college orchestra in America, was founded as an extracurricular activity at Harvard University in 1808. Its membership was often in the single digits and instrumentation varied greatly. In 1831–1832, for example, its instrumentation was "several each of 1st, 2nd, and 3rd flutes, a clarinet, 2 horns, one violoncello and 'part of the time a nondescript bass horn'."[4] In 1837 graduates of this organization founded the Harvard Musical Association.

The first attempt at forming a professional orchestra in Boston may have been in 1809, when Gottlieb Graupner (1767–1836), an oboist in Haydn's London orchestra who had immigrated in 1798, founded the Philo-Harmonic Society. Lasting until 1824, it had about 16 members and played in various locations. Graupner, who led the group from the string bass,[5] was also one of the founders of the Handel and Haydn Society.

In 1833 Lowell Mason founded the Boston Academy of Music. It operated an orchestra under the direction of George James Webb.[6] This orchestra was in turn succeeded by the Boston Musical Fund Society, an orchestra whose membership consisted of approximately half professionals and half amateurs; it presented six to eight concerts per year and had a quick succession of conductors: C. H. Mueller, F. Suck, C. C. Perkins, and J. C. D. Parker.[7] Although lighter fare was played by the ensemble during their early years, in 1841 they performed the first Beethoven symphony (the 5th) to be presented in Boston.[8] This orchestra performed fairly consistently through 1847 and then continued sporadically until 1855.

On December 9, 1843, the Philharmonic Society of Boston presented its first concert under the direction of J. G. Jones.[9] He was later followed by Messrs, Herwig, Schmidt, and Carl Zerrahn.

Meanwhile, the orchestra of the Boston Music Fund Society was largely displaced by the Germania Orchestra, comprised, as its name implies, of German musicians who had fled the 1848 political upheavals in their homeland. The Germania Orchestra was itinerant, however, traveling up and down the eastern seaboard. Elson comments:

> They gave most of their concerts in Boston, for of the musical cities this presented the freest field, yet they travelled about the country, and Philadelphia and other cities had thus good opportunities for studying a European model—a most necessary thing in those days of untrammeled and often misguided music enthusiasm.... It performed the most ambitious works, and together with the Handel and Haydn Society, gave Boston its first hearing of Beethoven's Ninth Symphony.[10]

In 1852 Boston Music Hall, the city's first permanent music performance venue, was built and, undoubtedly encouraged by this, the Germania Orchestra finally made Boston its home; unfortunately, the orchestra disbanded the following year. A number of the Germania musicians remained, however. Their flutist Carl Zerrahn (1826–1909) quickly became conductor of three major musical organizations: Handel and Haydn Society (1854–1895; 1897–1898) and two orchestras: the Orchestral Union (1854–1863) and the Boston Philharmonic Society (1855–1863); both were relatively successful ventures until derailed by the Civil War.

Following the war, musical life in Boston continued to improve. From December 23, 1865 until March 9, 1882,[11] the Harvard Musical Association presented symphony concerts under Zerrahn's conductorship and in 1867 both the New England and Boston Conservatories were founded. Though it afforded Boston's citizenry an exposure to great music, the orchestra's deficiencies both in quality and in range of repertoire[12] were in evidence when, in 1869 and 1870, Theodore Thomas's thoroughly professional orchestra visited. The need for a better local orchestra was readily apparent.

There were other concerts presented in Boston as well. Anton Rubinstein stopped in Boston during his 1872–1873 American tour and gave the city's music circles something to talk about through passionately conducting his own *Symphony No. 2 in C*, Op. 42, "Ocean." The most significant pre-Boston Symphony event, however, occurred on October 25, 1875, when Wagner advocate Benjamin Johnson (B. J.) Lang (1837–1909) conducted the world premiere of Tchaikovsky's *Piano Concerto No, 1 in B flat minor*, Op. 23, with Hans von Bülow as soloist. Though the Harvard Musical Association orchestra continued to flourish, an independent organization with a more comprehensive idea of repertoire, the Philharmonic Society (the second such Boston organization with this name), began giving concerts on October 24, 1879 under the direction of Bernhard Listemann. Having two semi-professional orchestras with two decidedly different outlooks, Boston was now on the cusp of transformation. The city's conservative music sage, John Sullivan Dwight (1813–1893), commented from an 1881 perspective, "The musical past of Boston, if she will truly read it in the light of the idea which can be traced through all stages of its progress, is to be cherished as the warrant of a providential mission, a pledge to higher duty, and the promise of a fairer future."[13]

This "fairer future" was made possible by one person, an individual of means who was also a philanthropist. Major Henry Lee Higginson (1834–1919), a New Yorker by birth, but a Bostonian since the age of four, was a self-made man. After two European sojourns of music study in the 1850s, he returned home with a vision—not of becoming a professional musician, but of establishing an orchestra based on those he had seen in Europe. Neither the time nor the circumstances were propitious as the country soon fell apart over the issues of states' rights and slavery. Higginson joined the Union army and fought in the Civil War, first as a lieutenant, then as a major, and finally as a lieutenant colonel, though throughout his post-war life he was referred to as "Major" in order to avoid confusion with an older cousin, Thomas Wentworth Higginson, who was also a Colonel. After the war, following failed business ventures in oil and cotton, he entered his family's brokerage firm, Lee, Higginson and Co., as a partner. Though profits were meager at first, the firm eventually became tremendously successful through wise investment in diverse interests, and in the process Higginson amassed a considerable fortune. His longtime goal of establishing a professional orchestra in Boston had become attainable. He reflected on the fruition of his dream in a letter to the members of the Boston Symphony Orchestra on April 27, 1914:

Gentlemen:–

Sixty years ago I wished to be a musician, and therefore went to Vienna, where I studied two years and a half diligently, learned something of music, something about musicians, and one other thing—that I had no talent for music. I heard there and in other European cities the best orchestras, and much wished that our own country should have such fine orchestras. Coming home at the end of 1860, I found our country in trouble, and presently in a great war. Naturally I took part in the war, at the end of which time I did various things, and at last came to our present office in State Street, where I was admitted as a partner.

For many years I had hard work to earn my living and support my life. Originally I had a very small sum of money, which had been used up in studying in Vienna and during the war. All these years I watched the musical conditions in Boston, hoping to make them better. I believed that an orchestra of excellent musicians under one head and devoted to a single purpose could produce fine results, and wished for the ability to support such an undertaking; for I saw that it was impossible to give music at fair prices and make the orchestra pay expenses.

After consulting with European friends, I laid out a plan, and after two very good years of business began concerts in the fall of 1881. It seemed best to undertake the matter single-handed, and, beyond one fine gift from a dear friend, I have borne the costs alone. All this is a matter of record, and yet it may interest you. It seemed clear that an orchestra of fair size and under possible conditions would cost at least $20,000 a year more than what the public would pay. Therefore, I expected this deficit each year, and faced contracts with seventy men and a conductor. It was a large sum of money, which depended on my business each year and on the public. If the concert halls were filled, that would help me; if my own business went well, that would help me; and the truth is, the public has stood by me nobly.

In my eyes the requisites of the Orchestra were these: to leave the choice and care of the musicians, the choice and care of the music, the rehearsals and the direction of the Orchestra, to the conductor, giving him every power possible; to leave to an able manager the business affairs of the enterprise; and, on my part, to pay the bills, to be satisfied with nothing short of perfection, and always to remember that we were seeking high art and not money; art came first, then the good of the public, and the money must be an after consideration....[14]

Although the management of the orchestra was an autocracy for the first 37 years of its existence, Higginson ran it with a great deal of common sense, feeling, and compassion.

On March 30, 1881, Higginson placed an editorial, "The Boston Symphony Orchestra: In the Interest of Good Music," in the major Boston newspapers explaining his sense of purpose. After presenting a case for the orchestra's need and expressing thanks to the Greater Boston community, he stated the following:

The price of season tickets, with reserved seats, for the whole series of evening concerts will be either $10 or $5, according to position.

Single tickets, with reserved seats, will be seventy-five cents or twenty-five cents, according to position.

Besides the concerts, there will be a public rehearsal on one afternoon of every week, with single tickets at twenty-five cents, and no reserved seats.[15]

With relatively inexpensive ticket prices and public rehearsals (which were essentially concerts), Higginson the philanthropist was clearly thinking of the good of the public. It is probably safe to assume that he would not have approved of the sobriquet "The Aristocrat of Orchestras" that was so prevalently attached to the orchestra during the 1950s and beyond.

It had been expected that Carl Zerrahn,[16] who had proven himself on so many occasions, would be the first conductor of the Boston Symphony, but Higginson instead chose Isidor Georg Henschel (1850–1934), after seeing him conduct his own *Concert Overture* at the March 3, 1881 Harvard Musical Association concert.[17] Henschel was primarily a vocalist and only thirty-one years old at the time. A fine musician, but no disciplinarian, he lasted three seasons in Boston, afterwards returning to England and a more successful conducting career—one for which he was eventually knighted.

The first concert of the Boston Symphony Orchestra took place on October 22, 1881 with the following complement:

- 13 1st violins
- 11 2nd violins
- 10 violas
- 8 cellos
- 8 basses
- 2 flutes
- 2 oboes
- 2 clarinets
- 2 bassoons
- 1 contrabassoon
- 4 horns
- 2 trumpets
- 3 trombones
- 1 tuba
- 1 timpanist
- 1 harp

Total: 72, including 4 temporary members[18]

Nearly all of these were local musicians. Higginson had asked Henschel to make sure of this for the first year, so as not to offend the Greater Boston music community. Ten years later, Theodore Thomas would make the same request in forming the Chicago Symphony.

During the Boston Symphony Orchestra's third season, Higginson returned to Vienna, searching for a successor for Henschel. Through one of his close friends and advisors there, Julius Epstein, Higginson was able to see Wilhelm Gericke (1845–1925) conduct and secured his services for the next five years. Gericke was the exacting perfectionist that the orchestra needed. During his first tenure (1884–1889), a number of foreign-born musicians of high caliber were added and the sound of the orchestra greatly improved. Even though their tenures ended before his arrival in Boston, Philip Hale was eventually able critique both of these conductors. The first time he saw Henschel perform at a Boston Symphony Orchestra concert, however, was not as a conductor, but as a vocalist. Hale was not impressed and labeled him "an uninteresting soloist."[19] Henschel would return to Boston twice as a guest conductor while Gericke would return as music director for a second tenure of eight years, starting in 1898.

Bostonians loved the orchestra that Higginson had bestowed upon them; its founding spawned a number of other musical organizations. Among them were the Fadette Ladies' Orchestra (1888–1927), founded by Caroline B. Nichols and Ethel Atwood; the Boston Orchestral Club (1885) and the Longy Club (1900–1917), both founded by Boston Symphony oboist Georgés Longy; the Boston Opera Company (1909–1914) and its successor the Boston Grand Opera Company (1915–1917); the Boston Flute Players Club (1920); and the Boston Saxophone Orchestra (1925), founded by Boston Symphony bassoonist Abdon Laus.

What brought Philip Hale to Boston in 1889 was the organist position at the First Religious Society in Roxbury of course, but he knew that in order to earn a decent living he had to have at least one additional source of income. He had done a significant amount of editing and reviewing in Albany and so it was only natural that he should seek employment as a music critic with one of Boston's newspapers. There was an astounding amount of concert coverage in the newspapers back then; sometimes there were more than a half dozen reviews of the same concert or set of concerts.

With its plethora of musical organizations, it was only natural that Boston would have a remarkable history of music journalism up to this point. In addition to the regular newspapers, there were a number of publications specializing in music. In 1820 the first music periodical appeared, John Rowe Parker's *The Euterpiad, or Musical Intelligencer*. This bi-weekly publication lasted four years. Parker also published the *Minerviad*, which was geared toward women.[20] *The Euterpiad* was followed a generation later by *Dwight's Journal of Music* (1852–1882), a remarkably successful publication edited by John Sullivan Dwight. Though conservative to a fault, it was quite influential in its time. Dwight also had a hand in the Harvard Musical Association. Far less conservative yet containing more caustic reviews was *The Metronome: A Monthly Review of Music* (1871–1874), edited by two brothers: Ambrose Davenport, Jr. and Warren Davenport, music critic for the *Boston Herald*, the *Daily Traveler*, and *Musical America*. Warren also served as a music critic for *The Folio* (1869–1895). Published in Boston by White, Smith & Co., its emphasis was on American music.[21] *Dwight's Journal*, *The Metronome*, and *The Folio* were only three of the dozen or so music periodicals that graced the tables of Boston's living rooms during the post-Civil War era.

Newspaperwise, the Boston music scene of 1889 had plenty of critics to go around. Three of the most influential were the aforementioned Warren Davenport, Louis Charles Elson (1848–1920), and William Foster Apthorp (1848–1913). Elson was a music theory and history professor at the New England Conservatory of Music who wrote for the *Boston Daily Advertiser*, *Courier*, and *Transcript*. Apthorp was also a New England Conservatory music history professor associated with many periodicals, namely the *Atlantic Monthly*, *Dwight's Journal*, and particularly the *Boston Evening Transcript*.

Hale's first newspaper job in Boston was that of music critic with the *Boston Home Journal*, a Saturday evening weekly published from 1876 to 1903. The *Home Journal* was not a broadleaf newspaper, but more of a magazine; its sixteen pages were divided into four columns each and there was a significant amount of space dedicated to the arts. Hale succeeded Charles Lemuel (C. L.) Capen, who retired in order to devote more time to teaching, composing, and editing. Capen did not stop writing entirely; he still submitted occasional columns to the *Boston Advertiser* and other media sources. Capen commented about the qualifications of his successor:

> Editor Boston Home Journal:
>
> Please grant me the liberty of taking this method of thanking the management of the *Boston Home Journal* for the very kind and sentimental reference, in last week's paper, to my former services as musical critic. Regarding my successor, I can

only say that your many readers are to be congratulated. The appointment of Mr. Philip Hale as your musical critic is one that cannot fail to elicit the appreciation of any true musician. His musical experience and education have been in one of the broadest and artistic of schools, and he has furthermore the enviable and deserved reputation of not simply being a virtuoso organist, but an artistic musician in the best sense. While congratulating both the management of the *Boston Home Journal* and the readers, I also feel that your new critic is to be congratulated. No one can realize so appreciatively as myself that any critic for your paper will be in a position well nigh unique for a journalist, in that the most unbiased opinions will be accepted and published and none other be solicited. This having invariably been the standard of the *Boston Home Journal* during my many years association with it, I trust there can be no impropriety in my congratulating so sincere and able a musician as Mr. Hale is known to be. Again thanking you most heartedly, believe me,

Yours sincerely,
C. L. Capen

Boston, Sept. 12, 1889[22]

The *Boston Home Journal* may have had limited reach, but it afforded Hale the opportunity of being able to review all twenty-four of the Boston Symphony Orchestra's regular subscription concerts. At that time the orchestra played at Boston Music Hall, located in the heart of downtown Boston,[23] not far from the *Boston Home Journal* office. Arthur Nikisch (1855–1922), a Hungarian, had just been hired as conductor and Hale was able to begin his Boston Symphony Orchestra experience right along with him. Both men were more than up to the task, though Nikisch may have had the rougher start. Upon hearing the orchestra for the first time in rehearsal, Nikisch made the well meaning but easily misinterpreted comment, "All I have to do is poetize."[24] Moses Smith comments:

> ....And poetize he did, to the frequent annoyance of reviewers, but the general public gladly assented to a mild deterioration in the Orchestra's technical finish in exchange for a new excitement in performances. The conductor became a cult, despite unconventional ways which caused eyebrows to be lifted among Boston society and disturbed even Higginson.[25]

Hale and other critics wanted him to do more than just poetize, of course.

Nikisch even mesmerized the orchestra by his style of conducting. A silent film clip from late in his career shows a commanding style of conducting with a very high conducting plane that forced attention to his piercing eyes.

At the age of thirty-five Hale was not wet behind the ears, but already an experienced critic with definite opinions and a growing reputation. His column for the opening concert of the 1889–1890 season, more than 1100 words, displays the enormous depth of knowledge in the areas of conducting, repertoire, performance practice, musical analysis, and biographical literature—plus a sense of humor that would characterize his style of critiquing:

> THE FIRST SYMPHONY CONCERT.—In applauding Mr. Nikisch, the patient and abiding work of Mr. Gericke should not be forgotten. He gave the orchestra technique. He taught it precision; he called attention to detail. Without the noble

range of the born conductor, he gave a cold and finished reading of whatever work was on his desk. He seemed to abhor contrasts; he shrank from great effects; he appeared at times to entertain a contempt for brass instruments. Gorgeous and daring coloring was not so dear to him as a pale monochrome. So the orchestra became under his leadership an admirable machine, which one looked at and admired. Not without reason, then did an irreverent New Yorker dub it, "The Boston Music Box."

The work of Mr. Gericke has made possible the first success of Mr. Nikisch. Rhythm, sudden contrasts, crescendos carrying all before them, depend first upon the technique of the performer. Well might Mr. Nikisch, in modestly acknowledging the praise of the audience, turn and point to the men who had so well carried out his wishes.

What Mr. Gericke lacked, seems to be the distinguishing characteristic of the musical nature of Mr. Nikisch. He is highly endowed with imagination, and this imagination is under control. One may quarrel with his ideas, but his ideas at least are interesting. Take for example the "Coriolanus" overture. Some musicians, men whose opinions are of weight, object to his reading of the second motive, which is said to portray the prayers of women, though for that matter the overture might as well be called "King Lear" or "Hamlet"; for it is simply great music. They say it was almost effeminate, untraditional, not as Beethoven wished it.

Pray, how did Beethoven intend for it to be played? Would he, himself, have directed it twice in exactly the same manner? We know by the testimony of his hearers that he played his own compositions f[o]r the piano with great freedom and almost capriciously.

Why should not a director be allowed to have his own conception of a work, provided that conception be a beautiful or effective one?

But some would say Mr. Nikisch did not show due "piety" towards Beethoven. Now there is a false and a true piety. Rubini was deservedly hissed when, not content with the great air in "Don Giovanni" as Mozart wrote it, he sang, instead of a sustained note, the phrase given in accompaniment to the violins. A pianist, however, who today plays a piece of Couperin exactly as it is written, overladen with ornaments added by the composer on account of the scanty resources of the instruments of that time, shows doubtful taste and false devotion. Again, the modern German organists in playing the works of Bach, play as a rule with full organ and say they follow in the footsteps of Bach. Yet, according to the testimony of Adam Hiller in his life of Bach, written only thirty years after the death of the latter, "he understood the art of combining the stops in a most cunning manner, and of using each according to its character"; and in Bach's correspondence, we find him asking that the tremulant of his organ be put in order.

Whether Mr. Nikisch's treatment of the second motive of the overture was traditional or not, it was certainly effective, particularly when towards the close it follows the warning notes of the horns.

The other numbers of the program were the Introduction to "Die Meistersinger," an entr'acte from "Rosamunde" and Schumann's Fourth Symphony.

In the beautiful music of Schubert the work of flute, oboe, and clarinet was excellent both in tone and phrasing. The reading of the Wagner overture was in many respects novel and as a whole impressive; agreeably distinct, with a fine sense of relative values of the parts in the most intricate contrapuntal passages.

There had been a good deal of comment about the choice of the symphony for the opening concert. It is without doubt true that the peculiar genius of Schumann did not lie in the direction of symphonic writing. He was a man of great ideas, with but little sense of orchestral color and a tendency to vagueness and uninteresting digressions.

The Schumann whom Zola apostrophizes as "despair itself, the ecstasy of woe, the end of all, the last song of mournful purity heard in air over the ruins of the world"—the true Schumann is seen in the Kreisleriana, the piano quintet, the Lieder. And yet what passages of wild grandeur and unearthly beauty does this often despised Fourth Symphony contain.

Its performance was a revelation. Even the first movement lost much of its inherent ugliness, and nothing could be more dramatic than the rest of the symphony beginning with the Romanze. The sixteen measures leading from the delightful Scherzo to the last movement were declaimed with overwhelming effect. The tones of the trombones, horns, and trumpets under the direction of Mr. Nikisch are no longer "pillowy protuberances."

The new conductor led quietly, at times a little too stiffly, without the score before him. If a conductor can dispense with the score, so much the better; for so can he exert more powerfully his personal magnetism, just as an orator who uses no notes plays more easily upon the passions of his hearers. To do this successfully a man must of course be favored by nature; and if he is able to memorize only a few bars, it certainly is then the part of wisdom to use a score of fairly coarse print.

The first afternoon audience was cold; it is true there were many present who had paid a high premium for seats which, I believe, Mr. Higginson originally intended for impecunious students and lovers of music. Possibly some of these good people were surprised at the absence of a calcium light; or they perhaps expected that Mr. Nikisch would be lowered from the ceiling to the director's stand by means of an invisible wire. The audience of the following Saturday night gave Mr. Nikisch a hearty welcome and a generous applause.

This first concert has shown conclusively that Mr. Nikisch is a conductor of rare endowments. Future concerts will show whether the "individuality" already complained of will prove to be individualism; whether instead of nine parts Beethoven and one part Nikisch we shall be obliged to have our Beethoven still more diluted. It will then be time enough to inquire into this bugaboo of "individuality" and ascertain whether the monster has horns and a real tail.

The program to-night is as rigorously German as was that of last week. Is Mr. Nikisch liberal only in matters of interpretation? And are we to go through a course of Mendelssohn this winter?[26]

The last two paragraphs of this column display what many would consider to be a rather supercilious attitude toward interpretation and programming. Rightfully or wrongfully, Hale assumed that he had some sort of bully pulpit from which he could evoke change. Less than three years earlier he had been studying in France and his eyes were opened to a different world of great music about which he had previously known nothing. Apparently he felt that he was now ready to take on the Philistinism in taste that John Sullivan Dwight had stamped on the majority of the Boston music populace—and the way to do that was to influence those with the greatest leverage. Olin Downes commented:

> In fact, the musical situation in the principal American cities, when he [Hale] appeared on the scene, was one of almost unrelieved Germanism, and we owe to Hale, as to no other critic that ever wrote in America, the recognition of Debussy, D'Indy, Franck and other composers of their school, the Russians, the modern Englishmen, and individualities in modern music, whose special qualities he was quick to perceive and uphold.[27]

Thus in the October 19th issue of the *Boston Home Journal's Art Journal* Hale placed himself into an adversarial role with Nikisch:

Mr. Nikisch and His Opinions

Mr. Arthur Nikisch unbosomed himself to a *Herald* reporter, and in last Sunday's issue of the paper appeared his estimate of Boston musicians.

"On being asked if he was pleased with the Boston Symphony orchestra as he had found it, he replied: 'I am more than pleased; it is magnificent. There are only two orchestras in Europe that can compare with it, and those are the orchestras at Dresden, conducted by Herr Schuch, and of Leipsig, which I my conducted until I came here'."

So, according to Mr. Nikisch, Europe is musically synonymous with Saxony. There is no first-class orchestra in Berlin, or in Vienna, or in Cologne, or in Hannover, or in Frankfurt, or in Munich. This will be interesting news to the people of these cities.

And how about Paris, Mr. Nikisch? Have you ever heard the orchestra directed by Lamoureax, and would you say as a musician that, in precision, rhythm, fineness in detail and breadth in conception, in orchestral technique, either the orchestra directed by the shrewd Schuch, whose rapid advancement at court was perhaps due as much to the charms of a fair wife as any overmastering ability as a conductor, or the Leipsig orchestra, which now mourns your departure, is superior? Are they not both inferior?

Have you heard of late years the orchestra of the Paris Conservatory, which long ago under Habeneck extorted praise from Richard Wagner, which now obeys Garcin? Have you heard any of the Berlioz concerts by the men under Colonne? Then there are orchestras in Russia and England, are there not?

But the good people of Saxony believe in Saxony and perhaps view all things musical through an Elbe fog, just as the famous Tartarin and his friends were influenced in their speech by Meridional mirage. Tarascon is not the only city in the world; nor are the great orchestras to be found in Saxony alone.

When asked about his programme, Mr. Nikisch said: "It will be my effort in arranging my concerts to encourage young American composers. I believe that there is a great deal of musical talent in this country, and I think that it ought to be brought out." And then he speaks in warm terms of Mr. Arthur Bird. He declares himself an admirer of Beethoven, Mendelssohn, Schumann, Wagner, *et al*, and he says nothing of the modern French and Russian schools. Let us by all means have the compositions of Americans brought to a hearing, and it is to be hoped that in this particular Mr. Nikisch will follow the example of Theodore Thomas rather than that of Mr. Gericke. Let us also have an opportunity of hearing the works of the modern French and Russian composers. Possibly the music of Borodine [sic], Cesar Franck, and Augusta Holmes would be more interesting to a Boston audience than the labored symphonic poem of some slavish imitator of Wagner, Herr This or Herr That.

What Mr. Nikisch says about Wagner is eminently sensible, though it may be a disappointment to the true, hysterical disciples of the "Master."

"With regard to Wagner, I don't think that his operas should be performed in concert. For perfect representation they demand the dramatic adjuncts of the stage. I make exception to five or six of his overtures, such as the overture to 'Die Meistersinger,' which, by the way, is to be [the] opening number on my first program, the 'Gotterdammerung' overture and the Vorspiel to 'Tristan and Isolde.'"

It is safe to say that he enters upon his work supported by the respect and kindly feeling of both orchestra and audience. Whether he preserves this respect until the end of his engagement rests entirely with himself. He has admirable musicians under him; behind him he has money. He has been heralded as a great leader. It remains to be seen whether he is a man of narrow mind, a bigot whose sole desire is to propagate *German* music; or a musician who asks of music only this: is it good or is it bad, regardless of its school, careless as to its origin or nationality.

Philip Hale[28]

The above rather caustic article was an opinion column, not a concert review. Still, Nikisch could not have appreciated it. In the following week's review, Hale laid off Nikisch's programming (it was still all Germanic) and instead went after program order:

THE SYMPHONY CONCERT—In arranging a concert program too little attention is paid to the limited capacity of the human ear. Either the concert is so long drawn out, or the program so unskillfully arranged, that the hearer, after an hour, is unable to receive musical impressions and leaves the hall jaded and depressed. Not without reason did the Italians compose operas which do not take over two hours in the performing, although at the opera the attention is in a measure diverted from the music by the action, costumes and scenery.

The concerts of to-day are as a rule too long. The interest too often flags with each successive number. To make an impression at the very start, to deepen this impression, to dismiss the audience hungry for music—this is no slight task. In this respect Theodore Thomas is unrivaled.

Now where is the proper place for a symphony? Mr. Nikisch seems to think it should be at the end. After an hour or more of music, the audience must hear the work which demands the most serious attention. Is this reasonable or natural?

It depends a little upon the nature of the symphony. If it be such a one as the "Haffner" of Mozart or the Ninth of Haydn, full of melody and life, as a final number it may be effective as a contrast to what has gone before. If it be one by Beethoven or Schumann or Brahms, let it be heard earlier in the evening. Why should that which demands the most careful attention be reserved until the ear necessarily has lost much of its powers of discrimination and enjoyment?

Is it rash to say that the symphony should be the second or third number of the program?

Nor is it by any means a universal custom to reserve the symphony for the last place. The first concert of the Paris Conservatory took place in March, 1828, and opened with Beethoven's Third Symphony. Looking over the program of successive years, it is seen that the symphony as a rule comes first. And in many German cities there is no fixed rule in regard to its place upon the program. The program is often divided into three parts, the second of which is devoted to the symphony.

The program of the second Symphony concert was:

Brahms	Variations on a Theme by Haydn
Goltermann	Andante and Finale from Concerto for 'cello in A minor
Mendelssohn	Overture, "Fingal's Cave["]
For 'cello:	
Bach	Air
Schumann	Traumerei
Popper	Papillon
Beethoven	Symphony No. 7[29]

Though Hale was eager to press his points, he was not out to discredit Nikisch. The fifth concert of the 1889–1890 season featured a trilogy of classical symphonic masterpieces: Haydn: *Symphony No. 88 in G*, Mozart: *Symphony No. 40 in G minor*, K. 550, and Beethoven's Fifth. As expected, Hale reviewed the performance of each symphony separately. He gave a very positive critique of the Haydn:

> ....The performance of this symphony was a triumph for the players and the conductor. It was the artistic triumph of the evening, and indeed of the career of Mr. Nikisch up to this date; for his "reading" was as artfully simple as the music itself. It was spontaneous, without any attempt of theatrical display. David Strauss, in his "Old and New Faith," acutely remarks that if you go to a concert where a symphony of Haydn is upon the program, you may be sure that if you are disappointed in it, the fault is in its performance. "And it can easily happen that the so-called 'best' orchestras will play it the worst. For they delight in spending their means of effect, such as the rough and sudden changes in strength of tone and tempo (upon which so many modern compositions depend), upon a music to which only the simplest execution does justice."[30]

Yet his critique of the Mozart singled out a perceived flaw in Nikisch's "heart-on-the-sleeve" romanticism:

> ....Now Mr. Nikisch has taken liberties in overtures by Beethoven and Weber for which he has been severely criticized. These were chiefly slight in tempo, generally found in connection with second motives and episodes. These liberties have found, on the one hand, warm admirers and earnest defenders; and the reasons for applauding instead of condemning are many. But take the first movements of the G minor symphony as played under Mr. Nikisch, was it as beautiful to the ear that night as it is the eye upon the printed pages? This wonderful child of inspiration and science is an allegro molto beginning with a melody given in octaves to the violins; the accompaniment is played by the other stringed instruments. It is an Italian song of restrained passion, of quiet intensity, such as is to be found in the first movement of Mozart's G minor quintet; it is direct, going straight to the mark, as terribly in earnest as many of the musical sentences of that old man Verdi. It stands at the very beginning of the symphony. Mr. Nikisch treated it sentimentally; he coquetted with it. It was beautiful, but it had as it were an artificial beauty; it was a woman bedizened and bedecked instead of the naked goddess, rosy and palpitating. Had this been the second motive instead of the first, there might have been a reasonable excuse; but surely at the beginning of a composition written so frankly and honestly, the rhythm should have been more sharply defined, and the melody given with more directness. I do not speak of any "traditions;" I do not speak of the "composer's intentions"; it seems to me looking at the score that in this case Mr. Nikisch failed to find the proper rhythm, and so the melody suffered; its sensuous warmth cooled and it became lukewarm. And the whole movement halted a little, and it seemed as though Mozart had put on airs of affectation.
>
> Yes, if the proper tempo is not found, the melody is ruined. How beautiful, for example, was the trio of the minuet in the same symphony; where if the "time" had been hurried one jot, the exquisite phrases allotted to the wind instruments would have been meaningless and confused. The minuets of Mozart and Haydn are often spoiled through the inability of conductors to discriminate between a scherzo and a minuet.[31]

The concert ended with the first of more than thirty performances of Beethoven's Fifth symphony that Hale heard the Boston Symphony play. His lengthy review[32] of it focused on the first five measures; fairly or unfairly, he also drew comparisons between this orchestra's performance and that of the Parisian Charles Lamoureux. To follow this up with a flex of muscle, he ended his review with these remarks:

> Six programs have thus far been presented to the music lovers of this city; and not one of them includes the work of a French composer. Is Mr. Nikisch acquainted with any of the compositions of the French school?[33]

This was written in 1889. The cosmopolitanism of the Classical era had long since given way to the Nationalistic styles of the Romantics. Though Impressionism had yet to make its mark, there was a noticeable difference between the German/British/American approaches to composition and the Franco/Russian. Hale had cast his lot with the latter. Not that he would always be, but at this point in his career his was clearly a Francophile. At the end of his review of the eleventh concert—one in which he extols Nikisch's reading of Beethoven's Second Symphony—his comments about the programming of the next concert, which pleased him, take a sardonic turn:

> Mr. Nikisch suddenly presents for the 12th concert a program made up of three novelties: a symphony by a Russian, a violin concerto by a Frenchman, and an overture by a German. Now an experience program-maker avoids extremes; still it is a delight to see at last the name of modern French and Russian composers upon programs which seem for three months to have been published solely in the interest of the Society for Propagating the German Faith.[34]

It would be presumptuous to say that Nikisch's widened scope of programming was in any way influenced by Hale's advocacy, though Hale's persistent call for a broadening of the orchestra's repertoire, even from the columns of the weekly *Boston Home Journal*, echoed throughout the symphonic community. The perceived amelioration of narrow programming, however, did not change the way that Hale would critique Nikisch's conducting; he continued to dole out either approval or disparagement—or both—as he saw fit. Sometimes a few carefully chosen words were all that were needed. The following is from a review of the seventeenth concert of the 1889–1890 season, in which Liszt's *Piano Concerto No. 2 in A* was performed:

> ....It is not too much to say that the playing of Mr. [Rafael] Joseffy was superb. His performance was eminently virile, yet although the temptation to pound was great, the pianist seldom forced tone into noise. His use of the pedal was remarkable; many bravura passages of exceeding difficulty were played without it, such is his marvelous technique; and his employment of the pedal-staccato was a liberal education to any observing student. Mr. Joseffy was listened to with profound attention and thrice recalled. Mr. Nikisch was unfortunate in his accompaniment.

American papers are still garrulous on the subject of Mr. Nikisch, says a London musical paper, who was really a god-send to the purveyors of "copy." One journal criticizes his attitudes in conducting, and another says that to do this is to reduce criticism to absurdity. But when a man perches himself on a high platform, and poses and gesticulates as part of the "show," opinions about his performance follow legitimately enough.[35]

Hale was quickly gaining a reputation. His sarcasm and wit were noted in New York's *Musical Courier*, where he was identified as "a critic who wields a trenchant pen and a musician of decidedly mature opinions."[36] One of these "decidedly mature" opinions had to do with his dislike for the cult followings that certain composers, particularly Wagner, had acquired. He was generally not fond of the music of Johannes Brahms, though it was not so much with Brahms, but rather with the Brahms idolizers, that he had a bone to pick:

> The blindest worshipper of Brahms could find no fault with the performance of the Symphony in C minor. In detail and as a whole it reflected great credit upon Mr. Nikisch and the orchestra. As for the symphony itself what will be the verdict of the future? Is it, as some would have it, the greatest orchestral work since Beethoven's Ninth? There is by the way much of Beethoven in this very symphony, and at times suggestions of the Ninth in themes, treatment of themes, and in coloring. No one will deny the breadth of the *adagio*, the gracefulness of the *allegretto* or certain overwhelming portions of the *finale*. The first and last movements however are crowded with material which seems superfluous and confusing; they share the reproach of Joncières in regard to the Second of Brahms when it was played in Paris in 1880: "It abounds in brushwood," And it must be admitted that owing to the length of the symphony and the lack of contrast between the movements it fatigues, particularly when placed at the end of a program.[37]

By the end of the 1889–1890 season, Hale had firmly established himself as a Boston Symphony Orchestra critic, and one to be reckoned with. It was also at this time that he entered Boston's social scene.

Since the middle of the nineteenth century, Boston had been dominated by a number of aristocratic, well-to-do families, many of which traced their ancestry back to colonial times. It was Oliver Wendell Holmes, Sr. who first used the term "Brahmin Elite" to describe what was in essence the Boston upper class of a modified Indian caste system. The Boston Brahmins were the pillars of the community—wealthy, highly educated, philanthropic, morally sound, religious, arts supporting—the Gnostics of their time. Cultivating their own accent ("a bet-tuh eye-deer"), this "ruling class" was self-perpetuating: their children attended the finest prep schools and private universities, and there was a significant amount of marriages among Brahmin families. Unfortunately, all of this led to a degree of exclusionism and snobbery.[38] Still, their contributions to society cannot be overlooked and, in general, Boston was the better for it.

The St. Botolph Club was and remains one of several private social clubs in the Boston area. Named after the patron saint of Boston (and from whom the original Boston in England received its name), it was founded in 1880. Its focus was on visual arts (periodic exhibitions were a feature), though this expanded to the other arts as well. As in the case of most of the other Boston clubs, its membership was limited by size (in this case, 125) and was by invitation only. For whatever reason, an invitation to membership was extended to Philip Hale and on May 31, 1890, he became a member.[39] Thus, just as Higginson and Isabella Stewart Gardner had done, Hale became a Boston Brahmin not by blood, but by association. It didn't stop here; the St. Botolph Club would be only the first of three such clubs that he would join.[40] He affectionately referred to St. Botolph's as "St. Bottle,"[41] though as Hale became more of a public figure, he bemoaned the lack of anonymity at the club. He wrote to his friend, composer Charles Martin Loeffler, in 1908: "Whenever we go to the St. Botolph there are persons who wish to see you and to ask me questions. There is no privacy there—not even in the privies."[42]

Sometime during the summer of 1890, Hale left the *Boston Home Journal* for a similar position with *The Boston Post*. Published six days a week, the *Post* had been in business since 1831 and had a much larger circulation. Hale's column, simply labeled "Music" or "Music Notes," varied greatly in length, probably due to the spatial requirements of the other news of the day. There was an anonymous commentary column, "Here in Boston," signed by "The Taverner" that usually appeared next to "Music." Though Hale would write regular nonmusic columns in the future for the *Boston Journal* and *Boston Herald*, it is doubtful that he wrote "The Taverner" for he would not join the Tavern Club for another two decades.

Hale's critique of the first symphony concert of the 1890–1891 season was consistent with what he had been writing previously; what would become his familiar trademark phrase, "The programme was as follows" now appears:

> The first of the series of concerts to be given this season by the Boston Symphony Orchestra under the direction of Mr. Nikisch took place Saturday evening at Music Hall. The programme was as follows:
>
> Overture—"Fingal's Cave" .... Mendelssohn
> Concerto in D minor, for two violins and
>   Orchestra of strings .... Bach
> Vivace. Largo. Finale (Allegro). .... Cadenza by Hellmesberger
>   (first time in these concerts)
> Symphony No. 3, in E flat, "Eroica" .... Beethoven[43]

He derided Nikisch's interpretation of the Mendelssohn:

> The programme chosen for the occasion was nowise remarkable—it was cut-and-dried, conventional obituary. In the Mendelssohn overture Mr. Nikisch tried to gain effects by a novel reading of familiar passages: the composition, as a whole, thereby lost in symmetry and it resembled more a potpourri than a coherent, well-proportioned work. The opening pages, on account of the slowness of the movement, became almost monotonous.

He also disliked the music in the Bach, but lauded the soloists:

> The concerto of Bach for two violins and string orchestra was exceedingly well played by the soloists, Messrs. Kneisel and Loeffler. The concerto itself, with the exception of the charming largo and Hellmesberger's skillfully constructed

cadenza, is tedious. Endless chains of passages in imitation soon become wearisome unless the attention is called away from the mere technical cunning of the composer. Lead men still rule us in the aria with imperious sway, and to even hint at the fact that the great masters were not always inspired seems to some as blasphemous as the conduct of Sydney Smith's friend, who ventured to speak disrespectfully of the equator. But the contrapuntal conventionalities of the past are as foreign to modern ears as the bravura airs of Händel. These men were great; they are still remembered in spite of the conventionalities of their time. Music changes with each generation, for it is subjective. The man of the seventeenth and eighteenth centuries is not the man of this nervous age, with its nervous diseases. The Bach of the concerto played Saturday evening is not the Bach of the "Passion," the "Well Tempered Clavichord" or the great compositions for organ.

He praised the performance of the *Eroica*, but had a warning for the conductor in dealing with H. D. Simpson, the orchestra's timpanist:

The symphony as a whole was well played, particularly the scherzo with its difficult horn passages. The liberties taken by the conductor in the first movement can easily be defended on musical grounds....

Mr. Nikisch should moderate the rage of his fell drummer. In a well-balanced orchestra the kettledrums should not always force themselves upon the ear, nor should the personality of the player be the subject of general comment.[44]

Six weeks later, he lodged a similar complaint:

The "Oberon" overture is evidently a favorite with Mr. Nikisch and as played by the orchestra under his direction it is a never failing delight. Throughout the evening, although the program itself was uninteresting, the playing of the orchestra was excellent. There were, it is true, occasional exhibitions of undue muscular exertion on the part of the kettledrum man, who has not by his playing given any adequate reason for his importation. Nor can the first clarinet be praised for his phrasing of the solo in the overture.[45]

New works were introduced as the season progressed. As what would become a pattern, Hale spent a large percentage of his column critiquing them, greatly reducing his commentary on standard works, especially if he had reviewed them before. He was keen on writing about American works, particularly if they had significant musical merit. One such work was the *Symphony No. 2 in B Flat*, Op. 32 by George Whitefield Chadwick (1854–1931). At that time Chadwick was making a career for himself as a composer, teacher, and organist. In the late 1870s, Chadwick had studied in Germany, particularly with Josef Rheinberger, with whom Hale would study a few years later. In 1897 Chadwick became Dean of the New England Conservatory and in the following year, with Ossian E. Mills, the school's bursar, would be instrumental in the founding of Phi Mu Alpha Sinfonia music fraternity. Hale wrote about the symphony:

Mr. Chadwick's Symphony brought this exceedingly interesting concert[46] to a close. It is a work of long breath, well-conceived, well expressed. It is the work of a musician by birth and breeding. It is an honor not only to himself but to his country. It shows a strongly-marked, well-defined individuality. You can never say when you hear it, "Mr. Chadwick is a disciple of X or Z." The music is that which comes out of Mr. Chadwick. It is his way of looking musically at musical things. Without speaking in detail of the many beauties of the work, the second movement must not be passed by. In the first place it is a scherzo, i.e., it is a jest. He uses the term as Schulert in the eighteenth century in his Sixth Sonata, as Monteverdi long before in his three-voice madrigals. It is not merely a conventional title applied to a fast movement of more passionate character with a romantic trio; it is a jolly jocose movement which approaches the edge of vulgarity. (And there are dealers in words who allege that true music must be tinged with coarseness.) The opening measures might serve to beat out the time to the heavy feet of roustabouts dancing on the levee. There is a smell of American soil in the same scherzo; a suggestion of the good-natured recklessness of the citizens of the States. We have as yet no truly American music; for the great number of compositions written by native composers, however excellent they might be, might be signed by foreign names. Perhaps the melodies written by David Braham for the plays of Edward Harrigan are the most serious contribution as yet to American music; for they are eminently characteristic; they suit the persons who appear in these sketches of life in New York, and you cannot imagine them sung with appreciation by the people of other lands. Now, Mr. Chadwick's scherzo could only have been written by an American, for its fun is intensely local, as is its color.

Mr. Chadwick conducted his own symphony and was loudly appreciated.[47]

The following week's program presented the critic with the uncomfortable circumstance of the conductor's wife as featured soloist. This unusual pairing presented Hale with a political as well as a musical problem. He had previously criticized Nikisch over and over again for his programming, conducting liberties, and balance, but now faced an expanded dimension. Most critics would have taken the easy way out, saying some complimentary things about Mrs. Nikisch and then quickly moving on, but Hale, of course, called it as he saw it:

Mrs. Arthur Nikisch, who sang publicly in Boston last week for the first time, appeared some time ago on a symphony concert at the Sanders Theatre, Cambridge, and then made a favorable impression, if applause be the outward token of sincere appreciation, and so Saturday evening she was most vigorously applauded before and after each group of songs. She is a mezzo-soprano; her voice is not of extended range, and it is naturally a pleasing one, for her medium register is of warm and sympathetic quality. Her high notes are weak, and she takes them badly; her lower ones are unstable. Her singing is more marked by the display of carefully studied taste and a cheerfulness of personality than by purity of tone production or technical skill. From the singing teacher's point of view, Mrs. Nikisch is not a well-trained vocalist; but she will undoubtedly be a favorite, for here as elsewhere, audiences regard more today the personal appearance and magnetic qualities of a singer than the use or abuse of the portamento. Her best work was observed in Brahms' song[48]. Her performance of the Mozart arias[49] showed the deficiencies of her technique and also established beyond a doubt that she was wanting in dramatic instinct; for nothing could have been more foreign to Mozart's music, the words of the libretto and the traditions, which have come down from the days of Mozart than Mrs. Nikisch's interpretation of these two immortal songs of passion. The accompaniments played upon the pianoforte by Mr. Nikisch were remarkably good.[50]

Hale was not entirely negative in his assessment of the singing; he was even complimentary about Nikisch's piano technique. It was, in his opinion at least, an honest mixed review. There was no vendetta here, no air to clear, and no vindictive pattern had been established. The following week Hale had nothing but good things to say about the orchestra's handling of the Chopin *Piano Concerto No. 2 in F minor*, Op. 21, Tchaikovsky's *Romeo and Juliet*, and Goldmark's *Rustic Wedding*, writing "The orchestra, under Mr. Nikisch, played a most sympathetic accompaniment [to the Chopin], and the two orchestral numbers of the program were exceedingly well played."[51]

Hale continued to write concert reviews for the *Boston Post* until December 1891, about a third of the way into the 1891–1892 season, when the trajectory of his career as a music critic suddenly skyrocketed. Three things contributed to this. The first was the invitation to be an associate editor of the *Boston Musical Herald*. This music journal, not to be confused with the *Boston Herald* newspaper, was the brainchild of George Henry Wilson (1854–1908), then program essayist for the Boston Symphony Orchestra. Rather than try to start up his own journal, Wilson acquired the "plant" of the journal from New England Conservatory[52] and made it his own by setting himself up as editor and publisher. His "new" independent journal started with Vol. XIII (November 1891), an issue of sixteen pages. Wilson was ambitious; he wanted a journal of rare quality; to do this he surrounded himself with a handful of associate editors, most of them being the most prestigious music critics he could find: Louis Elson (of the *Boston Advertiser*), whose chief role was to review new music, Benjamin Cutter (a composer who was to do preparations of Hanslick's critiques), Henry Krebiel (*New York Tribune*), W. J. Henderson (*New York Times*), and Hale. Henry T. Finck (*New York Evening Post*), Warren Davenport, and T. P. Currier were added later. To promote the *Boston Musical Herald*, Wilson took out advertisements in the Boston Symphony Orchestra program booklets. The following is from December 4–5, 1891:

This Afternoon
The December Number of the new
Boston Musical Herald
Can be bought at Music Stores and News-stands

Its special articles are by L.C. Elson, Philip Hale, Warren Davenport, Frederick Grant Gleason (Opera in Chicago), and Nathan Haskell Dole (who has written, from the only copy of the score in the country, an interesting article on Mascagni's new opera "L'Amico Fritz"). All the regular departments, including music in New York, by H. E. Krehbiel, and music in Boston by the Editor.

Subscription (beginning at any time) $1.00
Single Copies 10

SPECIAL ANNOUNCEMENT.

With the January number, the publisher will issue, free to subscribers, a picture of the

BOSTON SYMPHONY ORCHESTRA,

Being a reproduction in the Half-tone process of a photograph taken by H. L. Stebbin, e specially for this purpose...[53]

Hale's article in the December issue was "Two Foes to Criticism." In it he states, "The man who writes for a newspaper criticisms of musical performances has two dangerous foes: the publisher of the newspaper, and the reading public." It is essentially a diatribe lamenting the lot of the critic who writes an honest, negative review, the offended artist not wanting to buy future ads in the paper, and the publisher deciding whether or not to continue to employ the critic. It also tells of the audience member who, after reading the review, now feels foolish at having applauded a performance judged by the critic to have been of poor quality and, as a result, neither wanting to read any more reviews nor wanting to attend future performances. Most of the way through the article Hale describes the workaday role of the critic:

> Now the critic of a daily newspaper is obliged by the prevailing custom to write his notice immediately after the performance. He is obliged to write hurriedly; he is at the mercy of the night editor and the proofreader. He must write a readable notice and, too often, as George Moore puts it, "hysterical abandonment of critical reason is fomented in the red-pepper hours of spontaneous composition in a printing-office." He has but little time to weigh his sentences. He is tempted to accentuate unduly his phrases of praise or blame. And the man of midnight is a different being from the man of noon the next day....

The end of the article is bitingly satirical:

> So it is that there is a tendency in this country to settle questions of art by a showing of hands and the applause of the unthinking. "Reading articles" of a light and a gossipy nature are in many ways preferred to honest criticisms written by men of learning and convictions. They offend no one. They give interesting details concerning the parentage and the wardrobe of the singer. And they are often pleasingly illustrated.[54]

There were more articles to come. The *Boston Musical Herald* was a tremendous artistic success, but for various reasons it folded in 1893.[55] Two years later, many of its contributors, including Hale, found themselves writing for a new journal, *The Looker-on*, a monthly music, art, and drama magazine published by Whittingham and Atherton of New York.

The second thing contributing to Hale's spiraling success during the late Fall of 1891 was a change of employer. The *Boston Journal*, not to be confused with the *Boston Home Journal*, beckoned and Hale was more than ready for the call. The *Boston Journal*, which had started out as an evening newspaper in 1833, was now a daily paper that had a large Sunday edition. Hale was hired as music critic, but he also was given full reign over a nonmusical column, "Talk of the Day," of the "cabbages and kings" variety. Here he addressed all sorts of topics with his eloquence and wit. Though the humorist side of his personality often shone through, he didn't take it easy; these columns were thoroughly researched and he reveled in providing his readers with tidbits of knowledge and, occasionally, suggestions for further reading.

The *Boston Journal* also gave Hale star treatment. The Sunday paper usually consisted of five sections plus a magazine. On page four of the Department Section is where the banner "'Music and Musicians' by Philip Hale" would appear, usually at the top of the page and stretching across two to as many as all five columns. This was a much better newspaper home for Hale than he had experienced previously, and his relationship with the *Boston Journal* would last a dozen years.

The third item provided a foretaste of Hale's own destiny. It may have come as a complete surprise to those working on only the second issue of the *Boston Musical Herald* that the journal's founder, editor, and publisher George H. Wilson decided to leave town. This meant that Wilson would also be vacating his role as program essayist for the Boston Symphony Orchestra; his last program notes were written for the December 4th and 5th pair of concerts. There were many possible candidates to succeed him; Philip Hale was chosen. One could point out that Hale's position as an associate editor on the *Boston Musical Herald* could have given him a leg up to succeed Wilson, but Hale had written only one article for the journal to that point. It is more likely that Hale was recognized for the quality of the concert reviews he had written thus far. After the December 19, 1891 concert, *The Beacon* carried the following announcement:

> Since George H. Wilson's departure for Chicago, there to assume the secretaryship of the musical department of the World's Fair, the compilation of the notes for the programme Bulletin has been assumed by Mr. Philip Hale, who is sure to make his pages brilliant, diversified, and rich with the instructive fruits of knowledge and research.[56]

The Beacon's wording implied that Hale was to occupy the position permanently. It was a dream, and he had achieved it at the ripe old age of thirty-seven. The phrase "with Historical and Descriptive Notes Prepared by Philip Hale" appears for the first time on the cover page of the symphony's December 18–19, 1891 thirty-six page booklet. The program was a special one, commemorating the centenary of Mozart's death:

>   9th rehearsal and Concert
>   Programme In Memoriam W. A. Mozart
>
>   Overture to The Magic Flute
>   Arias from Don Giovanni
>   Masonic Funeral Music
>   Aria: "Dove Sono" from The Marriage of Figaro
>   Symphony in E flat [No. 39]

In addition to notes on the works performed, the Boston Symphony Orchestra program booklets had a special "Entr'acte," an article of extended length, usually on a subject related to one of the works on the concert. For this one, Hale put together "The Manner of Mozart's Death," featuring English translations of various accounts and directing those curious to further reading examples.

The December 24th and 26th pair of concerts featured a rather eclectic mix:

Handel:	Concerto for Strings and Two Wind Orchestras in F
Wagner:	Prelude, "Parsifal"
Rubinstein:	Ocean Symphony (Original version)

The Entr'acte for this program was "Opinions of Rubinstein," from the composer's autobiography translated by Aline Delano.

Hale's review of this concert for *The Boston Journal* pointed out the incongruity of the mix:

> I have more than once in these columns hinted at the absurdity of comparing together musicians of different centuries or even different generations. To solemnly weigh Handel and Wagner in the scales and then pronounce judgment is opposed to the spirit and the canons of modern criticism. The one, as well as the other, was an expression of his time. That is to say, each was in his way ahead of his time, but certain features, certain feelings of each century found fullest expression in the music of the one and in that of the other....[57]

Yet he was generally positive about the performance:

> The concerto was played with frankness and spirit. The work of the strings was generally to be warmly commended; the oboe solo passages were delightfully played; the horns were not always faultless in intonation or in quality of tone. The "Parsifal" prelude was played with great care, and the "Faith" motive was most defiantly proclaimed by the brass. The performance of the symphony was characterized by a brilliancy that was at times reckless.[58]

The program booklet of the next pair of concerts, January 1–2, 1892, does not have "with Historical and Descriptive Notes by Philip Hale," on its cover; in fact, there is no mention of any program annotator until October of that year, some nine months later. A statement by James M. Tracy of *The Boston Times*, however, verifies Hale's authorship of this booklet: "The analytical notes in the programme by Mr. Philip Hale are of great merit."[59] For the remainder of the season, however, the notes didn't amount to much and all of the Entr'actes were imported from other sources.

What happened? Hale was let go, not for the quality of his work, nor for his relationship with the orchestra, but because of the clout of one person: Arthur Nikisch. After taking aim at Hale's successor, Warren Davenport of the *Boston Transcript* confirmed what had happened nearly three years after the fact:

> In yesterday's *Herald* Mr. Woolf very justly arraigns Mr. Apthorp for the rubbish that he furnishes in making up the programme book for the Symphony rehearsals and concerts. Neither have Mr. Apthorp's effusions done him credit as regards the stability of his opinions and comments or the infallibility of his efforts as a historian. The man most capable of preparing such a book is Mr. Philip Hale, the musical editor of the *Journal*. Once during the time that Nikisch encumbered the position of conductor here Mr. Hale was engaged to compile this book, but after three his services were dispensed with, it was reported, by order of Nikisch because Mr. Hale saw fit to exercise his independence in his capacity as music critic, and not always to the credit of Mr. Nikisch's efforts. If I remember rightly, Mr. Hale's only objection to accepting the offer from the management was that his critical opinions in the *Journal* might not please Nikisch always, but this objection was waived by the management. Nevertheless, Mr. Hale's occupation was gone after the third issue of the book, Nikisch thereby, if the reports were true, being more potent than his managers. However Mr. Hale was eminently successful in his undertaking with the book, which is more than can be said of his successors.[60]

Thus, halfway through the 1891–1892 season, just as quickly as Hale had been put on a pedestal, he was knocked off it. His perceived "birthright" had been taken away. While support from other critics helped soften the blow, the scars from his dismissal would take a long time to heal. There was only one way for them to be entirely healed and that was through reinstatement. Hale, of course, had no way of knowing that that is precisely what would occur in the next decade. It is to Hale's credit that his write-up of the next concert, featuring the Cecilia Society chorus and the Shakespearean reader George Riddle (1851–1910), is consistent with his previous reviews, even with Mrs. Nikisch having a solo role in Schumann's Incidental Music to *Manfred*:

> The "Calling of the Alp Witch" was given with unusual delicacy and precision. The solo singers were adequate, although the unison passages of the "Incantation" were slightly marred by Mr. Meyn's singular habit of singing the two equal and final notes of a measure as though the first were dotted and the second of necessarily lesser value. In the "Hymn of the Spirits" the chorus was feeble; the requiem was sung with due effect.
>
> The applause of the evening, however, was given to Mr. Riddle, and deservedly: for he succeeded admirably in an arduous task. There might be a question as to his use of the "ascending scale"; possibly the last word of vanishing Astarte should be uttered as a reproach; but in view of the breadth and dignity and discrimination of performance, these and similar questions savor of hypercriticism.
>
> The concert opened with an excellent interpretation of the "Unfinished Symphony." It is interesting to note in this connection that the symphony was finished in 1891 by an earnest German named August Ludwig. His offense is aggravated by the fact that he has written a pamphlet in which he congratulates the world upon the accomplishments of his labor and the consequent satisfying of a long felt want. Incidentally he speaks of his own music in terms of warm approbation.[61]

It is interesting to note that Davenport's review of this same concert was much harder on Nikisch than Hale's, criticizing the programming and the conducting: "... never once was a sustained pianissimo realized. It does not seem to be a part of Mr. Nikisch's nature to conceive what sempre pianissimo means...."[62]

It would be a stretch to say that the sarcasm found in many of Hale's reviews of the 1890s stemmed from his losing his position; the acerbic side of his personality had been apparent as far back as his Albany days. Being the professional that he was, however, Hale kept the vast majority of his Boston Symphony Orchestra critiques on an even keel. He knew that the orchestra itself was not to blame. By and large he maintained a reasoned and restrained approach. Still, Hale needed an outlet for his inner rage and for this, either consciously or unconsciously, he identified not one, but two areas of great concern to him. The first was in the quality of the program notes written by his successor; the second centered on philosophical differences he had with *New York Tribune* music critic Henry Krehbiel (1854–1923) over Antonin Dvořák and what constituted American music.

Wiiliam Foster Apthorp, who assumed the role of Boston Symphony Orchestra program annotator on October 14, 1892, was well qualified for the position. He had already established himself as a critic of stature; his essay, "Some Thoughts on Music Criticism," formed part of a lecture "Musicians and Music-Lovers" that he had given at Lowell Institute during the 1886–1887 academic year. In this essay, Apthorp addressed the role of the critic:

> [The critic] must have a finer and more comprehensive point of view, and his highest function should be to let them [the readers]...listen to music with his ears....
>
> [Deciding what is good or bad] seems to me about as preposterous a position as a fallible mortal can well assume, and in this, as in most serious matters, it is hard to be preposterous without doing more harm than good.[63]

In his program notes, Apthorp was often quite verbose though, in Hale's opinion, sometimes not providing enough information. Hale thought that his own critiques should involve everything about the concert at hand—works, conducting, orchestral performance, audience—and program book. Everything was fair game. So, he clarified and enhanced information in the program books when he saw fit, thus creating ex post facto program note revisions. Sometimes he would simply refer to the "programme book," other times to "the compiler of the program-book," and still other times to Apthorp by name. The following is in reference to Bizet's *L'Arliesienne Suite no. 1*:

> The program book says that the Prelude opens with "a stern, march-like theme." Now this "march-like theme" is a march tune, and one that is well-known throughout France. It is an old Provencal Noel (or Christmas song), the "Marche dei Rei," the march of the Kings, the words of which are attributed to King Rene. The melody is two centuries older than the text. It is often called the March of Turenne.[64]

Hale also occasionally went on the offensive. Apthorp, who had an intense dislike for the music of Tchaikovsky, provided relatively scant information about the composer's *Pathetique* Symphony for its Boston premiere and it appears that Hale was livid:

> The program of the tenth Symphony concert, given last evening in Music Hall, Mr. Paur, conductor, was as follows:
>
> Symphony No. 6, in B minor, "Pathetique," Op. 74 (first time) .... Tschaikowsky
> Concerto for piano forte, in B major (first time) .... Henry H. Huss
> Overture to "Benvenuto Cellini" .... Berlioz
>
> The compiler of the program book saw fit to insert in the current number several platitudinous paragraphs masked as epigrams.
>
> For the same number he Englished an account of sundry dances of the time of Henry III, from "Les Origines de l'Opera," by Louis Leclercq. It is to be regretted that his courage failed him when he translated the description of the volte. He started out in fine feather, and the staid readers of program books were no doubt delighted to learn that "ladies who had well-turned legs could not afford to despise it (the volte), for they showed them freely.["] But why did he not pursue the interesting subject? Why did he not complete the paragraph ending "in keeping her skirts from flying in the air?" Why did he not follow the original (page 64), and quote from the good and free-spoken Tabouret? Why did he not tell the entertaining story of how Henry III, then Duke of Anjou, fell in love with Mary of Cleves

at a famous ball in 1572, when she danced the volte with prodigious vigor? 'Tis a tale of a shirt, and the curious can find it on page 66 of Celler's book.

The reader will find in this same program-book no information concerning the early history of Tschaikowsky's sixth symphony. And yet the question about its first performance is no more beyond conjecture than the "song the Syrens sang,["] or what name Achilles assumed when he hid himself among women.

The reader asks about this symphony. He finds in the program-book miscellaneous information and a pedagogic and imperfect view of the symphonic structure.[65]

Occasionally Apthorp slipped on the facts. Hale had no tolerance for this, and pointed out the errors. He knew within that he could have done a better job:

The program-book states that the Academic Festival Overture was written by Brahms in 1881. If the statement were true, it must have been composed hurriedly in the first week of January of that year, for it was performed early in the month at Breslau and Leipzig.[66]

Mr. Apthorp says in the program book of last night, "Coussemaker came out a year or two ago with a bulky volume, proving by carefully collected documents that Gregory the Great had next to nothing, if anything at all, to do with the establishment of the "Gregorian Chant."["]

Charles Edmund Henri de Coussemaker was in some respects a remarkable man, but he was not as remarkable as Mr. Apthorp would have us believe.

For Coussemaker died in 1876.[67]

The compiler of the program-book, speaking of Berlioz' "Childe Harold," says: "The work was first given in public at the Conservatoire in Paris on Nov. 23, 1834; but Berlioz introduced many alterations to the score afterwards. Paganini was present at the first performance; he expressed his delight with the work by sending Berlioz a check for twenty thousand francs the next day, which sum the poor composer devoted to paying off some crying debts, but especially to buying leisure to write his Romeo et Juliette Symphony, which he dedicated to Paganini."

But Paganini was not present at the first performance. He did not hear the work until Nov. 26, 1838. He had heard the "Symphonie fantastique" in 1833, and it was then that he asked Berlioz to write a piece of importance for the viola. Berlioz promised to write a viola solo which should express the "Last Moments of Mary Stuart," but he abandoned this idea, and finally wrote "Childe Harold."[68]

The program book announced that Goldmark was born May 18, 1832. As a matter of fact he was born in 1830.

Our old friend Friedrich Smetana figured on the title page of the program book as "Bedrich Smetana." This is accuracy with a vengeance.[69]

This "vengeance" was in force on March 14, 1897, when Hale devoted no less than 30 percent of his column on correcting Apthorp's notes on Felix Weingartner and Frederic Cowen:

And first a word about the program book. Weingartner's name is not spelled Weingaertner; or in other words the "a" is not modified.

The program book says Weingartner has written two operas. He has written three. "Genesius," "the third, was produced in Berlin, Nov. 15, 1892.

The program book makes no mention of Weingartner's strife stirring pamphlets: one on conducting, in which he has a bitter attack on the ultra-modern conductor; one published last year in which he attacks the present management of the Bayreuth festival. In each of these articles he roasts Nordica unmercifully. He has written other pamphlets, and when "Genesius" was produced in Berlin he made a savage reply in the newspapers to the critics.

The program book tells when Cowen's fourth and fifth symphonies were produced. It does not give the date of the first performance of the third symphony, the one played last night. This date is Dec. 18, 1880. Nor in the sketch of Cowen's life is there any allusion to his operas. "Signa," first produced at Milan in 1893, and "Harold," produced at London in 1895. "Pauline" (1876) is mentioned, but it was a failure, not "brought out with great success." There is no allusion to "Thorgrim," produced in 1889, which met with a happier fate.[70]

This was quite a tongue thrashing and yet, toward the end of the same column, Hale wrote, "Mr. Apthorp's remarks on Wagner's views are well worth reading."

Hale continued his quest for truth in program booklets throughout the decade. Perhaps his most scathing attack came toward the end of Apthorp's tenure, on the issue of the numbering of Tchaikovsky's *Violin Concerto*:

Mr. Apthorp in the Program-Book speaks of Tschaikowsky's concerto in D major, Op. 35 as "No. 2." Has Mr. Apthorp ever seen a copy of Tschaikowsky's concerto "No. 1?" Does he know what key it is in? Or can he tell who played the "No. 1" for the first time. Perhaps Tschaikowsky did write two concertos; but you will find no mention of them in the books. Tschaikowsky in his memoirs speaks of his "violin concerto." But he was a shy man and undoubtedly thought he should be contented with one work of this kind. Furthermore, the title- page of the score of this "No. 2" says "Concerto for violin." I fear that here is another instance of Mr. Apthorp's Olympian indifference to the facts, another instance of his dazzling inaccuracy. I say "I fear," for I cannot believe that Mr. Apthorp made such a blunder. He surely has the other concerto up his sleeve.[71]

This was not Hale's finest hour. The vast majority of his previous attacks had been directed toward Apthorp's notes, not to him personally. Indeed, there may have been no animosity between the two of them; both were members of the St. Botolph Club. In 1901 Apthorp stopped writing program notes for the Boston Symphony Orchestra; in 1903 he retired from the *Boston Evening Transcript* and retired with his wife to Vevay, Switzerland, where he remained for the rest of his life. A planned return to Boston never happened. Hale lamented this in a letter written on August 2, 1908 to Charles Martin Loeffler: "I hear Apthorp's return is postponed a year and I regret this very much."[72]

During the Spring of 1893 elements of change were sweeping through the Boston Symphony Orchestra. Hale was not alone in having incurred Nikisch's wrath. In a letter to Oscar W. Donner dated April 25, 1893, Henry Lee Higginson commented on Nikisch's behavior toward the end of his Boston Symphony conductorship, spurred on by the conductor's refusal to accompany the orchestra for concerts at the World's Columbian Exposition in Chicago:

DearDonner:

Mr. Nikisch has made me a great deal of trouble. He lost his temper because I would not keep him, for remember it was I who told him that I would not renew his engagement and advised him to make the Budapest bargain, and I absolutely refused the conditions which he made. He requested me to let him off on the $5000 which he is bound to pay for breaking his contract before the end of it if he carried out the season to my entire satisfaction; and, at the present date, which is the middle of the week just before our last concert, and just before our journey of three weeks, he has written a very insolent letter, declaring that he will not go on the journey unless I fulfilled certain conditions which are inadmissible.

He was told in writing on the 30th of March by me that the $5000 would not be demanded of him if he carried through the season to my satisfaction, which means simply that he will play his concerts as usual....

I have thought it possible that he might be raking some trouble for me in Vienna, and at one time I wrote to you a cable to suggest it and to ask you to look the matter up and contradict any fallacies which he might have uttered.

All these particulars about his late conduct with regard to leaving at once it is perhaps useless to tell until I telegraph you that you can tell it, as I do not want to make any trouble for him or for anybody else, and he may retract his follies; but I do not propose to be injured by him either there or anywhere else.

Mr. Nikisch pleads ill health, which no one else can see, for he looks as well as usual. He has been working more than usual because he has been playing in concerts for himself, all of which is against his contract.

The whole matter has been put in the hands of counsel and submitted to others, so that my own feelings should not guide me, and you can rely upon seeing from him several of the most remarkable letters that I have ever received, so far as insolence goes. For instance, at the present time he demands that a cheque for all that is due him to him, plus $2000, shall be given him at once, or else he will, not move an inch. His contract calls for pay each week in the regular way, and as he has always had pay in advance he knows that he can rely on getting his dues in the regular manner and without fail.

Yours very truly,
H. L. Higginson

Oscar W. Donner, esq.
Hotel Imperial, Vienna Austria[73]

Thus it was that Nikisch, having overstayed his welcome, returned to Europe and took over the conductorship of the Royal Opera House in Budapest. He was succeeded in Boston by the less flamboyant Emil Paur (1855–1932), an Austrian, who would serve as conductor of the Boston Symphony Orchestra for the next five seasons.

The remarkable World's Columbian Exposition in Chicago featured music from around the world. There the Boston Symphony Orchestra played two concerts and, separately, Antonin Dvořák conducted his Eighth Symphony. Dvořák had been lured to America during the summer of 1892 to assume the directorship of the National Conservatory of Music in New York at the then-unheard-of salary of $15,000 per annum. The invitation was from Mrs. Jeanette Meyers Thurber, who had founded the school in 1885 and who was the school's chief benefactor. Almost from the onset of his arrival, Dvořák displayed a passion for the music on this side of the Atlantic that was exotic to him—the music of African-Americans and Native Americans. On May 21, 1893, his most famous quote appeared in the *New York Herald*: "In the Negro melodies of America I discover all that is needed for a great and noble school of music."[74] This created quite a stir, and not just in New York.

Chief among Dvořák's supporters was the highly influential *New York Tribune* critic Henry Edward Krehbiel. An exact contemporary of Hale, Krehbiel was born in Ann Arbor, Michigan to German immigrant parents. Like Hale, he started to study law—but that is where the similarity ends. Unlike Hale, Krehbiel was largely self-taught in music and music criticism. He started as a music critic for the *Cincinnati Gazette* at the age of twenty in 1874, when Hale was still a student at Yale. And at twenty-six, in 1880, Krehbiel became music editor for the *New York Tribune*, a position he would hold for the remainder of his life. In addition to this work, he served as American editor for the 2nd edition of *Grove's Dictionary of Music and Musicians* and wrote program notes for the New York Philharmonic. Known to many as the dean of American music critics, and to those who knew him personally as "Pop," he carried in his brain a vast resource of musical knowledge. He championed the music of Wagner, Tchaikovsky, and Brahms, but at the start of the twentieth century, when the firm common practice period tonalities began to loosen, he did not support the music of Mahler, Richard Strauss, Stravinsky, Prokofiev, and Schoenberg. Krehbiel shared Dvořák's fascination for African-American folk music, even writing a book on African-American folk songs. Over his long and distinguished career he penned over a dozen other books on music, yet he is probably best known and respected for his 1921 translation and completion of Natick, Massachusetts native Alexander Wheelock Thayer's *Life of Beethoven*, the first reliable biography of the great composer.

Hale had a working knowledge of musical happenings in New York; from 1892 to 1898 he served as Boston correspondent for that city's *Musical Courier*, and many of his concert critiques were reprinted in that periodical. While he enjoyed having contacts there, he didn't care for the city itself. He later commented to Charles Martin Loeffler, "I would not live in that city if I had $100,000 a year."[75]

The New York Philharmonic's December 16, 1893 premiere of Dvořák's *Symphony No. 9*[76] *in E minor*, Op. 95, "From the New World," conducted by Anton Seidl at Carnegie Hall, was of great interest to him. Even before the event, the symphony prompted discussions about what American music was. Was this symphony truly American because it had been composed here, and/or because it employed African-American and Native American motifs? Or was it a Bohemian symphony, colored by American folkloric melodic lines? Positions were being taken. Being in close contact with the composer, Krehbiel had the upper hand, at least at the onset. On the day preceding the symphony's premiere, he published a 2,500-word essay, with excerpts, supporting the first position. James Gibbons Huneker, editor of the *Musical Courier*, disagreed, however, arguing that *the* American symphony had yet to be written.

Less than two weeks later, on December 29, 1893, the symphony was played in Boston for the first time. Just as Krehbiel had done, Hale published an extended essay about the work, although his was printed three days after the Boston premiere. Hale's essay took the opposing stance, maintaining that the work was not an American symphony. His review of the performance appeared in the same issue:

MUSIC

The Tenth Concert of the Boston Symphony Orchestra.

The program of the Symphony Concert given last evening in Music Hall was as follows:

Symphony No. 5, E minor .... Dvorak
Concerto for violin .... Beethoven
Overture "1812" .... Tschaikowsky

The question is not: Where did Dvorak find the thematic material for this new symphony?

The question is this: What did Dvorak do with the material after he found or invented it?

It is immaterial whether this symphony "From the New World" is American, Bohemian, or Celtic. The question is this: is the music good or bad?

*
**

Dvorak has here written a pleasing work, a work that abounds in melody, that shows the ingenuity of the trained musicians, that is brilliant in color. It is a work that will undoubtedly be popular, and deservedly popular.

He has succeeded in the main task and he has thus won glory enough.

*
**

But what is all this wild talk about the invention at last of "American" music?

Here is an excellent Bohemian composer. He is imported by the patroness of a music school, and at considerable expense. His dwelling in our country is undoubtedly, in a certain sense, an honor to us. He suddenly makes the discovery that "American" music must be built on Negro and Indian airs. He writes this symphony to prove his theory and found "American" music.

But let us ask a few questions.

If this symphony were played without any advance and explanatory notice in any European city, would a German, or Italian, or Russian, or Scot, or Frenchman say at once, "Why, this is American music!"

Would he not find any and all music but American?

Would he not find Scandinavian hints, Hungarian rhythm, Bohemian thought, Scotch melody; would he not find tributes to all nations; would he not admire the workmanship and leave the concert hall without a thought of Negro, Indian or native born white citizen of the United States?

*
**

The rhythm of the first phrase of the first movement is partly suggestive of the Southern steamboat and the plantation; but the rhythm is also partly European. The larghetto is full of Scotch and Scandinavian suggestion. The scherzo is anything you please; but, this may be said, as an exhibition of American characteristics real or alleged, as a musical exhibition of dash, "smartness," lack of reverence, and general devil-me-care, it is not to be named in the same breath with Mr. Chadwick's symphonic scherzo.[77] As for the finale, that, too, is what-you-will: there is a hint at "Yankee Doodle," but the temporary use of a transplanted tune does not make an "American" symphony.

Nor can you expect a Bohemian composer to throw off suddenly his nationality and forget it when he writes.

*
**

But there is much that is beautiful in this same symphony. First of all, it is cheerful and agreeable music. There is no touch of pessimism. The composer has the simple faith of a health child. There is the spirit of Nature. There is a thought of woods and fields. Simple and pleasing thoughts are expressed intelligibly. At times the thoughts are clad gorgeously in instrumental colors, but the beauty of the thoughts does not suffer thereby, nor is it puffed up or distorted. After one hearing, the slow movement seems to me the gem of the work.

....The playing of the orchestra was excellent. Mr. Paur conducted with authority, sympathy, and skill. The program was too long. The second and third movements, or at least the third movement of the concerto, might well have been omitted.[78]

When the symphony was repeated the following year in Boston, Hale's review was quite brief:

The anthropological symphony of Dvořák seems like an omnium gatherum of the folk songs of all nations, rather than the one, complete, inevitable identification of musical America. Viewed simply as music, it contains many delightful passages. The first two movements are the most satisfying: the scherzo and the finale seem somewhat monotonous, and long spun out on a second hearing.[79]

Hale heard the symphony many times throughout his career. Over three decades later, in 1929, he made the following somewhat more diplomatic observation:

Dvorak's symphony, which once excited controversy, has not been played here by the Symphony Orchestra since March, 1920. Today there is little or no talk about its origin, which at the time the symphony was first performed was misunderstood especially by those who shouted its praise, screaming: "It's 100 per cent American." The symphony is popular. The tunes are obvious. Some of them can be hummed and whistled as one is leaving the hall. There are otherwise interesting pages in the work. But when Dvorak was on his native soil, he rose to a greater height as a composer, than when he composed an oratorio for England and a symphony for the United States. The performance yesterday was all that could be asked, and the audience was greatly pleased.[80]

The diametrically opposed views expressed by Hale and Krehbiel at least partially reflect the differences of the writers' experiences in the cities in which they worked. New York was far more cosmopolitan, far more diverse, with hundreds of thousands of immigrants passing through then-new Ellis Island each year, choosing either to remain in its metropolitan area or to move to other locales. Boston was much smaller and far less ethnically diverse. There was no Liberty Enlightening the World there. The city had one large "minority" community, the

Irish, which made up about a third of its population. Even this proportion is somewhat overstated, as all of Ireland was part of the United Kingdom at that time, including the Protestant north. At this time, being born in Vermont, schooled in Germany and France, and working in Albany and Boston, Hale would have had little contact with persons not of his own race, let alone heard their music.

Boston was not diverse in terms of serious music either. Of the composers writing on this side of the Atlantic, those of the Second New England School, sometimes called the "Boston Classicists"—John Knowles Paine, George Whitefield Chadwick, Horatio Parker, Amy Beach, Edward MacDowell, Frederick Converse and others—dominated the American concert scene. All had been schooled in Europe and were contributing major romantic works to the orchestral repertoire. They weren't the first of America's symphonic composers—William Henry Fry and George Frederick Bristow preceded them—but they, as individuals and as a group, were quite successful. Together they represented Hale's view of the American music world. As for the Americanism in Dvořák's symphony, Hale had already heard parts of it in works composed three years earlier: the opening motif of the "Largo" dominating Chadwick's *Symphony No. 2* and the opening motif of Dvořák's "Finale" used in the opening movement of MacDowell's *Piano Concerto No. 2*. So for Hale, Dvořák's symphony was strictly a Bohemian work, not an American one. In a similar vein, Hale would have considered Gustav Holst's *Beni Mora Suite*, Op. 29, No. 1, a work where the composer incorporated tunes he had heard while in Algeria, as an English work by an Englishman, not as an Algerian piece.

Taking pot shots at Dvořák had not always been a pastime for Hale. Consider his 1892 comments about the composer's *Czech Suite*, Op. 39, originally intended as a serenade for small orchestra, a complement to his other two works in that form: the *Serenade for Strings in E*, Op. 22 and the *Serenade for Winds in D minor*, Op. 44 :

> There is spontaneity in the suite by Dvořák that is thoroughly delightful; that is sought in vain in later and more ambitious works by him. There is here no groping after an effect, no vague oracular shriek from a Bohemian tripod. The different numbers are not unlike cabinet pictures of folk life. The people are presented frankly in their simplicity and jollity. Such fresh and melodious music is welcome in the close air of Music Hall. The Dvořák polka makes more for musical righteousness than symphonic poems "in eight mystic devices and three paraphrases" or symphonies that are said to represent the struggle of Man with the Infinite. Nor is the furiant, known of old as the furie, to be despised. Perhaps in time we may become acquainted with the chodovska, the husitska, the Umrlec, the skakava, the strasak, and the baorak; for the Bohemians are a people of many steps, and Alfred in "Bohemian National Dances," writes of 136 distinct varieties in the manner of stamping, gliding, and leaping into the air.[81]

In his review of the same work five years later, however, Hale threw darts:

> ....There are charming passages in the Suite, which was written before Dvořák was a purveyor by appointment to English music festivals, or the director of a conservatory, or a buyer of gold bricks in the shape of Congo-Iroquois folk-songs. Welcome are spontaneity and freedom from anxiety.[82]

The above may appear to be racist from a twenty-first-century viewpoint, but unlike, say, John Philip Sousa's 1910 suite *Dwellers of the Western World*, Hale was neither building up nor degrading any particular race or nationality. He was only pointing out in a satirical manner what he considered to be the absurdity of the Krehbiel-Dvořák position. He continued to deride Dvořák in his columns as a composer who had sold out:

> Interesting, too, was Dvořák's "Carnival Overture," full of blood and leaping in the air and delirious delight. The contrasting andantino is charmingly orchestrated, but had the overture the strength, the swing of the Dvořák of old, before he wrote to English order and made a pilgrimage to Spillville, Iowa?[83]

And later, on the same overture:

> The overture, which Dvořák's publishers saw fit to name "Carnival," is specious music, decorative and all that, but I fear that it has no bowels.[84]

This scoffing even worked its way into his negative 1896 review of the Dvořák Cello Concerto:

> I confess I see no excuse in this enlightened age for a 'cello concerto, unless the concerto is very short and of two strongly contrast movements. The instrument is not well adapted to a work of long breath. There is a sweet cantabile, and then comes the bravura described by no less an authority than Hanslick as a chasing of flies up and down the strings. Now a little of this goes a great way. Add to this the inevitable monotony due to the somber quality of the instrument.
>
> Dvořák in this concerto, as in other late works of his, has run emptying. His themes are for the most part ultra-sentimental, or vulgar; his development of them is glided padding; the whole effect is one of insincerity rather than the naiveté that was truly one of his distinguishing characteristics before he wrote under contract for English audiences and English publishers. The second movement, an adagio ma non troppo, will undoubtedly be popular, and the 'cellist will reap a harvest of applause, but the music is neither lofty nor of real sensuous beauty; and we have a right to expect better things from the Bohemians. There are passages in the concerto that sound as though they were thought of originally for the alleged Negro Symphony, and were rejected; but rejected with care, saved for future use. As a whole the work is dull and no brilliancy of orchestration can remove the impression of dullness. Another sign of Dvořák's falling powers is his interminable good-by to a theme. He pumps his hands; he will not let it go, although they may be standing in a wind-swept corner.[85]

Even putting Dvořák aside, Hale continued his campaign against Krehbiel's position on what was American music. Sometimes it resulted in a piercing satire, even aimed at a composer and/or a piece he really liked. Edward MacDowell's *Suite No. 2*, Op. 48 "Indian," was premiered on January 23, 1896 by the Boston Symphony Orchestra in, of all places, New York. After praising the quality of the work, Hale wrote the following:

> ....That Mr. MacDowell took some or all of his thematic material from North American Indians doesn't interest me in the slightest. I go to a concert to hear music, not to study or discuss folklore.

Then these "Indian Tunes." Might not some returned warrior avenge himself upon the white oppressor by inventing some melody on the spur of the moment? Somehow or another, I always associate Indian tunes with Mr. Krehbiel. I see him in close confab with a plug-hatted venerable chief, as they discuss folk-songs over a jug of firewater. The phonograph is close at hand. The firewater begins to work and old Three-Tones-in-His-Voice chirps like a cricket. "Did you ever hear this, my pale-faced brother? Listen to the Scotch snap." The phonograph records the wondrous melody. Another drink, another folk-song, another burst of confidence to the phonograph. Why, the little jug is an anthology!

Mr. MacDowell may take his themes where he pleases, from an intoxicated chief who weeps at the name of J. F. [James Fennimore] Cooper; from Brer Krehbiel and his fellow explorers; from a relative of George Catlin; or from the rich storehouse of Mr. DeKoven. The question is: what does Mr. MacDowell do with the tunes after he takes them home?[86]

MacDowell actually felt much the same way that Hale did, stating, "So-called Russian, Bohemian, or any other purely national music has no place in art, for its characteristics may be duplicated by anyone who takes the fancy to do so.... Music that can be made by 'recipe' is not music, but tailoring."[87]

In his review of the same work nearly two years later, Hale wrote the following:

It is often stated that Mr. MacDowell's "Indian Suite" was inspired in a measure by Dvořák's so-called American symphony. When the Suite was played in Chicago Nov. 12, Mr. Arthur Mees, whose program-books are at the same time scholarly, sane, and interesting, fell into this error, and wrote that "Mr. MacDowell was undoubtedly influenced in turning to aboriginal American melodies by Dvořák's counsel, precept, and example."

Now as a matter of fact Mr. MacDowell had almost finished the Suite before Mr. Dvořák landed at New York.

*
**

I have discussed the Indian Suite twice at least in the Journal at considerable length, and I do not think it necessary to go over the same ground again.

Yet the temptation to speak of the fresh beauties in the detail revealed at each repeated hearing is strong, for the imaginative strength and the superb workmanship are not to be fully appreciated after one hearing. It is not a work that will be popular at once; I doubt if it will ever be popular in the common meaning of the term, for it is free from everything that is meretricious; it is without any taint of sentimentalism; it is without forced bizarrerie, and it avoids any panoramic detail that is dear to the superficial. But I know of few more remarkable pages of music than the unutterably sinister interruption in the movement entitled "In War Time" and the dirge that might well serve for the final In Memoriam of a once mighty race. In many respects, as in the higher qualities, as depth of thought and sustained flight of imagination, I place this work among the noblest compositions of modern times.

*
**

....I am enthusiastic over the triumph of a great composer, who has worked steadily and courageously in the face of discouragement; who has never courted by trickery or device the favor of the public; who never fawned upon those who might help him; who in his art has kept himself pure and unspotted.

I say in the magazine[88] of today that I believe Mr. MacDowell is one of the greatest composers now living. I do not say "American composers," for I include all composers in this statement, and in Art there should be no parochialism or chauvinism.

My belief is only riveted by the performance of last night, one that Mr. Paur, as well as Mr. MacDowell will remember with pride in years to come.[89]

Hale followed this up with a review in the *Musical Record*:

The concerto [*Piano Concerto No. 2 in A minor*] was more pleasing to the great majority than was the suite; but when the former reveals a man of talent, the Indian Suite stamps him as a genius. Is this a rash statement? Time will answer. Mr. MacDowell played with virility, dash, and dominating individuality.[90]

Another composer of the Second New England School whom Hale held in high esteem was Amy (Mrs. H. H. A.) Beach. He had lauded her solo performances on the Chopin *Piano Concerto No. 2 in F minor*, Op. 21 and the Saint-Saëns *Piano Concerto No. 2 in G Minor*, Op. 22. He also witnessed the premiere of her own *Symphony in E minor*, "Gaelic," Op. 32, of which he had the following to say:

Mrs. Beach is by no means the first woman who has written a symphony. A French woman, an admirable musician, wrote three, which were performed in Paris. Three English women have written symphonies, two of which have been performed in London. There are German women, whose names appear in the catalogue of symphony writers. The most remarkable was Aline Hundt, a pupil of Liszt, whose symphony in G minor was played at Berlin in the spring of 1871 and conducted by her in a manner that won the praise of critics who were prepared to scoff.

But any consideration of the part played by women in the history of orchestral works must be reserved for the Wednesday article.

Other thoughts suggested by the symphony of Mrs. Beach must be reserved till then. The election[91] is just now the one important thing and Art must sit quietly in the background.

*
**

It is fortunately not necessary to say of the "Gaelic" symphony, "This is a credible work for a woman." Such patronage is uncalled for, and it would be offensive. Nor is it necessary to say, "A praiseworthy endeavor." The endeavor is of little importance in art. The result is more to the purpose.

The crowded news columns only allow today the record of a few impressions. Let me say frankly that this symphony is the fullest exhibition of Mrs. Beach's indisputable talent. I think it should be ranked as a whole above her Mass, which was performed by the Handel and Haydn. The themes themselves may or may not be of importance; we will talk this over together later; certainly the treatment of them in the first, second, and fourth movements often excites honest admiration and gives a genuine pleasure. I except the slow movement, for it seems the most labored and at the same time the weakest.

First of all this music, as a rule, sounds well. For the jest is true, that there is music that is better than it sounds. Charming ideas of Schumann, for instance, are often shockingly dressed in orchestral robes. But in this symphony of Mrs. Beach there is the evidence of orchestral instinct rather than suspicion of loose experimenting. Some composers treat the orchestra as a child fools with a new box of blocks. There are grotesque combinations, impossible architectural devices. The child is surprised and delighted. Mrs. Beach wrote in this instance as though she were sure of the effects she had thought out. You do not at once feel that piano music has been fitted this away and that way and anyway to the orchestra.

Occasionally she is noisy rather than sonorous. Here she is eminently feminine. A woman who writes for orchestra thinks, "I must be virile at any cost." What Saint-Saëns said of Augusta Holmes is true of the sex.

Of the four movements, the second now stands out in sharpest relief. There is plenty of good stuff in the first; there is an elemental swing as well as a force that almost approaches grandeur in the finale; there are many excellent things in the detail on which I would fein dwell, but the scherzo is to me the most complete, rounded and truly musical of the movements.

Mrs. Beach, who was applauded heartily, acknowledged the tribute of the audience modestly.[92][93]

Hale was not being chauvinistic in his response; he liked this symphony. It was beyond him to be kind just because the composer was a woman; his was a level playing field. This in itself is manifested by the harsh commentary he had hurled three years earlier after the performance of the *Dramatic Overture*, Op. 12 by Margaret Ruthven Lang (1867–1972), daughter of conductor B. J. Lang. It was the first time that the Boston Symphony Orchestra had played a work by a woman composer:

The phrase *Place auz dames* should be without meaning on the concert stage.

The conductor of an orchestra should judge of the fitness of a composition proposal for performance without consideration of the sex of the composer.

A symphony is not good because the young and talented composer has suffered acutely from indigestion. A badly written song is still bad, even if the author sold newspapers at the age of six. The sufferings or the joys of the individual may color the composition and give it individuality, but its musical worth is not accurately determined by mere mention of sickness or health, poverty or riches, religious belief or sex.

A concert devoted to "the education of popular taste" should not be turned into a classroom exercise for the purpose of testing compositions of students for the discovery of merit or the correction of faults.

Nor should Music Hall be turned into a hothouse for the purpose of forcing talent.

It is the duty of a conductor to put gallantry in his pocket and examine carefully the score, even when the work is presented by a blushing maiden, a matron of reserve or a toothless crone.

*
**

These observations of a general nature may be applied in part to the case of Miss Lang, who has in the past given undeniable proofs of her possession of a musical nature. She has shown in certain songs with pianoforte accompaniment a pretty knack of melody, and her compositions have often been characterized by refinement and grace. But there is a mighty difference between a song and a "dramatic overture" for orchestra.

*
**

In the present instance Miss Lang has little to say, although she seeks many means of expression. Her themes are neither of marked originality nor of musical importance. The working-out is not so much working-out as working-after something. There is no apparent definite purpose, or the purpose is frittered away in search after effects. As an overture, the piece is amorphous. Dramatic, to be sure, is a comparative term, but in the common acceptation of the word, there is not one dramatic stroke in the whole work, nor is there a climax. As a fantastic tone poem, it is vague. Miss Lang finds at her disposal the orchestral paint box, and she colors her themes with this instrumental tablet and with that one; then she gains, occasionally, a piquant effect, a pleasing passage, but the whole lacks coherency and is diffuse.

In a word, this composition might well please the eye of a prudent and skilled teacher. He might look kindly at the pupil and say: "This is good; this shows promise; you are making progress. Now put it away and we will review your exercises in strict style." He would now be satisfied with "the spirit of the form" or "the sympathy with the form." He would demand the thing itself and not its impalpable atmosphere.

The overture was applauded and there was a vain effort made to call the composer forward.[94]

Such a review would have been devastating to any young composer, but Margaret Ruthven Lang rebounded quickly. Her overture *Witichis*, Op. 10 was performed by the Theodore Thomas Orchestra (Chicago Symphony) at the World's Columbian Exposition in August of that same year. Her orchestral works are no longer extant (possibly destroyed by her), but she did go on to compose more than 200 songs. In the years to come she remained loyal to the Boston Symphony: her subscription of ninety-one consecutive years set a record. In 1967 she was honored by the symphony with a concert celebrating the centenary of her birth.[95]

One composer that Hale consistently praised was Charles Martin Loeffler (1861–1935). Although he has occasionally been grouped with the Second New England School of composers, he clearly was not one of them. Loeffler always maintained that he was born in Alsace, on the border between German and France, but this was not the case; he was actually born in Berlin.[96] When he was a boy, Prussian authorities incarcerated his father, who died in prison. Ever since then, he denied his heritage, both with misstatement of facts and through the style of the music in which he wrote. In 1881 Loeffler immigrated to the United States; in the following year he was named assistant concertmaster of the Boston Symphony Orchestra. He became an American citizen in 1887.

Loeffler himself played the solo part when his *Divertimento in A minor for Violin and Orchestra* was premiered in 1895. Hale commented:

Mr. Loeffler was applauded enthusiastically for his performance and his composition. I can imagine easily an excellent and estimable person, fond on music, and learned in the primer of form, saying: "Oh yes, this divertimento is all very well as a show piece, and Mr. Loeffler played finely, but there is not much in it. No development of thematic material, and the variations in the finale are bizarre." Now Mr. Loeffler, as it seems to me, has a large sympathy for the modern French and Belgian decadent. He believes in tonal impressions, in effects of color, rather than in conscious plodding in the sonata ruts. The macabre is not distasteful to him.

He likes sharp contrasts. He delights in instrumental experiments. If he sought expression in verbal phrase he would cotton to Verlaine and Moréas and Rimbaud and Retté.

This divertimento shows clearly that Mr. Loeffler has a right to make experiments. There are strange or delightful effects throughout the work: as in the unison of harp and violas in the preambulum, the singularly effective use of muted trumpets in the eclogue, the alternate pizzicato in the finale. The romantic interrupts constantly the severe in the opening movement, as though it protested against the revival of old-fashioned precluding. Beautiful in thought and treatment is the eclogue, where no violins are used. The absence of the biting strings gives one some idea of how Mêhul's "Uthal," a one-act opera without fiddles, would finally exasperate the ear. Mr. Loeffler stopped his eclogue in time, or the audience might have uttered the famous cry of Grêtry, as he signed for a chanterelle, "Never mind the color of the movement," says an objector. "How about the thought?" Well, it was not spectacled, it was not dull; it was fresh and soothing and delightful.

Of course if you see the word ecologue and then feel a 6-8 rhythm and hear instruments associated with warm landscapes, flocks and herds, and high, indolent clouds, you are pastorally inspired. But without the name, the music might be "The Bride," or "Viola," or "As You Like It." In fact, you cannot in such music separate thought and color....To say that this is a creditable work is to talk like a pedagogue. It is indeed a fascinating composition, one that pricks suggestion and provokes moods.

And the composer played his difficult part with the accuracy, the brilliancy, the delicacy, and the purity that are so characteristic of him.[97]

In the years to come, Loeffler would become one of Hale's closest friends.

This concert, as in the case of nearly all, if not all, of the concerts of 1893–1898, was conducted by Emil Paur. Paur was not Higginson's first choice to succeed Nikisch. Higginson originally had wanted Hans Richter, who was unable to break his iron-clad contract.[98] Paur was born in Czernowitz, Austria (today Chernovtsky, Ukraine), and was a classmate of Nikisch when the two of them studied in Vienna. Paur's credentials were solid: he had previously conducted in Kassel, Königsberg, Mannheim, and Leipzig. As a conductor he was intellectual in his approach, conservative in his programming, and, to Hale's chagrin, was a proponent of Brahms. Paur was a literalist, conducting what was in the score; he did not offend, but at the same time he lacked the fire of Nikisch.

Just as he had done with Nikisch, Hale took Paur to task over programming, but perhaps, with a more reasoned approach. In a pair of reviews written during the first year of Paur's tenure, Hale bemoaned the fact that there was nothing performed to honor the memory of either Tchaikovsky or Gounod, both of whom had passed away earlier that year:

MUSIC

The Fifth Concert of the Boston Symphony Orchestra

Two composers of world-wide reputation died lately, Gounod and Tschaikowsky.

It is a matter of surprise and regret that the Boston Symphony Orchestra has not recognized this fact in any way whatsoever.

In certain towns of Europe, where music is regarded as an emotional art, it is the custom when a composer of great reputation dies to honor his memory, sometimes by exposing his bust or picture in concert hall or opera house, often by playing reverently one of his compositions.

But we are conservative here in Boston, and music is regarded here chiefly as an intellectual pursuit, something that makes for educational righteousness. Besides, neither Gounod nor Tschaikowsky was a German.

Or Mr. Paur may say "Gounod was a maker of operas; he was not a writer for orchestra alone. How can we honor his memory in a symphony concert?"

You have heard of the town of Leipsic, Mr. Paur; you have heard of the Gewandhaus concerts, and you are aware of the character of the said concerts. You also know how conservative musically are the good and the bad people of Leipsic.

Now I read in the Signale, No. 56 of this year that at the Gewandhaus concert given Nov. 2nd, one number of the programme was dedicated to the memory of Gounod. A march, described as "Feirlicher Marsch," by Charles Gounod, was played in honor of him. This may or may not have been "Marche Romaine;" the point is immaterial; the fact remains that the death of this Frenchman was noticed fitly in Leipsic, in the very temple devoted to the worship of "classical" composers.

And even Mr. Bernsdorf, who is generally ill at ease when he is obliged to hear modern music or write about it, paid the memory of Gounod a handsome tribute in his critique of the concert.

Gounod never visited this country, but Tschaikowsky was our guest. It is true that he conducted no one of his works in Boston. There was apparently no desire here to even see the illustrious composer. Yet, why should not his remarkable overture to "Hamlet" or to "Romeo and Juliet," or one of his symphonies be played in Music Hall to remind us of the world's loss?

As for that matter, it might not be uninteresting to hear the second symphony of Gounod or his nonetto[99] for wind instruments.

*
**

Others thought of remembering, according to their capacity, the death of Gounod, even if you, Mr. Paur, did not, you who have the resources of the Symphony Orchestra behind you, you who have the opportunity of inviting singers to join you in your work.

Such a tribute to the memory of the composer of "Faust" did not escape the thought of Mr. William Heinrich, the Manager of the New England Conservatory, or certain Roman Catholic churches in this town.

*
**

The programme of the symphony concert last evening was as follows:

Overture "Iphigenia en Aulide," Gluck: Double concerto for violin and 'cello, op. 102. Brahms: Symphony C major ("Jupiter") Mozart.

Brahm's "Double Concerto" was first played in public October 13, 1887, by Joachim and Hausmann, if I am not mistaken. It was then played at Cologne. Its first performance in America was by Max Bendix and Victor Herbert, January 5, 1889, at a Thomas Symphony concert in New York.

The concerto is in many ways a disappointing work. First of all it seems labored. The themes are neither fresh nor interesting. The thematic development is often ingenious, at times unreasonably intricate, as though the composer was so interested in a solution of a puzzle that he forgot that he was a musician. If there are occasional passages that are suggestive and almost beautiful, there are other passages in the first and third movements that are disagreeable without justification, and almost hideous. The andante is more endurable, and portions of it are charming.

The concerto is singularly arranged. Let us waive the question whether Brahms' choice of solo instruments was fortunate. The question here is, what employment did he make of them? He first of all, favored the cello. The violin part is extremely thankless, and it swarms with difficulties which seem needless and without any effect, even when they are conquered by such an admirable violinist as Mr. Kneisel. But neither the violin not the 'cello is so used individually, nor are they so used together that the hearer is able to listen to one dominating voice or two voices that compel attention. It is thought the orchestra had invited two guests to listen to the stranger's words or wit or wisdom; but afterward the members of the orchestra forgot good breeding and insisted on showing their guests how clever they themselves were and how much they knew.

The great fault, however, is that this concerto shows a poverty of imagination. There is technique galore; but there is little genuine music. Messrs. Kneisel and Schroeder performed their arduous task with skill and courage.

*
* *

The noble overture of Gluck, with the ending by Wagner, was finely played. And the overture is surely classic, if any music be thus termed. The Symphony of Mozart, with its Olympian serenity, its tenderness, its amazing mastery of technical problems, which are never allowed to seem problems to the hearer, was played with great care.[100]

[April 8, 1894]

The twenty-first concert of the Symphony Orchestra was given last evening in Music Hall. The program was as follows:

Funerale, Op. 23, No. 4 .... von Bülow
    (First ime.)
Symphony No. 3 (Eroica) .... Beethoven
Two movements from concerto for violin, No. 5, A minor, Op. 21 .... Molique
    II. Adante.
    III. Aegro
Tragic Overture, Op. 81 .... Brahms

The program of this concert was arranged as a memorial service in honor of the late Hans Guido von Bülow. As Bülow died the 12th of February, the tribute came late, but, as someone said, it takes a long time to bury a distinguished man.

Tschaikowsky, who is one of the greatest composers for orchestra in the last 20 years, died this season and Mr. Paur made no sign. His last symphony, a work hailed as a masterpiece in European cities and in New York, has not even been put into rehearsal here.

Gounod's death this season was mourned publically at the Gewandhaus, Leipsig, but Mr. Paur made no sign. And yet no one will argue seriously that Bülow outranks Gounod as a composer.

Not that Bülow is to be grudged this tribute. He was a great, if at times eccentric orchestra leader. His face, his playing of the piano, his sarcastic wit were well known in this town, and although there may not have been in the audience a sense of personal loss, as often happens when composers, strangers to us, die. Nevertheless, the tribute was deserved.

This tribute, by the way, would have been more complete if Mr. Paur had refused to put on the program one of Bülow's compositions; for this strange and versatile musician did not shine as a composer. To be sure, the orchestra might have played the overture to "Julius Caesar;" and in comparison with that dull enormity, the funerale is like unto a baleful star in the firmament.

The feature of the evening was the superb performance of the Heroic Symphony. Superb is a large, full word, often loosely used; but such a performance as that of last evening is rare. Not only was there scrupulous attention to detail; not only was there a fortunate and sane choice of tempi; but under the direction of Mr. Paur there was no thought of orchestral pedagogue or magnetic virtuoso. The only thought was, How great is this music; and not, How admirably the leader conducts. Although the first movement was not played in the fixed rigid spirit dear to some conservatives, the changes in tempo, slight, but effective, seemed the inevitable expression of the composer's ideas. The performance of the funeral march was free from theatrical extravagance; it was healthy and virile in its grief; there was no cheap expression of crape and tears: it was a lament with a mighty lamentation. Most excellent, too, was the rhythmic precision of the scherzo, and it may be here remarked that the pianissimo of Mr. Paur is a pianissimo, not a restless itch for a piano or a mezzo forte. The variations were played magnificently and it was a relief to find that the *poco andante* was not dragged out beyond recognition, and that simplicity was not turned into sentimentalism. All in all, it was a great performance, and Mr. Paur was seconded most ably by the men under his control.

G. Bernard Molique...concerto in Paris in 1836, and you were praised as a composer rather as a virtuoso....For years your concertos were a delight for violinists. But this is another age.

> King Pandien, he is dead
> All thy friends are lept in lead.

And to this restless generation your compositions for violin are in the limbo where are found pieces compounded of sugar and amiable bravura; yes, and your own oratorio, "Abraham," is there with many another vocal work, sacred or profane.

Mr. Roth played the peaceful numbers smoothly and with delicacy.

Molique, by the way, was born in 1803, not in 1802 as stated in the program book.[101]

The above review is almost a boilerplate of Hale's critiques of the 1890s, complete with criticism of the program booklet. Just as he bestowed praise upon Paur and the orchestra for their performance of Beethoven's "Eroica," he likewise criticized their backup work on the *Piano Concerto in B flat major* of Henry H. Huss:

> It may be added here that Mr. Paur gave loose reins to the orchestra. Certainly he might have shown more discretion, as soon as he realized the pianist's moderate strength.
>
> The performance of the orchestra throughout the evening was not flawless. Mr. Paur is getting to be too fond of violent contrasts, and forgetful of the fact that there must be measures in every work which demand moderation in treatment.

And was not the sublime theme of the last movement of the symphony taken at too fast a pace?[102]

All conductors develop idiosyncrasies and Paur was no exception. One of his was foot tapping. Hale came up with a humorous solution:

> Mr. Paur would certainly be horrified if he knew that his habit disturbed anyone prepared to admire him. The habit, if unconscious, is probably confirmed. Now what shall be done? Why should not Mr. Paur be presented with a pair of thick fur boots with felt soles? With them might be given a subscription list of "patrons and patronesses of music"; and the list might be headed with the motto "*Suaviter in modo*," or "Do good by stealth." Rubber boots are cheaper; but they would chafe the conductor in his more impassioned moments; they yield an unsavory smell; they have a cold, wet noise of their own, even when they are perfectly dry.[103]

All things considered, Emil Paur's tenure with the Boston Symphony Orchestra was a good one. Music-wise the orchestra responded to him well after the excesses of Nikisch, though Higginson, wanting to restore a more disciplined approach, considered five years to be sufficient. Hale paid tribute to Paur following the April 18, 1898 concert:

> Whether Mr. Paur remains or leaves, he may well be satisfied with his career in this town. As a musician, he has been faithful and effective. Not that I admire him in conducting works of all schools. I have found fault with him on several occasions and I see no reason to take back what I then wrote. On the other hand, I again pay glad tribute to his ability, remembering as I do performances of unparalleled brilliance. As a man he has proved himself worthy of all admiration. He has not wished to truckle, fawn, or cringe. He has kept steadily before him his duty toward his public and his art. Without arrogance, he has shown himself a man as well as a musician.[104]

Later that year, Paur was succeeded in Boston by a fellow Austrian conductor, Wilhelm Gericke. Paur's next two positions were with American orchestras, the New York Philharmonic (1898–1902) and the Pittsburgh Symphony (1906–1910). Both of these orchestras were having financial difficulties at the time; the Pittsburgh's funding was so bad that the orchestra folded at the end of Paur's term, unable to resurrect itself until 1926.

In the meantime Hale found himself busier than ever. The September 1897 issue of *The Musical Record* carried the following announcement:

> The next number of *The Musical Record* (October Edition) will be issued under the editorial management of Mr. Philip Hale, the well-known music critic of the city.[105]

For Hale, this was a dream. *The Musical Record* was well established—the first issue he was responsible for was No. 429. Here he had complete editorial control; he could write what he wanted and didn't have to answer to anyone. The time demanded of him by this journal meant that he would have to give up something, so he relinquished his position as Boston correspondent for New York's *Musical Courier*. An article in *The National Cyclopaedia of American Biography* (1910) included a description of Hale's journal:

> *The Musical Record* during the brief years of its existence under his editorship was a vehicle for information and comment on musical affairs that upheld the art from contact with petty personalities and sordid commercialism, and not finding sufficient support to justify the publishers in continuing it, its disappearance was felt as a personal loss by those who had to watch for it and know it through the lofty ideals of its editor.[106]

Hale edited the journal only until 1901; other things were looming on the horizon.

3

1900–1903

The twentieth century arrived in Boston eleven weeks early. On October 15, 1900, Symphony Hall was inaugurated, ushering in a new era not only for the Boston Symphony Orchestra, but also for the entire Greater Boston community. Its story deserves telling.

The building's predecessor, Boston Music Hall, had been home to the orchestra since the very beginning. In 1881, the year of the orchestra's founding, there were rumors circulating that Hamilton Place, the cul de sac on which the hall stood, was to be extended right through the building. To make sure that this would not happen and that the new Boston Symphony Orchestra would have a suitable place to perform, Henry Lee Higginson, the orchestra's founder, and his associates bought a controlling interest in the property.[1] As a result, the orchestra played its first nineteen seasons there. Boston Music Hall was not great; there were many problems of air quality, drafts, and—being located in the heart of downtown—outside noises. The acoustics were also problematical, to the extent that the organ that had been installed in 1863 had to be removed in order to place a sounding board above the orchestra. Higginson and others knew that the orchestra needed a better home and, since there were no other suitable halls in Boston, a new building had to be constructed. In a letter dated October 27, 1892, Higginson wrote to Charles Follen McKim (1847–1909) of the New York architectural firm of McKim, Mead & White:

Dear McKim,
This is a secret—please keep it absolutely.
Two or three of us have but the only feasible lot in Boston for a Music Hall—southern corner of West Chester Park[2], Huntington Avenue & a good small street—34,000 ft. in a parallelogram.
No hall is intended yet, & perhaps never—but if a very good offer for the present hall comes we might have to decide in haste....[3]

The following year saw a different threat to Boston Music Hall. As the city was growing, plans were made for a rapid transit elevated railway system for Boston. One of the lines was projected to be built right there. Higginson, who had recently foot the bill for the construction of Harvard University Stadium in 1890, was short of personal funds. This, however, did not dissuade him from hatching the brilliant scheme of forming a public corporation in order to raise the $400,000 necessary to construct a new hall. Within ten days, $402,000 had been raised, and this in the midst of the Panic of 1893.[4] Music Hall was now put up for sale.

In the meantime, McKim had three plans drawn up for the proposed hall: an ellipse, a shoe box, and a Greek amphitheater. A model of the latter was put on display in January 1894 at the nearly completed Boston Public Library, itself considered by many to be McKim's architectural masterpiece. Higginson, however, didn't buy into the Greek amphitheater plan; he and other backers preferred the shoebox design.

Finally, in 1898, after a four-year interval during which the economy greatly improved, Boston Music Hall was sold and the project moved ahead. Higginson retained control of the hall for a period of two years, which gave just enough time for the final planning and construction of what was originally referred to as the New Music Hall. Higginson contacted Wilhelm Gericke, who had just been rehired to conduct the symphony, for floor plans of the Leipzig Gewandhaus and Vienna Musikverein. These were not used directly, but were consulted in the face of some new time constraints. Eventually a new version of the old Boston Music Hall pattern accentuated with touches of the new Leipzig Gewandhaus was developed.

As time drew closer, Higgison and McKim sought the best talent possible to assure the success of the new hall. A young Harvard physics professor, Wallace Clement Sabine (1868–1919) was brought in to be acoustical advisor. Sabine was a real genius; while many of Symphony Hall's sightlines are not the best, the acoustics are phenomenal.

In March of 1899, plans and drawings of the new hall were published in the press. While generally meeting with acclaim, the plans did offer some problems for the then-ailing Handel & Haydn Society. Hale quoted the secretary of the society in his "Music and Musicians" column of May 21, 1899 before editorializing on what was obviously a perception problem in Boston at the time:

> I have on sundry occasions taken a shy at the venerable Handel and Haydn Society, but I read with a feeling approaching pain the report of the special meeting of this society held in Bumstead Hall May 15....
>
> Mr. Dow the Secretary of the society, made a speech, which was reported as follows in the Journal:
>
> "I want to talk about the business side of the society. With the present ideas followed out the society is assured of financial loss at the end of the concert season. We pay more for concerts now than any other society I know of. We have the Symphony Orchestra, expensive soloists—Mdm. Nordica at Easter cost the society $1000—and we have expensive advertising.... When Nordica was announced every buyer of tickets wanted to be assured before giving up his money that she would sing. And if this was so this year in Music Hall, what will it be when we move, as we are obliged to do? And where shall we go? The new Music Hall has no small rehearsal hall, and when I asked Mr. Higginson where we should rehearse and when, he said in the large hall, when it was not being otherwise used."
>
> ...Is the Boston Symphony Orchestra a luxury beyond the means of the Handel and Haydn? There is here an excellent orchestra for oratorio work, an orchestra that would show the conductor respectful attention and play to the best of its ability. I refer to the Boston Festival Orchestra led by Mr. Emil Mellenhauer.
>
> Are the solo singers too expensive? Why not engage then singers more reasonable, singers who will work harder and take their duties seriously? You pay $1000

to Nordica, a woman who is heart and soul in operatic work. She has a right to ask any price she thinks best; but, sure of her reputation, absorbed in more dramatic work, how much time you do think she would give to the proper study of an oratorio or cantata that is really of little interest to her? Are you always sure that such a singer will be present at rehearsals?

Look at the injustice done to singers in this town, singers that are capable, with fresh voices, worthy of every encouragement. I could easily name names of singers—and they are not of the old guard that in times past did valiant, faithful service—who would give pleasure in every one of the oratorios performed last season. They have the advantage of youth and enthusiasm. They would work patiently and industriously.

Boston is today a stepmother to singing children. She applauds at a Symphony Concert a poor singer like Mrs. Margaret Boye-Jensen; she perspires with joy over the false intonation and brutal tone production of shrieking and hawling German visitors; but she shuts her ears, not designing to listen to them that live within her gates.

And when a young Bostonian is applauded in the West or the Southwest, the incredulous old lady says, "How?" in spite of all her culture. "It isn't possible. Who is she? Bostonian? Why I never heard of her."

You must cut your coat according to your cloth. A well-fitting coat need not be lined and decorated with silk—especially when you have not the money to pay for the trimmings.

I might add that the pecuniary success attending the performances of "The Messiah" is largely due to devotional feeling and the power of association—but this is a purely personal belief; just as I believe that the public interest in oratorio as oratorio has waned gradually since the Symphony concerts became fashionable. At the same time, there are many people in this city who enjoy oratorio and would gladly support a society that could give them adequate performances at a reasonable price.[5]

Hale was right; the society has survived, and with Symphony Hall is its performance venue.

On June 9, 1899 ground was broken and a mere 15 months later, on September 22, 1900 the building was open for public inspection.[6] The name of the hall was still being decided during the late phases of construction. The initials "BMC" for Boston Music Hall were already cast in iron on the stair railings. Charles A. Ellis (1855–1934), manager of the Boston Symphony Orchestra, suggested naming it "Higginson Hall,"[7] but Higginson, out of modesty, never publically commented on the idea. Just how the hall was named is not known, but an article appearing in *The Boston Globe*, which featured a drawing of the inside of the hall, had the following heading:

NEW SYMPHONY HALL A PLACE OF BEAUTY

Perfect in all Requirements, a Delight to the Eye and the Heart—New Scheme in Ventilation and Heating—Acoustic Properties Perfect[8]

Whether or not this article served as a catalyst, the name "Symphony Hall" seemed quite appropriate and that was the name used by the time tickets and posters were printed for the opening concert.

The Inaugural Concert held on October 15, 1900 featured Beethoven's *Missa Solemnis*. This event was the most important that Hale had covered thus far. His column not only reviewed the concert, but included a tribute to Higginson as well. It also had information about the inauguration of the old Boston Music Hall. It is included here in its entirety:

NEW SYMPHONY HALL
A BRILLIANT AUDIENCE
THERE—FINE PERFORM-
ANCE OF BEETHOVEN'S
MISSAS OLEMNIS

(By Philip Hale.)

Symphony Hall was dedicated last night. The occasion will be memorable in the history of music in Boston. At last the Boston Symphony Orchestra has a fitting home. The orchestra itself has been for some years a Boston institution, one that identified and distinguished the city. In certain ways this society may be justly said to be unique. In the 18th century princes of Europe maintained orchestras for their own pleasure, and in the last half of this century the late Charles Lamoureux supported largely at his own expense the superb orchestra that he conducted; but it was reserved for Mr. Henry L. Higginson, a citizen of Boston, to see to it that the people of his town might have an opportunity of hearing at a reasonable price the best music performed by the best orchestra that money and experience could bring together and establish. Mr. Higginson pursued his course in the face of discouragement and obstacles in the early years. This statement seems incredible in the year 1900, but go through the annotated programs of the Symphony concerts, which are in the Allen A. Brown collection in the Public Library, and read the excerpts from the newspapers of 1881, and the immediately following years. Time is the true and great avenger. Mr. Higginson can now afford to smile at the petty suspicions and slurs and insults of the chronically disgruntled and the cheap intriguers who saw to art nothing but a business. Mr. Higginson is not a vainglorious man; but last night he might well rest content; he might have said with Paul: "I have fought a good fight"; and although he fortunately is not of the age of Simeon, yet might he have hummed to himself, as his right, the Nunc Dimittis.

*
**

The Music Hall that for 19 seasons was the home of the Boston Symphony Orchestra was inaugurated on a Saturday evening, Nov. 20, 1852. These societies took part: The Handel and Haydn, the Musical Educational Society, the Musical Fund orchestra, the Germania Serenade Band and Kreismann's Liedertafel. Mr. G. J. Webb was the chief conductor. Among the orchestral selections were the overtures to "The Magic Flute" and "Oberon," and the andante of Beethoven's Fifth Symphony. There were choruses from "The Messiah," "The Mount of Olives" and "St. Paul." And there was a star, a star of the first magnitude, a blessing star, for Alboni sang arias from "Norma," "La Fille du Regiment," and "Cenerentola," and she took part in a trio with Sangiovanni and Rovere from "The Barber of Seville."

*
**

Last night the program included a chorale of Bach, an address by Mr. Higginson, a poem by Mr. Owen Wister, and the stupendous mass of Beethoven, the Missa Solemnis in D, Mr. Gericke conducted. The chorus was made up of the Cecilia and others. The solo singers were Clementine de Vere, Gertrude May Stein, Evan Williams, Joseph S. Baernstein. Mr. J. Wallace Goodrich was the organist, and the violin solo in the "Benedictus" was played by Mr. Kneisel.

This music had not been performed often in this country. It is said that the first performance in America was at Cincinnati, May 19, 1880, under Theodore Thomas, with two quartets: Amy Sherwin, Annie Louise Cary, Campanini, M. W. Whitney—Annie B. Norton, Emma Cranch, Harvey, Rudolphsen. But my friend, Mr. August Spanuth of New York, the accomplished critic of the Staats-Zeitung, tells me that a performance was given at Steinway Hall, New York, May 2, 1872, by the Church Music Association, led by Mr. James Pach. Then there was a performance in New York May 3, 1882 when there were two quartets: Materna, Emily Winant, Campanini, Galassi (relieved by M. W. Whitney)—Mrs. Allen of this city, Emily Winant, Candidus, and Henschel. The first and only performance in Boston was by the Cecilia March 12, 1897, under Mr. Lang. The quartet was then made up of local singers who struggled bravely but ineffectually.

*
**

Some were disappointed, and perhaps not without reason, in the character of the musical part of the program. "Symphony Hall" and the dedicatory concert was without a symph[ony...]....Mr. Gericke showed his power over a chorus as over an orchestra, for seldom is a work of such colossal proportions given with a like minute attention to detail. In this respect the performance was truly remarkable. The solo singers left little or nothing to be desired. Their task was a most arduous one, and they fulfilled it technically and aesthetically.

And now a word about the Mass itself. I say "a word"; and yet an ingenious German by the name of Wilhelm Weber contrived to write a pamphlet of 133 pages about the work which is to him as an instance of plenary inspiration. There are overwhelming passages in this Mass, passages of transcendent beauty and grandeur, and there are also pages of tiresome fugue. The fugue was never the natural speech of Beethoven. Bach lived his monotonous, blameless life and loved his wives in turn and reared his children in counterpoint. Handel used the fugue as a giant rejoicing in his strength. César Franck thought in canon-form. But we know how Beethoven sweated over the fugues in this Mass; the singers also sweat; and, what is worse, do the hearers. But who can sit unmoved during the "Crucifixus" and the "Et Resurrexit"? What a masterstroke is the treatment of the phrase, "And he shall come again with glory to judge both the quick and the dead!" Or what shall be said of the marvelous beauty of the "Benedictus"?

*
**

It is to be hoped that other choral works may be performed from time to time under Mr. Gericke's direction. Oratorios or cantatas that have in time past been performed here perfunctorily and with little appreciation of their musical spirit might then be heard as the composer wrote them.[9]

The character of the above column as well as the previous one quoted regarding the Handel and Haydn Society's difficulties show that over the course of the past eleven years, dating from when he first came to Boston, Hale had developed a real caring attitude about the musical health of his adopted city. The bitterness of the early 1890s had worn off, to be replaced by a sense of verbal philanthropy. With the opening of Symphony Hall came concerts with intermissions, a welcomed respite, but there was also the establishment of higher ticket prices. Hale steered those unable or unwilling to afford the increase to the orchestra's new Thursday series at Sanders Theatre, on the Harvard University campus in Cambridge.[10] He also started to sparingly include letters from readers, if he felt them to be appropriate:

> I have received the following letter:
>
> Randolph, Mass.
>
> Mr. Hale:
>
> Through you may I say—"No tickets for standees" may give satisfaction to some of the seat-holders at Symphony Hall on Friday afternoons, but there are others. The absence of faces which have been familiar at concerts for a decade at least made many homesick to see them again. The writer holds a very fine seat in the parquet, but because he is able to do so is not disturbed when the lobby is filled with young, happy girls and young men who love the music and can only hear it that way. The Hall is a delight to eye and ear. After the draughts are adjusted, no one can find a flaw, but if one has to feel sorry at the time for the hundreds who are hungry for the exquisite music—"'tis pity 'tis true." Let them in—on the first floor at least. The doors at the entrance give ample chance for people to pass into their seats without using the side doors, if they happen to be crowded. Don't initiate the Hall with a policy of selfishness. "Narrow minds are very exclusive—but it requires broad minds and sympathies to be inclusive."
>
> TICKET HOLDER[11]

In the very same column, Hale spoke about his philosophy of reviewing, particularly about why he gave disproportionate coverage to various works performed at concerts:

> Some one, who neglected to sign her name, asked me last week, "Why did you not speak more at length about the pieces played at the Symphony concert Saturday?"
>
> Because, fair madam, there was only one new piece played. The Journal is a newspaper, not a musical magazine. Do you wish, at this late day a column of pretty or historical or educational talk about Beethoven's Symphony in C minor, with a discussion as to whether Fate knocks at the door in the first measures, or an inquiry as to the way the symphony might sound if it were to be re-orchestrated by, say—Richard Strauss or Mr. DeKoven? Or do you wish entertaining statements of fact concerning the appearance of subsidiary themes, codas and the characteristics of the oboe and bassoon?
>
> No, there are some things taken for granted, accepted, ticketed for many generations, and one of them is the 5th Symphony. And neither the "Euryanthe" overture nor the ballet-music from "Rosamunde" requires over a sentence in the year 1900, unless there be some singularity in the performance.
>
> Madam, the program to which you refer was a stupid one, and eminently unfit, with the exception of the symphony, for the first orchestral concert in the new hall. Now on Oct. 20, Mr. Theodore Thomas and his orchestra gave a concert in Chicago. Oblige me by looking at his program: "Jubilee Overture," Weber; Symphonic variations for orchestra and organ by Georg Schumann (first time);

Hungarian Dances (first set) Brahms; "Death and Transfiguration," R. Strauss; overture, "The Flying Dutchman," Wagner's Suite du ballet, "La Belle au Bois Dormant," Tschaikowsky (first time); Symphonic poem, "Mazeppa," Liszt. Last night Mr. Thomas brought out as novelties a Romantic Overture by Thuille and D'Indy's "Wallenstein's Camp." But Thomas is a skillful and catholic maker of programs.[12]

As substantiated by the last paragraph of the above column, Hale continued to express a definite interest in orchestral programming, reacting to a concert consisting entirely of excerpts from Wagner operas:

It was the custom some 20 years ago for conductors in Berlin to present programs devoted each to the works of one composer—Beethoven, Mozart, Mendelssohn, Schumann, Schubert, Haydn—and I believe there were actually "Spohr evenings." Of late years French conductors have tried "Saint-Saëns concerts" and "Massenet concerts" as well as concerts exclusively for the music of Wagner or Beethoven. Mr. Thomas in Chicago this season gave a "Beethoven Cycle."

The composers who bore an audience the least at such entertainments are undoubtedly Beethoven, Tschaikowsky and Wagner. No doubt the faithful Brahmsites, the initiated, the full-fledged mahatmas of the cult would enjoy—but "enjoy" is here a too frivolous word—would appreciate and ponder a concert to the sole glory of Johannes, the son of the double-bass player. Indeed I remember a Symphony concert here in April, 1897, when the program was composed of some especially dismal pieces by Brahms—among them the "Vier cruste Gesange." But that concert was in memory of the composer, and the courteous obligation of thus paying him respect enlarged the regret of the news of his death. Mozart and Haydn and Schumann and Schubert—their names are thrice honorable, but an evening of nothing but Mozart? Wild horses could not drag me to "An Evening with Mendelssohn," although the overture to "Fingal's Cave" is one of the most beautiful things in this sadly commercial world. A fascinating Tschaikowsky program might easily be arranged. That a concert was not thus planned after his death may be regarded as incredible by the future historian of music in this city. But would a Richard Strauss concert or a Cesar Franck concert be wholly endurable? I doubt it, although these names are as stars in the firmament.[13]

In addition to programming, Hale naturally had a definite opinion about the characteristics of good music. At the end of a scathing review of Serge Taneleff's *Symphony No. 1 in C*, he addressed this succinctly:

...Respectability cannot save a work; neither can the exhibition of acquaintanceship with form. Originality, depth, beauty, passion, and, above all, imagination—there must be at least one of these qualities. Nor does one scherzo make a symphony.[14]

In line with his keen interest in the vicissitudes of the Boston Symphony Orchestra, Hale reviewed and supported the efforts of its players. He had critiqued the Kneisel String Quartet a number of times over the previous decade and now, in 1900, the symphony's entrepreneurial principal oboist, Georges Longy (1868–1930), founded two professional ensembles. The Orchestral Club

(1900–1906) was dedicated to the performance of new works while The Longy Club, a wind ensemble of changeable instrumentation, was established along the lines of the Société de musique de chambre pour instruments à vent by French flautist Paul Taffanel (1844–1908) in 1879. Longy had been brought in as principal oboist for the Boston Symphony Orchestra in 1898, becoming the first French member of the orchestra's woodwind section.[15] In addition to the Longy Club and Orchestral Club, Georges Longy conducted the Boston Musical Association, the MacDowell Club, and, in 1908, a series of orchestral concerts financed by saxophonist Elise Hall. The first concert of the Longy Club was given on December 18, 1900 in Association Hall.

The programming of the Longy Club usually consisted of chamber music, with one larger work, featuring up to thirteen players, concluding the performance. Sometimes a piano was involved. Hale, of course, made general recommendations regarding repertoire from the sidelines: "Let us hope that in the future, Mr. Longy will give the most of his attention to the moderns."[16] Many important works—among them Richard Strauss's *Suite in B flat*, Op. 4, Gounod's *Petite Symphony*, and Dvořák's *Serenade for Winds*, Op. 44—were introduced to Boston audiences by this ensemble. Normally the Longy Club performed three concerts over a given season. When Longy retired in 1925, Hale dedicated an entire column to a description of Longy's work. Within it is a discussion of the Longy Club and its repertoire:

> In 1900 he founded the Longy Club, for the purpose of performing music written for wind instruments. The original members were Messrs. Andre Maquarre and Selmer, Hackebarth, Litke, Gebhard (pianist), with Mr. Longy as leader. There were necessary changes in the personnel from season to season until the club was disbanded in 1914.[17] Major Higginson was interested in the club and gave it liberal support. Would that the Boston Public had followed his example! A glance at the program shows the catholicity of Mr. Longy's taste. Among the works heard here for the first time were compositions by Bernard, d'Indy, Loeffler, Caplet, Bird, Lazzari, Herzogenberger, Malherbe, de Wally, Roeningen, Quef, Gouvy, Rietz, Longy, Hure, G. Faure, Lampe, Kovacek, Perihou, Kauffmann, Klughardt, Woolett, Handel, Weber, Grieg, Mouquet, Lacroix, Hahn, R. Strauss, Schreck, Magnard, Bumcke, Wolf-Ferrari, Mozart, Falconi, Enesco, Pierne, Reger, Cossart, Ravel, Fried, Moreau, Dukas, Debussy, Engene, Wagner, Diemer, Rimsky-Korsakov, Kriens, Florent Schmitt, Weingartner, Fiament, Strube, Loeillet, Juon.
>
> But these names do not give one an idea of the richness of the programs, for many other composers were represented by works that had been played once or twice in former years. The club was assisted by capable artists from time to time in order to bring out the more elaborate works by players of stringed instruments from the Symphony orchestra, by Armand Forest, violinist of Paris, who played here for the first time; by that admirable singer, Charles Gilibert, and Mme. Gilibert; by Mme. Sundelius, soprano; by Mrs. Richard J. Hall, saxophone, who was constantly a staunch friend and supporter of Mr. Longy in all his undertakings.
>
> These concerts, like the concerts of a similar nature heard many years before when the late Charles Mole, the first flute of the Symphony orchestra, was fired with a similar ambition, were caviar to the general. And in 1914 war broke out.[18]

Hale's reviews of the ensemble's concerts were consistent with his other ones, taking into account events surrounding the performances. On the final concert of the second season, the *Serenade*, Op. 40 of Cambridge, Massachusetts native Arthur Bird (1856–1923) was performed. The composer spent much of his life in Berlin and it was there in 1901 that this work for ten winds received the Paderewski prize for chamber music. The music critic for the *Berliner Börsen Courier* remarked, "It is distinguished for the freshness and spontaneity of its invention, as well as the clever craftsmanship and the clear and compact disposition of its different parts."[19] Hale wasn't entirely sold on the idea of prizes for musical works and commented:

> The fact that it is a prize piece would naturally awaken suspicion if not prejudice against it, for experienced composers who fully expect to win a prize refrain as a rule from marked originality, and walk calmly in well-trodden paths. They refrain studiously from the exotic, from that which startle, perplex, annoy. There was a time when Mr. Bird by orchestral pieces gave much promise, for he displayed melodic charm, and warm and varied harmonic and orchestral color. His ways for some time have been ways of pleasantness and ease, and he writes more and more conventionally. Surely he had no idea that this piece would ever be played by such admirable artists as those who did everything last evening to put his work in a favorable light. He might have written it for the ordinary wind instruments of a small German town. The music is smooth and respectable. The Adagio owed its charm chiefly to the fine playing of Mr. Lenom. The Scherzo is of operetta character, and the Finale includes a common ditty and a sufficient amount of commonplace counterpoint. The character of the judges in his competition is such that we are left to wonder concerning the character of the other chamber work entered for the prize. What must these other pieces be![20]

As in the case of all wind ensembles, the Longy Club had difficulty in attracting a sizeable audience. Hale commented on this more than once; he sent out a plea in his review of the ensemble's final concert of the 1902–1903 season:

> ...There were so few to hear it. Such performances are rare, even in Paris, or Brussels, the homes of wind-instrument players. These members of our orchestra excite the admiration of musicians in the cities they visit. Are we too much accustomed to them, that we miss the opportunity of hearing them? It does not seem to make any difference whether Mr. Longy and his associates produce new works or give the best of the classic repertory. The result is the same, the "patrons and patronesses" of music have not decreed that these concerts should be fashionable. Mediocre singers or pianists, either local or visitors, are approved, and the work is passed that they should and must be heard. But these artists—and I use the word discreetly—are passed by. Mr. Longy has made a brave endeavor. I should not blame him if with dignity he withdrew from the field. The abandonment of his concerts on account of non-support would be a reproach to the music-lovers of Boston and a blow to the prestige of this boastful city.[21]

Regardless of audience size, the Longy Club proved to be the most successful of Longy's ensemble efforts, at least in terms of longevity. It lasted through the spring of 1917, when the United States entered World War I.

Hale's major concern regarding the first season of the Boston Pops in Symphony Hall had nothing to do with audience size, but rather with the dictates of established societal mores, as professed in the following satirical article:

A SEDATE "POP."

Opening of 16th Season of These Musical
Entertainments and First in Symphony
Hall—A Carefully Conducted and
Most Respectable Affair.

The 16th season of the concerts known as the "Pops" began last night, with Mr. Max Zach as orchestral conductor.

Symphony Hall has now been thoroughly dedicated. First there was the elaborate performance of express dedication; the hall was dedicated to oratorio; there was a dedicatory organ recital; there was a dedicatory first symphony concert; and now the first "Pop" has been given, and the walls, ceiling and statues are acquainted with the smell of burning tobacco. Let us hope that thorough saturation with the smoke of this plant may improve the acoustical properties.

The floor was well filled last night, and some sat in the galleries, which might well be called the seats of the scornful; for the sight of elaborate dress, and a sea of white shirt front might well provoke a smile form the philosopher who is informed that the men and women at the tables are indulging themselves in Bohemian amusement. He might reply that there are several Bohemians; one without a seaport; one with a seaport; a Bohemia known to artists and jolly men and women who are not too anxious about their dress or social position; and Bohemia in Boston, a province in which some of the inhabitants wonder when others will begin to be joyous, and some are uneasy; for they are not sure that their own respectability is fully appreciated by their neighbors of the evening.

"Pop," I am told, is an abbreviation of "Popular." The abbreviation suggests merriment; the pop of champagne ordered by some ostentatious person who would never dream of ordering the wine if it sneaked out of the bottle; the pop of other corks, descending humbly to ginger-beer, and there is a pop even to alkalithia, if the corkscrew be deftly handled.

The "Pops" are supposed to be popular entertainments; light and gay and pretty music, light refreshments and pleasing drinks; permission to smoke; and genuine informality. Liberty—but not license, except for the beverages that are served.

Is it not true that of late years the "Pop" has become a "function," rather than a careless entertainment?

Mr. Comee surely does not wish that the frequenters of these concerts should consider them as formal occasions. I know that this is furthest from his thought.

The old feeling and the old enjoyment might return if there were two or three improvements carried out this season. The rails of the pen might be taken down and all tables considered as unreserved. First come, first seated, should be the motto. Any distinction on the floor kills democratic and contagious pleasure. If anybody wishes to show the public that he has a beautiful dress suit, he should be allowed to exhibit it, although the dress suit habit—especially when a black cravat is worn with a tailed coat—is almost as destructive to soul and body as the back-habit. And should not the prices of admission be lowered? I am aware that Messrs. Ellis and Comee are able to run their own business; and I remember how the Ferguson family of Philadelphia made a large fortune, but I like the managers of these concerts, and I would fain see the hall crowded with men and women, young and old, gossiping, flirting, laughing, wounding, if not killing care, and incidentally listening to the music, which should never be too loud to interfere with the long-winded story of the venerable Mr. Borax, or to drown out the amorous whispers of the youth who sits under the shade of a miraculous hat. It would be a pleasure to see visiting from table to table whenever the spirit moved a visitor. The word "Pop," as here applied, should regain its true meaning; it should not be used to characterize a concert attended solemnly by men and women who dress slowly for it and look skew-eyed at rakish youths and pretty girls and wonder where "those persons" live.[22]

The year 1901 turned out to be a watershed year for Hale. On April 5, his rather lengthy article, "Operatic Extravagance," appeared as the Entr'acte in the Boston Symphony Orchestra program book. The reason for the appearance of this article is unknown to the author. It could be that it was secured by William Foster Apthorp, then on the verge of retirement, or by Henry Lee Higginson to serve as a type of "re-audition" for Hale. Whatever the case, after a period of nearly ten years, Hale was reinstated as program essayist for the orchestra that fall. This time it would stick; he held the position for the next thirty-two years, nearly the remainder of his life. During the previous decade the quality of Hale's reviews and articles had placed him among America's foremost arts critics, but his greatest work still lay ahead. Thus, just as the twentieth century had arrived eleven weeks early for the Boston Symphony Orchestra, it arrived nine months late for Hale.

As was briefly the case ten years earlier, Hale served two masters: the Boston Symphony Orchestra and the *Boston Journal*. By the time Hale assumed the position of program essayist, his *Boston Journal* concert reviews generally had less edginess than those at the start of his career. He had a vast wealth of knowledge in his memory or—if he happened not have certain things memorized—then knowledge of a vast selection of resources that provided him with aesthetic as well as factual backup. This was apparent in his review of Brahms' *Academic Festival Overture*, which opened up the first concert of the 1901–1902 season:

> Johannes Brahms desired to give thanks publicly to the university of Breslau because he had received from the illustrious dignitaries of the University the degree of Doctor of Philosophy. How best could he express his thanks in music? By something stately, pompous? Or by something profound and cryptic? Brahms acted with shrewdness in the matter; he took for his thematic material well-known students' songs. These songs are familiar throughout Germany, and it is not as though a composer called upon, for instance, to write an appropriate overture for the approaching jubilee at Yale should take songs peculiar to that college; nor is it as though a composer should take "Eli Yale" and "Fair Harvard" and a Dartmouth or a Williams song for his themes. Wherever Brahms' overture is heard by a German student, whether of Heidelberg, Bonn, Berlin, or Breslau, the themes are old friends and common property.
>
> Brahms was not wholly unacquainted with the joyous nights of German students. In the early fifties Joachim spent summer months at Göttingen, where he studied, especially history and philosophy. Brahms, or as he was known among his friends, "Johannes Kreisler, Jr.," visited him there, and they no doubt assisted lustily in the exercises of the "Kneipe."

And yet the nearest approach to spontaneous joy in this overture is the introduction of the famous "Was kommt dort von der Hoeh." For once Brahms is mirthful. Most of the overture is dry, chiefly on account of the orchestration, for this master of structure was color-deaf. As for the finale, with the "Gaudeamus Igitur," a tune known to all American students and young women who find delight in students, it reminds one in treatment of Weber's handling of the Saxon National Hymns at the end of his "Jubel" overture.[23]

This was the first concert in nearly a decade for which Hale was both reviewer and essayist. After reviewing the remaining works on the program—Lalo's *Violoncello Concerto*, Liszt's *Fest-Kläng*, and Beethoven's *Symphony No. 7*—Hale added the following disclaimer:

> The orchestra is again together after a long vacation, which to many of the players was only a vacation in name. It is fairer, then, to refrain from speaking of performances in detail until the players are fully under control to each other. It would also be unfair to refrain from saying that the performance last night was often creditable to conductor and men and worthy of the high reputation of the orchestra.[24]

Hale was being careful, of course. The memory of what had happened ten years earlier was still fresh on his mind; he did not want to bite the hand that fed him. Unfortunately, Hale's hedging heightened an already perceived conflict of interest that did not escape those who were close to him. Many of Hale's *Boston Journal* reviews were reprinted in the *Musical Courier*. A mere nine days later, the following acerbic "counter-review" by one identifying himself only as "Pro Bono" appeared in that periodical:

> VERSUS PHILIP HALE, POOR MAN!
> Boston, Monday
>
> Dear Musical Courier:
>
> I see by this week's issue of your paper that you are once more following your pernicious habit of not permitting your critics (alleged!) to speak the truth. Now, there's Philip Hale! I've known Phil. since he was a boy. I had a hand in his education. I know that as a critic for a daily paper he cannot ventilate his true pent up emotions, and I always hoped that as an associate of yours he might be allowed to write just what his musical acumen dictates. Of course you wouldn't write against the Boston Symphony for the world, and so you have probably given poor Mr. Hale spiritual advice in advance. I attended the Boston opening. And wish I had spent my money on "Floradora," up on Broadway. Why? Well, I might as well tell you at once that as a musician, trained before the mast, I am accustomed to orchestras which are led by the director, and not to one which takes the director by the hand and conducts him! That's the Boston epidemic now! Take my word for it! You know me! That orchestra, and this is not after dinner either, is the finest in the world! Such material! Such instruments! Such individual intelligence! And the management! Where can you find men like Higginson, with his brown trousers; Ellis, of the genial heart; copious Fred. Comee, and that fine, kindly man, L. H. Muggett? Wouldn't these brains build up any organization from Tammany Hall, the D. A. R,'s to the Mafia? I "guess" they would! Now, what is the difficulty? They have the hall, the orchestra, the management, but not the director. Saturday

night I wanted to be umpire, and call down good paternal advice to Gericke, but I was afraid of waking up the audience he had so carefully put to sleep! It wasn't a square deal anyway.

You know, if you remember anything outside of the trusts, that "Academic Overture" of Brahms! Well, after the men came on stage and knelt in prayer to Kneisel, they yawned and stretched themselves and then Gericke came along. He had on clothes, but not much hair. It took some time for him to get his glasses on, and then when Mr. Higginson squeezed a dollar to make the eagle mourn—they were off! It was a great start! The men were just a little ahead of the conductor, but he jumped a hurdle and caught them. It's sad enough when Brahms tries to be kittenish through the medium of a full orchestra and a heavy score, but it's sadder still when a director works like yeast to see the joke, to be young, joyous, devil-may-care in the seeing. Gericke didn't do this. He took it seriously. It hurt his feelings. It made you feel like rag-time at a funeral. That's probably the way it made him feel. Then when salty tears were gathering, ouí!—the men got ahead! But Gericke's a routine director and was—out at first! He felt so pleased, was such a surprise! The men looked quite annoyed, as they had evidently counted on winning. I lost $10 betting on the men, because I know and believe in them. There's Kneisel, and Schroeder and Loeffler—I felt sure they would win. Life is full of these disappointments; you know how it is. While my dismay was still fresh from the bat, a shock of black hair and a pair of "googling" brown eyes escorted a 'cello on the stage. It was *Fest-Kläng*! Play! He struck into the broad opening movement of the Lalo Concerto, and somebody behind me dropped a brass button down my back and my hair sat up! This little, wee, titan possesses tone, temperament, trills, technic to beat the whole band back of him! Such a sincere, manly youngster, such sincere, manly art is a rarity even in these days. Did you ever notice his down-bow staccato? Then again legato playing as he has it in his wrist is a gift, a direct gift. Another feature is, if Gérardy sings the same theme one hundred times—and you know how Lalo treats his themes—he sings it differently. It tells a new phase of the story. While he is essentially a temperamental player, he never overdoes; you don't find him portamento going up and down the strings or exuding undue sentiment. The trouble is that an untemperamental conductor is a skull and cross-bones to a temperamental soloist; the orchestra pulled back badly at times, but Gérardy woke up the audience just the same. This was a treat indeed, and we felt braced for the Liszt number.

It's a curious study about magnetic currents. A man like Paur or Nikisch holds his men as in a vice from the moment he steps on stage. Gericke or Thomas establishes it only at times. You can see it born and wane and disappear. Gericke starts in all right for the climax—the kind he knows about, you know; he goes along for a few bars when suddenly he loses hold of the men and that climax cometh not. Same thing, when the men work up momentum to a high pitch, where drums, trumpets, pianolas, Aeolians, &c., are all toiling, he can't work them down to a pianissimo until the middle of the next number. Thus Boston cannot have true artistic climaxes or pianissimos, because there is no architect there to build them. What's a symphony without shading, nuance, color? This is to get us over to the Liszt number mentioned above. I want to forget it. You know how effective the full stop of an orchestra is, and how the silence throbs and throbs with anticipation of the continuation of the story. When the Boston Symphony strikes a rest, it stops—just stops—that's all, and it's a time for conversation. It is more irritating when an organization like this continually just misses it than anything you can conjure up. An orchestra *cannot* play itself. Already the standard raised by Nikisch and Paur has been lowered, although the orchestra itself has improved. The woodwinds have been augmented you know and they do great work. I never heard the theme for oboe in the Beethoven Seventh played so beautifully, and the duet for two oboes and two clarinets was delightful.

The second movement was flawless. Mr. Gericke's inability to color and contrast was never more apparent than in the Scherzo and Trio. You remember all the "tootling" the woodwinds have to do in this movement and the drawn tones or pedal points (any old thing you want to call them) which stand still on one note and whistle. Well, my wife said to me: "Pro Bono, can't you sit still?"; but I just writhed in agony. I thought the whole world consisted of unshaded pedal points and "tootling" tubes. You ought to hear Paur color and shade this difficult movement, which sounds frivolous and even impudent after the grandeur of the second movement unless it's played with refined understanding. The finale has odd scoring, hasn't it? Think of the trumpets and violins forte against the woodwinds! Still the strings were less in Beethoven's time, we mustn't forget that. The last movement was a scramble, a run-for-your-life scramble—and then I came away. The audience was not once aroused to spontaneous applause save by Gérardy. This is the whole truth and I am sorry Phil. isn't permitted to tell it. What's the use of having a critic if you coach him all the time? Still he has troubles of his own! An organist and a music critic in Boston! That would feaze a haler man than Hale.

I could write lots more, but I am tired now, and my wife says the beer is getting stale. Any time you want the truth told just call on me. I have a useless supply on hand, for we only get paid in the world to lie. I am, in sorrow for your misdeeds (will be seventy-five my next birthday),

PRO BONO OF BOSTON

P.S.—*Not Pro Bono!*[25]

The P.S. is probably a humorous indication that this person didn't usually work for free. So who was Pro Bono? The prima facie clues indicate that this was someone Hale knew as a child (perhaps a teacher in Northampton), that this person was an expert in several areas—the affairs of the Boston Symphony Orchestra, conducting and conductors, and the music performed that evening—and that the writer was a seventy-four-year-old married male. There were many candidates; one would imagine that this was written by a retired symphony player or retired music critic. It would not be much of a stretch to say that since the letter itself is eloquently written as a satire under a pseudonym, it could have been written by the same humorist who often expressed himself in his columns through such fictional personalities as "Young Chimes," "Old Chimes," and "Herkimer Johnson"—in other words, Hale himself!

In 1954 Warren Storey Smith, who had been music critic for the *Boston Transcript* and *Boston Post* toward the end of Hale's career, wrote an article for *Musical America* celebrating the centenary of the birth of four distinguished music critics: Henry Krehbiel, Henry T. Finck, William J. (W. J.) Henderson, and Hale. In addition to making a reference to Hale's use of "Herkimer Johnson," Smith commented about Hale's refinement as a critic:

A kindly man by nature, Hale was known as "Philip the Terrible." The German-born pianist and pedagogue, Carl Faelten, who had felt the rough side of Hale's pen, called him a "bulldog" (making it rhyme with "dull rogue"). Hale mellowed considerably in his later years. On leaving a Jordan Hall debut recital he remarked that since there was nothing good to say about the pianist, he would discuss the program.[26]

It is interesting to see how Hale's program essays stack up against those of his predecessors. George H. Wilson, the Boston Symphony Orchestra's first essayist, began in the symphony's second season writing a single sheet labeled "Music Hall Bulletin."[27] According to extant programs in the Boston Symphony Archives, facts sometimes would be printed on the backs of the program sheets and translations provided in a thin accompanying pamphlet. Over Wilson's nine-year tenure, this expanded to thirty-two pages. Wilson was not overly concerned with the music itself and rarely supplemented the facts with any personal scholarship. William Apthorp did, but occasionally misfired on the facts. Robert B. Nelson comments:

> It is quite interesting to compare the notes on the same musical selections by these three writers: Wilson, Apthorp and Hale. The most obvious distinction is the steady spiral toward accurate information that would be both informative and interesting to concert-goers....As regards analysis, it has been noted that Wilson was more journalistic than musical and Apthorp was more musical. Compared to Apthorp's contribution, Hale differed, in general, only in brevity, requiring two pages to Apthorp's three.[28]

Hale was indeed more succinct than Apthorp, and his insistence on accurately presenting the facts and details, even if it brought embarrassment to those who should have known better, was a trademark of his from the very start. His program booklets served as vehicles for both educating and entertaining the symphony audience. They generally contained 500–1500 word essays on each work performed—facts about the composer, origin of composition, instrumentation, musical analysis, and previous performances. Sometimes there would be insufficient material available to him about a given work; in that case he would provide relevant literary diversions from ages past, often gleaned from Greek mythology. Warren Storey Smith commented, "Hale's knowledge, as his program notes attested, was encyclopedic. At one time or another each one of them had interests far removed from music."[29] In addition to information about the programmed works, he provided an Entr'acte of roughly 1,500 words for the middle part of the booklet. These were either by him or taken from another source. In the case of the latter, Hale always gave credit where credit was due. Hale's joy in the presentation of scholarship, whether it was the result of his own work or the work of others, could be described as a form of enlightened cherishing. He was educating Boston and he relished it. James Gibbons Huneker, editor of the *Musical Courier*, comments:

> ...Philip Hale wrote a masterpiece in miniature about Jack the Ripper, entitled "The Baffled Enthusiast." We had a Philip Hale cult then. No wonder. An artist in prose, he literally educated Boston in the gentle art of paganism. Why, even in such a deadly task as inventing analytical notes to Boston Symphony Orchestra programmes, he brings a touch that lightens the inherent dryness of the subject.[30]

This "deadly task" resulted in Hale having a very full plate, though he still continued writing for other periodicals on the side. His *Musical Record* met its demise in 1901, but immediately he became a co-editor, along with Louis C. Elson and Henry T. Finck, of a new periodical named *Musical World*. While Vol.

I (1901) was under the editorial leadership of all three of them, Vol. II (1902) had only one editor—Hale. Most of this volume was given over to articles on women musicians, both as composers and performers. Several of the articles had no author cited, although these were clearly Hale's work. He had always had an interest in women musicians—his wife Irene was one, of course—and the whole volume comes across as an expansion of his November 4, 1896 *Boston Journal* article on women symphonists. For whatever reason, Hale did no more editing for *Musical World* beyond this volume, though he did continue to write anonymous articles for *The New Music Review*.

As his stature among his peers grew, Hale was often sought out for information or advice. Richard Aldrich (1863–1937) became music critic for the *New York Times* in 1902, a position he would hold for the next nineteen years. He wanted to know about the directors of Boston's choral societies and asked Hale for information. This would have been readily at hand for Hale, who was more than happy to comply:

Jan 5/1903

Dear Aldrich:

Apollo Club-still running—Conductor last season and this: Emil Mollenhauer.
　In 16th season in 1889 Turned into the Boston Singers Society.
　Boyleston Club-Osgood. The Boston Singers, led by him, bust at the end of season 1890–1891.
　Cecilian still led by Lang.
　Euterpe was never a choral society. Devoted to Chamber Music. It bust years ago. End of season 1889.
　Arlington Club-W. G. Winch. Then Chadwick. It bust over a dozen years ago.
　Add Choral Art Society-W. Goodrich, Conductor of 2nd season.
　The Boston Singers Club-H. Tucker Conductor also 2nd season.
　I wish to congratulate you on your latest prefaces to Schirmer's operas. They are exceedingly well done. Happy New Year.

Yrs
Ph. Hale[31]

As time went by, Aldrich and Hale became good friends, as did their wives. The following brief series of correspondence shows Hale going out of his way to find out information about an opera that was new at the time:

Feb 24/08

Dear Richard,

Just a line to say I am looking up Dolores by Breton (Tomas).
　3 acts, text by José Felin [?] First performance Madrid, Theatre of the Zarzuela in March 1895. Performed at Milan, Dal Vermetta [?], Jan 19, 1906
　It was so popular in Madrid that it was parodied "Dolores, de cabeza o el colegial atvzvido," text by Gravés, music by Arnedo.
　More soon. For another opera by Breton, see Hanslick's "Fünf Jahre Musik" p. 2.
　I have written Mrs. Aldrich this mail.

Yours as ever,
Philip Hale[32]

Dear Richard:

<u>Dolores</u> was performed in Prague in 1906. You will find a description of the first act in the Signale for that year nos. 23–24 pp. 391–3.

By the way, did I leave in the room I occupied a pamphlet edition of Maeterlinck's <u>Pelleás</u>; the front cover was gone or had gone—or done gone.

Sincerely,
Philip Hale[33]

Feb. 26/1908

Dear Richard:

Thank you for the package. I did not mean to hurry you. I did not remember whether I left Maeterlinck's play or not.

Here is some more <u>Dolores</u> information.
1st performance in Madrid March 16, 1895
Italian version by E. Godesciani.
Voice & piano score published at Madrid in 1895.

---

3 acts with orchestral Prelude.
Scene in Calatazud, Aragon. 1830–1840.
I think the libretto is taken from Rama [Dama?] by José Feliú y Codina.

Original cast at Madrid-Spanish text of course

Dolores	Mme. Corona
Gaspara	Mme. Castellanoi
Lazaro	Mr. Simonetti
Celemino	Alcantera
Melchiorre	M. Mastres
Patrizio	Visconti
Rojas	Sigler
Mulattiere	Vera

Best wishes to you both.

Yours sincerely,
Philip Hale[34]

4

1903–1917

1903 was a year of many changes for the Boston Symphony Orchestra and for Philip Hale. Romanian-born Franz Kneisel (1865–1926), the orchestra's concertmaster since 1885, had formed a professional string quartet, the Kneisel Quartet, shortly after his arrival in Boston. He and the other three members of the quartet—second violinist Julius Theodorowicz, violist Louis Svečenski, and violoncellist Alwin Schroeder—decided to break with the orchestra and devote themselves to a chamber music career centered in New York, though Schroeder would return to the symphony for a brief two-year stint in 1910–1912 and Theodorowicz would rejoin it more permanently in 1917. An anonymous letter in the *Musical Courier* addressed their departure:

> ...It is reported that Mr. Higginson was very angry with the Kneisel Quartet for resigning from the orchestra, on the ground that they did not give him "notice" enough. But they gave just as much "notice" as he ever gives anyone, and a good deal more than he usually gives. He evidently did not like the "taste of his own medicine."[1]

The loss of these players, especially Kneisel, was a real blow to the orchestra. It created a period of instability in the concertmaster position over the next two decades, resulting in a succession of occupants in that chair: E. Fernandez Arbós (1903–1904), Willy Hess (1904–1907, 1908–1910), Carl Wendling (1907–1908), Anton Witek (1910–1918), and Frederic Fradkin (1918–1920). Richard Burgin would break this trend with conviction, occupying the chair from 1920 until 1962. As if the departure of the Kneisel Quartet were not enough, Charles Martin Loeffler, the orchestra's assistant concertmaster since 1882, also left in order to focus his efforts on composition.

In spite of this rather high turnover in key personnel, things were improving for the players, if not musically, then at least in terms of personal stability. At Wilhelm Gericke's insistence, a pension fund was established. Special concerts were created, with proceeds earmarked for the fund. The first such concert was held on December 27, 1903 and featured such works as "Ah! fors' i lui" from Giuseppi Verdi's *La Traviata* and "Juliet's Waltz" from Charles Gounod's *Romeo and Juliet*. The second, held on April 13, 1904 was a much grander affair, culminating with Beethoven's Ninth Symphony. Hale commented about the program and the fund itself:

PENSION FUND CONCERT

> The Boston Symphony Orchestra gave last evening, at Symphony Hall, a concert in aid of its pension fund. The organization was assisted by the chorus of the Handel and Haydn Society and by Mrs. Kileski-Bradbury, Miss Pauline Woltmann, Mr. Theodore Van Yorx, Mr. Myron W. Whitney, Jr., and Mr. Sullivan Sargent. The programme consisted of Beethoven's "Egmont" overture, Mozart's Quintet from "Cosi fan tutte," and Beethoven's Ninth Symphony, in D minor, for solo voices, chorus, and orchestra.
>
> A good deal has already been written about in these columns and elsewhere concerning the purpose of these concerts and that purpose must be by this time generally understood. The musicians have by their own efforts established a fund destined to aid members of their organization after they have become old or incapacitated for service. This fund they propose to increase by giving occasional concerts. It is an independent and praiseworthy effort, and deserves the encouragement of all loyal music lovers in the community. Last evening the audience was small. Doubtless the opera season is an unfortunate time for the giving of other music entertainments; but there seems no excuse for the vast barren spaces in the hall. It is needless to dilate upon the quality of the concerts offered. This programme may not have been as alluring as a more varied, and more generally modern, programme would have been, but it was an admirable program for all that, and it is most regrettable that, together with the prospect of a fine performance and its good cause, it should not have aroused more public enthusiasm.
>
> Of the performance, it is needless to speak in detail. Mozart's quintet was gracefully sung. The symphony was given a spirited reading; the chorus sang with good volume and intonation, and the orchestral portions, especially the first three movements, elicited warm applause.[2]

Hale was passionate about supporting the players through these concerts. In his review of a 1908 pension fund concert conducted by Max Fiedler and featuring works by Liszt, Wagner, and Tchaikovsky, he spoke again about audience size, this time adding a note about the quality of the orchestra:

> The cause for which the concert was given and the nature of the program should have drawn a much larger audience. Some may say that there should have been a soloist, an admired prima donna or a formidable pianist; but at whatever concert of the Boston Symphony orchestra a virtuoso assists, however famous he or she may be, the orchestra, after all is the dominating soloist, the true virtuoso. It might be reasonably supposed that any opportunity of hearing this superb orchestra would fill the hall to overflowing.[3]

Sometimes guest conductors were brought in for these occasions. Richard Strauss conducted an entire concert on April 19, 1904 and Georg Henschel, the orchestra's first conductor, was brought back on November 25, 1905 to conduct Beethoven's overture *Consecration of the House*, Op. 124 on a concert that was otherwise conducted by Gericke.[4]

The year 1903 also witnessed the Boston Symphony Orchestra performing the inaugural concert of a new performance venue. New England Conservatory's Jordan Hall was dedicated on October 20 of that year. Located only one block away from Symphony Hall, the new hall provided a badly needed additional concert venue for the city. Seating a little over 1,000 people, Jordan Hall's acoustics are very good, though they do not quite compare with those of Symphony Hall. Most of its respective vantage points, however, are superior.

Sometime during the summer of 1903, Hale left the *Boston Journal* and became the music critic of the *Boston Herald*. At the beginning his duties were about the same as before: to review concerts and to write a nonmusical column, "As the World Wags." While on the surface this change of employer may appear to have been a lateral move, it was not. Hale may have been lured to the *Herald* by any one or all of three things: a better salary, a wider circulation (meaning a wider audience), and/or better stability. Whatever the case, Hale "celebrated" his new position with a gargantuan 5,000-word essay in the July 5th *Sunday Herald*, "The Attitude of American Critics toward Music," in which he not only provided the reader with a history of American music criticism, but also discussed the contributions of a number of his contemporaries.[5] Hale was now 49 years old, the end of the normal life expectancy for an American at the turn of the twentieth century. Somewhat miraculously, he stayed at the *Herald* for 30 years—the remainder of his career. Hale's decision to go with another employer turned out to be propitious, for in October 1917 the *Boston Journal* was bought out by the *Boston Herald*.

During this first three years at the *Herald*, Hale's Boston Symphony Orchestra reviews were uncredited. Such anonymity may have been the result of some type of understanding between the newspaper and the orchestra, or it may have been Hale's choice; nobody wanted a repeat of the 1891 debacle. Still, it appears that this was carried to an extreme since many of his other columns written for the *Herald*, including those having nothing to do with the orchestra, also remained anonymous. On October 18, the same day that his review of the symphony's opening concert was published, his enormous article "Opera in English and in Foreign Tongues, and the Relation of Language and Music" was published without his name on it. Of course, everybody knew that Hale was the new *Herald* music critic. This was confirmed by an editorial that appeared in the *Musical Courier* in early November:

> The Boston Symphony Orchestra was on its first circuit tour for the season last week, and therefore did not perform in Boston; hence we are unable to print an article from the pen of Philip Hale in this issue of the paper. It was asking too much of Mr. Hale to expect him to write on the same subject about the same time for two papers. In the Boston Herald his articles are unsigned, therefore in their reproduction in The Musical Courier they become more valuable by being credited to him. The daily papers should always have the names of their critics signed to their criticisms, especially in New York, because here sometimes criticisms are written which might be credited to the baseball reporters, or to the golf reporters, or the yacht reporters. As it stands now, whenever The Musical Courier reprints the Boston Herald criticisms it brings into prominence the fact that Philip Hale is the recognized music authority of that paper.[6]

The opening concert of the orchestra's 1903 subscription series was held on October 16. Though Hale had written some informative articles for the *Boston*

Herald earlier, this was the first review he wrote for them. He picked up right where he left off; his style remained the same:

SYMPHONY SEASON OPENS

The Overture to "Euryanthe,"
as Usual, Heads the List.

Concerto by Tschaikowsky, Entr'acte by Bruneau and Symphony by Brahms Complete the Programme—Wilhelm Gericke is the Conductor Again This Year.

The program of the first concert of the 23rd season of the Boston Symphony orchestra at Symphony Hall, last evening, Mr. Gericke conductor, was as follows:

Overture, "Euryanthe"	Weber
Concerto No. 1 in B-flat minor for piano	Tschaikowsky
Entr'acte, Symphonique from "Messidor" (First ime)	Bruneau
Symphony No. 2 in D major	Brahms

The overture to "Euryanthe," in Europe, as well as in this country, often serves as [the] opening or closing piece at a first symphony concert of a season. Thirty years or more ago, when negro minstrels were fashionable as well as popular entertainers, the opening chorus, or, to speak by the card, the "opening load," was an arrangement of a chorus from "Ernani," and it was titled "O Hail Us, Ye Free!" Had not this particular chorus been sung, the audience would have been suspicious of the jests, songs, dances and farces that followed. So, too, there was a time when all popular concerts began with the overture to "Zampa" or the overture to "Massaniello" or the overture to "Poet and Peasant." In concerts of a more dignified nature "Euryanthe" is accepted by many as the fitting announcement of the beginning of another season.

There is reason other than mere caprice for this choice. The overture is not without a certain old-fashioned but veritable pomp; it has the spirit of ceremony which the admirers of Weber call "the chivalric spirit." What Mr. Apthorp was fond of naming the characteristic Weberian upward rush—in other words, the flourish peculiar to Weber, his signature, which was his mannerism—contributes no doubt to the general feeling of pleasurable expectation and promotes what Athenaeus held to be one of the chief ends of music—"a gentlemanlike joy."

It would be perhaps an idle task for an ultra-modern to insist that the only music in this overture that appeals to the men and women of the younger generation is that of the short episode which was originally intended to accompany a pantomime scene on the stage, a scene of old-fashioned romantic melodrama, with tomb, kneeling heroine, gliding ghost, and an eavesdropping, intriguing woman. In these few mysterious measures Weber thought far beyond his period. The ultra-modern might say that the rest of the music is decorative and that the decorations are substantial until they are cumbrous; that the melodies are like unto a cameo-brooch worn by a faded woman who remembers nights of coquetry and dances long out of fashion, that the few measures of counterpoint show Weber as a plodding amateur. Nevertheless, the conventionally jubilant swing and the impetuous pace make their way in a concert hall even in 1903.

So, too, the choice of a symphony by Brahms was in this instance judicious. The symphony in D is the most genial of the four, the most easily accepted by an audience, for if there are pages of supreme beauty in it, as toward the end of the first movement, so there are pages that are Mendelssohnian in the form and in the rhythm of the easily restrained melodic thought. Mendelssohn, a shrewd composer, seldom, if ever, committed the blunder of surprising an audience. As in the theatre, so in the concert hall, an audience does not wish to be left in doubt, and in this symphony, which is in reality a storehouse of beautiful things, there is every now and then a passage that is acceptable by the hearer as an agreeable commonplace.

The entr'acte from Bruneau's "Messidor" is a prelude to the fourth and last act of that opera, for which Zola wrote the libretto in prose. In the opera house the curtain rises toward the end of the prelude and the final measures are enchained with the music of the scene. The entr'acte is built on five typical themes, for Bruneau invented themes to typify situations or to serve as symbols. An earnest commentator assures us that there are at least 26 of these themes and they must be mastered for the purpose of prompt identification, or the hearer sits in his seat with as foolish a face as that of Parsifal standing during the communion scene in the castle of the Holy Grail. The themes in the entr'acte typify Spring, Sowing, Water, Love, and Toil.

In the opera house, these themes may suggest what has gone before, serve as a summing up of preceding action, or awaken thoughts concerning the outcome of the story. In a concert hall this entr'acte sandwiched between a concerto and a symphony can be considered only as absolute music. The themes are merely melodies without esoteric significance. As absolute music, the entr'acte is a pleasing work. The themes are fresh; they are introduced with apparent spontaneity; they are not too laboriously combined; and the orchestration is ingenious and sonorous. Bruneau is a composer concerning whom there is a marked difference in opinion even in Paris. A man of decided convictions, a critic who wrote bravely and honestly, he inevitably made enemies. Let us hope that we shall have an opportunity of hearing more of his music and of judging for ourselves. He has composed a symphonic poem, "The Sleeping Beauty," which will soon be played at Chicago, and excerpts from his latest opera, "L'Ouragan," have been warmly applauded in Parisian concert halls.

Tschaikowsky's first piano concerto has been played many times in Boston since it was first introduced here and to the world, by von Bülow in 1875. Last night the pianist was Mr. Harold Bauer and his performance was a memorable one, memorable for rhythm and passion. Tschaikowsky was an oriental in his love of rhythm and color, in his delight in rhythmic iterations, in drum beats or in haunting phrases that repeated do not weary, but take possession of the hearer and fret his nerves till he is mastered by the spell, till he thinks and dreams or would fain act to that compelling rhythm.

It has been said of this great tone-poet of longing, anguish and despair, that he at times is melodically trivial or coarse. His melodies have a direct appeal: pathetic, they stab at the heart; but their gaiety is not that of the idle dancer. Let the tune be at first ever so spritely, sadness creeps in, and the sadness is ever so poignant in the expression of the melancholy. Tschaikowsky might well have written the dance tunes for the revelers in Poe's wild tale; music that now halted strangely, that shuddered in its measure, knowing the approach of the masked Red Death. In this concerto how suddenly the merriment of the French dance tune in the second movement is chilled! And how the dance fades away as at command.

Now Mr. Bauer not only appreciated the essential spirit of this concerto, which is too often misunderstood or belittled by being turned into a mere show piece, but by an intellectual force charged with artistic passion, he interpreted the music and revealed Tschaikowsky's soul, a soul that, as we now know from the composer's correspondence, was full of strange contradictions; the soul of a man shy, now distrustful; and now confident of his genius—one yearning for affection, yet suspicious and inclined toward misanthropy; a man of the loftiest and noblest aspirations, vexed by his grievous mental ailments.

The concerto is to be taken as Victor Hugo took Shakespeare—in bulk. It is enough to say of Mr. Bauer's performance that never before did the work seem so colossal in proportions, so tenderly beautiful, so rhythmically entrancing and irresistible, so demoniacally, and yet so nobly, passionate. The long continued and repeated applause was merely the attempt of the audience to show in a measure its profound appreciation of the concerto and Mr. Bauer's artistic worth.

All in all, a concert of unusual interest. Mr. Gericke was warmly greeted, and he conducted with fervent authority. His reading of the first movement of the familiar symphony was perhaps especially admirable in a concert that even at the very beginning of the season was often worthy of the reputation of the orchestra at its zenith. Mr. Arbos, the concert master; Mr. Ferir, the violin player, and other new members were in their respective seats. Mr. Krasseit, the 'cellist, will be present at the next concert.[7]

Taken at face value, the above review was what one would have expected from Philip Hale at this point in his career. There was less coverage of the more familiar works though, rather surprisingly, there was in-depth detail about Tchaikovsky and his concerto; the soloist was lauded. The Bruneau, on account of the readers' unfamiliarity with the work as well as the composer, received a significant amount of coverage. The *Music Courier*, however, instead of simply reprinting Hale's review, preceded it with the following editorial:

Before reprinting what Philip Hale thought and wrote in last Sunday's Boston Herald on the opening of the twenty-third season of the concerts of the Boston Symphony Orchestra it may be well to state that for the first time in ten years seats for these concerts were on sale at Symphony Hall, and that at the auction sale of tickets for the season there was a loss of about 25 per cent on the Friday afternoon sales and of about 10 per cent on the Saturday evening sales. As compared to the sums received last season.

Two reasons are assigned for this manifestation of decreasing interest. The one is the absence of attractive solo stars, which is proved by the fact that the prices of the tickets for the concerts when [Dame Nellie] Melba is to appear are advanced by the ticket speculators to figures far ahead of the average concerts, which indicates that Boston musical culture is no lower and no higher than the music culture of this star ridden town.

The second reason assigned for the falling off of income is the self evident fact that Mr. Gericke as a conductor fails to draw. Naturally The Musical Courier, like other critical sources, has its theory for this. People very soon tire of academic orchestral conducting, and they will find in this city this approaching season the reason why so many European communities have become interested and fascinated by some of the men who are coming over here to conduct the Philharmonic concerts. Most of these men have graduated and are no longer academicians, but are demonstrators of authority. Mr. Gericke is an amiable time beater. It will be observed that Mr. Hale, who is suffering from the fact that he is writing for a daily paper, which like all dailies, cannot afford to be independent, cannot afford to print the truth. Mr. Hale, as will be seen by the following, does not enter upon any criticism of Mr. Gericke's conducting. It will be observed by students of these phenomena that the daily music critic can always freely criticize the absent composer and the transient guest, but the local musician, the local music institution, with their permanent pull, cannot be treated unfavorably by the critic, because the owners of the daily papers, being the slaves of public opinion, cannot afford to have the truth printed in their columns.[8]

The criticism of Hale's lack of commentary regarding Gericke's conducting did not stop there. *The Musical Courier* printed the following a week later:

Mr. Gericke Again.

To The Musical Courier:

After reading your altogether discriminating introduction to Philip Hale's account of the opening Symphony Concert in this town, many of us were in the condition of the minister of the gospel who thanked the man for swearing for him. Many of us have wanted to say just what you said in that introductory paragraph, but, to use the New England vernacular, "we dassant."

Everyone likes Mr. Gericke personally. It is generally conceded that he conducts with uncommon accuracy. Indeed, as a patron of the Symphony concerts said to me lately: "He conducts with the precision and certainty of the Pianola." And there you have it. The personal distinction and the individual warmth to which the Pianola lays no claim, clearly these do not belong to Mr. Gericke. The loss is manifest. And some of the town people, who remember Nikisch and Paur, or who have happened to hear Wetzler in New York or Scheel in Philadelphia, are beginning to find fault—in a thoroughly gentlemanly and Boston way, to be sure, but nevertheless to find fault and the fault-finding spoke loud in the sale of season tickets a fortnight since.

There are other criticisms of Gericke besides his academic style of conducting. His manifest opposition to modern compositions and more particularly his contempt for anything and everything American do not count as virtues, even in a slow and poky town like Boston. Then, we were not a bit pleased because he did not secure Richard Strauss for at least one concert, and because he did not, many of us did not take season tickets, but have saved our pennies to hear Scheel's Philadelphia players when they come to town and for a trip or two New Yorkward to hear Strauss and the other novelties to be there later in the season.

Back Bay.

Boston, Mass., October 27, 1903.[9]

Reasons for Hale not directly attacking Gericke's conducting most likely had to do with Hale's position as program essayist, but there was probably more to it than that. For one thing, Hale felt that Gericke, the disciplinarian, was doing his expected job in establishing a high performance bar for the orchestra, placing the focus on music making rather than on himself. For another, there had developed a mutual and respectful relationship between the two men. Hale's relationship with Nikisch had been outwardly antagonistic and, according to his own words, he really did not personally know Paur. Gericke, however, had a very different personality from his two immediate predecessors. Though not flamboyant, he was much more amicable and, early on, he had acquired at least a functional command of English. He was approachable and Hale liked that.

Gericke did not have an easy time during this season. This was his sixth straight year of conducting the Boston Symphony Orchestra, one year longer than any of the orchestra's previous conductors had stayed. Altogether though, it was his eleventh year, counting his earlier 1884–1889 tenure, which meant that Gericke had conducted the orchestra for more years than Nikisch and Paur combined. Overall, he was well liked and well respected, though a vocal minority, such as those writing cowardly anonymous criticisms, suggested that his Boston tenure should have ended at five years. As if such verbal assaults were not enough, there were other problems that lie beyond his control. The programming of what was to have been the Hector Berlioz centenary concert had to be modified twice. The securing of the services of operatic soprano Nellie Melba, a major draw, had much to do with this, but when she developed a cold, a last minute change was in order. Hale commented:

> Mr. Gericke had bad luck with the programme of this concert. The programme, as originally planned, was in commemoration of the centenary of Berlioz, which could not be celebrated on Dec. 11—the birthday of Berlioz (1803)—for this week the orchestra will be giving concerts out of town. The original programme included the Symphony performed last night, the overture to "King Lear," and orchestral excerpts from "The Damnation of Faust." For certain reasons beyond his control, Mr. Gericke was obliged to change the programme and therefore the centenary of the birth of the great Frenchman, the creator of modern orchestration, the creator who has not been surpassed by any of his disciples or imitators, will not be celebrated at these concerts, in which his name has been honored since the beginning. It is interesting to note in connection with this the Berlioz anniversary programme prepared by Theodore Thomas for the concerts of the Chicago Orchestra Dec.11–22.
>
> Overture, "Benvenuto Cellini"; recitative and aria from "Les Troyens" (Miss Marguerite Halli); symphonie fantastique; Ball scene and love scene from "Romeo and Juliet"; invocation, minuet, "Dance of the Sylphs"; romance, "My Heart with Grief is Heavy" (Miss Halli)' Rakoczy march from "The Damnation of Faust."
>
> And then Mme. Melba took cold and was unable to sing the airs from "La Clemenza di Tito" and "Hamlet" to the keen disappointment of all, and not merely those who go to Symphony concerts for the sake of the soloists, male and female after their kind. The justly celebrated climate of Boston delights in sport with golden-voices sopranos. Mme. Melba, however, will delay her departure and sing later at a Symphony concert.
>
> The concert, then, was purely orchestral: The symphony by Berlioz remained; there was the Academic Festival overture of Brahms, in which the composer was less academic than his wont; "The Voyode," an orchestral ballad by Tschaikowsky, which was produced here in the form of a transcription for brass band at a Sousa concert Dec. 9, 1902, and the Wedding March from "A Midsummer Night's Dream," which was introduced unexpectedly in honor of the day, which was to Maj. Henry Higginson a wedding anniversary.[10]

Being the professional that she was, Melba did appear with the orchestra three weeks later to sing Handel's "Sweet Bird" and Ophelia's "Mad Scene" from Thomas's *Hamlet*.

On April 2, 1904, Gericke programmed Anton Bruckner's unfinished ninth symphony, a rather severe work. Hale commented:

> ANTON BRUCKNER'S
> SYMPHONY GIVEN
>
> Unfinished Work of the Composer
> Played in Boston for the First
> Time at Concert of Sym-
> phony Orchestra
>
> ----
>
> MUSIC THAT VEXES
> AND IRRITATES NERVES
>
> ----
>
> Mendelssohn's Overture to :The
> FairM elusina" and a Beethoven
> Overture Also Given—Miss Mu-
> riel Foster Sings
>
> ----
>
> The programme of the 21st concert of the Boston Symphony orchestra, Wilhelm Gericke conductor, in Symphony Hall, last evening, was as follows:
>
> Overture to "The Fair Melusina" .... Mendelssohn
> Aria, "Che Faro Senza Euridice" .... Gluck
> Symphony No. 9, unfinished .... Bruckner
>   (first ime)
> Songs with piano:
>   "Gute nacht" .... Dvorak
>   "Von Jenseits" .... Rachmaninoff
>   "Mutterlaenderlei" .... R. Strauss
> Overture to Leonore, No. 2 .... Beethoven
>
> Anton Bruckner died before he finished his ninth symphony. This symphony was performed at Vienna Feb. 14, 1903, and the first performance in the United States was at Chicago the 20th of last February. Just before Bruckner died he said, "I undertook a stiff task. I should not have done it at my age, and in my weak condition. If I do not finish the symphony then my "Te Deum" may be used as a finale. I have nearly finished three movements. The "Te Deum" was performed in Vienna as the Finale. The unfinished work has been performed in several German cities, and in Munich alone it has been played at least three times.
>
> The symphony as performed last night is on the whole less endurable than preceding works of the same composer. We do not use the word "endurable" with offensive intent. To listen to a symphony by Bruckner is literally a test of endurance; for although there are sublime pages in some of the symphonies—pages that are apocalyptic in sweep and grandeur of vision—there are many more pages that are perplexing or childish. To use a homely phrase Bruckner's music soon "gets on the nerves;" not to excite, nor to thrill them, but to irritate and vex them. It is a long time between this composer's intoxicating drinks.

We are not told whether the ninth symphony was revised by the composer fully to his satisfaction. The manuscript contains dates of completion, but such dates are not always a sure index of a composer's unchangeable approval. The fastidious Tennyson revised constantly many of his earlier poems long after publication, and the changes were not always advantageous. It is highly probable that the three movements are as Bruckner wished them. They are certainly in his familiar manner; they show the weakness known of old, and here and there is a page so lofty and irresistible that it makes us wonder at the tiresome twaddle that precedes or follows.

The opening measures, the preparation and the announcement of the chief theme, these are powerfully conceived and expressed. After these measures there is an intolerable amount of flat and vapid sack to a bit of nourishing bread. The scherzo is by far the one movement most sustained in the interest. It is original and often piquant. There are impressive moments in the third movement.

There are the old, elemental faults: a lack of conformity of thought so that there is no apparent organic structure. The music has a series of views. The ear, as, in the other instance, the eye, becomes tired through disappointment and is quickened only for a moment. There is no continuous rhythmic pulse that beats to the end. Bruckner is as a child who puts building blocks in a row, and has neither the inclination for the skill to construct a building, either solid or fantastical. His melodic thought is often dry, and the endless repetitions dampen the soul. His wild admiration for Wagner leads him to the imitation of his idol's harmonic devices, or at times to deliberate and respectful quotation.

There is no need of going into the political quotation of pitting Bruckner as a Wagnerian against Brahms and his passionate press agent Hanslick. There is Bruckner's music in this ninth symphony; and if, to complete the familiar speech, there it will remain, we fear it will be to the world at large as on a dusty shelf. It was once the fashion to publish volumes entitled "Elegant Extracts," but a score of such musical quotations is hardly suited to concert use.[11]

The Boston Symphony orchestra performed no fewer than four different symphonies during that month: Bruckner's Ninth, Haydn's 97th in C (listed as No. 7) on April 12th, Beethoven's Ninth in D minor at a Pension Fund concert on April 13th, and Beethoven's Eighth in F, conducted by Richard Strauss, at the April 19th Pension Fund concert mentioned earlier. Hale's review of the latter pays tribute to Gericke's work; it occupies fully one-third of the column:

PENSION FUND
CONCERT A TREAT

Richard Strauss Makes His First Appearance as Conductor of SymphonyO rchestra—Performance Was Triumph for All Participating

----

MR. GERICKE ALSO COMES
IN FOR MUCH PRAISE

Work of the Orchestra Was Result
Of His Long and Arduous Labors
In Bringing It to the present
State of Perfection

Dr. Richard Strauss conducted last evening in Symphony Hall, by special arrangement of the Pension Fund committee, a concert of the Boston Symphony Orchestra. The programme was as follows:

Symphony No. 8	Beethoven
Prelude to "Tristan and Isolde"	Wagner
"Don Juan"	R. Strauss
"Don Quixote"	R. Strauss
Love scene from "Feuersnot"	R. Strauss

The performance was as much of a triumph for Mr. Gericke and the players as it was for Dr. Strauss, composer and conductor. The supreme virtuoso qualities of the orchestra as a body, the remarkable euphony and the exquisite balance of timbres, the plasticity and the now instinctive phrasing—these characteristics that make the orchestra famous—are due to the artistry of the players, and, above all, to the discipline maintained for so many years by Mr. Gericke. He first established the brilliant reputation of the orchestra, and through his untiring vigilance this brilliance has been preserved of late years. Without his work in the past, Dr. Strauss' task last night would not have been so easy, nor would his triumph have been so assured.

It is well to remember this, for it is easy to forget it. We all, accustomed to the best, over familiar with it, are inclined to sigh for new readings, novel effects. We welcome that which has been hitherto unknown; we cherish it for a season; and then that, too, becomes stale. Conductors will in the flight of years come and have their little day; they will blaze and their light will go out or be forgotten. When the history of this orchestra will be written, the name of one conductor will be enduring in the inseparable association with the name of Maj. Henry Higginson. Mr. Gericke will be remembered as the conductor who gave the orchestra the qualities that set it apart from other bands of players, who, by his taste, intelligence, skill and authority carried out and brilliantly the noble purposes of the founder and the maintainer of the Boston Symphony Orchestra.

The features of the concert were the prelude to "Tristan" and Strauss' "Don Juan." The Prelude was played with infinite yearning and splendid passion, and the performance of the tone-poem was distinguished by dash, brilliance, the demoniacal spirit that fired the breast of the pursuer of the ideal woman.

The performance of the symphony was not one of unusual merit. There might have been some curiosity as to the pace of the second and third movements under Dr. Strauss; but no sane person expected surprises in reading. For the music does not admit of marked surprises, and the conductor who attempt to be revolutionary with this symphony would deservedly excite suspicion as to the sincerity of his art. Here and there Dr. Strauss made perhaps a nuance to which we were unaccustomed, but his reading as a whole was conventionally sound, and the music itself did not gain or suffer by any slight innovation.

Mr. Gericke took infinite pains this season in the rehearsal of "Don Quixote." The performance under his direction was masterly. The compositions itself did not appeal to us, either as programme music or as music without an explanatory text. The performance under Dr. Strauss was not in certain instances as memorable as that under Mr. Gericke, and it strengthened our opinion concerning the value of the work itself. There is a display of amazing technical ingenuity; there are startling orchestral effects; the variation that represents Don Quixote discoursing in lofty speech concerning the ideal is of rare power and beauty; but, on the other hand, much of the music is unintelligible without a text or tiresome with it.

"Don Quixote" is to us the least interesting and successful of Strauss' larger works, and the music belittles and degrades the finest gentleman in all fiction. Such was not probably the intent of the composer who wished to perpetrate a fantastically practical joke. Don Quixote in Cervantes' tale met with all manner of strange adventures; he was mocked and maltreated by worldly wise persons, by men and women of high and low degree; but the Don Quixote of the immortal romance is himself never ridiculous; he is enviably noble when is most abused.

There was a very large audience and there was unbound enthusiasm. Dr. Strauss was recalled again and again, the distinguished composer and conductor well deserved such honor. He shared the applause modestly with the orchestra and with Mr. Krasseit, whose "cello playing in 'Don Quixote' merited the public recognition."[12]

Guest conductors were, at that time, a rarity for Boston and Hale's review, though full of praise for Strauss discouraged acceptance of him as a cult figure. Hale strived to give credit where credit was due. He was not the only one to credit Gericke with developing the orchestra into a world-class institution. The person closest to the orchestra since its inception, Henry Lee Higginson, had the following to say long after Gericke's departure:

H – H.   December 28, 1918

Dear Mr. Gericke,

Now that the war is finished, I can write to you and express the strong hope that you all four are well and content.

But first let me say this: When people speak of the Boston Symphony Orchestra and of its beauty, its style, its perfection, they add: "Gericke made the orchestra." I have known this and said this for many years past. Philip Hale repeated it at the Tavern Club dinner last week; Dr. Muck said it to me in Berlin in 1910, and has said it again—"Gericke made the orchestra."

To me this means much, for do you know a better orchestra? Has any orchestra in existence played more concerts or more variety of music, or to more audiences? Has any orchestra done more to stimulate good music in any land, or given more peace and happiness? I know of none; and if this is true, Wilhelm Gericke has been a great benefactor to men, women and children of our day. We have given perhaps four thousand concerts....[13]

The following letter from Hale to Gericke probably referred to Strauss's conducting of Beethoven's Eighth, although it could have also referred to Gericke's conducting of Bruckner's Ninth, since the reviews of the other two symphonies mentioned above were favorable:

Boston April 21, 1904

My dear Mr. Gericke:

I was touched as well as pleased by your note, more gratified than I can tell you.

I wrote only what I thought while I sat at the concert. I was much hurt by the absurd applause after the movements of the Symphony, which was none too well performed. So when I got down to the office and began to write, I said to the public what I should have liked to say from my seat in the gallery. I always write what I think and feel, for I could not write in any other way. No doubt I am often wrong in judgment, but I am sure you know that I am at least sincere in my opinion, however poor it may be.

I beg of you not to be discouraged by any seeming indifference to the part of the audience, for I believe that at heart the Symphony audience is your warm admirer and supporter; but audiences, like men and women, are sometimes thoughtless, and like children gape with wonder at anything that is new.

Thank you again for the generous expression. Would you be so kind as to send me the titles of the excerpts from "The Ring," for as we publish an index with the 24th program book, the printer will need plenty of time.

> Yours very sincerely
> Philip Hale[14]

Early in the 1904–1905 season, Paul Dukas's symphonic poem *The Sorcerer's Apprentice* was performed in Boston for the first time in a concert that also featured Beethoven's Fourth Symphony, Wagner's Overture to *Tannhäuser*, and Joachim's *Hungarian Concerto*. As one would expect, Hale spent half the column on the Dukas:

> Paul Dukas' "Sorcerer's Appretice" is now seven years old—at least it was first played in Paris in 1897. Theodore Thomas' orchestra has played it twice in Chicago, and Mr. Van der Stucken produced it in Cincinnati last season. The composer, who was born at Paris in 1865 and studied at the conservatory in that city, has written comparatively little, but that little has excited attention and commanded respect: an overture to "Polyeacte"—two other overtures have not been published—a symphony, and a formidable piano sonata that takes 40 minutes in performance even when the pianist is urged to do his best.
>
> All these works are eminently serious. But Mr. Dukas, like many serious persons, has his light moments. The "Sorcerer's Apprentice" is his best joke.
>
> It is a musical illustration of Goethe's ballad of the same name, the story of the apprentice who, in the absence of his master, tried to work one of his more remarkable tricks, that of turning a broom into a water-carrier, and by not knowing the words to end the spell, was nearly drowned. The tale is a pleasant one, and it was told still more delightfully by Lucian, the satirist, centuries before Goethe. Where did Lucian hear it, or who told it before him?
>
> Dukas has made a singularly picturesque and effective transliteration into music. Many young Frenchmen have glib and colored orchestral expression, but, unfortunately, their thought is insignificant or scrappy. Dukas has striking thoughts, the gift of developing them logically; he is clear even when he is most fantastic in his orchestral speech and, above all, he has fancy and imagination. There is no attempt at mosaic work; there is no interlinear translation.
>
> "You know the poem?" asks the composer: "now what do you hear in this?"
>
> After the introduction which prepares the mood of witchcraft of haunted rhapsody or of mysterious Egypt, the small works, and its chief theme, developed, varied, swells with the wretched apprentice's terror, and then enters the vexed and saving sorcerer. The spell is broken. The broom is again a broom.
>
> The scherzo was played brilliantly and Mr. Gericke is to be thanked for producing here this excellent example of the better modern French school and congratulated for the performance itself.[15]

He ripped apart the Joachim, which introduced Willy Hess to the Boston audience:

> Mr. Willy Hess, the new first concertmaster, made his first appearance in America since he attained man's estate. When he was 10 years old he played here in Music Hall with Theodore Thomas' orchestra (in 1869), as "Master Willy Hess." He chose last night Joachim's "Hungarian" concerto, a very long and for the most part labored and tedious work. Mr. Listemann, who delighted in Herculean feats, played the whole of it at a symphony concert in 1881.
> Insatiable violinist! Could not one movement suffice?
> Messrs. Kneisel and Winternitz were more discreet and compassionate; they were content with one movement. But perhaps Mr. Hess wished to perform a pious duty in honoring his master, Joachim.
> Mr. Hess, who was cordially welcomed and heartily applauded after each movement, made a most favorable impression in spite of the handicap of the concerto itself. He displayed the confidence and agility of the virtuoso and the phrasing and the musical intelligence of the experience concertmaster. The music did not call for, did not allow, in fact, any exhibition of deep emotion, but whenever there was opportunity, there was a display of amiable sentiment without trickery or exaggeration. The violinist was presented with a wreath.[16]

As was consistent with Hale's other reviews, the Beethoven and Wagner works were scarcely commented upon since they were familiar to the audience.

The question may arise as to how much of a Francophile Hale was by the time he wrote this review. After all, his own edition of *Modern French Songs* in two volumes was published that same year.[17] In the review, at first glance, his commentary on the Dukas was positive, the Joachim negative. Yet within the Dukas, Hale took a jab at lesser French composers. As far as his dislike for the Joachim, Hale called it as he saw it, and he did praise Willy Hess's performance. While being a display piece for the soloist, Joachim's concerto is somewhat of an endurance test for the audience, and the focal point of the concert was the Boston premiere of Dukas's 11-minute scherzo, not the 45-minute concerto. Hale's advocacy of performing single movements of symphonies or concertos is, of course, nothing new. He was after quality and practicality here, and his praise or condemnation of a work itself had nothing to do with the nationality of the composer who wrote it.

Returning to the Francophile question, Hale was very eager to encourage the acceptance of "modern" French music. In December 1905, French composer Vincent d'Indy became the first person ever to guest-conduct the Boston Symphony Orchestra during a regular subscription concert. *The Sorcerer's Apprentice* was again on the program. The remainder consisted of Cesar Franck's *Psyche and Cupid*, Gabriel Faure's suite from *Pelleas et Melisande*, and two of D'indy's works: *Symphony No. 2 in B Flat*, and *Istar*. Hale commented:

> For the first time in the history of this orchestra, a foreign conductor was invited to lead it as a guest. The innovation was a tribute both to the younger school of French composers whom he so worthily represents. This school is "young" in the freshness and vigor and modernity of its musical views, opinions, tendencies rather than in the respective ages of its most distinguished members. It is characterized by the purity and the nobility of its artistic aims and purposes....

Of late years, Mr. Loeffler, and after him Mr. Kneisel, Mr. Lang, local pianists and singers, Mr. Longy, Mr. Paur, and above all Mr. Wilhelm Gericke have made us acquainted with composition of this modern school. Nor is this interest, this acquaintanceship, something sudden. Boston has always been willing to hear what composers of any nation had to say. Its German population is not so great that by showing a chauvinistic spirit it succeeded in Germanizing thoroughly and narrowly the musical taste. Nor did the Germans, who did the pioneer work here, and to whom we owe much, display an illiberal spirit. The "Waverly overture, by Berlioz, who is still a modern among the moderns, was played here 54 years ago, and this great master was applauded in Boston long before the Berlioz cult was fashionable in Paris. The conductors who brought out these works were for the most part Germans as were the members of the orchestra who played them.[18]

It wasn't just modern French music that Hale was selling here; it was continued expansion of the orchestral repertoire, an expansion that he felt had existed in Boston for some time, even in the Dwight era of the mid-nineteenth century. About the same time as d'Indy's guest appearance, the orchestra was accused of having an embargo against American music. Hale responded with one of his longest articles, detailing every American composer and composition that the orchestra had programmed since its inception in 1881.[19] Higginson also addressed the issue, saying "All the conductors have been willing to play American music when it seemed to them good enough, and they have been liberal in that way."[20] It was this sense of well-roundedness that Hale sought to preserve.

In addition to repertoire, Hale was also concerned about appropriateness of setting. In December 1904, the first time he had heard Faure's suite from *Pelleas et Melisande*, he praised it, but only after issuing this caveat:

Stage music almost always suffers when it is transferred from the theatre to the concert hall. The prelude is no longer the quickener of anticipation. It cannot serve to prepare a sympathetic mood. It no longer contains hints and auroral flushes. The entr'actes become in the concert hall absolute music; they neither comment on the scene that preceded nor prepare for that which is to follow. On the other hand, there is this comparison: the music when performed in the concert hall is heard, while in the playhouse it is generally lost in the din of assembling and in the chatter.[21]

Hale was also concerned with appropriateness of setting for classical period works and five months later questioned the programming of Wolfgang Amadeus Mozart's *Symphony No. 38 in D*, "Prague," K. 504, even though it is scored for a sizeable classical complement:

However well this little symphony of Mozart may be played as regards euphony, proportion, general fitness—and it was played exceedingly well last night—the work is nevertheless ineffective in Symphony Hall. It would undoubtedly be a pleasure to hear it, and works of a like nature, performed by a small but carefully chosen band of players in a hall no larger than, say, Chickering. Then the old music would have more than a historical interest. It is true that large orchestras were assembled occasionally in Mozart's period for special occasions—orchestras of 200, and even of 400, were not wholly unknown in Vienna—but these conditions were rare, chiefly in aid of a pension fund for musicians. The orchestra of the opera house in Prague, where the symphony was first performed, included only six violins, two violas, and two basses. No doubt other strings were added for concert purposes, but the symphony was designed for a small orchestra in a comparatively small room.[22]

Such in-depth commentaries regarding programming notwithstanding, Hale once again came under criticism for not leveling judgment against those onstage:

> Of course we do not now expect Mr. Hale, our noted critic, who is usually so caustic and severe, to tell the truth about the very management that pays him, it is said, a goodly sum per week to compile the programs of these concerts.
> Is not independent criticism out of the question under such circumstances?
> How he would have made "mince meat" of Mr. Arbos last year, or Mr. Grisez this season, had they been unlucky enough to have appeared in Boston without the prestige of the Boston Symphony Orchestra to support them? In his criticism of both of them we have the spectacle of Mr. Hale making excuses for their shortcomings.
> The question is often asked: Do any of the critics attached to the great Boston newspapers really dare to write the truth? Why do they allow misstatements to appear all the time?
> A subscriber[23]

Hale wasn't so concerned with vindictive rhetoric; he was more concerned with capturing the moment. He had actually written his opinion of what a review should be months earlier, in a *Sunday Herald* article:

> A musical review should breathe the enthusiasm of belief, the joy of appreciation and the equal joy of rejection. For this reason there is much to be said in favor of the criticism written immediately after a performance for a morning newspaper. The music is surging in the writer's head; he is under the spell; or he is fully conscious of the composer's vain attempt to put him in another world, to enwrap him in a hitherto unknown atmosphere. He has no time for wary or commercial reflection. The article is within him, and it must out.
> The criticism is for a day, and it should perish with the day.[24]

Throughout his career Hale had a number of hidden associates, fellow musicians, and dramatists who would supply him with an almost constant stream of all sorts of printed materials—announcements, journals, program books from both the United States and abroad, etc. Sometimes the most unlikely person would help him out:

> 1087 Boylston St
Feb 11 1905
>
> My dear Mr. Gericke:
> Thank you very much for the programs. I suppose the Sinding Suite is the "Episodes Chevalieresques" in F major.
> It is too bad about the impossibility of getting extra instruments this season and I sympathize with you fully in the matter. When you return from New York I

should like to call on you and talk this union matter over. In some way or other the public should know you are hampered in the production of modern works with a thunderous orchestra. But of course I shall say nothing till I see you. We can then talk about the <u>Eroica</u> as you suggest—but surely you know best about this.

I wish you all good luck on the trip—weather, trains, audiences—and embouchures of horn and trumpet players. With kindest regards to Mrs. Gericke, Mrs. Plummer & Miss Gericke, believe me.

Yours sincerely,
Philip Hale[25]

Of particular interest is the second paragraph, where Hale writes about extra instruments and union matters. The Boston Symphony Orchestra was not unionized then, though there were two local musicians' unions in the city, one black and one white. The black union was reported to be one of the most active in the country while the white union dated all the way back to 1863. Hiring in extra musicians probably would have meant paying them union wages, something Higginson would have been against. Whatever the case, perhaps with Hale's help, the problem was either solved or avoided and the orchestra was able to program Gustav Mahler's enormous *Symphony No. 5 in C-sharp minor* in February of the following year.

Just as Gericke supplied Hale with programs, Hale was more than happy to return the favor, starting in the second paragraph of the following letter.

Boston, May 18/1905

My dear Mr. Gericke:

I was very sorry not to be in when you called and much pleased by your letter. I have been busy, for I have to write from one column to two columns a day editorial articles for the Evening Edition of the Herald, but I hope to get into the country soon. Before I leave, however, I shall give myself the pleasure of calling on you and Mrs. Gericke.

I have the Philharmonic (Berlin) and the Dresden Royal Orchestra programs if they would be of any use to you in the hunt after "novelties."

Loeffler wrote to me that he was much impressed by Theodore Y Sayes's

Symphony, which he heard lately at Brussels, and I believe the work is to be played in London.

Mr. Brown brought back a good many new scores from Europe this spring for the Public Library. They are in the Brown room, on the top floor.

You must be glad at the thought of soon leaving the city and breathing true country air.

Believe me, I appreciate fully the many pleasant things you have written me. We all, whatever we do, have our cares, anxieties, trials, especially when we try to do what seems to us our duty. A word, then, from one who has your high sense of artistic sincerity and honor means much to me.

With best regards to you all, as ever.

Yours sincerely
Philip Hale[26]

The above provides some detail about how busy Hale was during this time of his life—so busy that he now left the very thing that brought him to Boston, his church position in Roxbury.

The 1905–1906 season turned out to be Gericke's last. He had spent 13 years on the podium of the Boston Symphony Orchestra, a record that would not be broken until Serge Koussevitzky passed it in the late 1930s. Though Higginson publically stated that the reason for Gericke's departure was the latter's homesickness for Vienna, the real reason appears to have been salary. When Gericke was hired for his second stint with the orchestra starting in 1898, Higginson offered him $10,000 per year; Gericke was able to negotiate this up to $12,000.[27] Over the years, another $500 was added to Gericke's salary for expenses, making his total package $12,500. In early 1906, Gericke asked Higginson for a raise and was refused.[28] By late March Gericke's resignation had become public and a farewell dinner was arranged. Hale commented to Charles Martin Loeffler:

> April 26. 1906
>
> Dear Martin: The lists of names signed to the call for a dinner for Mr. Gericke on Tuesday Evening reminded me of "the Happy Family" that Mr. P. T. Barnum used to exhibit. Are you going to sit between Mr. Fallten and Mr. Gericke? I cannot go.[29]

That fall Gericke was succeeded by Karl Muck, a German conductor of Swiss citizenship. Muck, considered to be one of the top two or three conductors in the world, was eminently qualified. He had been principal kapellmeister at the Royal Opera House in Berlin since 1892 and held a PhD in philology, classical literary scholarship. Holding an honorary German passport bearing the Kaiser's signature, he was "on loan" to Boston. Though not as personable as Gericke, Muck was a skilled conductor and one who was able to win over his public in a short amount of time. He also bolstered the quality of the orchestral forces through the hiring of thirty-five of the finest players that he knew—twenty-seven Germans and eight Austrians.[30]

Upon his arrival, Hale wrote an article that not only addressed Muck's qualifications, but mentioned those of his predecessors as well:

CONDUCTOR MUCK AND
THE LIST OF SOLOISTS

The Twenty-sixth Season
Promises to be One of
Unusual Interest

The 26th season of the Boston Symphony Orchestra, which will open Oct. 12, 13, promises to be one of unusual interest. First of all there is the engagement of a new conductor. The engagement of Dr. Karl Muck is a radical departure from the traditions. He is the first conductor of an established, widely recognized reputation who has been engaged to conduct the concerts of the Symphony orchestra. The others, Messrs. Henschel, Gericke, Nikisch, and Paur, were at the time of their assuming the leadership comparatively unknown men as concert conductors. Mr. Henschel was known only as a singer, pianist, composer; Mr. Gericke was one of the conductors of the Vienna Court Opera; Mr. Nikisch was the first conductor of the Leipsig Stadt Theatre, and Mr. Paur, after serving as opera conductor in Cassel, Koenigsberg and Mannheim, succeeded

Mr. Nikisch at Leipsig and then at Boston. Only one of these four conductors had had much experience as a conductor of symphony concerts: Mr. Paur had led the subscription concerts at Mannheim. No one of them was then ranked among the great virtuoso conductors. They all had their reputation to make, and much of their reputation today is founded on their work with the Boston Symphony Orchestra.

Nor should the respective service of each one in turn to the orchestra and to the community be forgotten. Mr. Henschel, as the first in order, had an unenviable task, but the catholicity of his programmes and the fine taste displayed in making them broadened the knowledge of the public and raised its level of appreciation. Mr. Gericke made the orchestra a virtuoso instrument, on which Mr. Nikisch played romantically and poetically. Memorable performances were given by Mr. Henschel's successors: Performances of Schumann's Symphony in D minor and Tschaikowsky's "Romeo and Juliet" under Mr. Nikisch; of Tschaikowsky's "Pathetic" symphony, Strauss' "Thus Spake Zarathustra" and the entr'act from Chabrier's "Gwendoline" under Mr. Paur; of symphonies by d'Indy, Franck, and Mahler, and of Strauss' "Don Juan" and "Don Quixote" under Mr. Gericke—we name at random, for the history of the orchestra is full of brilliant, glorious debuts.

But the connection of Dr. Muck with...Prague, with the Vienna Philharmonic Orchestra, with the Wagner festivals at Bayreuth, and his many appearances as a "guest" in the opera houses and concert halls of Europe have made his name familiar to all who follow the news of the musical world. They know him as a virtuoso conductor, one of the "stars" who now rival famous prima donnas, tenors, violinists, and pianists in exciting attention, applause, and hot and long-continued discussion....

Facts and Rumors

Although Dr. Muck has never visited America, it has not been for lack of opportunity. As long ago as 1893 he was considered as a possible conductor of the Boston Symphony orchestra. It will be remembered that after the sudden departure of Mr. Nikisch a contract was made with Dr. Hans Richter whereby he was to become the successor of Mr. Nikisch, but Dr. Richter, for some reason that has not been explained, broke this contract. When Mr. Ellis was in Berlin last spring Dr. Muck showed him a letter which Richter had sent him at the time, in which he urged Dr. Muck to go to Boston as a substitute. Dr. Muck, who had just completed his first season with great success, would not listen to any proposition for him to leave the city and his position.

In the last year of Mr. Maurice Grau's direction of the Metropolitan Opera House of New York, Mr. Grau endeavored to persuade Dr. Muck to come to New York for the opera season, and he made him an offer of a salary which was unquestionably the largest that had been offered to a conductor. Dr. Muck refused to consider this offer. Since that time at least one other attempt has been made, but in vain, to induce him to come to this country.

One of the many absurd statements which have been published in this country and in Europe sine Dr. Muck's engagement is that he will come to Boston "on trial." A man of his reputation does not go anywhere "on trial." His position in Berlin is one of the most desirable and the most coveted in Europe. His services are constantly demanded by leading opera houses and orchestras of the continent. And what counts even more than this in Germany—he has for years enjoyed the personal friendship of Emperor William.

That Dr. Muck has engaged himself in Boston for only one year is due to his own desire. His leave of absence from his duties had to come directly from the Emperor.[31]

A letter from Hale to Gericke, written several months after the latter's departure from Boston, comments briefly about his personal contact with Muck before revealing his take on the city's musical scene as it existed at that time:

> 1087 Boylston St.
> Dec. 9, 1906
>
> My dear Mr. Gericke:
>
> I have often tried to find time to answer your most interesting letter, and believe me I have often thought of you and missed you and yours. Never have I had so little time for myself.
>
> Boston is the same curious town, small and one-sided, yet pleasant to live in. I have seen very little of Dr. Muck. What I have seen was pleasant. He is an excellent conductor in some ways, and in other ways he does not especially interest me, but, like yourself, he is honest, sincere and conscientious in his work. His wife is an agreeable woman who takes her life quietly. In other aspects the musical world is unchanged. Wallace Goodrich is to conduct three orchestral concerts. The orchestra is all made up of Union men! About 50 of them. The concerts are to be in Jordan Hall. There is not much interest in visiting pianists or violinists, though there are many of them. Fewer subscriptions to the Cecilia and the Choral Art than last year.
>
> It is all opera in New York. The critics there do not care much for Geraldine Farrar. Hammerstein at the new Manhattan Opera House has some fine singers. The Kneisel audience in Boston has dropped in size and quality, and the Symphony Quartet has a small audience. This is the village news. I see Mr. Gaugengigl occasionally and he always talks of you, as do many others. I wish you were living here—but there is more to interest you in Vienna. The Herald changed owners last October, but the change did not affect me. I some ways I think the paper has improved some. I take the program books of the Vienna Philharmonic and from them and the programs in them I have some idea of musical life in your town.
>
> We had a delightful visit in St. Albans and there was much talk about you all. See Miss Endicott once in a while. But I have hardly any time to be sociable. Saint Saens was here and played so fast that the orchestra could hardly keep up with him. Rosenthal played wonderfully and others have played in a mediocre manner. I do not think we shall have any opera here.
>
> This note is only an apology. I hope in a week or so to send you a more satisfactory letter. Meanwhile give my kindest regards & remembrances to all in your household and believe me always your friend and admirer who misses you.
>
> Philip Hale[32]

Muck's arrival was perhaps the most exciting musical event that occurred in Boston during 1906–1907, but on a national level it may not have been the most newsworthy. Richard Strauss's notorious opera *Salome* had its world premiere at the Dresden Court Opera on December 9, 1905. Hale was on hand to witness its January 22, 1907 American premiere at the New York Metropolitan Opera.

Hedwig Lachmann's German translation of Oscar Wilde's play served as Strauss's libretto. Containing such items as the Dance of the Seven Veils and a final scene where Salome kisses the severed head of John the Baptist, the play itself had been banned in England for some time, yet Strauss had made the decision to incorporate the entire play into his opera. The day after the New York premiere of the opera, a 4,000-word condemnation written by Henry Krehbiel appeared in print. Hale's review, however, was quite positive, though it contributed to the work's notoriety. James Gibbons Huneker commented:

> His [Heinrich Conreid's] "Salome" production, with Alfred Hertz conducting—and he is a sympathetic conductor of Richard Strauss—would have been a musical event of importance had it not been for the notoriety of the affair. Our music critics, all God-fearing men, with imaginations devoid of the morbid or salacious, were thrown into a tumult by Philip Hale, who called their attention to the fact that Salome was a degenerate suffering from a rare and "beautiful case"—as the diagnostics say—of necrophilia. No one had ever heard of the disease except for madhouse doctors or readers of Kraft-Ebbing [sic] and the poetry of Maurice Rollinat. The conjunction of Oscar Wilde's name completed the havoc. A scandal ensued. Here was a chance to get back at haughty Richard Strauss, who had dared to flout local criticism. The opera was withdrawn.... Philip Hale must have smiled more than once at the effect on our unsophisticated souls of his verbal firebrand. There is no more "degeneracy" in the magnificent outburst of savage exultation and poignant passion of Salome over the head of John the Baptist than in Isolde's loving lament over Tristan—his, too, is a dead skull.[33]

In addition to his review, Hale contributed significant background information to Lawrence Gilman's 85-page operatic guidebook on *Salome*.[34]

Later in the season the American violinist Maud Powell took Boston by storm in a performance of the *Violin Concerto in D minor* by Jean Sibelius. Hale mentions her in a letter written to Loeffler while on vacation during the following summer:

THE BOULDERS
JACKSON, NEW HAMPSHIRE
August 21/1907

Dear Martin,

I had a very pleasant time with you last Thursday. If you want to go to Paris don't think of doing anything for me. In the first place, there's nothing I really want. As I told you my aim now is to get free from things.

The scenery is stunning from this house. I expect to be here until Sept. 1 or about then. My plans afterward are not yet determined.

I have read a singular book "Une nuit au Luxembourg" by de Gourmont.[35] I suppose you know it. Much of it is exceedingly distasteful to me.

Was it not Maude McCarthy[36]—not Maud Powell—who decided to drop the fiddle and bow to study theosophy? I think you mentioned the latter.

Mir ist ganz würst.[37] I lead a lazy life. Hours of meals are all wrong from a sanitary point of view, but I accommodate myself. I am wading through Anatole Frances' Pierre Nozière[38]—which I had never read before.—but I find it hard work to read.

Take care of yourself if you go to Europe and bring yourself back. I hope your head is better.

With best wishes to the Fays—Miss Fay and Mr. Fay—
I a m

Yours affectionately
Philip Hale

I expect to get back to Boston about Sept. 12—for a day. Then I hope to return to Osterville.[39] [40]

In the above letter Hale wrote about "wanting to get free of things," yet this did not occur; in fact, just the opposite happened. Perhaps it was the result of the loss of extra income from his Roxbury church organist position or the resignation of a newspaper colleague that caused him to undertake even greater responsibility. Whatever the case, in 1908 Hale found himself to be both music and drama critic for the *Boston Herald*. Banner headings over entire pages, such as "Stage and Music by Philip Hale" and "Dramatic and Musical Review by Philip Hale," became the norm for Sunday editions. Added at various times during his career were such items as "Weekly Comment," a summary of the week's performing arts events, and "Notes and Lines," a column taken largely from his program notes that also included annotated listings of coming events. Professional theatrical performances as well as those at universities were often covered by him.[41] In terms of literary clout, Hale had now arrived at the zenith of this career. This standing was not something he had particularly strived for, but rather it coincided with the natural trajectory of his talents as a writer.

The fall of 1908 brought a change of conductors to the Boston Symphony Orchestra. Karl Muck, who had been so impressive in his short two-year engagement, was appointed music director of the Berlin Royal Opera House and therefore could not remain in Boston. Upon resigning his position, at least temporarily, Muck recommended his friend and former classmate August Max Fiedler to take his place. Hale wrote what he could to give his readers a favorable impression of the new conductor:

> The coming season brings to the orchestra and to Boston a new conductor, the sixth that has been at the head of the organization. When it became definitely known last year that the services of Dr. Muck could not be retained for another season, a thorough canvass was made of all the great conductors of Europe who were available, and final choice settled on Max Fiedler of Hamburg. Mr. Fiedler has made his career exclusively as a conductor in concert work and his career has been comparatively short, for he was in the prime of life before conditions enabled him to take up the baton. He has been a conductor only 13 years, but his rise in his branch of the art has been extraordinarily rapid, until today he is ranked among the few great conductors of the world, and his services as "guest" are in constant demand in the musical centers of Europe....
>
> Mr. Fiedler is famous as a man of catholic tastes. He is a strong upholder of modernism in music, being one of the best and most influential friends the young composers of Europe have. He is also famous as an interpreter of Brahms, Beethoven, and Schumann. He is said to be skilled in the making of programmes. He is married—his wife is an English woman—and he speaks English fluently.[42]

Other changes were on the horizon in Boston. Beginning on December 4, 1909, Hale's reviews started to appear one day after the first of each pair of subscription concerts. Before that, they had appeared two days after. Whether or not this affected Hale's work routine is not known; it is impossible to discern any overall difference in the quality of his reviews before and after this date. A more significant change, however, was the establishment of a new professional performance entity in Boston.

Opera had always been a questionable affair for the city during the nineteenth century. Finally in 1908, through the generosity of Eben Dyer Jordan, Jr. (1857–1916), an heir to the Jordan Marsh fortune, a permanent opera company was established and a new opera house built on Huntington Avenue, two blocks west of Symphony Hall. On November 8, 1909 the Boston Opera Company gave its first performance, Amilcare Ponchielli's *La Gioconda*, with Lillian Nordica in the title role.

The Boston Opera Company was highly touted in the press. This was something new and exciting. Hale regularly covered the performances, of course, and was quite supportive. The opening of the company's second season secured a center column headline at the top of the first page of the *Boston Herald* on November 8, 1910:

> BOSTON OPERA
> SEASON OPENS
>
> ———
>
> A Noteworthy Production of
> Boito's "Mefistofele," with
> ContiC onducting
>
> ———
>
> THREE NEW SINGERS APPEAR
>
> ———
>
> Brilliant Array of Society Fills
> Boxes; Elaborate Gowns
> in Evidence[43]

An ambitious enterprise, the Boston Opera Company offered some 20 different operas each year; by the start of the fourth season, there were 68 soloists lined up.[44] Still, there were organizational issues and no music directorship was ever set in place, though Felix Weingartner was essentially its featured conductor from 1912 to 1914.

In spite of its high mindedness and the quality of its offerings, the company's fortunes floundered. This was the result of a number of things: Jordan's gradual withdrawal of financial support, an ill-conceived and ill-timed tour to Paris (purportedly to show the Parisians what opera in languages other than French sounded like), and the start of World War I, which severely limited the availability of guest artists. Henry Lee Higginson tried to secure support for the company from Isabella Stewart Gardner,[45] but even he was unable to save it and in May, 1915 the Boston Opera Company declared bankruptcy. Later that year, there was an attempt by the Chicago Opera Company's Max Rabinoff to resurrect professional opera in Boston. This venture, called the Boston Grand Opera Company, also went bankrupt.[46]

It is difficult to assess any impact that either opera company and the new opera house may have had on the programming offered at Symphony Hall. There had always been an eclectic mix offered at the venue, including a number of presentations, both musical and nonmusical, that had little to do with the Boston Symphony Orchestra. The following advertisement appeared in the program book for October 29, 1909:

> Symphony Hall, Thursday Afternoon, November 4,
> At 2:30 and Wednesday Evening, November 17, at 8:15
> ISADORA DUNCAN
> IN CLASSIC DANCES
> Orchestra of 55, Gustav Strube, Conductor assisting
> Tickets $2.00, $1.50 and $1.00
> Now on Sale[47]

Gustav Strube, a member of the first violin section of the orchestra since 1890, served as conductor of the Boston Pops on and off from 1898 to 1912; he also conducted many non-Boston Symphony concerts. He was also a composer; his *Concerto for Violoncello and Orchestra in E minor* was premiered by cellist Heinrich Warnke and the Boston Symphony Orchestra in the week prior to the Isadora Duncan event. In 1913 he left Boston for Baltimore, where he became a faculty member at Peabody Conservatory and, in 1916, the founding conductor of the Baltimore Symphony Orchestra.[48] The "Orchestra of 55" in the advertisement quoted above would have had many Boston Symphony Orchestra musicians in it, as moonlighting by symphony players, forbidden by Henry Higginson a quarter of a century earlier, had become accepted practice by this time. The focal point of this performance, however, was Isadora Duncan's manifestation of Richard Wagner's comment about Beethoven's *Symphony No. 7 in A*, Op. 92 being the "apotheosis of the dance." Her performance left such an impression on Hale that he recalled it in his review of the same symphony when it was played at a regular subscription concert the following year:

> It was little over a year ago that Isadora Duncan danced the "Interpretation" of three movements of Beethoven's seventh symphony. At the time, and a year before in the same hall, there were some who scoffed at her presentation, and spoke with a fine show of indignation concerning the "desecration" of the symphony.
> And yet, when yesterday the strangely solemn strains of the Allegretto were heard, the vision of Miss Duncan came into the mind and remained until the end of the Finale, with its Dionysiac joy. And there also came the thought of music composed by Eric Satie and orchestrated by Debussy, "Gynopedies," performed here almost six years ago by the Orchestral Club. To this music, as to Beethoven's Allegretto, Grecian youth might well have danced with the gestures that have come down to us on frieze or vase.
> The symphony was well chosen to commemorate Beethoven's birthday 140 years ago, for it ranks among his greatest works, and this is to say among the greatest of all musical compositions. The symphony is nearly 100 years old. Think how wildly applauded orchestral compositions that were new and surprising only 20 or even 10 years ago are now moribund or smugly entombed forever!
> There is not a note of the symphony that [has] not been long familiar to a modern audience. Even when conductors do their best, which is the worst, to give an unfamiliar, a personal reading, the music soars above them that would twist and shape it according to their own device.

In the performance yesterday the music was allowed to go on its way, and was not too personally conducted. The Scherzo was finely played; the mysterious passages in the course of the first movement were more than ordinarily effective, and the orgy of joy at the end was not for once the frenzy of a red-capped, drunken mob.[49]

The New York Philharmonic Society appeared in Symphony Hall for the first time on February 26, 1910 as part of the orchestra's New England tour. At its helm was Gustav Mahler, more famous during his lifetime as a conductor than as a composer. In his review Hale was eager to extol the virtues of Mahler's conducting, yet was quick to provide some incisive commentary about the orchestra itself. Mahler had been having difficulty with his then all-female board of directors (the Vienna Philharmonic would not even have female members in its orchestra until late in the twentieth century). Hale, while hinting that there had been some problems with the Philharmonic's governance in the past, stayed clear of discussing this:

BOSTONP REMIERE
OFP HILHARMONIC

Reorganized New York Society
in Concert Show Capability
For Great Sonority, Emotion
and Brilliance

By PHILIP HALE

The Philharmonic Society of New York, Gustav Mahler, conductor, gave its first concert in Boston last night in Symphony Hall. The program was as follows:

"Fantastic" Symphony	Berlioz
Suite for Orchestra	Bach
Overture "Leonore" No. 3	Beethoven
"Till Eulenspiegel"	Strauss

Mr. Mahler was already known to Boston as a poetic conductor of great operas. Last night he revealed himself as a most accomplished and highly imaginative symphonic conductor. He is in the first rank of interpreters, not as a sensational virtuoso, not as one endeavoring to excite applause by novel and singular readings of old scores, not as one whose figure should overshadow the composer, but as one genius who understands another, has the ability and the willingness to share his appreciation with the audience, and is practical in his reading of the finest poetry, whether it be lyrical, epic, or nobly fantastical.

Even the most skillful conductor is dependent on his orchestra, however carefully he may have shaped it for his purpose. The Philharmonic Society is now in its 68th season. It has been under many distinguished conductors. It has had its experiences and vicissitudes. Its government was for a long time peculiar. Its concerts in New York—and I have heard its concerts at intervals since 1888—were often brilliant and often commonplace. It numbered in its ranks for years excellent, mediocre, and poor players. It had unusual routine experience, and on occasions it could surprise and delight its hearers.

At present, it is probably artistically stronger than at any time in its history, and by its concert last night it showed conclusively the beneficial results of the reorganization and of the discipline under Mr. Mahler.

It might be said that in some respect the orchestra might be improved. To name the less worthy is unnecessary, and it is also unnecessary to name certain distinguished artists now members of the orchestra. The work of the superior members and of the inferior was known to all last night by solo passages. No doubt, present weaknesses will in time be strengthened. It is enough to say that the orchestra is now far more homogeneous than it has been in the past; that it is now a mighty instrument for Mr. Mahler to play on at his will; that it is capable of great sonority without extravagance in tone; that it can be both emotional and brilliant.

The compositions chosen for performance were all familiar, except Mr. Mahler's arrangement of movements from two suites by Bach (the second and the third), with the use of a "piano-harpsichord" to fill out the "continuo," played by the conductor.[50] The movements were well contrasted, and they were performed with amazing freshness and vitality. The well known air was sung with a refreshing absence of sentimentalism, yet with true feeling.

Some may object to the manner in which the piano-harpsichord was used, and complain of too much freedom in invention, but if they were asked what they would have, they would be at a loss for a reply. This instrument, with its peculiarity of tone, gave a suggestion of Bach's period, without suspicion of undue archaism. A suite of Bach is often expressionless and dreary in performance. The music that is sometimes merely as dry bones was last night living flesh, radiant with beauty. Nor could anyone justly say that Mr, Mahler in his reading departed from the letter of the spirit.

A few seasons ago Mr. Weingartner gave an impressive performance of Berlioz' "Fantastic" symphony. The performance last night was equally impressive, though in some respects it was differently conceived, as in the famous thunder passage given at the end of the third movement on the kettle drums. Mr. Mahler's reading gave the idea of distance, and it was thus more in accordance with Berlioz' wish. Mr. Mahler's reading of a whole was careful, but not meticulous in detail, overpowering in moments of wild fantasy, charmingly poetic in its tenderness, and at all times superbly imaginative.

In the overture, he let Beethoven speak for himself and in Strauss' ever delightful rondo there was rare exhibition of clearness in the exposition of the general structure; there was rhetorical brilliance; above all there was there was an ever pervasive sense of humor. And how charming was the opening—"Once upon a time"—in its unaffected simplicity.

Mr. Mahler showed himself the great conductor in many ways in his choice of tempi; in his control of rhythm; in his infinite wealth of dynamic gradations; in his sense of continuity; in his expression of detail without checking the melodic line in obtaining powerful effects without sacrifice of tone. And in the carrying out of his purposes he was gladly" and ably seconded by his players.

The size of the audience did not reflect credit on the boast of Boston that she is a musical city. Those who had the pleasure of hearing this unusually excellent concert were enthusiastic, and Mr. Mahler was applauded to the echo.[51]

Unfortunately, this was Mahler's first and only appearance with the Philharmonic in Boston. Three months later, in February, 1911, he resigned from the orchestra due to illness and three months after that, on May 11, died in Vienna. In November of that same year, the orchestra returned to Boston in an all-Wagner concert, conducted by Mahler's successor Josef Stransky. Hale, having had his fill of all-Wagner concerts, took on the programming:

It is to be regretted that the program was composed wholly of Wagnerian compositions. The regret did not come from any false piety toward Wagner or from the wish that his arias and scenes should be performed only on the operatic stage. There is now no wild discussion over this once mooted point; it is no longer thought advisable to tie at least one disputant in a chair; for Wagner is today as calmly and reasonably discussed as though his name were Rossini or Donizetti. But a program of works by several composers would have afforded a more favorable opportunity of judging the orchestra and the conductor. It is said that the program of yesterday was not planned by Mr. Stransky; that he wished to conduct a symphony by Beethoven.[52]

Stransky was not nearly the musician that Mahler was. Hale recognized this, of course, but wanted to at least give him a chance. He continued:

Mr. Stransky made a very favorable impression. His personality as a man is pleasing and it colors strongly his interpretation. This is half the battle in these days, when Beethoven and Berlioz, Brahms and Richard Strauss must be personally conducted if they expect to find favor with an audience. Mr. Stransky seems to be a man of authority and taste, a fiery nature who exercises self-control; a poetic soul who is not extravagantly dirhythmic. Nor does he apparently take himself too seriously.[53]

Hale, however, could not avoid making allusion to Stansky's predecessor:

The Philharmonic Orchestra, composed for the most part of seasoned, experienced players, had for its last conductor a famous drill-master with a rare gift of interpretation—where the symphonic work on his deck appealed to him. Mr. Stransky came to an orchestra distinguished for its routine work. It was not to be expected that he would mold it anew in a few weeks. Under his direction yesterday it played with fine precision, with a full sonorous body of tone in passionate and stormy passages, with marked elasticity in rhythmic and dynamic changes, and with an inspirational vitality. While Mr. Stransky was free in his management of movement, there was always a sense of continuity and what Walter Bagahot said of the best novel—that it should constantly go ahead—may well be applied to the performance of a musical work.

The orchestra, led by Mr. Stransky, was always interesting, often truly poetic and eloquent in interpretation. Mme. Gadski sang with her accustomed fluency, and was recalled many times after the finale of "Tristan." It is to be hoped that Mr. Stransky and the Philharmonic will visit us again.[54]

Hale's hopes were realized and the Philharmonic returned to Boston the following year. This time the programming was eclectic. Hale now was able to see Stransky conduct in a variety of styles and did not hold back in his criticism:

PHILHARMONIC
SOCIETYH ERE

———

Great Crowd Hears New York
Orchestra Led by Mr.
Stransky.

———

MISCHA ELMAN SOLOIST

Symphony Hall Audience Is Enthusiastic Over Program of Familiar Works

By PHILIP HALE

The Philharmonic Society of New York and Mischa Elman, violinist, drew and audience yesterday afternoon that filled Symphony Hall. Many stood. The program was as follows: Weber, overture to "Euryanthe;" Beethoven, symphony No. 5, C minor; Strauss: Love Scene from "Feuersnoth;" Brahms, concerto for violin, (Mr. Elman, violinist); Liszt: Symphonic Poem, "Tasso."

This orchestra is fortunately not a stranger to Boston. It visited the city with Mr. Mahler as conductor. Last season it came here with Mr. Stransky—exactly a year ago yesterday—and the program was devoted wholly to music by Wagner, although it was said at the time that this program was not of the conductor's making; that he wished to play one of Beethoven's symphonies. Yesterday he had his way.

The characteristics of this orchestra are well known to concert goers. Chief among them are plasticity, a well established routine proficiency, a sonority that is brilliant when brilliance is required. The various choirs are well-equipped, though our old friend Mr. Reiter is still inclined to play solo in ensemble. The strings are incisive rather than oily: the wood-wind as a body has precision, and the flutes and bassoons are especially good; the brass has tonal quality even in fortissimo passages. New York may well take pride in this orchestra, and not only on account of its long and honorable history.

The program contained no hope for a Sunday afternoon audience, but the audience of yesterday was enthusiastic without partiality. Even the performance of the well-worn "Euryanthe" overture was so enjoyed that Mr. Stransky was obliged to bow several times out of acknowledgement, and the concerto of Brahms, which cannot justly be described as ear-tickling or hair-raising, was applauded as though Mr. Elman had poured molasses and lighted rockets, pinwheels, and a set piece with a soaring American eagle. All this showed that a huge miscellaneous and holiday audience will enjoy good orchestral music provided the performance be interesting. Mr. Elman's full, rich, beautiful tone and his amazing sureness in technic made many forget, while they were under the spell of the violinist, the inherent dryness and forbidding austerity in many of Brahms' pages.

Mr. Stransky evidently wished to dot all the "I's" and cross all the "t's" in the symphony. He was not always willing to trust Beethoven's own expression, and so he then emphasized, italicized, over-elaborated, gave undue importance to measures that have insignificance in themselves, as though he read in them an esoteric meaning. Now, he was not sensational in this; he was painstaking, serious, and sincere; but what was the result? In his desire to give an elastic and emotional interpretation, to avoid the cold accuracy and choking rigidity of an academic reading, he often checked the flow of musical ideas, and little details were brought out so prominently that they disturbed the long melodic line to which they should have been subordinated. This was particularly noticeable in the second movement, although the first movement and the Scherzo did not escape injury. The Finale was played with marked effect, nor did the interest flag after the first pompous and triumphant announcement. In fact, Mr. Stransky's talent was more fully displayed in this Finale than in the preceding movements.

It has been said that a singer should sing his pauses. This truth was established long before Mr. Plunket Greene's printed advice to his erring brethren and sisters of the concert stage. But the pauses may be so long and so frequent that the song, weary of waiting, impatient at repeated interruptions, disappears and will not be coaxed back.

When there is the desire to be continually effective, and the striving is apparent, climaxes are discounted. There are portentous hints that disappoint; the effect that should be like a thunder-clap has been anticipated.

It is enough to say that the orchestral performance was almost always interesting, often brilliant. Mr. Elman's treatment of the concerto was engrossing, and not merely through the rare sensuousness of tone and virtuoso ease. He is to be thanked for refusing to gratify the insatiate appetite of encore-fiends.[55]

There was also a change in Boston Symphony Orchestra programming, as Fiedler's approach—long concerts offering works that were often in great contrast to one another—stood in opposition to Muck's more conservative focus on program unity. Neither Fiedler's program length nor his flair for the dramatic went unnoticed by Hale, as is evidenced in his February 15, 1911 review of what must have been a truly remarkable concert:

BOSTON HEARS
BUSONI'S MUSIC

Part of a Too Long Program
of 16th Rehearsal of the
Symphony Orchestra

PIANIST IS THE SOLOIST

Plays Extracts from Suite from the Music to Gozzi's
"Turandot"

BY PHILIP HALE

The 16th public rehearsal of the Boston Symphony orchestra took place yesterday afternoon in Symphony Hall. Mr. Fiedler conducted. Mr. Busoni was the pianist. The program, was as follows:

Prelude to Lohengrin	Wagner
"Don Quixote: Fantastic Variations"	Strauss
Concerto No. 3, C minor, for piano	Beethoven
Extracts from the Suite from the music to Gozzi's "Turandot"	Busoni

Only four of the eight movements from Busoni's suite were played, and yet the concert was too long. The prelude to "Lohengrin," beautiful as it is, might well have been omitted. Busoni's music was played for the first time in Boston, and it only would have been fair to him if the whole suite, with its contrasts, had been heard. As it was, marches succeeded each other, and as all the music was necessarily exotic in character, the monotony of the march movement was without relief. The "Nocturnal Waltz," "Dance and Song," "In the Women's Apartments" and the march, "Altoum," were not played.

This music was written by Mr. Busoni for Gozzi's dramatic fable, "Turandot," known to some through Schiller's version, a "tragic-comic fairy tale."

The story is of a beautiful and haughty princess in China, who did not wish to wed, and so her suitors were given three riddles to guess. Many thus lost their heads, but at last, the Oedipus appeared. Mr. Busoni has said that the themes of his score are borrowed from oriental melodies and he therefore believes that he has improved upon conventional orientalism.

Music that is composed for the theatre often loses half its effect when played in a concert hall. This is true of Bizet's suites taken from the music to "L'Arlesienne" and of Faure's suite derived from his music to "Pelleas and Melisande." It may be said of Busoni's music, heard yesterday, that it is distinguished chiefly by its entertaining instrumentation and its oriental atmosphere. This music may justly be called amusing. It was a mistake to produce it when "Don Quixote," a series of variations, was played at the same concert; but the composer was present as the soloist and the opportunity to pay him a compliment was therefore not neglected. It might be well before the season closes to perform the whole suite. Yesterday Mr. Busoni was called out after the "Turkish finale" and warmly applauded.

He had already given pleasure by his performance of Beethoven's concerto in C minor, which had not been played here for many years in any important concert. The concerto is a favorite with some European pianists, possibly on account of the finale, which is delightful from beginning to end as an example of Beethoven in light and playful mood, showing a gaiety that is at once contagious. Mr. Busoni's performance of the first two movements was characterized by fluency, a fine sense of proportion and a faultless and highly polished mechanism rather than by warmth and spontaneity. Yet it should be remembered that only the middle movement calls for any marked expression of sentiment, and the sentiment of this Largo is contemplative, not deeply emotional or passionate.

The performance on the whole was a fine exhibition of highly developed and well controlled technic. Yet there is this to be said: Mr. Busoni did not attempt to modernize the music in any manner. He let it speak in its own way, with its archaisms, its old formulas. When the language of Mozart was heard in Beethoven's music, the pianist was Mozartean in interpretation. There are a few passages in this concerto that hint at the greater Beethoven, as in the coda of the first movement, and in the still effective and at that time surprising enharmonic changes in the finale. These passages were brought out by Mr. Busoni unostentatiously, but in memorable fashion. The most salient feature of his performance was the brilliance of the last movement.

It was quite a pleasure to hear "Don Quixote" again, for it contains some of Strauss's noblest and inspired music. There are few more eloquent pages than those in which Don Quixote is supposed to reason concerning the ideal and those that portray his death. These passages are enough to put Strauss with the immortals. Yet there are some who ignore this music and dilate on the "absurdity" of imitating sheep and employing a wind machine. They seek for eccentricity and that which is bizarre, and have no ears for the strains of solemn and pathetic beauty.

The performance on the whole was one of the most noteworthy of the season. Perhaps Mr. Fiedler was occasionally didactic in his interpretation, as though he wished to explain this or that variation to the audience, but in view of the general and great merit of the performance this objection might well be considered hypercritical.

> Mr. Warnke's interpretation of the violoncello part was masterly in every way. The technical difficulties were surmounted with ease; the tone was varied and beautiful; the different sentiments were fitly expressed, and the music of the death scene was played with true emotion. Mr. Ferir in tone and interpretation stood side by side with Mr. Warnke, and the orchestra played magnificently.[56]

Fiedler had firmly established himself as a conductor willing to take risks, also one who was willing to cater to the audience when necessary. Thus, he became a favorite in the eyes of many concert-goers. It appears, however, that Fiedler was seen by Higginson merely as a caretaker, a replacement for Muck until the latter would be able to reclaim the orchestra's music directorship. Although this was known by a chosen few, the public remained largely unaware and Higginson naturally wanted to keep it that way. August Spanuth, editor of the Berlin publication *Signale für die Musikalische Welt*,[57] referred to Fiedler in a negative manner. Hale in turn cited the article. Spanuth, a former New York music critic, had quite a reputation; he would be sued by the *New York Times* for slander later that same year over false accusations about one of their reporters telegraphing fabricated interviews to him.[58] Hale wrote to Higginson, obviously in response to the latter's inquiry:

> 1087 Boylston St Boston
> Feb 6, 1911
>
> Major Henry L. Higginson:
>
> Dear Mr. Higginson:
>
> I know Mr. Spanuth slightly—I have met him once or twice—but I have known him as a writer for a long time. I believe him to be honest, not malicious, but at times wanting in tact and writing without a fine regard for another's feelings from a wild desire to tell the truth or what he considers truth.
>
> In the present instance, i.e. in the Signale article from which I quoted, he makes a statement bluntly that would again hurt Mr. Fiedler's feelings; but if anyone should remonstrate with Mr. Spanuth, he would be surprised and would probably say: "But isn't it the truth?"
>
> I should take pleasure in writing to Mr. Spanuth in the hope of setting him right, but I think he is now fairly aware of the facts. I shall remind him that Mr. Fiedler was engaged temporarily, for a specified time; that his "removal" is merely the ending of his engagement which has been honorable to him and satisfactory to the audiences of New York and other cities as well as Boston.
>
> The people in Boston probably know the reasons why Mr. Fiedler leaves. I think any allusion to the matter in the Herald might wound him rather than sooth him.
>
> Tomorrow I'll leave a copy of Mr. Spanuth's article at your office. Please do not trouble yourself to return it. Believe me.
>
> Yours sincerely
> Philip Hale[59]

It was undoubtedly through his contacts with Higginson and others, as well as his reputation as a writer, that Hale became a member in two more Boston Brahmin social clubs. He had long been a member of the St. Botolph Club, but now became involved in the Thursday Evening Club and The Tavern Club. The Thursday Evening Club had been founded in 1846 with eight members as "The

Warren Club," named after the acclaimed Boston anesthesiologist John Collins Warren. Its goal was to promote social and scientific conversation. By the time Hale joined it on November 28, 1911,[60] the club's invitation-only membership had expanded to 160. Meetings were held biweekly at members' homes. In the club's centennial address given on October 24, 1946, Reginald Fitz cited various inventions displayed at club meetings:

> The telephone in 1876 when Mr. Bell placed two instruments in adjoining rooms, permitting members to talk to one another by the new device, Mr. Edison's phonograph in 1878; electric light fixtures in 1881, and in the same year, pictures of a horse in motion by means of instantaneous photographs—the forerunner of motionp ictures.[61]

Though he never hosted a meeting of the club, Hale was the featured speaker on no fewer than five different occasions, extemporizing on such topics as "Boston Newspapers," "Theatrical Conditions in Music," and "Bohemianism in Literature." In his acceptance letter to Harold E. Ernst to speak on the latter topic, Hale displayed his characteristic modesty, writing "I'll try to make it good."[62]

Founded in 1884, The Tavern Club catered more to a clientele with artistic and literary interests, its 126-member active roster[63] being a virtual "Who's Who" of the Boston arts world. Its membership has included such persons as Arthur Foote, Artur Nikisch, Josef Adamovsky, George W. Chadwick, Bliss Perry, Oliver Wendell Holmes Sr. (the club's founder), Oliver Wendell Holmes, Jr., John Singer Sargent, Augustus St Gaudens, Edmund Tarbell, Mark Antony DeWolfe Howe, Henry James, Horatio Parker, Frederick Cabot, Henry Lee Higginson, John Fitzgerald Kennedy, and William Weld.

Hale became heavily involved with the inner workings of the club, serving as librarian, vice president (twice—1916–1928 and 1931–1934), and as an ex-officio member of the Executive Committee. It was during his first term as vice president, around Valentine's Day, 1917 that a celebration of some sort was held. It appears that members were asked to write poems about themselves; then again, certain members may have been "roasted." Whatever the case, the poem about Hale is uproarious:

<u>TavernC lubV alentine</u>
<u>1917</u>
<u>PhilipH ale</u>

When I was a baby boy,
I was known as "Mother's Joy."

Then I grew older until
I became "Our Darling Phil."

Next a weedy, lawless lad,
Learn to smoke and swear like mad,
Drank my bitter beer and ale,
The fellows called me "Sporty Hale."

> Since I've grown to man's estate,
> I am mistress Fashion's Mate.
> Sporting a flowing tie and wear
> A checkered vest and bang my hair;
> And my name, should you inquire,
> Is Mr. Philip Hale, Esquire.
>
> Listen, while I tell to you
> Some few things that I can do:—
> I can criticize a play;
> Write a "column" every day,
> Telling how the old world wags,
> Full of wisdom, wit, and gags;
> For I am, so people say,
> A walking 'cyclope-di-a.
> Know a lot 'bout music, too—
> Leastways, people think I do,
> Though if truth be told, I swear,
> I think more of eyes and hair,
> Shapely ankles, luscious lips,
> And slender, curving, lithesome hips,
> Than all the music Wagner made
> Or Paderewski madly played.
>
> So, if an artist's young and fair
> Though like a rasp her voice is,
> I say that it cannot compare
> With Patti's tuneful noises;
> But if she's ugly, old, and fat,
> Yet sings like a Madonna,
> I say that all she sharps are flat,
> And otherwise dog-gone 'er.
>
> ***************
>
> Wisdom and Wit and Modesty,
> Maidens both coy and frail,
> All make obeisance to me,
> Their Mentor, Philip Hale.[64]

Documentation concerning the year when Hale became a member of this club is somewhat confusing at first glance. The name "Philip Hale" appears in the 1894 edition of *The Rules of the Tavern Club of Boston, with a List of the Officers & Members*,[65] yet later editions of the same volume list Hale's membership as dating from 1912. There are at least two possible explanations for this discrepancy. It could be that Hale was elected in 1893–1894 and then allowed his membership to lapse for the next 18 years. More likely, however, is that the Philip Hale in the early listing was not a Philip Hale the music critic, but rather Philip Leslie Hale (1865–1931), the Boston impressionist artist who would have just started to teach at the Museum of Fine Arts following great success in Europe. Undoubtedly, Philip Hale and Philip Leslie Hale knew each other; coincidentally, both wrote columns for the *Boston Herald*.

By the start of the 1912–1913 season, Max Fiedler had returned to Germany, first to Hamburg, then to Berlin, and Karl Muck resumed his conductorship of the Boston Symphony Orchestra. Though criticized for his wildly diverse programming, Fiedler had been able to maintain the orchestra on a high technical plateau and, therefore, was able to deliver a finely tuned world-class musical organization to his successor. Muck had finally severed ties with the Berlin Royal Opera House, where he had conducted well over 1,000 performances. Hale commented:

> Not without regret has he left the orchestra of the Berlin Royal Opera House. Many of its players have grown up under him, and the ensemble, which is justly famous, is almost wholly the result of his labors lightened by the devotion of the men to the leader whom they will sorely miss. He realizes, however, the unique advantages of the position in Boston; the absolute freedom given to his wishes, musical judgment and taste.[66]

Muck's return was eagerly anticipated by the public. The bidding for selected seats in Symphony Hall for the 1912–1913 season produced an average price that was higher than that of the previous season.[67] His season opener was triumphant:

**WARM GREETING
FOR DR. MUCK**

———

Audience Enthusiastic at Opening of Symphony's 32nd Season

———

PROGRAM IS ALL ROMANTIC

———

Beethoven's "Eroica" and Liszt's
"Mazeppa" Features of
Afternoon

———

By PHILIP HALE

The program of the public rehearsal that opened the 32nd season of the Boston Symphony Orchestra yesterday afternoon in Symphony Hall was as follows:

Symphony No. 3 "Eroica" .... Beethoven
Overture "Roman Carnival" .... Berlioz
Symphonic poem No. 6, "Mazeppa" .... Liszt
Prelude to "The Mastersingers" .... Wagner

The 32nd season opened brilliantly. As soon as Dr. Muck came upon the stage, after an absence of four years, the great audience paid him heartfelt and flattering tribute; nor need he doubt for a moment the sincerity of this welcome; an exhibition of respect of respect and admiration for him as conductor and as man; nor was in this instance the fanfare of the orchestra merely traditional and perfunctory. Dr. Muck acknowledged the welcome with grace and dignity, as was his wont.

> He nothing common did or mean
> Upon that memorable scene.

In view of the conditions that attended this concert—a conductor whose methods are unfamiliar to some in the orchestra, the limited acquaintanceship established by a few rehearsals, the presence of new players—the performance was unusually brilliant. The program was a romantic one throughout, for the Beethoven of the "Eroica" is still to be reckoned with as a romanticist.[68]

The heart of Muck's repertoire was German and romantic, but he was open to programming the music of composers of all nationalities. In 1913 he conducted Cesar Franck's *Symphony in D minor*, still considered at that time to be quite modern in its harmonies, and touted the music of the French impressionists. He drew the line at expressionism, however, and Hale quoted him in an October 3, 1912 interview:

> The Herald has already reported the fact that the music of Arnold Schoenberg was recently hissed in London when it was produced by Henry Wood. Dr. Muck said that he cannot understand Schoenberg's music. "He puts C major, D major, E major in juxtaposition, without any harmonic pretext known to even radicals, and the result to me—well, I do not understand it, and it is hard for me to believe that the composer is sincere. Now, Debussy's harmonic scheme, while it is highly original, is logical and effective."[69]

Two years later, however, in what seems to have been a courageous move, Muck programmed Schoenberg's *Five Pieces for Orchestra*. The critic from the *Boston Globe* referred to the work as "Schoenberg's Absurdities" containing "Caterwaulings of Woe."[70] N otH ale:

MISSH INKLE
SHOWSS KILL
AS SOLOIST

———

Symphony Orchestra's Playing
of Schoenberg Pieces Re-
ceived with Dignity

———

By PHILIP HALE

The eighth Public Rehearsal of the Boston Symphony Orchestra, Dr. Karl Muck conductor, took place yesterday afternoon in Symphony Hall. Miss Florence Hinkle, soprano, was the soloist. The program was as follows:

A Faust Overture	Wagner
"Voi che Sapete"	Mozart

Five pieces for orchestra:
  Presentiments, The Past, The Changing
  Chord, Peripteta, The Obbligato Recitative
    First Time in Boston
	Schoenberg

"Ave Maria" from "The Cross of Fire"	Bruch
Symphony in G, (The Surprise)	Haydn

Bill Nye said, many years ago, that the music of Wagner was better than it sounded.[71] Arnold Schoenberg says today that his own music is better than it sounds.

The pieces played yesterday are extraordinary. It is easy to say that the composer is a maniac or a poseur. Neither statement would be accurate. Those who have read his treatise on harmony know that he is a man of unusual knowledge, force, originality. Those who heard his quartet last season know that he can write music of uncommon beauty and towering imagination in a more familiar form.

It would also be easy to say that when Strauss' "Till Eulenspiegel" was first performed in Boston, the majority in the audience thought the music chaotic, incomprehensible and the composer mad. Today, in comparison, with Schoenberg's pieces this symphonic poem is as clear as music by Haydn. Remember, too, that when Debussy's "Nocturnes" were played twice in succession at Chickering Hall they were thought to be incomprehensible.

These instances will not answer the objectors to Schoenberg. What is to be said of his five pieces? Personal impressions are interesting chiefly to the person impressed. No two persons hear music in the same way. I could make little out of the first and third pieces. There are fine moments in "The Past" and "The Changing Chord"; beautiful suggestions of mood; strangely beautiful effects of color. Nor is the fourth piece wholly inexplicable. To argue for or against this music, which might be of another planet, after even several hearings, would be presumptuous and even foolish. It took many Bostonians, well acquainted with orchestral and chamber compositions, a long time to familiarize themselves with the idiom of Cesar Franck, and later with that of Debussy. These composers, however, are not so fundamentally radical, anarchistic, as Schoenberg.

Thomas Hardy in that noble prose epic, the description of Egdon Heath, asks if the exclusive reign of orthodox beauty is not approaching its last quarter. "The new vale of Temple may be a gaunt waste in Thule; human souls may find themselves in closer and closer harmony with external wearing a somberness distasteful to our race when it was young. * * * The time seems near, if it has not actually arrived, when the mournful sublimity of a moor, a sea, or a mountain, will be all of nature that is absolutely consonant with the moods of the more thinking among mankind. And ultimately, to the commonest tourist spots like Iceland may become what the vineyards and myrtle gardens of South Europe are to him now, and Heidelberg and Baden be passed unheeded as he hastens from the Alps to the sand dunes of Scheventingen."

When Schoenberg's Five Pieces were performed for the first time in London, and in Chicago, there were scenes of outspoken disapproval. Yesterday the behavior of the audience was highly creditable to Boston. There was smiling; there was giggling at times; there was applause. Nobody rose to remonstrate. Nothing was thrown at Dr, Muck and the orchestra. There was no perturbation of Nature to show that Schoenberg's pieces were playing; the sun did not hasten its descent; there was no earthquake shock. It was as it should have been in Boston.

Miss Florence Hinkle has a beautiful voice which she uses with rare skill. The Canzona of Chreubino, sensuous in its supposed passion, should be sung by a darker voice to gain full effect. It served yesterday to display the art of Miss Hinkle in sustained and flawless song. The lyrical measures of Bruch's "Ave Maria," conventionally suave, were sung with unexaggerated emotion, and the singer gave dramatic importance to the agitated passages that in themselves are of a perfunctory and meaningless nature. It has been said by some that Miss Hinkle is a cool, impassive singer. They probably mean by this that she is not spasmodic and hysterical. Seldom at Symphony Hall concerts of late years has there been such a delightful display of pure vocal art as that of yesterday.

Dr. Muck gave an eloquent reading of the Faust overture in which there are hints at the Wagner to come. The symphony of Haydn, admirably performed, is not among his most interesting.[72]

During these years, and one might say for the remainder of his life, Hale was seen not only as a member of the established "old guard" of music critics, but now also as an individual who had reached the upper echelons of Boston's social hierarchy; his advice on various matters was eagerly sought by friends and colleagues. Hale wrote the following letter in response to a request from singer Clara Kathleen Barnett Rogers (1844–1931) who had been teaching voice and diction at New England Conservatory since 1902:

>Osterville Mass
>September 22/1912

My dear Mrs. Rogers:

I was glad to hear from you and also glad to heaven that you are eager to improve the English enunciation and pronunciation of poor wretches, to better their slovenly diction. I am sure your influence will be of weight and the Conservatory is undoubtedly a fine field to work in. (By the way, the Fogler sisters have sent me a circular, saying that they purposed to teach English for singers after the method of Miss Somebody Duty Jones of London).

We all as a people speak English in a careless and often incorrect manner, and it is not surprising that so many American singers are almost or wholly unintelligible. Whenever I hear an English Soubrette in a musical comedy, I am delighted with the distinctness of her enunciation and the euphony of her diction. Yet talk with the same girl and she might be a Cockney in familiar speech. Now—Why? In what lies the difference?.[73]

Henry Higginson, who supported myriad educational institutions at various levels, had been a Fellow of the Corporation of Harvard University since 1893. He was also a Trustee of New England Conservatory. It was probably in the former position that he wrote to Hale, seeking his advice about candidates for a facultyp osition:

>January 12, 1915

Dear Mr. Hale:

Have you any idea about Thomas C. Hill who is a teacher in the musical department at Cambridge? As I have the responsibility of looking him up, I ask for your real opinion, which will not be quoted to anybody. He does pretty well, but has not, I should suppose, the balance or catholicity which are desirable in a teacher of students. I would not have a man slur the new music, and I would not have a man slur the old music. I do not know Mr. Hill personally, but do know that he comes of excellent people, as you do, and respect him.

You are aware that in any great institution like the University we are apt to get medium or ordinary men—men of fair parts and no more, and who inspire nobody.

I shall be very much obliged to you if you can tell me what you have to say,— and please bear in mind that your opinion will be put in the fire if you wish after it is read and digested.

Do you know a young man named Clifton or something of that sort, who has graduated lately and who is, I believe, at the present time in France, and have you any notion about his quality [?]

I hope that you enjoyed the great Li[s]zt concert as much as I did.

I am, with kind regards,

Yours truly,
[HLH]

Philip Hale, Esq.,
1087, Boyleston Street
Boston, Mass.[74]

Hale responded quickly:

1087 Boyleston St[.]
January 13, 1915

Major Henry L. Higginson:

My dear Sir:

I am sorry to say that I know nothing about Mr. Thomas C. Hill. In fact I never saw his name or heard of him until I received your letter. This is not an argument against his ability, for unless he should be actively engaged as a composer, conductor, pianist, I should not be apt to know about him.

But I do know something about Mr. Chalmers Clifton, having met him and having seen him conduct a large orchestra. He is a man of unusual musical talent, one that I am sure will make his mark. I know him personally only slightly, but his conducting was admirable. Furthermore I am told by good judges that he has ability as a composer. He is a modest young man of pleasing address. Whether he has the gift of imparting knowledge is another matter, of which I am not qualified to judge.

Yes indeed I enjoyed the Liszt concert. I have never heard a finer and more impressive orchestral performance here or in Europe. Dr. Muck is a wonderful man—and what a wonderful instrument you have given him to play upon.

With my best wishes,

Yours sincerely
Philip Hale

P.S. You speak of Mr. Clifton as living in France. It is my impression he is now in Cambridge or Boston.[75] Mr. Edward B. Hill knows his address.[76]

Two years later Higginson requested that Hale do a confidential evaluation of Edward Burlingame Hill[77] and, in the following year, an evaluation of "Messrs. Spalding, Hill, and Heilman of the Music School of Harvard U.—especially if they are good teachers."[78]

From May 14 to May 26, 1915 the Boston Symphony Orchestra performed a series of 13 concerts at the Panama-Pacific International Exposition in San Francisco. Held officially as a celebration of the opening of the Panama Canal, this world's fair unofficially demonstrated the city's resiliency in rebuilding itself after the devastating earthquake of 1906.

Concerts were held in the fair's Festival Hall, a large dome-shaped building that seated over 3,000. In addition to band and orchestra concerts, the hall featured well-attended recitals by acclaimed organists.[79]

The printed Boston Symphony programs had the trademark brown covers then in use for the orchestra's subscription concerts. Program notes and commentary were by Hale, of course, but there were no Entr'actes and advertising appeared only on the back covers. Nearly all of the concerts followed the order of performance: symphony first and overture last.

Muck's tour programming was, as one might expect, primarily German (including two all-Wagner concerts), though two works of the Second New England School of composers—Edward MacDowell's *Indian Suite* and George W. Chadwick's *Symphonic Sketches*—were also included. In addition, there were four concerts dedicated to music of particular lands—two French, one Italian, and one Russian.[80] Camille Saint-Saëns and John Philip Sousa were in attendance at the first French concert for a performance of the former's *Symphony No. 3 in C minor*, Op. 35 "Organ."

Hale reiterated his assessment of Muck in a remarkable expository written at the end of the 1915–1916 season in which he addressed his philosophy about what determines the success of a season, soloists, and programming:

The success of the Boston Symphony Orchestra in a season of 24 concerts (48 in all) does not depend on the number of unfamiliar compositions produced or the number of the soloists.

It should be remembered that it is not now easy to obtain the orchestral parts of comparatively new or even the parts of old ones. (Thus it is said that no parts of Schubert's "Unfinished" symphony can be purchased in this country.

The soloist, as a rule, disturbs the concert. The chosen concerto or aria seldom fits in the general scheme of the program. If the soloist is a celebrated person he or she becomes in the eyes of many the feature of the concert. What goes before the solo is heard with indifference; after the soloist leaves the platform the orchestral music—overture, rhapsody, what-not, serves as a hat-and-overcoat piece. But soloists are still necessary to attract some to the concert hall. The attraction is probably not so potent as in former years, when the first question asked was, "Who is the soloist this afternoon?" More are now interested in the purely orchestral music. It is true that some men, such as Messrs. Caruso, Kreisler, McCormack and Paderewski, would draw a crowd to a Symphony concert no matter what the character of the orchestral music might be. There is always a huge audience for a favorite prima donna.

Dr. Muck's programs have been adversely criticized. We have shown the injustice of one reproach: that they were exclusively German. But it has been said that they have been strangely arranged; that inferior music has been played. Some wish that well known symphonies of Haydn should be shelved and they wonder why one should be forced to hear at regular intervals the first and second symphonies of Beethoven. There were a few programs this season that were trying; that of April 14–15 for example: Humperdinck's overture to "The Forced Marriage"; Dvorak's violin concerto; Haydn's symphony in D major; truly a program to strike terror to the stoutest soul. Such instances, however, were few, very few. If there are some who grow restive at the thought of too many orthodox compositions in good and regular standing, to quote the old formula of letters applying for membership in a sister Congregational church, there are others who denounce all "ultra-modern" pieces, are hardly reconciled to Richard Strauss, and look on Debussy as Anti-Christ—poor Debussy, who is even now becoming a classic, so swift is the march of the years, so shifting the expressive forms of music.

Any fair-minded person of a receptive nature, experienced in hearing orchestral concerts, will now remember familiar works that were made fresh and vital by the beauty of performance. For it is not extravagant to say that the performance of the orchestra under Dr. Muck week in and week out has never been equaled in this city. Performances of this nature are in all probability not heard in any city, European or American. There may be a brilliant performance of this or that piece in Paris, Vienna, Dresden, London, Chicago, New York, but where are 24 concerts of a similar nature so conspicuous for technical perfection and supreme interpretation to be heard? These concerts in Boston are so remarkable, they have been so remarkable under the leadership of Dr. Muck, that they are now taken by too many as a matter of course.

For the Boston Symphony orchestra is not merely one that contains certain accomplished virtuosos; the orchestra is a virtuoso. It is an instrument that, having been brought to a state of perfect mechanism by Dr. Muck, responds to his imaginative and poetic wishes. He stands there calm, undemonstrative, graceful, elegant, aristocratic; a man of singularly commanding and magnetic personality, even in repose. The orchestra is his speech, the expression of the composer's music as it appeals to the conductor's brain, heart, and soul.

It is now hardly possible to think of the orchestra without the vision of Dr. Muck at its head as the interpreter of beauty and brilliance. Fortunate, thrice fortunate, is he in having at his command this orchestra, largely his own creation; wholly the superb interpreter of composers as he understands them, as he shares in their own emotions, confessions, declarations, griefs and longings.[81]

Muck continued this great success into the 1916–1917 season with a wide range of programming, from Loeffler's *Hora Mystica*, Busoni's *Turandot Suite* (both featuring choruses), Strauss's one movement piano concerto *Burleske*, and Cherubini's overture to *The Abercerrages*, to a string orchestra performance of Beethoven's *Grosse Fugue*, Op. 133. The latter, presented at the third concert, was not one of Hale's favorites:

Beethoven wrote a formidable fugue as the finale of his string quartet op. 120 [sic, 130]. When the quartet was first played in Vienna 90 years ago this fugue was condemned. The publisher, Artaria, prevailed upon Beethoven to write another finale. The fugue was performed here by the Kneisel quartet in 1907. It has been played by all the orchestral strings in New York, at a Theodore Thomas concerts, and in Chicago at a concert of the Chicago orchestra.

This music of Beethoven may interest students as a specimen of fugal writing. Played by a quartet it has little or no aesthetic charm. The greater number of pages are dull when they are not ugly. When the music is played by all the strings in an orchestra the inherent ugliness is intensified. The hearer's only enjoyment is in observing the precision of the players. He says to himself: "Here are between 50 and 60 men fiddling with all their might and main. How well they keep together!"

On the night of April 26, 1890, Mr. Arthur Nikisch, then conductor of the Boston Symphony Orchestra, conducted Paganini's "Moto Perpetuo" played, as the program stated, by 32 violins. The violinists stood in an imposing row. We remember the occasion well. The sight of 32 men doing the work of one excited the audience to frenzy. This clap-trap performance, which should have been accompanied by the illumination of Bengal lights, provided the heartiest applause of the season of '89-'90. Yesterday the players, with the exception of the double basses, remained seated. The audience made no ardent demonstration of enjoyment or approval. Perhaps if the men had all stood there might have been an exhibition of at least moderate rapture.[82]

Meanwhile, the international climate had grown ugly very quickly. What started out as a regional European war in 1914 had escalated dramatically and by early 1917 German U-boats were sinking American merchant ships in the North Atlantic. On April 6, the United States entered the war. Muck, a German-born Swiss citizen who had a German passport signed by Kaiser Wilhelm II, felt increasingly uncomfortable and offered to resign. He was at the end of his five-year contract and leaving at this point would present both him and the orchestra with the opportunity to make a clean break. Higginson, however, convinced him to remain. In terms of artistry, Muck had been reluctant to depart; under his musical directorship, the Boston Symphony Orchestra had become one of the finest, if not the finest, orchestra in the country.

Recognizing the greatness of the orchestra, the Victor Talking Machine Company of Camden, New Jersey initiated a series of orchestral recordings with them. From October 2 through October 5 the entire orchestra, though severely restricted by the limitations of acoustical recording, was able to cut ten 12-inch 78 r.p.m. sides.[83] This resulted in an aural documentation that was incredible for its time. The orchestra appeared to be on top of the world, but two cataclysmic though unrelated events occurring over the next three years would knock it off itsp edestal.

5

1917–1933

In addition to its Symphony Hall subscription concerts, the Boston Symphony Orchestra regularly performed at other venues along the Eastern Seaboard. On October 30, 1917 the orchestra played the first of three concerts that season planned for Providence, Rhode Island's Infantry Hall. Only an hour from Boston by train, concerts in Providence and Worcester, Massachusetts, were seen as local concerts, with the players returning home afterwards.

By late 1917 anti-German sentiment was running high. The Germans were considered the aggressors in World War I and the US government felt it had to protect its citizens through any means possible. This resulted in passage of the Espionage Act of 1917 and Alien Enemies Act. Naturally, there was some overreach and overreaction as hysteria spread across the country. German-Americans quickly declared their loyalty to the United States. Many Americanized their surnames: Schmidt to Smith, Schumacher to Shoemaker, etc. German language courses were dropped from high school curricula and German-speaking rural enclaves, such as those in Breese, Illinois or Hermann, Missouri, quickly shifted their language to English. Even the music industry was not immune. The Metropolitan Opera revised its programming for the 1917–1918, eliminating offerings in German, and some music history texts were written that ignored the contributions of German composers. Austrian-born violinist Fritz Kreisler was banned in Pittsburgh.[1]

Among those fueling the fire of public opinion was Australian-born John R. Rathom (1868–1923), the editor of the *Providence Journal*. Rathom was a pro-war extremist, publishing exaggerated accounts and fraudulent charges in a series of articles both in his newspaper and in *The World's Work*. Thus it was when the Boston Symphony Orchestra, then still dominated by German and Austrian musicians, performed their first wartime concert in Providence, Rathom was quick to seize upon an opportunity. He placed the following editorial in the *Providence Journal* the morning of the concert:

CONCERNING DR. MUCK

The Boston Symphony Orchestra is to appear in Providence this evening under the leadership of Dr. Karl Muck.

Professor Muck is a man of notoriously pro-German affiliations and the programme as announced is almost entire German in character.

It has been said that Dr. Muck has not yet played any patriotic American air at his concerts, whereas Mr. Damrosch began his New York season with a patriotic address and "The Star-Spangled Banner" and Mr. Stransky included the national anthem and an American symphony in his initial program for the year.

It is as good a time as any to put Professor Muck to the test. The Boston Symphony Orchestra should play "The Star-Spangled Banner," in Providence to-night.[2]

Rathom had thrown down the gauntlet, the result being that a great deal of misunderstanding and misrepresentation soon followed. A rather lopsided account of what occurred that evening appeared on page 1 in the *Providence Journal* the next morning:

AMERICANA NTHEM
ENTIRELY IGNORED

———

Symphony Orchestra Does Not
Play "Star Spangled Banner"

———

TICKETS REFUSED TO MANY

———

Request Made of Manager Ellis
Concerts by Nine Providence Societies is Not Granted— -Hunga-
rian, Russian and German Selections Are Played.

The Boston Symphony Orchestra did not play "The Star Spangled Banner" at the concert here last evening.

Despite the request of representatives of nine local societies and the Rhode Island Liberty Loan Committee, telegraphed to C. A. Ellis, manager of the organization in Boston, earlier in the day, Dr. Karl Muck conducted his musicians in a programme of Russian, Hungarian, and German selections, ignoring the American anthem entirely.

Moreover, scores of prominent men and women who went to Infantry Hall expecting to buy tickets at the door, were met with a blunt refusal on the part of the management to accommodate them, although there were several vacant rows at the back of the hall. Many of them appealed to Mr. Ellis, only to be met with the statement, "We have sold all the seats we care to sell."

At the Billy Sunday preliminary banquet in the Narragansett Hotel last evening, Rev. A. Z. Conrad, pastor of the Park Street Congregational Church, Boston, in speaking of the work the church had to do in making our army invincible with the spirit of God, said he was glad to see that so many representative societies had petitioned the "The Star Spangled Banner" be played at the Symphony concert. He read the names from a copy of the Evening Bulletin he held in his hand.

"Any man who wields a baton under the Stars and Stripes," he said, "and isn't willing to play it, shouldn't be allowed to live under them; in Boston, Symphony Hall is the only public hall where the Stars and Stripes are not displayed, because Dr. Karl Muck will not permit it."

The orchestra expected trouble last evening. Col. Henry L. Higginson of Lee, Higginson & Co., the patron of the organization, made the trip here with the musicians and returned with them to Boston. Mr. Ellis said that this was "because of the editorial in the Journal and the telegram sent by the women."...

"Will the orchestra play 'The Star-spangled Banner?'["][a *Journal* representative] asked Mr. Ellis.

"I think not," Mr. Ellis replied. "The Boston Symphony Orchestra played it every night for 10 weeks during the pop concerts in Symphony Hall, Boston, where it was appropriate. We have announced our programme for to-night and people have purchased their tickets to hear this programme, and I think it will be well worth hearing."

"I received the telegrams requesting 'The Star Spangled Banner' this afternoon, signed by [names listed below]. Not one of these names appears on our list of subscribers for the season."

"You say the orchestra played the national anthem in the pop concerts; the Journal representative continued. 'Did Dr. Muck lead that?'["]

"He does not lead the pops concerts," was the answer.

"Has he ever lead 'The Star Spangled Banner?'["]

"I do not know."

"I received the telegrams requesting 'The Star Spangled Banner' this afternoon...."]

The joint message was as follows:

"We the undersigned earnestly request that 'The Star Spangled Banner' be played by the Boston Symphony Orchestra this evening, Oct. 30, at Infantry Hall:["]

MRS. EMMA WINSLOW CHILDS, President Chopin Club.

MRS. HAROLD J. GROSS, President Monday Morning Club.

MRS. GEORGE S. MATTHEWS, Vice president MacDowell Club, and chairman of the music committee of the Rhode Island State Federation of Women's Clubs.

MISS MARY S. WINDSOR, President Schubert Club.

MISS VIRGINIA BOYD ANDERSON, presiding officer, Rhode Island State Federation of Musical Clubs.

MRS. GEORGE HAIL, President Northeastern District National Federation of Musical Clubs.

MRS. JAMES E. McCONNELL, President, the Chaminade Club.

MRS. GILBERT C. CARPENTER, First Vice President of the Chaminade Club.

Mr. West's telegram read: "The Liberty Loan Committee of Rhode Island requests that "The Star Spangled Banner" be played by the Boston Symphony Orchestra at the concert to be given in Providence to-night."[3]

Most of the above article was factual. The request by the heads of music clubs to have "The Star Spangled Banner" performed at the concert during wartime was in itself quite understandable. If the article is accurate, then it was Ellis who was approached about this and, in retrospect, probably showed poor judgment in the matter. One area in which he displayed good judgment, however, was in restricting the concert to subscribers, thus greatly reducing the opportunity for a public demonstration inside the hall during the concert. Higginson, who upon arrival was consulted by Ellis about "The Star Spangled Banner," quietly pocketed the request. The orchestra had been rehearsed and the concert had been set, with Tchaikovsky's *Fourth Symphony*, Wagner's "Elisabeth's Greeting" from *Tannhäuser*, Liszt's *Prometheus*, Wagner's settings of *Three Poems*, and Beethoven's *Overture to Egmont*.[4]

The main problem with the above article is that about half of it contains opinions from people such as A. Z. Conrad who, through disseminating misinformation, placed the blame on the conductor. Muck, of course, knew nothing about the request. Philip Hale would never have written such an article. People's opinions were important to him, but he did not use people as pawns, let employ their opinions for the purpose of fear mongering. Rathom, on the other hand, used these opinions as fodder for the following incendiary editorial, released the next day:

THE CASE OF DR. KARL MUCK

Dr. Karl Muck, Conductor of the Boston Symphony Orchestra, is a creature of Germany and a dangerous alien enemy.

He was born in Darmstadt, graduate at the gymnasium in Würzburg, studied at Heidelberg and Leipzig, conducted at Zürich, Salzburg, Brünn, Graz and Prague, and received from the Kaiser the title of "Königlich preusserischer Generalmusikdirektor."

As Conductor of the Boston Symphony Orchestra he has grossly offended every patriotic American by his refusal to render our national anthem. His attitude toward his audience in Providence on Tuesday evening was one of studied contempt.

Mr. Ellis, his manager, moreover put himself in the same category with Dr. Muck by his pitiful and damnable excuse that the programme had been fixed and could not be changed. What can any reasoning American think of a statement like this?

There is no room for a man like Muck on the concert stage of America. He has no business conducting the Boston Symphony. We are at war with his country and we cannot tolerate his defiance and outrage of American patriotism.

Dr. Muck should be withdrawn at once and forever from the American stage and placed where he belongs—behind bars in an internment camp.[5]

The next evening Higginson, having reassessed the situation and undoubtedly bowing to public pressure, announced to the Symphony Hall audience that "The Star Spangled Banner" would be performed at all future concerts. The *New York Times* carried the news:

DR. MUCK RESIGNS,
THEN PLAYS ANTHEM;

Higginson Announces at Boston Concert
Symphony Director's Offer to Quit.

ACCEPTANCE NOT CERTAIN

But the Symphony Orchestra
Will Play "The Star-Spangled Bonner" at
All Its Concerts.
Muck Offers Resignation.
Career of the Director.
Played "All German" Programs.
Criticized by Damrosch.[6]

A slip reading "The National Anthem will be played as the closing number of the programme" was then inserted into all of the orchestra's pre-printed programs.[7] For those yet to be printed, this notice was included at the bottom of the program order page. This still did not satisfy New York zealots who claimed that the particular arrangement of "The Star Spangled Banner" being used was, in itself, defamatory. Nor did it satisfy those in Baltimore, who quickly cancelled a November 6th concert. Later it was revealed that the arrangement had been completed by the esteemed Irish-American cellist and conductor Victor Herbert. Zealots also claimed, as the *New York Times* had printed, that Muck was forcing all-German programming down the throats of tour audiences. The 1917–1918 Boston Symphony Orchestra's trip programs, however, indicate this not to be the case. Some of the programs featured Wagner, but Wagner was Muck's specialty.[8]

It is not surprising, then, that the Boston Symphony Orchestra cancelled its remaining 1917–1918 Providence concerts. Rathom responded with a vicious January 15, 1918 editorial:

> The cancellation of the Boston orchestra's dates in this city opens the way for a series of concerts by the Providence organization with a better financial outlook than ever before.
>
> Many subscribers to the Boston Symphony concerts will have a substantial sum returned to them through the decision of its management not to continue the concerts here this season. The suggestion is made that this money can be profitably used in subscribing to three concerts by the local orchestra, which has done good work for many years and lately increased its technical reputation.
>
> The Providence Symphony Orchestra should receive, in view of the failure of the Boston organization to appear in this city, a heartier support than heretofore. There ought to be no doubt of the success of the plan to enable it to carry through a three-concert programme in Providence during the present winter.
>
> Our home orchestra is no means rival to any stellar organization in the country. And it lacks both the jelly fish management and insolent Prussian leadership that has given us good riddance of the Boston Symphony.[9]

With such anti-German hysteria raging in the press, it is amazing that the orchestra was able to continue functioning in any sense of pre-war normalcy. Yet, in its December, 1917 catalogue, The Victor Talking Machine Company announced the release of the first Boston Symphony Orchestra recordings. These included the "Finale" of Tchaikovsky's *Symphony No. 4 in F minor*, Op. 36 (two 12-inch sides) and Wagner's "Prelude to Act III" of *Lohengrin* (one 10-inch record). The Tchaikovsky "March Miniature" from his *Suite No. 1* followed soon thereafter.[10] The announcement was accompanied by a quote from Muck:

> Yesterday when I arrived I was feeling very pessimistic. I had heard no satisfactory records of a symphony orchestra. I did not believe they could be made—but today—I am very much surprised. I am very pleased. These records sound like a symphony orchestra.[11]

Also notable during this season was the January 21, 1918 Boston premiere of Gustav Mahler's *Symphony No. 2*, "Resurrection." Hale, who had been quite impressed with the composer's *Symphony No. 5 in C-sharp Minor* when Wilhelm Gericke conducted it in 1906, was not so inclined toward acceptance of this earlier work:

PLAYM AHLER'S
SYMPHONYH ERE

Work Shows Little Genuine
MusicalV alue—Chorus
Is Powerful

PERFORMANCEI S
TRIUMPH FOR MUCK

By PHILIP HALE

The Boston Symphony Orchestra, Dr. Muck, conductor, assisted by May Peterson, soprano, Merle Alcock, alto, and the great chorus trained by Mr. Townsend, performed Gustav Mahler's Second Symphony last night in Symphony Hall. There was a very large audience. The symphony was performed for the first time in this city.

The final chorus by its sheer dynamic force, with the voices of many singers, the frenzy of an enlarged orchestra, the roar of organ and the peal of bells, undoubtedly affected the nerves of the hearers. They were for the moment thrilled. The question is whether it was worth while listening for an hour or more to the preceding movements of the symphony to experience a thrill.

It is known that Mahler was bitterly opposed to the program notes when his symphonies were performed. It was his habit to ask that only the indications for the movements should be printed on a program. Notes he abhorred, whether they were b iographical, a nalytical, e xplanatory....

It is to be regretted that Dr. Muck spent his rare talent and the excellent resources at his command in the preparation and performance of a work that has so little genuine musical value. Mahler could not have complained of the performance. In his lifetime, when he conducted the symphony abroad and in New York, he never had such an admirable orchestra and chorus. If he had been present last night he would have shaken warmly the hand of the conductor; he might have embraced him. But the splendor of the performance did not glorify the music itself. It still remained now blatant, now wildly pretentious, now of leaden dullness; with here and there hints at ideas that came to naught in the expression; with a few pages of pleasing commonplace; showing too often a surprising lack of taste, a clumsiness in orchestration, the belief that din is necessarily dramatic, that brute force is artistic strength.[12]

Thus Hale joined Higginson in continuing to support Muck on an artistic basis. This, however, was no indication regarding how Hale felt about the war. Though he never served in the military, Hale was a patriot. In a letter to Richard Aldrich dated March 17, 1918, Hale mentions that he was cancelling his subscription to the *Saturday Evening Post* due to "Villard's pacifism."[13] He had reasons; of the 125 Tavern Club members, 40 were in active service.[14]

Public sentiment against Muck continued to grow, and on March 25, 1918 he was arrested. The following appeared in the *Boston Herald*:

DR. KARL MUCK
ARRESTED A S
ALIEN ENEMY

Symphony Conductor Is
Taken as He Leaves
Motor Car at His Home

LOCKED UP IN BACK
BAY POLICE STATION

Federal Authorities Silent
Regarding Possible
Recent Evidence

Dr. Karl Muck, director of the Boston Symphony Orchestra, was arrested at his home, 50 Fenway, at 11:30 o'clock last night, by policemen and agents of the department of justice. He was taken to the Back Bay police station and lodged there for the night, under the charge of Lt. Mulligan. The arrest was made at the instance of U. S. Dist. Atty. Boynton, Asst. U. S. Atty. Judd Dewey being directly in charge of the arrest.

Dr. Muck will be charged with being an alien enemy. He will be taken to the federal building this morning and afterward probably be transferred to the East Cambridge jail. It was intimated last night he will remain at the East Cambridge jail for some time.

UNDER SURVEILLANCE

Dr. Muck has been under surveillance for some time, probably since the incident of some months ago, when it was charged he refused to direct the orchestra in playing "The Star-Spangled Banner" at a concert. It is significant that Dr. Muck's arrest occurs at a time when that incident, with its accompanying popular indignation, its defense of Dr. Muck on the part of Maj. Higginson and others, and other circumstances had begun to pass from the public mind. A member of Dist. Atty. Boynton's staff when asked last night if evidence had recently been found against Dr. Muck, said that he was not at liberty to say.

The arrest was decided upon late last evening. Policemen and department of justice agents kept vigil on the Fenway residence from about 8:30 until 11:30. Dr. Muck, they learned, was either at a play or at some social affair. Immediately upon the arrival of his limousine at his home a policeman stepped to his side, identified him, and told him he was under arrest.

SURRENDERS WITHOUT PROTEST

He immediately expressed his willingness to give himself up and walked with the officers from his home to the station.

At the station house he was put into a cell. Since no bail is obtainable in such cases, there he was forced to remain throughout the night, undergoing, no doubt, the same sensations as would any other man for the first time lodged in a cell.

The cell in which he was imprisoned in former days had held many a famous confidence man, robber and murderer. But never before has one of the greatest musicians in the world gone through the experience of spending a night in it.

The police officers in charge of the station granted him no more favors than they did any of the other prisoners. His bed was just as hard as that of the men in the adjoining cells on either side, and his tin drinking cup was of the same model as theirs.

Lt. Mulligan declined to make any statement concerning the arrest of the noted musician, other than to say that Dr. Muck was being held for the department of justice, and that he had been ordered to make no comment whatever on the case.

"My husband's arrest is preposterous." Mrs. [Anita] Muck declared at her home. "I have no knowledge of what the charge could be, and I am sure it will prove to be a farce. I know he will be released right away, for Mr. Ellis told me so."

Mrs. Muck spoke with a marked German accent, and appeared to be very much disturbed by the action of the authorities. She refused to believe that they could bring any charge against her husband.

Dr. Muck was to conduct tonight's Bach's "Passion According to St. Matthew," a production which has been in preparation all winter. An orchestra, a chorus of 400 and a boy choir of 80 have been taking part in the rehearsals.

When a reporter phoned the home of Maj. Henry L. Higginson, financial backer of the Symphony Orchestra, early this morning, a member of the household who answered said that since Maj. Higginson is suffering with a slight illness, it did not seem best to disturb him for the purpose of asking him to make a statement concerning Dr. Muck's arrest....

PLAYS ANTHEM HERE

Dr. Muck explained that "The Star Spangled Banner" was not a suitable musical composition for an aggregation of such artists as his musicians were. He disclaimed any lack of respect to the flag or the nation.

He tendered his resignation to Maj. Henry L. Higginson, founder and chief sponsor of the orchestra.

Upon the declarations by Providence citizens that Dr. Muck had declined their request to play the "Star Spangled Banner," Maj. Higginson made the following statement:

Dr. Muck never knew that a request for the "Star Spangled Banner" had been made until after the concert was over and he had returned to Boston. None of the orchestra members knew of the request until they reached Boston."

Maj. Higginson explained that the request had been made to Mr. Ellis, the orchestra manager, and himself, and he had ordered Mr. Ellis "to do nothing to change the program, which had been made up and rehearsed."

On the afternoon of Nov. 2, when the storm of protest over the Providence was at its height, the orchestra, with Dr. Muck leading, precipitated a tremendous patriotic demonstration here in Boston by playing the national anthem for the first time. Announcement was made that the anthem would be on the program at every future concert of the orchestra.

Though this appeased somewhat the sentiment against the conductor, the clamor of protest against him has continued. A few days ago Brooklyn was added to the cities in which the orchestra is barred....[15]

At least the *Herald*'s report was objective. However, the *New York Times*, itself not immune to occasional yellow journalism, had an article heading that led readers astray:

ARREST KARL MUCK AS AN ENEMY ALIEN;

Federal Authorities in Boston May Prefer
Charges Under the Criminal Code.

CLAIMED SWISS CITIZENSHIP

Conductor Spends Night in a Cell—Asked
for Passports to Europe Yesterday.
Refusal to Play National Anthem.[16]

That evening the Boston Symphony Orchestra concert featuring Johann Sebastian Bach's *St. Matthew Passion*, planned for months, went on as scheduled, though without Muck. Ernst Schmidt, a member of the first violin section who had previously conducted the Boston Pops, was chosen to conduct for the remainder of the season. Well aware of Muck's arrest, Hale took the high road in his review and did not comment about it. Instead, he wrote a characteristic review, critiquing the music (in fact, heavily criticizing the composer), and giving credit where credit was due. Of interest is the fact that Ernst Schmidt is listed as "Ernest" Schmidt. This could have been a printer's error or a deliberate attempt to downplay the conductor's lineage:

BACH'S PASSION
MUSIC GIVEN

All the Matthew Production
Heard at Symphony Hall
At Two Sessions

SCHMIDT CONDUCTS
IN PLACE OF DR. MUCK

By PHILIP HALE

The whole of Bach's Matthew Passion music was performed yesterday in two sessions, afternoon and evening, in Symphony Hall, by a chorus of 400 voices—prepared by Stephen Townsend—a boy choir of 80, the Boston Symphony orchestra and these solo singers: Florence Hinkle, soprano; Merle Alcock, alto; Lambert Murphy, tenor; Reinald Werrenrath, baritone; Herbert Witherspoon, bass; Arthur Myers, tenor. John P. Marshall was the organist. Alfred De Voto the pianist. Ernest Schmidt conducted.

Camille Saint-Saëns, a sympathetic and profound student of Bach, declared over 30 years ago that the performance of that great master's choral works is now a chimera. "There can be only more or less curious attempts; attempts made for the joy of scholars and library rats; but they are far from being the realization of the work imagined by the composer.["] Saint-Saëns then spoke of instruments employed by Bach which are now out of date, of the music written for a small chorus, swarming with complicated phrases, leaps to far-off intervals, trills, all sorts of difficulties; of extremely dangerous pages for the solo singers.

Some musicians, as Robert Franz, have believed in the enlargement and enrichment of Bach's score for the Matthew Passion. Purists have objected to Franz's tinkering and patching. They have argued in favor of performances exactly as Bach gave them in the St. Thomas Church at Leipsic [sic]. The introduction of clarinets especially disturbs them. The management of Symphony Hall, in its announcement of the concert yesterday, stated that "it is an anachronism to introduce into the score an instrument like the clarinet which was invented years after Bach's death."

Bach died in 1750. Let us waive the question whether J. C. Denner of Nuremburg "invented" the clarinet about 1700 or merely modified the then existing chalumeau or schalmei. A mass composed by a Belgian in 1720 contains a clarinet part. Le Poupiliniere of Paris imported two German clarinetists and they played in the Concert Sprituel. Rameau employed clarinets in 1731. Clarinets were used in J.C. Bach's opera "Orione," produced in London in 1763. The boy Mozart in London copied an overture of Abel that contained clarinet parts. In 1771 Mozart at Milan wrote for clarinets. A clarinet solo was heard at a concert in Philadelphia in 1769. Clarinets were heard in New York concerts as early as 1764....

[Dr. Muck put all of his] time as well as all of his skill to a reverential reconstruction of the score. The result was as interesting as it was effective, but it could not transport the players back to the Leipsic of the composer's period. Nor was it successful in relieving the inherent monotony of many pages, but this was not Dr. Muck's intention.

There are two ways of considering a performance of the Passion Music: one is to view it as a religious service; the other is to treat it as one would treat any concert work. If the music is to be regarded as any other sacred composition performed in a concert hall and without religious service, the performance of the whole work is a mistake. Certain songs, irksome to the singer, boresome as music, without truly emotional or religious significance, seldom expressive of the text, might be omitted with advantage to the composer. Did anyone yesterday afternoon find musical pleasure or religious benefit from the soprano solos in the first part? Only those who believe in the plenary inspiration of Bach would insist on the performance of every page. Bach could be as dull as any Kapellmeister in Eisleven. The purely decorative arias in the Passion Music might well be omitted. Even Mme. Hinkle, with her excellent voice and art, could not turn the long aria in the second part into a thing of beauty. Or hardly mitigate its barbaric ugliness.

When the Matthew Passion was first performed at Leipsic there were probably religious exercises between the two parts. In the concert hall the performance must be considered as a performance of any sacred composition.

It may then be said that the performance yesterday was an extraordinarily impressive one, admirable in nearly all respects, one not likely to be surpassed here in the coming years. It was far superior to any one that we have heard in Germany. Mr. Townsend had brought the chorus to a high degree of proficiency. The tonal quality and plasticity of the great body of singers were remarkable. Dr. Muck in the final rehearsals had so completed the preparation that Mr. Schmidt, called suddenly to conduct, found his task greatly lessened. Nevertheless he should be warmly praised for carrying out so well Dr. Muck's intentions. In the second part there were times when the accompaniment of solo singers in arias was not sufficiently subdued, but those instances were not many.

Mr. Murphy's reading of the narrator's music was a constant delight; his enunciation was so clear, his diction had so great significance. Not too dramatic, he steered clear of sentimentalism. Mr. Werrenrath's singing of the music of Jesus was marked by rare dignity, by an expressiveness that was intelligent as well as emotional. Mme. Alcock again displayed a beautiful voice and vocal and aesthetic understanding. Nor should Mr. Longy's playing of the oboe obligato in the first part be forgotten.

There was a large and deeply interested audience. The performance will be repeated with the same singers next Tuesday.[17]

Hale, wanting to give every opportunity to Schmidt, covered the remainder of the orchestra's season with scarcely a reference to Muck. One week later, however, Louis C. Elson of the *Boston Advertiser*, while complimenting Schmidt on his ability to handle the orchestra in such dire circumstances, commented, "Mr. Ernst Schmidt can scarcely swing the baton of Dr. Muck."[18]

Though the orchestra's season was saved, the printing of falsehoods, such as the last sentence of the *New York Times*' March 26, 1918 heading, continued to feed the rumor mill for many months to come. Higginson was very aware of the power of the press and when it was mistakenly reported in the *Herald* that Muck had been dismissed by the orchestra, he wrote the following rather terse letter. Even though Hale had nothing to do with it, Higginson addressed his lettert oh im:

October 29, 1918

Dear Mr. Hale:

This is for you—as a matter of justice,—and for use if need be.

I notice that the "Herald" speaks of Dr. Muck's dismissal—in an accidental paragraph. I have no objection to the word, and I approve of his dismissal from the Tavern Club.[19]

Here are the facts: He never refused to play the "Star Spangled Banner." To the contrary, at my first request for it in November, he pleasantly agreed,—and resigned. He feared internment, so he said to me. I laughed at the fear. I told the Friday audiences these facts at the time. Later, in February, I decided that he should go at the end of the season, and so told a friend and asked him to note the fact. About March 1st Dr. Muck came to me and resumed his request to resign. I agreed, and fixed the end of the season—May 4th, 1918.

There are the exact facts.

Then came the arrest, &c., and the United States attorney here said that he was arrested on the ground of an "Enemy Alien." In November and December I sought and strictly followed the instruction of the United States attorney here—Mr. Anderson, and of the Legal Department in Washington.

It is well that a gentleman in your position should have this record. My compelling reason for keeping him was that I made a bargain with the public for thirty-five years and had kept it absolutely. Neither Dr. Muck nor I were of consequence in comparison with the national question. If I had believed that he had sinned in any way against our country, I should have dismissed him at once. To this day I have no reason to believe that he did so sin.

> Yours truly,
> H. L. Higginson

Philip Hale, Esq.[20]

Hale responded, "What you said about Dr. Muck interested me. I am sorry that some misinformed person used the word 'dismissal' in the *Herald*."[21]

On March 31, 1918 Higginson wrote a letter to the US Attorney General requesting permission for Muck and his wife Anita to travel to Germany via Holland and Scandinavia. In it he stressed "Muck's absolute propriety, honesty, and honor."[22] Higginson obviously wanted to protect Muck. At that point in time, however, he was oblivious to the dark side of the conductor's personality: Muck was a womanizer.

At the point of his arrest, or shortly thereafter, federal agents raided Muck's residence at 50 The Fenway in Boston's Back Bay. They discovered no incriminating evidence about Muck's being an enemy alien, but did find a treasure trove of love letters from Rosamond Young, an impressionable and rather naïve nineteen-year-old heiress from Milton. She was an aspiring soprano, appearing as featured soloist on the December 17, 1917 Boston Symphony Orchestra concert at Worcester's Mechanics Hall.[23] She was also scheduled to sing on the January 15, 1918 Providence concert that was cancelled. Agents followed up on the love letters lead and searched her bedroom while she was out riding. There they found letters from Muck (written in both German and English), pictures of him, and a key to a deposit box which turned up still more letters, mostly from 1914 to 1915, when Rosamond would have been underage.[24] In addition to confirming marital infidelity, a recurring pattern in Muck's life (including an affair with soprano Emmy Destinn and possibly one with concertmaster Anton Witek's wife), many of these letters display an extreme anti-American sentiment. The following is a bowdlerized version of one that was eventually published in *The Washington Times*:

> My dearest [Rosamund],
>
> I fail to find words to express my joy over your decision to renew our friendship, which you so cruelly broke off in a matter of despondency. I feel happy to know that you no longer feel worried.
>
> You say, and you are right in saying so, [Rosamund] darling, that my martial [marital?] entanglements make it hard for you to continue our hitherto pleasant relationship. But can't you see, darling [Rosamund] how much harder it is for me to renounce the love that grew between us so sublimely?
>
> Must we, for the sake of foolish sentiment that is imposed on us by others, forswear the love that is divine and impressible by common language. No, [Rosamund] darling, a thousand times no! You are mine and I am your slave. And so we must remain...It will perhaps surprise you to learn that to a certain extent Madame Muck knows our relationship. She has a noble heart and her mind is broad beyond the comprehension of the swinelike people among whom we must live a while longer....
>
> And it will be only a very short time when our gracious Kaiser will act upon my request and recall me to Berlin. Once there, through the good offices of my

beloved friend Minister Schmidt, our Kaiser will be prevailed upon to see the benefit to the fatherland in my obtaining a divorce and making you my own. Then darling

Please be considerate of

YOUR KARL[25]

Regardless of the type of relationship they had, the fact that Rosamond had accompanied Muck across state lines meant that he would have gone to trial under the Mann Act.[26] Given a choice by the authorities to either face this trial or be detained as an enemy alien, Muck naturally opted for the latter. The charge: violation of the US postal laws.

Early on, the original letters were shown to Ellis and Higginson, who felt a deep sense of betrayal. The revelation that Muck was not the person that Higginson thought him to be was essentially the straw that broke the camel's back and one of the factors that contributed to Higginson's rapid physical decline. Federal agents agreed not to make these letters public and they were kept in storage in Washington, DC. After the war, however, Felix Weiss, a former agent who had access to the files, was bribed by the *Boston Post*, Hale's former employer, into illegally obtaining copies of the correspondence for the newspaper.[27] Hence, beginning November 9, 1919, the *Boston Post* ran a 12-part exposé of Muck with bowdlerized versions of the conductor's letters. Other newspapers quickly followed suit.

On April 6, 1918 Muck was taken to Ft. Oglethorpe, Georgia, an internment camp where he would spend the remainder of the war. Anita took lodgings in Chattanooga, Tennessee, located only seven miles to the north; she was allowed to see her husband quite frequently. She died in Germany in 1921.[28]

At its peak Ft. Oglethorpe housed approximately 3,400 people, primarily noncombatant enemy aliens. The facility where Muck was interned housed the elite and the artists. Though still an internment camp, the facility had a library, sporting facilities, arts and crafts, gardening, educational classes, a biweekly newspaper, and a sizeable music program. Muck, quite bitter, wanted nothing to do with the latter and Ernst Kunwald (1868–1939), former conductor of the Cincinnati Symphony and the only other conductor to be interned, cheerfully became the de facto dean. An orchestra was formed, named the Tsing-Tao Orchestra after the German protectorate in China. Muck was talked into conducting the orchestra only once, on December 12, 1918, which resulted in a riveting performance of Brahms' *Academic Festival Overture* and Beethoven's *Eroica*.[29] It was the last time Muck would conduct on American soil. He was finally released in July 1919 and departed for Europe with Anita shortly thereafter, on August 21. Muck continued his conducting career in Germany, serving as music director of the Bayreuth festival until 1930 and the Hamburg Philharmonic until 1933, resigning in protest when the Nazis came to power. Despite his despotic tendencies Muck was no Nazi, although on his 80th birthday he received a plaque from Adolph Hitler. Muck died on March 3, 1940.

In the United States, the name Karl Muck had become so synonymous with amorality and anti-Americanism that steps were taken to expunge the memory of Muck's association with the Boston Symphony Orchestra. This was accomplished in part by expurgating him from their joint legacy: the recordings made with The Victor Talking Machine Company. Muck's name was no longer included on any new copies of the four sides of the orchestra's recordings already released, and production of the remaining six sides was halted. It wasn't until 1995 that the five surviving sides of this group would be released, as part of a historical CD set.[30]

On May 4, 1918 Higginson, by then eighty-three years old and in ill health, turned control of the Boston Symphony Orchestra over to a board of trustees headed by Judge Frederick P. Cabot. In a letter to Richard Aldrich written on January 4, 1920, Hale commented about Higginson's departure:

> Maj. Higginson acted badly for a year before he died towards the orchestra. From a letter he wrote me after Dr. Muck had been interned I know that he professed pacifistic faith in him to the last. In spite of his constitution, I think that his heart was badly shaken by Muck's conduct. Not a word from him—if he had nominally remained [,] the orchestra after Muck's withdrawal would have saved much trouble and financial loss. At present, I am glad to say, the hall is absolutely full at all concerts, and everyone is cheerful. One reason, I believe why he [Higginson] did not endow the orchestra by will is that his fortune was much less than was supposed....[31]

At the end of the 1917–1918 season, the orchestra dismissed eighteen Germans, including Ernst Schmidt. This may have been a moot act as a total of twenty-nine German members of the orchestra were interned.[32] Higginson commented to Gericke from a post-war perspective:

> Last May I gave up the orchestra, and it is now in the hands of an able committee who are managing it well and giving excellent concerts. All the Germans have been dropped and the Austrians kept. Rabaud, an admirable French conductor, is at the head, and the work should go on well. But I often long for a concert such as you gave us—Haydn, Mozart, Beethoven, Schubert. Only a Wiener Kind can play Schubert. You, Nikisch and Muck were great conductors, and the others were good.
>
> I like to say these things to you, because you have deserved them and because you are remembered by many, many people with deep respect and affection....
>
> I was very sorry to give up the orchestra, but there was no help for it. Naturally the war made certain things very difficult.[33]

With the war still raging in 1918, the board of trustees was not about to hire another German or Austrian to replace Muck. Myriad telegrams were sent to Allied and neutral countries about available conductors yet, with the vicissitudes of war, they were unable to hire one until July of that year. Then they played it safe, hiring Henri Rabaud (1873–1949), conductor of the Paris Opera, a composer, and a conservative programmer. With these two acts—dismissal of the Germans from the orchestra and the hiring of Rabaud—the orchestra passed through a dramatic artistic transition, shifting its orientation from German to French.

Rabaud's tenure, however, was doomed from the start. Because of the late hiring date—he was not even announced until September—and complications of getting across the Atlantic during wartime, Rabaud was unable to get to Boston for the start of the 1918–1919 season, thereby missing the first two concerts. As a substitute, the board of trustees brought in Pierre Monteux (1875–1964), then conductor of the French wing of the New York Metropolitan Opera. Monteux had experienced a series of extremes during the past few years. He had been conductor of the Ballet Russes in Paris from 1911 to 1914, which included conducting the notorious premiere of Igor Stravinsky's *Le Sacre du Printemps* (*The Rite of Spring*). That feat alone thrust Monteux into the upper echelon of the world's conductors. When war broke out, however, he found himself a private in the French army for nearly two years, seeing service at the front until Serge Diaghilev convinced the French government to allow Monteux to take the Ballet Russes on an American tour. At the end of that tour, Monteux was hired by the Met.

In a letter dated November 3, 1918, Hale commented about Monteux as well as the possible conductor search to Higginson:

> Mr. Monteux made a most favorable impression on orchestra and public. Mr. Rabaud, no doubt, will be a worthy successor, but as he probably can stay only this season, the committee would not make a serious blunder if it should engage Mr. Monteux for 1918–19, provided it cannot secure Mr. Toscanini. I am not sure that Mr. Monteux would not in the end be the more capable man for this specific service....[34]

It is interesting to note that in this letter, Hale went far beyond his roles of music critic and program essayist in making recommendations about conductors. His suggestions were, of course, personal and moot to a degree since Higginson was no longer controlling the orchestra at this point. It is not known whether Higginson responded or whether he forwarded Hale's suggestions.

So, was the hiring of Rabaud merely a stopgap measure? In the index of Bliss Perry's 1920 book on Higginson, Rabaud is listed as "interim conductor."[35] Hale's letter also seems to add weight to this. In his reviews of Rabaud, however, Hale never mentions this possibility and was quick to praise the conductor:

FOURTH CONCERT BY SYMPHONY

Mr. Rabaud Gives Delightful Reading of Schubert's "Unfinished" Work

REPEAT THE SAME PROGRAM TONIGHT

By PHILIP HALE

The fourth concert of the Boston Symphony Orchestra, Mr. Rabaud, conductor took place yesterday afternoon in Symphony Hall. The program was as follows: Schubert, "Unfinished Symphony;["] Grieg: piano concerto (Mme. Olga Samaroff, pianist); Saint-Saëns, Symphony in C minor, No. 3.

When Joachim, one of the most impotent and stupid conductors we ever knew, was about to give a performance of the "Unfinished" symphony, he asked many musicians of Berlin what they thought the pace of the second theme, first announced by the violoncellos in the first movement, should be. Some conductors sentimentalize this theme, dragging the pace until the song becomes lackadaisical. Mr. Rabaud is a musician of taste and judgment; he did not fall into this error. The symphony is eminently Schubertian in its beauty and in its weakness. For the most part the composer pipes his songs of innocence as the boy heard by William Blake; but in the first movement there are measures of a grandeur that is seldom found in Schubert's compositions. In these measures we recognize the Schubert that conceived the "Doppelgaenger," the "Gruppe aus Tartarus," the "Dwarf" and a few other songs in which dramatic force comes before charming lyricism.

Mr. Rabaud gave a most impressive interpretation of these measures. The whole movement by the force of the contrast gained thereby. As for the second movement, which shows Schubert's tendency toward prolixity, and is so inferior to the first that one rejoices because the symphony was left unfinished, all that is to be done with it is to let the composer pipe his pretty tunes. Some day a conductor may have the courage to play the first movement alone, a noble fragment, comparable with that torso in literature, the "Hyperion," of Keats.

Schubert wrote "Current a Calamo." It was otherwise with the Saint-Saëns of the C minor symphony. We doubt whether his head were hot and his feet cold when he was engaged in the composition; but that head was full of invention and contrapuntal skill. We spoke last Saturday, discussing Saint-Saëns' symphonic poems, of the clearness and the logic of his musical thought. These qualities are as fully displayed in the symphony, which is nore of a triumph of workmanship. The serenity of the adagio, the fantastic presto, and the majesty of the section before the brilliant coda, with its jubilant blasts of brass, are imaginative pages, not merely the carefully written measures of an accomplished technician. The symphony had been heard at these concerts on at least four occasions. It was also played here by this orchestra when the composer was present, but as pianist and composer, not as conductor. Never was it so interesting, never so imposing, as it was yesterday under the direction of Mr. Rabaud.

When Mme. Samaroff played here with the orchestra from 1906 till late 1909, her performance was distinguished chiefly by a peculiar brilliance. Her treatment of emotional passages left one cold. Yesterday one noticed a change of style. Her touch had more poetic quality. She was lyrical rather than defiantly theatrical, although there was sufficient force in the stormier pages. This concerto, which some think has had its day, gives delight solely by its purely lyrical quality; not by any suggestion of folk dance; not by the bravura measures and the crashing apotheosis, which are of decidedly secondary quality. Mme. Samaroff did well to discriminate in this manner; to sing rather than to disclaim. In doing this, she unfortunately too often made the mistake of underemphasis. There were times when the piano part, being of the first importance, was heard only with strained ears, so that the first movement was on the whole pale, without vitality. Nor was this in any way the fault of Mr. Rabaud, whose accompaniment was sympathetic and delightful throughout.[36]

From the above critique, it would seem that Hale had heard the Grieg piano concerto once too often. Yet when this concerto was performed the next time, a little more than two years later, with Pierre Monteux the conductor and the eccentric Percy Grainger the piano soloist, he was quite complimentary:

Mr. Grainger played the familiar concerto in a delightfully musical manner. Not relying solely on fleetness and brilliancy, he gave a finely conceived and detailed performance of the first movement, too often read in a perfunctory manner by pianists impatient to show what they "can do" later when insistent demands are made on technical proficiency. And so, well-worn as this concerto is, yesterday it had fresh life, nor was the workmanship displayed by the composer the only attractive feature of the music itself.[37]

Rabaud's initial contract was for just one year. Some accounts state that his season was not a success, yet reviews do not bear this out. Whatever the case, either by his own choosing or that of a board of trustees eager to sign Monteux, Rabaud vacated his post at the end of the 1918–1919 season and returned to Paris. In 1922, upon the resignation of Gabriel Fauré, he became director of the Paris Conservatoire.

Monteux was ready to step in; he was already in the country and was immediately awarded a five-year contract. He grabbed the bull by the horns from the very start. His October 31, 1919 concert was truly remarkable, featuring three Boston premieres of major works as well as an incredible star soloist: Haydn's *Symphony No. 85 in E flat*, "La Reine" ("The Queen of France"), Stravinsky's *Firebird Suite*, and Serge Rachmaninoff performing his own *Piano Concerto No. 3 in D minor*.

RACHMANINOFF WILDLY CHEERED

Pianist in Impressive Performance at Fourth Symphony Concert

"QUEEN OF FRANCE" BY HAYDN SCORES

By PHILIP HALE

The fourth concert of the Boston Symphony Orchestra, Mr. Monteux, conductor, took place yesterday afternoon in Symphony Hall. The program was as follows: Haydn, Symphony, "The Queen of France" (first time in Boston); Rachmaninoff: Concerto No. 3 for piano and orchestra (first time in Boston); Stravinsky, Suite from the ballet "The Fire-Bird" (first time at these concerts). Mr. Rachmaninoff was the soloist.

It is a surprising fact that the orchestra played Haydn's Symphony for the first time; nor have we been able to find the record of performance by any orchestra in Boston at a public concert. Haydn's symphonies were heard here often in the last years of the 18th century, and it is more than probable that "The Queen of France" was one of them; but there is no means of identifying any one of these Symphonies, for they were entered on the program as "Grand Symphony," "Overture," or "Full Piece."

Bülow once spoke of "The Queen of France" as "a miniature symphony to be performed in a miniature room by a miniature orchestra," and he referred sarcastically to a performance of it by "60 fiddlers and six tooters." Now Haydn wrote "The Queen of France" for Paris, a city that was accustomed to large orchestras. He wrote it for the "Concert de la Loge Olympique," a society that replaced the "Concert des Amateurs," and this orchestra numbered 40 fiddles, 12 violoncellos, eight double basses, and the usual number of wind instruments. It is not likely that "The Queen of France" was first performed by a little orchestra.

Yesterday the string section was somewhat reduced and the wood wind was doubled. Would the symphony seem fresher, more sparkling, if it were performed in a little hall by a small orchestra? We doubt it. As it was played yesterday the first movement and the trio of the Minuet gave special pleasure. The variations of the pretty French song of old time do not stray so far from the theme itself as to relieve the movement from the reproach of monotony.

Mr. Rachmaninoff played his third concerto 10 years ago in New York. The performance was the first one. The prevailing mood of the music is one of sadness, a melancholy now subdued, now defiant; hardly relieved until the final outburst of hope, joy, what-you-will, by capricious episodes, as if one forced oneself to take a more sanguine view of life and then sank back, resigned to fate, or rebellious. The first movement is the most imaginative, the most impressive. We know of few first movements, if any, in the repertoire that equal it. The attention of the hearer is at once riveted; the mood is at once established. Low mutterings as of "the compulsive millions of men" under a leaden sky; the sadness of it; the thought of a brooding, sinister Fate, not quite ready to deal the final blow—thus this music may be characterized without extravagance, without any laborious attempt at fine writing. The intermezzo, while it is interesting, often poetic, falls below this Allegro. Nor is the Finale, in spite of the exciting moments, the contrasting episodes and the thrilling apotheosis, equal in musical and psychological importance or in technical construction to this constantly sustained, firmly knit, inevitable first movement. Yet the two last movements in another concerto would make their irresistible way. It would be a pleasure to speak of the workmanship displayed, of the character of the melodic and harmonic schemes of the skilled orchestration. The performance by the pianist was a remarkable one, remarkable even for Mr. Rachmaninoff. The pianist and the composer were one and the same being. Thoughtful, imaginative, brilliant as this performance was, the virtuoso did not allow one to forget the music or regard it as merely an opportunity for the display of the pianist.

The orchestra played as if inspired, with even more than its customary elasticity, tonal strength and beauty in solo passages and in ensemble. The great audience recalled Mr. Rachmaninoff again and again. Seldom has a pianist received so flattering a tribute in Symphony Hall.

Information in the program book about first performances of Stravinsky's works was gained from contemporary French and English journals, and from supposedly authoritative annals. Yet, in some instances, this information is inaccurate. Thus there was a performance of "The Fire-Bird" in London, led by Mr. Monteux, before Rhene-Baton conducted it. Mr. Monteux also conducted the first performance of "Petrouchka" in Paris and the first performance of the opera "Le Rossignol" at the Paris Opera. How the contemporary journals could be so mistaken is not easily comprehended.

The performance of the suite from "The Fire-Bird" brought pleasant recollections of the ballet. To anyone that has seen this ballet, the music in concert form, however detachable it is, is less significant. On the other hand, seeing a ballet, one necessarily too often disregards the music. In the Suite the sport, the fascinating dance of the Princesses, and the charming Lullaby—which, by the way, Mr. Monteux interpolated—are the most effective as concert music. The "Danse Infernale," away from the stage, suffers the most severely of all the movements. The performance of the Suite was exceedingly brilliant.

The concert will be repeated tonight. There will be no concert next week. The program of November 7, 8 is as follows: Berlioz, Symphony "Harold in Italy" (Mr. Denayer, solo viola): Chadwick, "The Angel of Death," Symphony poem (first time here); Chabrier-Mottl: Bouree Fantastique. Mme. Povia Frijsh will sing an air from Franck's "Redemption" and these songs with orchestra: Duparc, Invitation au Voyage; Moussorgsky, Hopak; Bloch, Psalms 137 and 114.[38]

From the programming of this concert as well as that listed for the next, it is apparent that Monteux was renewing the orchestra primarily along French lines—even the Haydn symphony had a French connection. This approach didn't bother Hale, of course. What did bother him, however, was the out-of-town perception that the Boston Symphony Orchestra had gone downhill. He commented to Aldrich about statements made by New York music critic James Gibbons Huneker:

> ...I love Jim the man, but I have been secretly disappointed in his critical work for the last two years. He seems to me to be without judgment. That means his constant trumping of Walter Damrosch? Why does he keep harping on the "once great [estate?]" of the Boston Orchestra? Over here we are...proud of it and think it better than ever. We are also foolish enough to like Mr. Monteux and we prefer him to Dr. Muck.— this without thought of the latter's Germanism. The strings under Dr. Muck had lost quality. Now they sound as they did under Mr. Gericke.[39]

In January 1920 Monteux's contract was extended. Hale was ecstatic and commented, "The trustees of this orchestra and the city of Boston may well be congratulated on the reappointment of Mr. Monteux for a term of two years."[40]

To the Boston populace, it now appeared that the orchestra had clearly moved beyond the crises of the recent past. The optimism was short-lived, however, as a compete break with one particular entity of the past—Higginson's benign dictatorship—resulted in a heightened degree of labor unrest. Post-war inflation was beginning to take its toll on the players. In October 1914, the minimum salary for Boston Symphony Orchestra members was $1400. This had not changed in five years. On February 6, 1920, a letter was sent from violinist Rudolf C. Ringwall to Judge Cabot. This letter, signed by nearly all of the orchestra personnel by sections, asked for a raise of $1,000 (to $2400) starting with the 1920–1921 season.[41] Three weeks later Cabot received another letter, this one from the players saying that they had formed a union, the Boston Symphony Orchestra Members Association.[42]

The orchestra's American-born concertmaster, Fredric Fradkin, supported these efforts. Fradkin had toured with Monteux on the 1916 Ballet Russes American tour and was initially hired by the Boston Symphony as Rabaud's concertmaster in 1918. Later, his contract was extended to cover 1919–1920 and 1920–1921.[43]

Tensions were escalating and it appeared that a strike was inevitable. Representatives of the Detroit Symphony Orchestra were already in Boston, doing some informal recruiting of players and it was reported that the Philadelphia Orchestra was about to do the same. On Wednesday, March 3, Cabot sent letters to both orchestras.[44,45] The following evening, at Sanders Theatre on the Harvard University campus, there was a heated exchange of words between Fradkin and Monteux. Things came to a head the following day, at a Friday afternoon concert at Symphony Hall, when Fradkin remained seated after Monteux had motioned the orchestra to stand. Hale, who had astutely stayed away from commenting about the Muck situation in his reviews, was greatly offended by Fradkin's insolence. Not surprisingly, he addressed the incident in his review of the concert; what is surprising is that his account of it takes up more than half the review:

SYMPHONY GIVES
17TH CONCERT

Ovation Acclaims Greatest
Success Achieved in
Thirty Years

FRADKIN INCIDENT
MARS PROGRAM

By PHILIP HALE

The 17th concert of the Boston Symphony Orchestra, Mr. Monteux conductor, took place yesterday afternoon in Symphony Hall. The program was as follows: Berlioz, Fantastic Symphony; Malipiero, "Pauses of Silence"; Borodin, "On the Steppes of Central Asia"; Wagner, overture to "The Flying Dutchman."

When Mr. Monteux came on the platform he was greeted with extraordinarily hearty and prolonged applause.

After a brilliant performance of the symphony—a performance that has not been equaled here for 30 years, that has been approached only by the one given by a visiting orchestra led by Mr. Weingartner in Symphony Hall, Mr. Monteux was, naturally recalled. He was recalled again. He then invited the orchestra to share in the applause. All stood, except Mr. Fredric Fradkin, the concert master. Whatever personal disagreement there may be between the conductor and concert-master—the reports published in the newspapers have been exaggerated and evidently one-sided—the platform of Symphony Hall is not in the course of a Symphony concert the place to air a real or fancied grievance. Mr. Fradkin, by not rising with the others, acted discourteously toward the applauding audience. When he left the stage for the intermission many in the audience hissed him for his rudeness. When he returned some, especially in the second balcony, applauded; there was also some hissing; some in the orchestra were so tactless, not to say discourteous, toward the audience, as to join in the applause. Mr. Fradkin had the assurance to stand up this time. He bowed to the audience and the orchestra.

As soon as Mr. Monteux reappeared there was a mighty counter-demonstration. The applause was enthusiastic; it grew louder and louder until the great audience stood for some time, clapping hands vigorously; there was also cheering. Mr. Monteux then went on with the concert.

It was a deplorable scene. Nothing like it had happened in the history of the orchestra. May nothing like it happen again! No player, before yesterday, had allowed personal feeling to overcome him so as to forget the observance of common courtesy toward men and women that were generous in their support and in their appreciation of the orchestra to which he belonged.

The symphony is an amazing work; not only because it was first played 90 years ago when Beethoven had not been dead four years and young Wagner was studying at Leipsic; not only because in orchestration it was a revelation; it is amazing today by reason of the wild imagination, the flaming romanticism, the audacities in musical thought and musical expression. If Berlioz had not lived, the men that came after him, Wagner included, would have been obliged to work out painfully their own orchestral salvation. The influence of this genius, a man practically self-taught, a master of no instrument, brilliant as critic and essayist, a poet when writing a treatise on instrumentation, profoundly unhappy, unappreciated in his own city until long after his death, a self-torturer; the influence of this man is still felt throughout the musical world.

After the scene that has been described, the audience was hardly in a quietly receptive mood, yet there was again wonder at the moods of Malipiero's "expressions," music that 50 years from now may be to hearers as simple as Haydn's is now to us; there was enjoyment of Borodin's Sketch and Wagner's engrossing overture.

The concert will be repeated tonight. The program of next week is as follows: Mendelssohn, Overture, Nocturne and Scherzo from his music to "A Midsummer Night's Dream"; Loeffler, "A Pagan Poem" (piano, Mr. Gebhard, English horn, Mr. Speyer); Glazounoff, Symphony No. 6, C minor.[46]

Hale, of course, had been a Boston music critic for over thirty years at this point in time, yet one wonders if his particular accolade about this performance of the Berlioz *Symphonie Fantastique* being "a performance that has not been equaled here in 30 years" was written primarily to offset the Fradkin incident. Hale may have had even more to say about the latter, but he was very busy, covering the Chicago Opera Association's production of Debussy's *Pellas et Melisande* at the Boston Opera House that evening.

The orchestra's board of trustees met that same evening and voted to terminate Fradkin's contract. Cabot immediately sent news of the board's action to Fradkin: "...In pursuance of this action of the Trustees you are hereby notified that you are dismissed from the Boston Symphony Orchestra Inc. I enclose a check for $234.38 in payment of your agreed compensation to the time of dismissal."[47] This all occurred over night; the following morning the press printed the entirety of the board's letter, news of Fradkin's intent to sue the orchestra over his dismissal, and an apology from Fradkin to the public:

I humbly apologize to the audience and to the public, if they feel I have offend them in any way by not rising and joining in the tribute to Mr. Monteux....

When the conductor turned around to bow his acknowledgements for the third time he signaled for the orchestra to rise, but I remained seated. From the unexpected ovation I strongly felt that something or other had been planted to uphold him in his tiff with me and to get the audience to show its disapproval of my action in joining the union, and their approval of Conductor Monteux's action in showing his disapproval of the same.

I felt deeply hurt, as it appeared to me as if the audience was trying to impress upon me, by the cajolery of something that failed to show on the surface, that I was agitating a movement of some kind that was distasteful, or spelled propaganda, although I am a naturalized America citizen and have been for years.

This tremendous demonstration to Mr. Monteux came after the first Berlioz symphony, and it was so pronounced that I didn't rise because I felt the applause offered was not intended for me.[48]

That same day, March 6, 1920, in a meeting held across the street from Symphony Hall, the seventy-four union members asked the board of trustees to reinstate Fradkin. When this didn't happen, thirty-five of the ninety-one players in the Boston Symphony Orchestra went on strike, refusing to play on the concert that evening. Cabot and Monteux tried to convince the players to stop the strike, but to no avail.

The walkout did not set well with either the board or symphony patrons and the following morning the *Boston Herald* listed the names of all thirty-five strikers as well as what instruments they played.[49] Wishing not to waste any time, the board offered individual hearings to those strikers wishing to remain with the orchestra. These took place with Cabot at Symphony Hall from 2:00 to 5:00 p.m. on Sunday, March 8. Only three of the strikers, including Ringwall, took advantage of the offer and asked for reinstatement. Their requests, however, were rejected by the board.[50] Two days later Cabot sent a letter to each of the strikers announcing their dismissal. Thus, within two years, counting the dismissal of the eighteen German players during the war, the orchestra had lost at least fifty-three members—a disaster that would have shut down just about any other performing ensemble.

The board, needing to quell concerns among symphony patrons, published a three-page letter of explanation in pamphlet form:

BOSTON, MASS., March 10, 1920

To the Supporters of the Boston Symphony Orchestra:

Recent events have produced a condition in the affairs of the Boston Symphony Orchestra which calls for a frank statement from the Trustees.

It should be said at the outset that the termination of Mr. Fradkin's connection with the Orchestra bore no relation to his activities on behalf of the musicians' union. Mr. Fradkin was concert master, and as such had the special duty of maintaining the standards and discipline of the Orchestra. Under such circumstances his conduct was a breach of discipline and a discourtesy to the Orchestra's audience, which, in the light of his contracted obligations, would have required prompt and decisive action by the Trustees at any time.

The question of the affiliation of members of the Orchestra with the American Federation of Musicians, through the "Local" known as the Boston Musicians' Protective Association, is not of recent origin. The general problem confronted Major Higginson early in the thirty-seven years of his maintenance of the Orchestra. He took and resolutely held the position that the artistic ideals of the Orchestra he had established required absolute liberty in its management...Shortly after the present Trustees assumed the conduct of the Orchestra, this question was raised again. The Trustees made no objection to the affiliation of members of the Orchestra with the Federation of Musicians, provided it could be brought about consistently with those ideals of the Orchestra which had become its most cherished traditions. The rules of the Association, as then shown and explained to the Trustees, were not consistent with such ideals. Substantially they provided for the "closed shop":— that is, only members of the Association could play in the Orchestra....[51]

The letter continues, with explanations about the difficulties the orchestra would have had in obtaining certain players had the orchestra been unionized.

The middle portion deals with finances—securing additional funds through an extension of the Pops season and in securing a large endowment. After again slamming the American Federation of Musicians for the rigidity of its rules, the board ended with a reiteration of what it considered its altruistic nature:

> The trustees of the orchestra have for their chief concern its continuance and development as the splendid instrument of art and civilization into which it has grown through its nearly forty years of existence. Their concern is for the exceptional, the best; the concern of the Federation is, of necessity, for the general, the average. The trustees believe that in a conflict between the rules representing these two ideals, they cannot accept the second, and that an upholding of the first will make in the long run not only for the higher standards of art but for the better interests of the members of the Orchestra.[52]

The position of the board was very clear, and the pamphlet idea worked. Dozens of letters were sent in support. There was another effort on the part of the players to unionize the orchestra in late 1925,[53] but the board once again staved off the attempt. It wasn't until 1942 that the Boston Symphony Orchestra became the last of the nation's professional orchestras to unionize.

The orchestra had been crippled by the strike, but not destroyed by it. There were still fifty-six players who had not struck and, fortunately for the orchestra, the strike itself had not obliterated any sections entirely. Thus there remained a key core of players who could then be supplemented by the hiring of additional personnel as needed. Still, Monteux had to replace twenty violins and violas; thus, the programming was affected. Of the works projected for the March 13th concert, mentioned at the end of Hale's previous review, only the Mendelssohn was retained. Heinrich Gebhard was still the piano soloist, but Loeffler's *Pagan Poem* was replaced with yet another performance of Grieg's *Piano Concerto in A minor*, and Glazounov's *Symphony No. 6 in C minor* was replaced with Beethoven's *Symphony No. 4 in B flat*, Op. 60, which features the smallest instrumentation of the nine. Hale commented briefly on this in his review, the first post-strike concert:

18TH CONCERT
OF SYMPHONY

Great Audience Welcomes
Conductor Monteux
And His Players

FINEP ERFORMANCE
STIRSE NTHUSIASM

By PHILIP HALE

The 18th concert of the Boston Symphony Orchestra, Mr. Monteux, conductor, took place yesterday afternoon in Symphony Hall. The program, necessarily changed from the one announced last week, was a s follows: Mendelssohn: Overture, Nocturne, and Scherzo from "A Midsummer Night's Dream"; Grieg,

Concerto for piano and orchestra (Mr. Gebhard, pianist); Beethoven: Symphony No. 4.

The great audience welcomed Mr. Monteux and the faithful men of the orchestra warmly. The enthusiasm showed conclusively appreciation of the stand taken by the trustees and of the loyalty shown by so many valuable, distinguished players. It also showed a confidence in the future and the glory of the orchestra, a confidence not to be shaken.

The performance deserved the hearty applause that punctuated the concert throughout. It is hardly necessary to write at length concerning the music itself. Mendelssohn's overture and Scherzo are still delightful. Would that he had always written in this vein, for he was, first of all, a romanticist, never so happy as when excited by a fantastical subject, as by Shakespeare's comedy, or "The First Walpurgis Night," or by a scene in Nature, as in the overture to "The Hebrides." In the Nocturne we note the peculiarly suave sentiment that too often degenerated into rank sentimentalism, as in many of the "Songs without Words." Mr. Wendler, horn, and Mr. Laurent, flute, contributed so greatly to the success of the performance that they were obliged to come forward in acknowledgement of the applause; the applause was also for whole orchestra. The Scherzo was played with the utmost delicacy and crispness and the wood-wind choir covered itself with glory.

Admirable, too was Mr. Monteux's reading of the symphony which, with the exception of the Adagio, is not among the great works of "the deaf man of Bonn," as he was recently characterized by a flippant critic. Here, as in the performance of Mendelssohn's music, there was ever-present clarity and a fine sense of proportion.

Is Grieg's concerto becoming shop-worn? Mr. Gebhard's playing of it was brilliant, rather than poetic or romantic. The better portions of the concerto are surely romantic. In the first movement he appeared to be in a restless mood; the lyric passages were not sufficiently elastic; more than once a phrase sung enchantingly by the violoncellos was repeated by the pianist rigidly. It should be remembered, however, that Mr. Gebhard played at comparatively short notice.[54]

Hale wasn't finished with post-strike commentary just yet. It is apparent from his review three weeks later that he fully supported the board's position, especially the point about establishing an endowment. He was now sixty-six years old. At an age when most people would have been retired, he was enjoying his work fully; thirty years of critiquing Boston Symphony Orchestra concerts and nineteen years of writing program notes had turned Hale into the orchestra's biggest fan. He praised the strings' performance of Georg Friedrich Händel's *Concerto Grosso No. 5 in D* and Bedrich Smetana's overture to *The Bartered Bride*, complimenting the newly hired players while launching a vector toward those who had struck:

There was a triumph of strings in Handel's concerto and in Smetana's overture. Mr. Monteux had confidence in the new members; his confidence was fully justified. It may be said without exaggeration that the present section of second violins is the most capable in the history of the orchestra. Admirable, too was the work of the other players on stringed instruments. All were severely tested; all acquitted themselves gloriously. The young blood in the orchestra of today is more than a fair exchange for the phlegm of past seasons. The new members and the old were on their mettle.

> Now is the time for the trustees to make an energetic, unrelaxing "drive" for the desired endowment. The orchestra, today, is a superb body of players; it will even be a more magnificent institution at the beginning of next season. The great ability of Mr. Monteux as disciplinarian and interpreter is fully recognized. Interest in the "new" orchestra, which contains nearly all the famous players of the past, is at its height. The great public, not only the audiences, should take pride in the orchestra as a civic institution. It should also forbid insidious German propaganda to work its mole-like way in matters of art.
>
> Mr. Monteux has proved that as a program-maker he is far from being a chauvinist; he welcomes music of all nations, provided the music is good.[55]

The last sentence of the second paragraph is an admonition about the combination of politics and art. Ever since his earliest days in Boston, Hale had fought against the predominance of German music in the Boston Symphony Orchestra's programming. The symphony now had a conductor whose approach to programming was something more pleasing to him. Of course, Hale had no idea at this point how prophetic his phrase "insidious German propaganda to work its mole-like way in matters of art" was. The next dozen or so years would give rise to the Nazi party, who would publish lists of composers whose music would be forbidden to be heard over the airwaves and in the concert hall.

One of the final concerts that spring was a pension fund concert featuring the Harvard University Glee Club and its conductor, Dr. Archibald T. Davison. Hale himself held fond memories of having accompanied the Yale Glee Club as a student some forty-five years earlier. He commented:

> Harvard University may well be proud of the Glee Club and the conductor of it. It should be remembered that the personnel necessarily changes with each graduating class. This makes the task of drilling the more arduous.
>
> There was a time when the Glee clubs of Harvard and Yale sang chiefly college and popular songs for their own amusement and for the pleasure of the alumni in the cities the cubs visited...Dr. Davison has taught these students intelligently, musically; he has not overstrained them, for they sang yesterday with delightful spontaneity, yet with a careful regard for nuances of expression, with a mastery of dynamic gradations. In piano passages there was security of intonation; when full vocal strength demanded, tonal quality was not lost. Especially noteworthy was the performance of the music by Lotti and Leisring, a performance that might excite the envy of any male chorus composed of picked professional singers who had long worked together.
>
> It was a pleasure to hear the choruses from [Anton Rubinstein's] "The Tower of Babel." When this oratorio was performed by the Handel and Haydn Society in 1883 the music given to the Shemites and the Hamites was thought to be extremely oriental. In 1920 young composers, French, Americans, English, when their musical thoughts turn eastward, are more oriental than the orientals themselves.
>
> It was a happy thought to call in the assistance of the Harvard Glee Club for this occasion. The club responded in most generous spirit. Let us hope that these singers next season may be heard in some important work for male voices and orchestra at a subscription concert.[56]

The following year the Harvard Glee Club would be joined by the Radcliffe Choral Society, which Davidson also conducted, on a Boston Symphony Orchestra subscription concert featuring music from Wagner's Parsifal.[57]

At the end of the 1919–1920 season, Monteux had his sights on hiring a permanent concertmaster. With lingering effects of the recent war still being felt in central Europe, Monteux turned toward the north and asked Georg Lennart Schneévoight (1872–1947), conductor of the Royal Stockholm Philharmonic Orchestra, for suggestions. Schneévoight recommended Polish-born Richard Burgin (1892–1981) who had worked with him not only in Stockholm, but also in Helsingfors (Helsinki), and Christiania (Oslo). Schneévoight then arranged for a visa for Burgin so that he could go to Paris to play for Monteux. Burgin commented:

> I played for Monteux at his home. He told me that unfortunately his piano playing was very poor and he could only play some of the harmonies once in a while. He asked me what I wanted to play from the standard repertoire—Tchaikovsky, Brahms, Beethoven. I played a section of this and that for about 45 minutes in all. He didn't bother me about orchestral works because he knew I'd been concertmaster for Schneévoigt for five or six years. Nevertheless, I thought I'd better tell him that I was not too familiar with contemporary music outside of Germany since the conductors whom I knew didn't care much for contemporary music. In Sweden we had had to play twice the nine Beethoven symphonies, and symphonies by Bruckner and Brahms. I told Monteux that I knew very few things in the French repertoire and that I wasn't familiar with modern compositions. He replied very charmingly, "Neither do I know modern music. Nobody can tell what's going to be composed, but I hope I will conduct it and we'll study it together."
>
> Well, Monteux evidently liked my playing and he told me to return to London immediately and sign a contract. The manager of the BSO, Mr. Brennan, was still in London, but had to leave for America the next day by boat. I succeeded in getting a permit to go to London, which was very difficult at that time. I reached Mr. Brennan, signed the contract to go to Boston, and that was how Monteux engaged me.[58]

It was the start of a stable conductor–concertmaster relationship the orchestra had not previously known. In his amazing forty-two-year tenure in Boston, Burgin served as concertmaster for only three conductors: Monteux, Koussevitzky, and Munch. At least some of this had to do with the manner in which he was treated. While retaining his position as concertmaster, Burgin also became conductor of the Boston Symphony Orchestra's Young People's Concerts (1924–1934), then guest conductor of the orchestra on an annual basis, then assistant conductor (1927–1943), and finally associate conductor (1943–1967).

Monteux and Burgin worked together over the next four years to mold the sound of the string section. These were their "salad days," with the twenty-eight-year-old Burgin meeting and planning daily with the forty-five-year-old conductor. By mid-season Hale was ready to fully endorse Monteux's efforts. He spoke highly of the conductor on a personal level at the beginning of a review that contained hints of satire:

11TH CONCERT
BY SYMPHONY

Performance of Debussy's
"La Mer" Poetic and Impressive

ISOLDE MENGES AS
SOLO VIOLINIST

by PHILIP HALE

The eleventh concert of the Boston Symphony orchestra, Mr. Monteux conductor, took place yesterday afternoon in Symphony Hall. The program was a follows: Schubert: Overture in the Italian Style, C-major; Haydn, "Military" Symphony; Bruch: Concerto for Violin, G-minor, No. 1; Debussy, "La Mer." The solo violinist was Isolde Menges, who played with the orchestra for the first time.

The feature of this concert was the performance of "La Mer." There have been five performances before yesterday, but no one of them was so poetic, so impressive. We sometimes wonder if the symphony audience fully appreciates what Mr. Monteux is doing for music in this city; if it fully appreciates his catholicity of taste as shown by his programs; his interest in the work of the younger composers of all nations; his skill as a disciplinarian and as an interpreter of works ancient, modern and ultra-modern. He is a singularly modest man, not one to blow his own horn; not one to make a sensational display; he is not a parlor-lion, seeking to make himself "popular" by gaining the sweet influence of ladies. A man of a refined nature, well-informed, courteous, he is devoted to his art and his family. No conductor since Mr. Henschel has been so fortunate in program-making, and Mr. Henschel as a conductor was the veriest amateur learning his trade at the expense of the orchestra and the audience. It is not extravagant to say that the concerts this season have, on the whole, been the most uniformly interesting in the history of the orchestra; some of them have been the most brilliant. We are fortunate, indeed, that this most musical conductor dwells here and is in command.

Is "La Mer" to be ranked among Debussy's greater compositions? Some years ago M. Louis Laloy, always an admirer of Debussy, welcomed, apropos of "La Mer," when he called a happy change in Debussy's art: at first wholly an impressionist, he came to adopt more simple forms, more precise ideas, a more solid construction, more vigorous rhythms, without losing anything of his finesse or his freshness. It is true that in "La Mer" the developments are largely planned; the three sections might be called the first movement, the Scherzo, and the Finale of a symphony; but this does not make the music any more beautiful. There is much in the saying of Plotinus that fire surpasses other bodies in beauty because it obtains the order of form "and is the most subtle of all, bordering as it were on an incorporeal nature." There is more intensity, more power in "La Mer" than in the preceding orchestral works of Debussy; there is also the indefinable, entrancing subtlety.

If one says, "But to me the ocean is different from this," the answer is that the ocean is what one sees and feels in its presence. To the sailor the ocean is not so mysterious as it is to the landsman. Quote the famous line of Aeschylus, or poems of Byron, Swinburne, Whitman, to him, and he would find nothing in them. In this music of Debussy is what the word "ocean" suggests to the imaginative. Mr. Jones may long for a prolonged orchestral storm. Mrs. Jones may miss the rocking that she finds in the first movement of "Scheherazade;" to Miss Jones the ocean is only an excuse for showing herself liberally in a becoming bathing suit. The poetry of the ocean, sportive, tender, capricious, ironically jovial, sublime, terrible, escapes this amiable family. What to the three is this music of Debussy?

Whether Schubert's overture was written in mockery of Rossini or in admiration of his genius—the latter hypothesis is the safer—the fact remains that Rossini did the thing much better. (There is an eloquent tribute in the December number of the Chesterian of London by—of all men in the world—Alfredo Casella).

There are perhaps a dozen of Haydn's Symphonies seldom played that would be agreeable to hear. We found the "Military Symphony," in spite of the admirable performance, for the most part dull. Even the bass drum, the triangle and the cymbals do not save it. Did Haydn introduce these percussion instruments to arouse the three-bottle gentry and the bulbous matrons of London from their slumber?

Miss Menges showed a rich tone and emotional feeling in Bruch's hackneyed, mushy and splurgy concerto. She has, undoubtedly, what so many singers fondly think they have, viz. temperament. It is unfortunate that she has not learned to play with greater bodily repose, with authoritative ease and poise.[59]

Some may have argued that Hale was being a Francophile here: chauvinistic to the French while disparaging to the German speakers. After all, his critique of the music in Debussy's "La Mer" was quite positive while that in the Schubert, Haydn, and Bruch was negative. Yet this argument is negated by his review of the orchestra's 17 subscription concert that year (March 4, 1921), in a critique of the *Symphony No. 3 in A minor*, "Scottish," by Felix Mendelssohn, a composer whose music he often did not enjoy:

As the ultra-radical Alfredo Casella astonished his countrymen and others by praising the music of Rossini, so Darius Milhaud, a composer of ultra-modern tendencies, has surprised Frenchmen by stating that Mendelssohn was the greatest classic of the 19th century. The symphony played yesterday—Mr. Monteux and the superb orchestra gave an eloquent performance—is about 80 years old. Hearing it, one can grasp Milhaud's meaning; for Mendelssohn, a stickler for form, yet occasionally a romanticist, observed the orthodox conventions with constant attention to a beauty that had not the strangeness in its nature commended by Bacon in his essay. It was very seldom that Mendelssohn let himself go as he did in "The First Walpurgis Night." He seldom screamed, for screaming would not have been well-bred. He measured carefully his effects; he made his points neatly. Over-praised in his lifetime, too long a fetish in England, he has since been under-rated. He was the incarnation of musical orthodoxy. His radical feeling, if he had any, is not to be detected in his music. He never exulted in it as Mr. Bloch does today.

Yet, when all is said, this "Scotch" symphony contains beautiful and delightful pages. The work has not aged greatly; it is fresher than many orchestral works written a few years ago. Only in the sentimental Adagio does one find the weaker Mendelssohn, the composer of many "Songs without Words." Without using Scottish tunes, he gave the symphony a Scottish character, for he had been impressed with his visit to Holyrood; by the story of Mary and Rizzio; by the melancholy surroundings. The melancholy is gentle, contemplative in his music; the composer was not in the doleful dumps; and in the gay and exquisitely scored scherzo the Mendelssohn, constitutionally joyous—joyous always in gentlemanly fashion—is revealed. The performance without pauses, as the composer wished, was an exceedingly fine one. After the great performances of the Brahms symphony last Saturday night, after the performance of Mendelssohn's symphony yesterday, the doubting Thomases, if there are still a few, who sigh for "a conductor that is in sympathy with German music" and speak disparagingly of the orchestra, which was never in a higher estate, should hold their peace.[60]

Hale's last sentence rings true, as a look at the orchestra's 1920–1921 trip programs reveals that Monteux's programs were just as German as Muck's.

In a way, the orchestra was experiencing a renaissance in the early 1920s, with an infectious piqued sense of discovery in the works brought out by Monteux. Among the major compositions that Boston audiences heard for the first time were Kalinnikoff's *Symphony No. 1 in G minor*, Griffes's *The White Peacock*, Mahler's *Symphony No. 1 in D major*, Ravel's *La Valse*, Saint-Saëns's *Carnival of the Animals*, Dohnányi's *Violin Concerto*, Stravinsky's suite from *Pulcinella* and *Le Sacre du Printemps*, Vaughan William's *Fantasia on a Theme by Thomas Tallis*, and Holst's *The Planets*. Monteux even paid tribute to his predecessor, Henri Rabaud, by programming his "Dances from the Opera *Marouf*," and made sure the orchestra paid tribute to its American roots with Frederick Converse's *Symphony in C minor* and George Boyle's *Piano Concerto in D minor*. Hale was careful in his reviews to reach as wide a readership as possible, translating titles into English where appropriate (Saint-Saëns's *The Carnival of the Animals*) and even going overboard to a degree, referring to Ravel's *The Waltz* without including its original title.[61]

Hale showed no signs of slowing down, either personally or professionally, and on November 9, 1922 became a member of the Massachusetts Historical Society.[62] This was not a social club, but a place where he could do additional research. It was also convenient, located on Boyleston Street near The Fens, on his way to and from Symphony Hall. He also had other interests, particularly in reading, and was a fan of Herman Melville's writings. In a letter dated October 22, 1921, Melville's granddaughter, Eleanor Melville Metcalf, offered a copy of Raymond Weaver's biography of the author to Hale.[63]

The year 1923 witnessed the start of a substantial change of personnel in the music criticism industry. The *New York Tribune*'s Henry Krehbiel died on March 20. Later that spring, Hale's friend Richard Aldrich was preparing for retirement from the *New York Times* and Henry Theophilus Finck, likewise, from over forty years at the *New York Post*, though he would stay another year. Aldrich had been music critic for the *New York Times* since 1902. Olin Downes, then music critic of the *Boston Post*, one of Hale's former newspapers, was up for the job, but had reservations about taking it. Hale commented to Aldrich and offered advice on the matter:

15 Keswick Street

Boston, Massachusetts
April 29/23

Dear Richard,

I was talking with Downes Friday. He thinks that he can't live in New York with wife and children—live decently on less than $10,000. I tried to reason him out of this idea.

Dr. Brennan thinks Hughes of the Daily Telegraph (London) is the man for you; that he told Brennan when he was here that he would like a job in this country above all things. Hughes, as you know, is a man of genuine acquirements, a North of Ireland man, but a Protestant. He certainly could come for half of what Downes thinks is necessary, probably for less than that. After all, I don't wish to butt in, but I think Hughes worthy of consideration. Importing a man from London might give the <u>Times</u> greater prestige than picking one from the Boston tree.

I wish for my own sake that you were going to stay, if only for the sake of my knowledge of what takes place musically in New York. Gilman is too flowery, too precioux, too "Corinthians" as Matthew Arnold would say. To be sure there's Wm. J. but the Times should have as good a man as possible. As ever, I am

Yours sincerely,
Philip Hale[64]

As it turned out, Hale himself was being considered for the position. London *Times* music critic H. C. Colles had been a guest music critic for the *New York Times* but was now returning to the other side of the Atlantic. Adolph Simon Ochs, owner of the *New York Times*, probably didn't want to see Aldrich leave either and came up with the idea of Aldrich and Hale sharing a position starting in January 1924. The timing, however, was all wrong for Hale. The following letter shows his reluctance:

15 Keswick Street
Nov. 11, 1923

Dear Richard,

It is needless to say that I am greatly complimented by Mr. Och's suggestion that I should succeed Mr. Colles for three months. I should enjoy working for The Times and with you, though if I were in the office I should insist that we share the leaders. "Drink fair, be fair, whatever you do."

But—, although I have no written contract with the Boston Herald or the Symphony Orchestra, I do not think it would be honorable for me to leave them in the middle of the season. Furthermore, even if the editor and the management were consenting, at the end of my three months, I might find myself replaced in Boston—for no man is absolutely essential to newspaper or incorporated body. Furthermore—here I have a house which I have been improving at considerable expense. I could not leave Irene in it alone; I doubt I could sell or rent it in advantageously in January. And at the end of three months, I might be homeless. If the proposal were at the opening of the season, I should feel more hopeful about the advantageous result of an engagement in New York.

Believe me, I have considered the matter seriously and appreciate the flattering nature of the proposal and your interest in the matter. You are at liberty, of course, to share this letter with Mr. Ochs and I wish you would thank him for his thought of me.

I have taken the liberty of suggesting on the opposite page critics who might serve more than acceptably The Times.

I have not spoken to Irene about your letter, for she is at present in a nervous condition due to overwork in house settling, etc.—nothing serious, but disturbing.

With my kindest regards to your wife, believe me, as ever.

Yours affectionately,
Philip Hale

Mr. Strangways—I'm not sure about the spelling—of the Times.

ErnestN ewman

Squire of London

E. T. Baugham of London

M.J ean-Aubry

Does not Calvocoressi write in English?[65]

This was not the only offer that Hale turned down. At about the same time he had been approached by Ferris Greenslet of the Houghton Mifflin Company about writing a book:

Boston Nov. 25/1923

Dear Greenslet,

Pardon my long delay. It's very complimentary to me that you should wish a book from me, but, as I have written Mr. Wyman, I have neither time nor inclination. Newspaper articles are ephemeral. We change opinions with our skins. At least once every seven years, and I should hate to see articles of mine in covers. Thank you just the same. It is only fair to tell you that I have made the same answer, declining, to a firm in New York, also to one in Boston. This was some years ago, when I was perhaps more sure of myself.
Believeme .

Yours sincerely,
Philip Hale

Ferris Greenslet Esq
Boston[66]

During the preceding week, on November 16, Roland Hayes (1887–1977) performed with the Boston Symphony Orchestra at Symphony Hall. It was the first time that an African-American soloist had performed with the orchestra. It was not, however, the first time that Hayes had performed at Symphony Hall; six years earlier he had given a solo recital there to a full house. In 1920 he had gone to Europe, studied with Georg Henschel, and achieved international stardom. The Boston Symphony Orchestra concert on which he performed featured Dvořak's *Symphony No. 7 in D minor*, Moussorgsky's *Night on Bald Mountain*, Roussel's *The Rose-Colored City*, and Hayes singing Mozart's "Un Aura Amorosa" from *Cosi fan Tutti*, Berlioz's "The Repose of the Holy Family" from *The Flight into Egypt*, and two spirituals: "Go Down, Moses" and "By-and-By." Hale was ecstatic about Hayes's singing:

> It is very seldom that a Symphony audience is permitted to hear as admirable singing as that yesterday which came from Mr. Hayes. Not only is the voice beautiful in itself; vocal skill, aesthetic taste, and genuine feeling also distinguished his performance. There is a tenor who can sing Mozart's music, and not merely in correct and academic fashion. Notes had their value; they also had their significance. His singing of the scene from "The Flight into Egypt"—and here Berlioz is at his best in intimate expression—was characterized by a fine appreciation of the text, by sympathetic simplicity. The Negro Spirituals were sung with a fervor, a pathos, a conviction that were free from the talent of sentimentalism or of exaggeration.
>
> The accompaniment written by Mr. Rudolph for "Go Down Moses" struck one as too heavy, if not labored. Perhaps a lighter performance of it would have removed this impression. The accompaniment to "By and By," written by Anthony Bernard, a conductor in London, is appropriate and charming. Mr. Hayes was warmly greeted and enthusiastically applauded.[67]

The Monteux years had set the Boston Symphony Orchestra on the cutting edge of the musical world. That is why it came as a surprise to the public that in the spring of 1924 his contract was not renewed. The board cited the policy established by Higginson more than a quarter of a century earlier of not hiring conductors for more than a five-year period. This, of course, was ludicrous as two past conductors—Gericke and Muck—had retained their posts for longer periods of time. In April 1924, before the announcement was made, Monteux had confided to Burgin that he was leaving Boston "for purely personal reasons."[68] Monteux had recently separated from his second wife Germaine and their two children, and had now moved in with Doris Hodgkins, an American divorcée with two children of her own. The Muck scandals were still fresh on people's minds. The board's imposition of the five-year limit, then, appears to have been an excuse in order to avoid the possibility of facing the consequences caused by another conductor's problematic behavior. They need not have worried. Monteux and Germaine divorced in 1927; he and Doris Hodgkins married almost immediately thereafter and remained so until his death thirty-seven years later.

A successor to Monteux was found quickly, if not already preselected. Serge Koussevitzky (1874–1951), a Russian bass player with entrepreneurial tendencies (he had his own orchestra and publishing house), was conductor of the State Orchestra of Petrograd (St. Petersburg) shortly after the first revolution. In 1920, he fled the Soviet Union and went to Paris, where he organized and conducted a series of prestigious concerts bearing his name. When he started conducting in Boston in 1924, he unintentionally became the center of controversy. The ubiquitous anti-German hysteria of World War I had now been replaced, courtesy of the Bolshevik Revolution, by a "Red Scare." Was Koussevitzky a communist? No, but something written by Hale in his first program notes of the season inadvertently caused some people to think twice. In his quest to stay current, Hale used the name "Leningrad," which the Soviets had used to replace "Petrograd." Moses Smith comments:

> ...The tempest in a teapot, as it turned out to be, was precipitated by Philip Hale's innocent reference to "Leningrad" in his notes for the program-books of the Boston Symphony Orchestra [the name had been changed from Petrograd to Leningrad, following the death of Lenin the previous year]. Conservative Boston took alarm. Courtenay Guild, one of Boston's leading citizens, told a newspaperman, "If we are expected to pay reverence to Lenin to please the leader of our Symphony Orchestra, it may be desirable to look for a new conductor in spite of the undoubted musical abilities of our Russian visitor."[69]

Never to let an opportunity pass, *The Boston Post* carried the following in bold 1-inch letters:

OBJECT TO LENINGRAD

> Patrons of Symphony Blame New Director for
> Soviet Name of Russian Capitol in program[70]

This spawned a nationwide fury in the press, even with Koussevitzky retorting in the same issue:

I would be the last to wish to honor Lenin and Trotsky. I have left my country because of them and the terrible things they have done. I had a fortune of more than a million dollars in your money and it is gone—all gone—they took it from me.

I could not understand why the capitol city of my country should be called 'Leningrad' in the programs of our orchestra. But I hesitated to speak about it to others than my wife and secretary. I stifled my prejudice against this very objectionable word because I feared I might offend some very good Boston friends...Now the matter is cleared up. I hope we shall never see that word in the programs of the Boston Symphony Orchestra. I think that in a few years—perhaps five years, surely within ten—Russia will recover sanity, and this great and beautiful city will again be known to all the world as St. Petersburg or even Petrograd.[71]

Further repercussions faded; Koussevitzky had successfully cleared the air. The clarification of place nomenclature had no effect on Hale, however, who still referred to the city as "Leningrad."

In addition to this rather awkward start with the public, Koussevitzky had difficulty in establishing himself with the orchestra. Monteux was a conductor who could audiate almost anything, that is, sit down with a score and hear via inner hearing what the music sounds like. Koussevitzky, who did not have this inculcated at an early age, could not do this from the start; he had to work things out for himself through rehearsal with the orchestra. For this he relied heavily on Richard Burgin and musicologist (and humorist) Nicholas Slonimsky. Burgin comments:

...Unlike Monteux, but similar to many conductors, Koussevitzky lacked the natural ability to hear music with his inner ear, an ability that is necessary for studying scores. He did have the ability to listen to music when it was performed. Despite his outstanding talent, Koussevitzky's musical experience and knowledge lay in his intuition more than in education. His greatness as a conductor came from his ability to project his natural talent despite the obvious shortcomings in his musical education.

So when Koussevitzky came to Boston, he needed quite a bit of help, musically, and he made a happy choice in employing Nicolas Slonimsky as his private assistant. Slonimsky, whom I knew very well and was in practically daily contact with at the beginning of Koussevitzky's tenure, was an outstanding musician, in fact, unique. Slonimsky did everything for Koussevitzky that he needed, he prepared and coached Koussevitzky in every detail of the music he would conduct, from reading and analyzing the scores to playing everything for him on the piano. He also acted as Koussevitzky's musical secretary. In a word, Slonimsky was a very important person for Koussevitzky, probably one of the reasons why Koussevitzky did not leave the BSO in discouragement after the first couple of seasons, when he and the orchestra went through a natural, but sometimes very rocky period of adjustment.[72]

In his review of Koussevitzky's October 10, 1924 debut with the orchestra, Hale also addressed the issue of audiation, not from the viewpoint of one who knew about the conductor's limitations, but from his own perspective:

When Mr. Nikisch succeeded Mr. Gericke he said after the first rehearsal, delighted by the technical proficiency and euphony of the Boston orchestra: "All I have to do is poeticize."

Mr. Monteux left a superb instrument, the work of his own creation, for Mr. Koussevitzky to play upon.

No conductor, however expert, and no orchestra, however elastic and responsive, can in a week or 10 days, become so intimate in relationship that the players are the unfailing interpreters of the conductor's eloquence and passion. Further acquaintance will undoubtedly be to the advantage of these players and their conductor. His talent, his genius will shine the more brilliantly; his limitations, if he has them, will the more clearly appeal.

Yet this, in all justice may now be said. Mr. Koussevitzky has a commanding figure and that indefinable quality known as magnetism, which works his spell on orchestra and audience. When he faces his public he is neither arrogant nor obsequious. He at once inspires confidence, expectation, curiosity. These are all valuable qualities for a conductor to possess in these nervous, restless, questioning years.

It is evident that Mr. Koussevitzky is imaginative; that while he can be sensuous in gaining effects of color, this sensuousness is controlled by a cool head. He probably approves the famous paradox of Diderot. He surely sympathizes with the dictum of Mozart: "Music should sound." There is no fear in his breast of pedantic saws and cold or stuffed traditions; he thinks for himself; he feels the music in his own way; he hears its appeal without caring how it appealed or appeals to others.

He knows that melodic figures should be sung, yet he is not given to sentimentalism. He realizes the value of tonal proportion. When he delights in strong contrasts, it is not merely to win the applause of the unthinking. He is dramatic, but yesterday he was not theatrical.

These are hasty impressions made by his leadership at one concert. It is always rash to prophesy, but, after all, is it rash to predict that the season of 1924–1925 will be a brilliant one?[73]

Indeed, Koussevitzky's first season was a success. Of particular interest was a concert devoted to works of Stravinsky. In addition to suites from *The Firebird* and *Petrouchka*, the composer appeared as featured soloist on his *Concerto for Piano and Wind Orchestra*:

The concerto, dedicated to Mme. Koussevitzky, completed and produced last spring, is another matter. The composer tells us that it is a sort of 17th century passacaglia or toccata i.e., 'the 17th century viewed from the point of view of today.' Does he mean by this that we should hear the old music as we think we should have heard it in that century, or that composers of the 17th century, if they were brought to life and allowed to hear modern music, would adapt the old forms and contrapuntal weavings to suit the present taste? Academic questions not calling now for laborious consideration. The question is this: is the concerto heard yesterday merely an intellectual effort, an attempt to straddle centuries far apart, or is it music that is emotional in the nobler meaning of the word, or a masterpiece of enchanting brilliance? The concerto, after one hearing is not to be fulsomely praised, not to be carelessly dismissed as jejune and futile. There is a curious mixture of styles—the hearer is suddenly transported from the formalism of Bach's time to a modernity of expression which is not of the highest order. In the rhythm there is at times the suggestion of the Negro influences that is now felt on the other side of the Atlantic. There is a succession of styles rather than a continuity of individualism. This is more surprising, for Mr. Stravinsky as a composer is above all an individualist, neither following a school nor belonging to one. It is easy to recognize and admire in this concerto technical facility, as it was easy to recognize by Mr. Stravinsky's performance of the piano part, the grim earnestness with which he pursued his inexorable plan. Purely aesthetic, call it sensuousness or call it emotional, enjoyment was derived almost solely from the melodic section in the middle of the work.

A remarkable man, this Igor Stravinsky: a fascinating, perplexing, at times irritating personage in the world of music: an inventor and master of rhythm and orchestration, and as such a one he influences and will influence others. Whether he will prove to be an apostle of sweetness and light, a torchbearer down the years to come will be for those who come after us to decide.

Yesterday the hall was full of his glory and in this glory Mr. Koussevitzky and the players shared.[74]

Another highlight of that season was not the performance by a composer of his own work, but that of the composer's work by his teacher. Aaron Copland (1900–1990) was still in the beginning stages of his career when Nadia Boulanger (1887–1979), his composition teacher at the Fontainebleau School near Paris, came to the United States on a concert tour set up by the New York Symphony. She played the solo part on the premiere of his *Symphony for Organ and Orchestra* under the baton of Walter Damrosch. Shortly thereafter, she performed it in Boston. Hale commented:

Mr. Copland, born in Brooklyn, now living in New York, having studied in this country, went to Paris in 1921, where he continued to study, returning to this country last summer. His teacher in Paris was Miss Nadia Boulanger, who yesterday played the organ part of the symphony dedicated to her.

A good many were yesterday shocked by this symphony; perhaps affronted, regarding it as a personal insult to subscribers eager to hear music that they knew and liked. Yes, there are some, and they are voluble, who resent the putting of unfamiliar works on Symphony programs. They have no curiosity about what is going on in the musical world. They have ears, but they do not hear, and they are unwilling to hear, unless the new composition is by a local composer with whom they have at least a bowing acquaintance.

Mr. Koussevitzky is to be thanked for courageously introducing new works even when they are of a strong design, even if they are apparently ugly at first hearing, provided always that composers have really something to say, however raucous or hysterical their speech; but these composers must not stammer; they must not be detected in the act of experimenting.

Mr. Copland is now 24 years old. His symphony, written in 1924, was produced in New York last month. The music is definitely planned and gives proof of the composer's talent. It is an honest work, this symphony, though some may with equal honesty think this talent is here misguided. They may cry out against pages that are noise, not sound, of acid harmonies that have not the saving grace of exciting surprise, that leave the hearer indifferent or bored. But the Prelude, in the nature of a reverie, has decided character; it established and maintains a mood. Here the composer is simplest and most effective. His stormy outbursts later are too often futile orchestral ragings with occasional measures that are grotesque in their puffing and snorting. The rhythmic freedom with its constant changes is noteworthy as showing the influence of Stravinsky, an influence observable in other ways.

It is not an atrocious crime for a composer to be young; but youth is yeastly in its strivings, and it has its idols. The Stravinsky idol towers in the musical cathedral, and many are the young worshippers. Its brightness is excellent and the form thereof terrible, as in the image seen by the dreaming Nebuchadnezzar. Its head may be of gold; its breast and arms of silver; but its feet are part of clay.

In Mr. Copland's Symphony there is much brass, there is clay; but there is also something of the silver, if not a little gold.

The performance of this difficult work was brilliant...Miss Nadia Boulanger, an organist of established reputation in Paris, played solo and ensemble pages with technical skill and as an accomplished musician.[75]

Hale's critique of the work was generally positive, in accordance with and in support of the practices in programming that Monteux had exercised and that Koussevitzky was now continuing. At this point in time, however, Copland's music was not particularly well received by others. The heading of Warren Storey Smith's column in the *Boston Post* for this same concert read: "Barbaric Music by Symphony—Copland's Work Brutal—Woman Organist Soloist."[76] Hale would have the opportunity to critique at least three additional works by Copland in Boston, the world premieres of *Music for the Theatre*, *Two Pieces for String Orchestra*, and the *Piano Concerto*—the latter receiving one of Hale's most negative reviews of later years.[77] Unfortunately, Hale would not have the opportunity to hear any of Copland's popular "Americana" works as these were all composed after 1934.

During his first season Koussevitzky took a two-week break period in January and had Henry Hadley, associate conductor of the New York Philharmonic, fill in. This break became a yearly tradition and guest conductors of Koussevitzky's choosing, many of them more famous as composers, were brought in. The result was that the orchestra and its audience were given an exposure to different creative artists. Before Koussevitzky's time, guest conductors were a rarity. The list of January guest conductors during Hale's tenure as program annotator included:

Henry Hadley	1925
Michael Press and Eugene Goosens	1926
Alfredo Casella and Ottorino Respighi	1927
Sit Thomas Beecham and Maurice Ravel	1928
Enrique Fernandez Arbos (the former Concertmaster) and Artur Honegger	1929
Eugene Goosens and Alexander Glazounov	1930
Henry Hadley and E. Fernandez Arbos	1931
Chalmers Clifton and Gustav Holst	1932
Albert Stoessel	1933

This respite worked its wonders; Koussevitzky returned refreshed each time, though there were naysayers who commented that he invited only weak conductors in order to make himself look good—and Koussevitzky did have his share of self doubts—this was neither the purpose nor the effect. Hale commented upon the conductor's return on January 29, 1926, from one such break:

If Mr. Koussevitzky had any doubt concerning the respect and affection in which is held by the great musical public, that doubt must have been dispelled by the glowing tribute paid him yesterday afternoon when he came on the platform of Symphony Hall after his vacation of a fortnight.[78]

In addition to established guest conductors, the early Koussevitzky era was characterized by a phenomenal number (some would say an overload) of world premieres, nearly one for each pair of concerts, and by first-rank composers being invited to perform their own newer works with the orchestra, particularly piano concertos. Stravinsky and Copland have already been mentioned. Among the others were Darius Milhaud (*The Carnival of Aix—Fantasy for Piano and Orchestra on the Ballet "Salade,"* 1926), Serge Prokofieff (*Piano Concerto No. 3*, 1926 and *Piano Concerto No. 5*, 1932), Bela Bartok (*Piano Concerto No. 1*, 1928), and George Gershwin (*Second Rhapsody,*1 932).

Koussevitzky was always searching for the new. Sibelius's final symphony was performed in Boston on December 10, 1926, only two years after its completion. In his review of it, Hale brought up a very poignant and prophetic question about the composer's future:

> The symphony by Sibelius, published last year, was played in Philadelphia by the Philadelphia Orchestra on the third of last April. Sibelius is now 61 years old. Will he live to write his nine symphonies? For some composers wish to rival Beethoven in this respect, forgetting that he purposed to write a tenth, not remembering that among the ancients seven was a sacred number. Bruckner and Mahler wrote their nine; the latter indeed left sketches for a tenth. Of composers living, Nicolas Miaskovsky has written his eighth and he is only in his 45th year.
>
> The question, after all, is whether Sibelius still has something to say in music. He could be content to rest his fame on earlier works than this symphony, works which show a strong, sometimes oppressing and depressing individuality. Perhaps his leading characteristic is a peculiar somberness. There are times when he has even seemed a "dismal Jemmy," but there was no denying his rugged strength, his disdain of cheap bids for immediate popularity.
>
> Ingenious and imaginative critics have argued that Sibelius could not write otherwise because he has lived for the most of the time in Finland, and as a fervent patriot, has been influenced by the landscapes and the seascapes, the lowering sky, the blasted heaths, the forbidding wildness of the natural scenery, and by the thought of Russian domination. These critics have found in his music fierce winds, stormy billows, desolate stretches, the cries of sea birds, etc., etc. Travelers inform us that Finland is a delightful, hospitable land; that the landscapes can smile, that winds and waves are no more furious than in our own country. Nor is it safe to say that a composer is inevitably influenced by his own environment. We forget whether Buckle has anything to say about the influence of natural scenery and climate on composers. Tschaikowsky saw Italy and wrote an Italian caprice, but he took Russia with him and composed his caprice in Russian. The Spaniard will not have Bizet's "Carmen." Auber was a Parisian of the boulevards; he seldom went beyond them; he never visited Naples, yet in the market scene of "La Muette de Portici" he caught in a marvelous manner the Neopolitan spirit.
>
> Nor is it prudent to assert that a composer is always influenced by his mood. Beethoven wrote one of his most joyous symphonies when he was in particularly doleful dumps.
>
> In all probability Sibelius would have composed in the Sibelius manner had he lived in Rome, Paris, Chicago. His is too strong a nature to be easily affected by sky, climate, city. In this seventh symphony one does not find the freshness, the wild charm, the tragic and sinister darkness associated with much of his music. It is scholarly rather than spontaneous, nor do the themes have the former distinction and personal quality. The first section, as of a long lamentation increasing in sonority, is at first impressive, but the very persistence of the mood leads the hearer

to long for a contrasting section or even a lyric episode. That the symphony is solidly constructed is beyond question. So solidly that one recalls the criticism of the confused young man in "Great Expectations," who when asked by an actor what he thought of his performance, said it was "massive and concrete."

As for "Finlandia," suddenly added to the program, though it was composed before Finland lost her identity as a nation, and is of so patriotic a nature that the performance was for a time prohibited in Finland, the thematic material is wholly Sibelius's own, not derived from folk tunes, or national anthems. The dynamic force of the music excites stormy applause, as it did yesterday, but this symphonic poem, or what-you-will, is not to be ranked among the best works of the composer.

The more advanced Stravinskians regret that the master wrote "The Firebird." It is too melodious, this music, too "obvious," they say. But it is eminently beautiful to the ear, fascinating even in the concert hall, without the sight of the situations and the dancing, without thought of the legend.

An interesting concert in which Mr. Koussevitzky and his players gave us of their best, which reminds one of the motto on the bags of "Lone Jack" tobacco: "Or to seek no farther; better can't be found." There will long be grateful remembrance of the manner in which Bach's concerto was performed, especially of the Andante, played with genuine simplicity that is of the highest art. Steinberg published his arrangement fifteen years ago, and Mr. Milhaud, the pianist of the next concert, brought it out in Philadelphia when he, as guest, conducted the orchestra of that city in January, 1923.[79]

Ironically, just as Hale was penning his remarks about Sibelius, the composer stopped writing almost entirely. Sibelius would live another three decades, but composed no orchestral works after 1926. Hale mentioned that *Finlandia* was added to the program later, undoubtedly as an audience pleaser, but its addition was indicative of a less-than-salient trait of Koussevitzky.

While the conductor was lauded for his overall handling of the music directorship, there was one thing he did repeatedly from the very start that irked both critics and audiences alike: last minute changes. Moses Smith comments:

> ...The newspaper critics, however they might outdo each other in praise of Koussevitzky's performances, were agreed from the outset. They all condemned his practice of changing announced programs. They felt that it showed small regard for the institutional character of the Boston Symphony concerts; for the right of the audiences to know in advance what they were going to hear and, if they wished, to prepare themselves for the hearing. Philip Hale, the program annotator, was especially annoyed, of course, because the changes often came too late to allow a corresponding substitution in his printed notes. On one occasion, indeed, Koussevitzky's casualness in changing a program three times before it assumed final form provoked from Hale the rebuke, "After this, announcements in the Program Book of forthcoming concerts should be headed: 'Subject to Change.'"[80]

This became so infuriating that Hale mentioned it in his review of the first season's penultimate concert:

> Mozart's Symphony in C major (K. 425) [No. 36, "Linz"] had been announced and notes about it were in the program book. As the book was in the press it was too late to substitute notes for Schubert's Symphony [No. 5 in B flat, D. 485]. Why the change was made is a question answered only by "So the conductor wished."[81]

Hale followed this up by writing about the Schubert symphony in the style of a brief program note, educating his readers in print that which was denied the concert audience. He was not pleased with the substitution and uncharacteristically leveled an attack on the Schubert supporters in the audience:

> There are still in Boston men and women who believe in the plenary inspiration of the long-acknowledged great composers. To these believers the name "Schubert" was enough: anything signed by him must be good. And so there was clapping of hands, the customary, yet barbaric, manner of showing rapturous enjoyment.[82]

Koussevitzky probably would have read or at least been informed of Hale's commentary. This could have led to a conflict between conductor and critic, much as what Nikisch had had with Hale more than thirty-five years earlier. Yet this was not the case: Koussevitzky had an entirely different mindset from Nikisch and did not view Hale's words as an attack. In spite of the fact that Koussevitzky did not always enjoy a good relationship with the press, he did have a great deal of respect for Hale and saw him as a supporter of what he was trying to accomplish. He commented about this in an interview appearing in *Life* magazine a decade after Hale's death:

> The worst troubles I have had in America have been with the critics. Again, not as much in Boston as in other places. Luckily, during my first years there we had two prominent critics: Philip Hale and H. T. Parker. Hale was the greatest music critic of his time. Parker had an exceptional intuitive feeling for new music. These two men were never destructive, not even about the most ultramodern compositions. They both wrote with genuine good will.[83]

As it turned out, Koussevitzky survived the first few difficult years. His relationship with orchestra personnel improved greatly over time, his programming continued to be eclectic, and his quarter of a century with the orchestra, particularly notable for the establishment of the Berkshire (now Tanglewood) Music Center and the Koussevitzky Music Foundations, marked his tenure as the greatest of any Boston Symphony Orchestra conductor to date.[84]

An enormous leap for the orchestra in terms of expanding into the Greater Boston community and beyond occurred during Koussevitzky's second season. On January 15, 1926 it was announced in the media that the Boston Symphony Orchestra would start broadcasting their Saturday night subscription concerts over radio station WEEI. This first series of broadcasts was made possible through the beneficence of Brookline resident Winfred S. Quimby, who donated $1,000 per week.[85] The date of the first broadcast was January 23rd. This entry into the electronics age was followed up a little more than two years later with the first electronic recordings made by the orchestra. Over a decade had passed since the release of four of the ten acoustical sides conducted by Muck, and significant improvements had been made in the recording process since then. The new electronic recordings were still done for the Victor Talking Machine Company (which, after its merger with RCA, became Radio-Victor Corporation of America and, eventually, RCA Victor); only this time the orchestra was recorded at Symphony Hall. Between November 13, 1928 and October 1930, when the Great Depression started to take its toll, more than sixty 78 r.p.m. sides were cut.[86]

The first works to be recorded with the electronic process were Stravinsky's Suite from *Petrouchka* and *Apollon Musagète: Pas de Deux*, as well as Ravel's "Suite No. 2" from *Daphnis et Chloé*.[87] The latter was performed by the orchestra in concert during the following year, 1929. Hale commented:

> Ravel's Suite is as if it had been planned with the express purpose of displaying the euphony, sonority, brilliance and elasticity of the remarkable orchestra conducted by Dr. Koussevitzky. One can easily think that led by a respectable but prosaic man of routine experience the music itself might occasionally seem purposeless, if not trite, especially as it does not in the concert hall accompany action in an appropriate stage setting. As played under the conditions stated—a virtuoso orchestra with an understanding, poetic, magnetic conductor in full sympathy with the composer—the music has kaleidoscopic beauty, the performance is incomparable. One might ask whether in this instance a conductor and his men do not with the material produce such glowing effects that Ravel, if he were listening, might say to himself, "Did I really write this music? Did I expect it to be so beautiful in the actual performance?["][88]

As witnessed by the above, at this point in time Hale was calling the conductor "Dr." Koussevitzky, as were other members of the Boston Symphony Orchestra community. In June of that year, Koussevitzky had received an honorary Doctor of Laws degree from Harvard University; he actually wrote a dissertation for it, "Concerning Interpretation."[89] Hale himself had been bestowed with an honorary Doctor of Music degree from Dartmouth during the previous year.[90] It is not known, however, if Koussevitzky ever referred to Hale as "Dr."

In the spring of 1930, for no apparent reason other than Koussevitzky's personal preference, the Boston Symphony Orchestra had a Brahms festival. Moses Smith commented about the festival, recalling a well-known story about Hale:

> The press gave much attention to the Festival in advance as well as in review. Philip Hale recalled the legendary suggestion that the old Boston Music Hall have a red light over a sign, "This way out in case of Brahms." He also recalled that MacDowell taught his dog to play dead at the mention of Brahms' name.[91]

Hale's general lack of enthusiasm for the composer's music did not show in his reviews, only in the fact that of the festival's six concerts, he reviewed only the two that were subscription concerts. By this time Hale was seventy-six years old, well past the age when most people would have retired. There were other members of his staff who were quite capable reviewers and he had started to farm out a number of assignments to them, although he was still music and drama critic at this time.[92]

The year 1930–1931 was the orchestra's Fiftieth Anniversary season and Koussevitzky wanted to make it something special. He had yearned to take the orchestra on a European tour, but the money just wasn't there. What he was able to accomplish, however, was phenomenal.

Koussevitzky had two real coups up his sleeve: The first was a reconstruction of the very first Boston Symphony Orchestra concert with their original conductor, Georg Henschel, now Sir George Henschel, at the helm. Only six of the seventy-two 1881–1882 players were still alive, but Henschel was now a youthful eighty and more than up for the task. This October 10, 1930 concert, the first subscription concert of the season, was broadcast; it was also a part of the Tercentenary of the founding of the Massachusetts Bay Colony. There was much advanced planning and Hale was a part of it. He wrote to James Lincoln Huntington, Secretary of The Tavern Club:

> PHILIP HALE
> 15 KESWICK STREET
> BOSTON
>
> [n.d.]
> Dear James,
>
> Judge Cabot thinks The Tavern Club should give a dinner (or luncheon) to Sir George Henschel who will conduct the symphony orchestra—as resurrected from Oct 1881. He will be here next week and the week after—
>   More poorer for your elbow,
> From
> PhilipH ale
> Dr. James Lincoln Huntington
>   Secretary[93]

Henschel's arrival was highly touted in the press. Olin Downes wrote a huge article about it for the *New York Times*. In his anticipatory *Boston Herald* "Concerts" column of October 5, 1930, Hale covered the history of Higginson's hiring of Henschel and then followed with a look at contemporary press criticism of the conductor:

> Any one can learn by consulting the newspapers published during the three years of Mr. Henschel's conductorship that the concerts were often bitterly criticized: that criticism of the conductor was often savage. Even his friend Mr. Apthorp, writing to the Evening Transcript in 1911 about the early years, said that the choice of the conductor was made "without due circumspection"; that Mr. Higginson was "in plain English paying Mr. Henschel a high salary for those days, for learning his trade in public." It should not be forgotten that there were "unfortunate elements" in the orchestra. Bernhard Listemann, the concert master, a remarkable violinist in certain ways and a sound musician, was a nervous, high-strung man, constitutionally unfit for the position. He was wont to hurry the tempo; he insisted on playing the music in his own way; without the intention of usurping the conductor's throne, he could not follow any conductor. Then there were intrigues against Mr. Henschel in the orchestra and out of it.[94]

Six days later Hale reviewed the concert. Not only is the review quintessential Hale, it also provides an 1881 retrospective from a 1930 perspective:

> The first concert of the Boston Symphony Orchestra's 50th season took place yesterday afternoon in Symphony Hall. Sir George Henschel—in 1881 Mr. Georg (sic) Henschel was invited to conduct the opening concert of the of the Anniversary season, for as the first conductor of the orchestra he arranged the program for the first concert given in Music Hall on October 22, 1881. This program with one exception—the substitution of the Prelude to "The Mastersingers of Nuremberg"

for Weber's "Festival" overture—was as follows: Beethoven, overture to "The Consecration of the House"; Gluck, "Cite fato senza Eurydice" from "Orfeo ed Eurydice"; Haydn, symphony B flat (B. & H. No. 12) [No. 102]; Schubert: ballet music from "Rosamunde"; Bruch: Penelope's Sorrow from "Odysseus"; Wagner, the prelude to "The Mastersingers of Nuremberg." The substitution of Wagner's music for Weber's is to be regretted, for the program of 1881 in full would have given the audience of yesterday a better idea of what those assembled in Music Hall 50 years ago applauded or condemned as "radical," "too modern," "anarchistic."

If Wagner's Prelude is left out of consideration, the program of 1881 now seems respectable enough, respectively prosaic, or as some would say, dull. What conductor today would put the "Consecration of the House" in rehearsal if Beethoven's name were signed to it? Yet for many years in the history of this orchestra the overture was solemnly performed and reverently heard. Suppose a composer in 1930 should hand this work to Dr. Koussevitzky or Mr. Toscanini or Mr. Stokowski and ask for a performance?

Haydn's Symphony No. 12 [No. 102] is not one of his most characteristic works. Schubert's music was charming 50 years ago and delights the ear today; nor in this instance is Schubert's prolixity fatal. What prima donna in 1930 would deliberately choose Bruch's air from "Odysseus"? But for several season's Bruch's "Odysseus," "Arminius," "Achilleus" were regarded by the orthodox as masterpieces of choral song. How paltry, how labored this air of Penelope seemed yesterday after Gluck's great air! The singer at the concert in 1881 was Annie Louise Cary, yesterday Margaret Matzenauer. Far nobile sonorum!

It would be interesting to know how many in the audience yesterday were at the concert of 50 years ago; and of those, how many display the mental and physical activity of Sir George? He conducted with the force and the gusto of a young man exultant in the direction of a great orchestra. It is doubtful whether as a young man of 31 he conducted with the same confidence and vigor.

When Dr. Koussevitzky and Sir George appeared on the stage there was now the customary scene of homage, audience rising, applauding while standing, all in a friendly and joyous spirit. Dr. Koussevitzky spoke a few words, not merely by way of introduction—for Sir George's name and reputation have long been known even to those who have never seen him conduct, never heard him sing—but as a graceful tribute to the man who had the arduous task of the first years and now must rejoice in the present splendor of the orchestra—nor did Dr. Koussevitzky neglect to remind the audience that it was Mr. Higginson's courage, one might say his artistic obstinacy in the face of too many discouragements as well as his princely munificence that enabled Sir George and his successors to carry out their own musical aims and win at last the world-wide fame acknowledged even by rivals.

The occasion yesterday was one of sentimental reminiscences. Hearing the music was associated to some, perhaps to many, with memories of the past; of singers who once gave delight, but whose lips have long been dumb; of violinists and pianists whose brave deeds are now a tradition. But here is Sir George amazingly buoyant, enthusiastic, virile....[95]

With this concert, Hale had now seen every one of the conductors employed by the Boston Symphony Orchestra during his lifetime guide the orchestra through a complete program.

Henschel's concert was indeed a tremendous success, both in conception and realization, yet for Koussevitsky and the orchestra this was just the beginning. In the months prior to the season, the conductor was able to convince the board of trustees to commission works from ten internationally renowned composers for this celebration. His hope was that the resultant compositions would remain in the repertoire in perpetuity as living testimonials to the orchestra. Of the ten works commissioned, eight were ready for performance during the Anniversary season. The dates of their premieres are included in parentheses:

Edward Burlingame Hill: *An Ode* (October 17, 1930)
AlbertR oussel: *Symphony No. 3 in G minor* (October 24, 1930)
Ottorino Respighi: *Metamorphoseon modi XII* (November 7, 1930)
SergeP rokofiev: *Symphony No. 4* (November 14, 1930)
HowardH anson: *Symphony No. 2*, "Romantic" (November 28, 1930)
Igor Stravinsky: *Symphonie de Psaumes*, for chorus and orchestra (December 19, 1930)
ArthurH onegger: *Symphony for Orchestra* (February 13, 1931)
PaulH indemith: *Konzertmusik*, for strings and brass (April 3, 1931)[96]

Of these eight, the most often performed remains Stravinsky's *Symphonie des Psaumes* (*Symphony of Psalms*), the paramount work of his neoclassical period. Its Boston premiere followed on the heels of yet another Koussevitzky-instigated festival, the orchestra's Beethoven Festival, held on December 2–6 at Constitution Hall in Washington, DC. The concert featuring *Symphony of Psalms*, however, did not feature its world premiere; that occurred in Brussels six days earlier under the baton of Ernst Ansermet. As expected, Hale had much to say:

...The orchestra was assisted by the Cecilia Society, which had been trained by its conductor, Arthur Fiedler.[97]...The p ianist was M r. Samromá.
It has been said that Stravinsky of late is deeply religious; that he may devote himself to the glorification of God in music. This rumor possibly arose from the fact that he dedicated his "Symphonie de Psaumes" to the orchestra, but composed it, as he states on the title page, "to the glory of God." And so Bruckner intended to dedicate his unfinished ninth symphony to the Lord God Omnipotent. But is this new symphony of Stravinsky the devout more musical, more poetic, more imaginative than the compositions written in his supposedly pagan state? It surely is a less engrossing work, less interesting musically than the worldly played yesterday and premiered at Paris last December. Stravinsky should remember that he can show religious devotion in a ballet even if Apollo is his hero or in music that fascinates in jazz rhythms or by the suggestion of them. He might say with Sir Thomas Browne[98]: "For even that vulgar and tavern music, which makes one man merry, another mad, strikes in me a deep fit of devotion, and a profound contemplation of the first composer."
Stravinsky went to the Psalms for inspiration, choosing the sonorous texts of the Vulgate Verses of the 39th (the number in the King James version), Verses that are a prayer, an entreaty; from the 40th in which the Psalmist rejoices that his cry was heard, that he was taken from the horrible pit, the miry clay; and the 150th in which the people are urged, and all things that have breath, to praise the Lord with the sound of all manner on instruments. His choice of instruments for these psalms is peculiar: no violins, no violas, but five flutes, many other wind instruments, a harp. He called for two pianos. Although the psalmist wished organs and high sounding cymbals to give praise, Stravinsky would not be the man to be so literal in his orchestration.
It is to be regretted that the repetition of the symphony did not take place as first announced, for much that was strange, almost foreign to the text, might have seemed pertinently eloquent. Schoenberg's arrangement of Bach's organ prelude

and fugue might better have been omitted. Without the repetition, the concert was too long as it was. The orchestral interludes are the most baffling portions of the symphony at first hearing. They seem to be purposeless: hardly designed to put one in the mood for the following text; not a musical commentary on what has preceded. Was it the composer's endeavor to be Hebraic in his music? Hebraic in spirit, after the manner of Ernst Bloch—but not too reminiscent of the synagogue? The ending of the first psalm is indeed beautiful, originally beautiful; so is the treatment of the Alleluia later. And Stravinsky escaped the temptation of making the Psalm of Jubilation one prolonged shout. There is a most effective passage in it to be sung in a subdued manner, as by worshippers in awe of the majesty of the Lord. The symphony is of such importance that it demands a second hearing, one not too long deferred.[99]

Jesús María Sanromá, the Puerto Rican pianist who regularly performed with the orchestra, was the soloist for Stravinsky's *Capriccio for Piano and Orchestra*, also on the program. It is not known whether he was one of the two pianists required for *Symphony of Psalms*. Regardless, *Capriccio* was better received by the audience than *Symphony*. Hale ended his review of the concert tongue-in-cheek: "And so yesterday, the worldly Stravinsky triumphed as far as the audience was concerned over Stravinsky the devout."[100]

The two remaining commissioned works were performed during the following season:

Aaron Copland: *Symphonic Ode* (February 19, 1932)
MauriceR avel: *Piano Concerto in G*(April 22,1 932)

The Copland work was completed in time but, due to its rhythmic complexity, Koussevitzky convinced the composer to rebar it, and that meant postponing its premiere by a year.[101] On the other hand, Ravel interrupted work on his commissioned concerto in order to write his other work in the genre, the *Concerto for the Left Hand*, for Paul Wittgenstein. Even when he finished the *Piano Concerto in G*, Ravel allowed it to be performed many times by Marguerite Long on a European tour before its Boston premiere, which then occurred simultaneously with its Philadelphia premiere—both instances being a slap in the face to the commissioning body.[102]

There was an eleventh unheralded work in this set as well, an anonymous *Overture* performed on October 31, 1930. The composer turned out to be Koussevitzky himself.

In the early 1930s then, in the midst of the Great Depression, this outstanding combination of guest composer-conductors and commissioned works provided Hale with a fitting coda to his long career. When his own vast musical knowledge and wisdom are added to the mix, it is evident that Hale was at the epicenter of a brief golden age in the dissemination of classical musical thought—as a living, breathing entity—to the public. Hale's mind was as sharp as ever, though physically he was starting to feel his age. In a letter dated April 27, 1930 to Frances Sharf Fink, a contributor to the *Boston Herald*, the *Christian Science Monitor* and the editor of *The Jewish Advocate*, Hale mentioned that his eyesight was "starting to fail somewhat, from hard work."[103] This, however, did not prevent him and Irene from traveling to England later that spring, or to France two years later.[104] Still, there were other physical ailments; in August of 1931 he wrote to

James Lincoln Huntington that he was unable to attend a meeting of the Tavern Club Executive Committee as he was nursing a "game leg."[105] This malady was still affecting him two months later as Mark Antony DeWolfe Howe mentions missing him at the Tavern Club,[106] and by July of 1932 another ailment, neuritis, was crippling his right hand.[107]

That Hale relished writing during this era is obvious, but this does not imply that he let up on his criticism. He still called things as he saw them. The following is from March 28, 1931, the fourth concert of a Bach festival on which Cantatas Nos. 20 and 85, *Concerto for Two Violins in D minor*, and the *Orchestral Suite No. 3 in D* were performed:

> Bach the writer for instruments outvied yesterday, Bach the writer for human voices. The first part of the concert [instrumental] was the more pleasing to the audience; the more creditable to the composer. For Bach, like Mozart and Beethoven, was not always inspired; the three could write as dull and barren music as the humblest of their now forgotten contemporaries.[108]

Mozart also got his due, in Hale's review of his *Requiem*:

> It may have surprised some that a Requiem should be performed as a concert number in the week before Christmas, yet in this period of financial depression when many dividends are either dead or moribund, there was a certain fitness to the selection.
>
> One might reasonably wish that the Requiem had been by another composer; not necessarily Berlioz or Verdi, though it would be a joyful experience to hear either of these great requiems conducted by Dr. Koussevitzky; but, say Cherubini's Requiem in C minor.
>
> For Mozart left his work unfinished, and what he had completed is not always worthy of him....
>
> There are a few lovely passages in this requiem, but in the pages of sustained loveliness, as the "Lacrymosa" and the "Hostias" Mozart wrote only eight measures of the former; Sussmayer completed it and wrote the whole of the "Sanctus," "Benedictus" and the greater part of the "Agnus Dei." Nor is it blasphemy to say that in this Requiem there is no page of such tender, prayerful, religious feeling as the "Pie Jesu" of Cherubini's work in C minor, or many parts of celestial beauty in Verdi's. Nor can the many fugal pages of Mozart be justly described as dramatic or religious. In his time fugues were expected in music for the church, but those in this Requiem do not rise to the height of grandeur. And one might justly say that if it were not for Mozart's name, the mystery connected with the commission given to him by the man in gray, and Mozart's pathetic ending and lonely burial in a pauper's grave, this Requiem would not be included among his greater works.[109]

Haydn was also in for it, less for the quality of the music than for the way in which it was perceived and presented. The following is from a concert performed on April 1, 1932 in honor of the bicentennial of Haydn's birth. Three of Haydn's symphonies (Nos. 1; 94, "Surprise"; and 104, "London") were performed as was the *Violoncello Concerto in D* (the only one known by the composer at that time):

> It was meet and proper that the first and last symphonies of Haydn should be performed on this occasion. It is always a pleasure to hear Mr. [Gregor] Piatigorsky.

Four works by Haydn and three of them in D major? Only the brilliant performance of orchestra and soloist took away the reproach of inevitable monotony....

Haydn's first symphony played with a reduced number of strings gave opportunity for the exquisite euphony and technic, elasticity of this section. As regards the contents, one recognized the characteristics of the later Haydn. The other symphonies chosen [Nos. 94 and 104] are so well known—were known to our maiden aunts in the 60s [1860's] by four-hand arrangements for the piano—that it is hardly necessary to discuss them; yet it may be said if Aunt Lucinda and Aunt Vashti died long ago, the symphonies seem to have eternal youth, though an audience today does not find the "surprise" of the loud chord overwhelming. As one said in the corridor yesterday, "We have had too many surprises in the contemporary works we have heard this season and last to be startled by Haydn."

Haydn wrote the violoncello concerto for his friend Anton Kraft, the capable solo violoncellist of Prince Esterhazy's orchestra. Would honest Anton have recognized the work yesterday? Several have tinkered with it, adapted it to suit "modern taste," decked it with all manner of furbelows and frills to enhance the glory of the virtuoso. It would have been interesting to hear the concerto exactly as Haydn wrote it.[110] Anton would have wondered at Mr. Piatigorsky's performance; praised his technical proficiency, admired the purity of his tone, the brilliance of his bravura, but might he not have said, "This instrument, as it is played, sounds to me more like a violin than a violoncello"? and might he not have exclaimed now and then: "How sweet! Perhaps a little too sweet!"[111]

Piatigorsky returned as a guest soloist one year later, as solo cellist on Richard Strauss's *Don Quixote* and—as in the case of the Haydn, with authenticity in performance practice mattering little—Mozart's *Horn Concerto No. 3 in E flat*, K. 447, "freely transcribed by G. Cassado." Hale commented:

Mozart befriended a poor devil of a horn player by writing four concertos and one rondo for him. This man Leitzeb [Leutgeb] had come from Salzburg, where Mozart had known him, to Vienna, where he had little luck and was in debt. Mozart thought little of these concertos; Gaspar Cassado, a Spaniard of Barcelona, took it into his head to transcribe the third concerto for the violoncello: saying to himself, Mozart never wrote a 'cello concerto; what a pity! The larghetto is beautiful, whether it is played by Mr. Boettcher, the admirable first horn of the orchestra at a Young People's Concert (1928), or by the accomplished Mr. Piatigorsky, master of a beautiful tone and refined, aristocratic technic. The other movements give an example of Mozart taking it easy in his commiseration of an old colleague's sad plight.[112]

Thus it was that the only Mozart horn concerto that Hale heard at a subscription concert turned out to be a transcription. One can only hazard a guess at what Hale may have said about the last movement in particular had he heard this concerto played on its intended instrument.[113]

One week later, Hale wrote what appears to have been his final Boston Symphony Orchestra concert review. The bulk of it is included here, not because the concert itself was particularly remarkable, nor for any special treatment that Hale may have bestowed upon it, but simply as closure to a truly incredible career:

The program of the 21st concert of the Boston Symphony Orchestra, Dr. Koussevitzky, conductor, given in Symphony Hall yesterday afternoon was as follows: Haydn, Symphony in E flat major (Salomon No. 19) [No. 99]; Loeffler, "Evocation" for orchestra, female chorus, and a speaking voice (first time in Boston); Walton, "Belshazzar's Feast," for mixed voices, baritone solo and orchestra (first time in the United States). The chorus was the Cecilia Society, Arthur Fiedler, conductor; David Blair McCloskey was the baritone soloist.

The symphony was not too familiar. It had been conducted by Mr. Gericke in 1886; by Dr. Koussevitzky in 1926.[114] The perfection of the performance yesterday gave the symphony an importance that it otherwise would not have had. The music is characteristically melodious and suave, with a charming slow movement, a minuet that for Haydn is commonplace, and with the two traditional movements that in this instance are not conspicuous, but of the routine order.

Loeffer's "Evocation" was composed for the dedication of Severance Hall, the home of the Cleveland Symphony orchestra. It was eminently proper that he should have been invited to contribute a composition for that occasion. Mr. and Mrs. Severance, the donors of the hall, were friends of his, and Mr. Sokolov, the present conductor of the orchestra, was not only an intimate friend: he was a former pupil and at the time was a member of the Boston Symphony orchestra. It was known by donors, conductor, and the Cleveland audience that Loeffler's contribution would be worthy of the occasion. He took the text from fragments of the Greek anthology which in themselves are musical, telling of the building of a beautiful temple of the Muses; of Pan and the nymphs who loved him; of the Singing Stone which Phoebus lifted on his shoulders for the temple, the stone on which the god laid his Delphic harp. There was need of Mr. Loeffler's exquisite taste and subtle instrumentation to clothe this idea and the poetic expression of it in fitting tones. The occasion was not one for pompous strains and exultant fanfares, the ordinary stock-in-trade of composers summoned to a similar task. There was need of a poet-musician, imaginative and capable of voicing his imagination, mindful of the use to which a beautiful hall would be devoted.

Who but Loeffler would have bethought him of a viola-harp for Apollo's instrument? Who but Loeffler would have thought of Pan and the nymphs in connection of a hall in Cleveland? And so we have a poetically musical fantasy that took one look to a world when beauty was worshipped. Here again we have the Loeffler of pure musical thought and of sensitive expression; who shuns the obvious but is not persuaded that barrenness of ideas, that polyphony, or atonality, and tortured instrumentation are convincing proofs of originality. His musical mind is Greek, not Judaic.

Walton's "Belshazzar's Feast" was written for the Leeds Festival and the famous full-throated Leeds chorus. Years ago Dr. Whasby laid it down as a maximum in rhetoric that "elaborate stateliness is a worse fate than the downliness and languor which accompany a very loose style." Thomas De Quincy in answer quoted the sentence "Belshazzar the king made a great feast to a thousand of his lords and drank wine before the thousand." De Quincy said, "Reading these words, who would not be justly offended in point of taste had his feast been characterized by elegant simplicity?"

Osbert Sitwell selected the text from the Bible and arranged it for Walton. The composer refused to be spectacular or melodramatic in his music for the handwriting on the wall. The words are given to a baritone in recitative with a few with a few ominous, lugubrious measures for cymbals, drums and gong. The male chorus translates them and fortissimo succeeds the pianissimo, as if the captive Jews were already preparing the overthrow of Babylon. Note also the dramatic orchestral touch after "The King was slain." The only sustained spectacular pages are those in march time, where the gods of gold, silver, wood, stone, iron and brass are praised.

What might be called the purely musical pages are devoted to Jews weeping by the waters of Babylon and commanded to sing a song of Zion. The choruses of exultation at Babylon's fall and praise to the God of Jacob are full of Judaic fury. This persistent fury—not to say noise—is almost without relief, and one wishes that the Israelites might rest their voices for at least a few minutes. The chorus and the baritone had a trying task, but they did not falter. The orchestra made light of difficulties. Dr. Koussevitzky, who is to be thanked for bringing out this noteworthy work, conducted his forces with enthusiasm. As "Belshazzar's Feast" is to be repeated on Monday night there may be occasion for further comments on this episode i n B iblical h istory. . . .[115]

6

Aftermath and Conclusion: 1933–1936

As usual, Philip Hale's April 1, 1933 *Boston Herald* review announced the next pair of Boston Symphony Orchestra concerts, in this case to be held two weeks later, on April 13 and 14. The April 14th review, however, was not by him, but signed with the initials of another writer, "E. B." It may very well have been the first subscription concert that Hale had not reviewed in nearly forty-four years. His April 1st review gave no indication that he would not be reviewing the next concert, nor was there any indication on E. B.'s review that Hale had resigned his position, though everyone around him knew that his retirement was imminent. He was now seventy-nine years old, rapidly losing his sight and the use of his right hand.

The administration at Harvard University may have sensed Hale's retirement and on June 22nd conferred upon him an honorary Master of Arts degree. At the commencement ceremonies, Harvard President Abbott Lawrence Lowell referred to Hale as an "acute and learned critic, striving to promote the art of music and improve the public taste."[1]

Retirement from work, however, did not mean retirement from life and Hale continued to be active in Boston's social world the best that he could, actually serving a second term as vice president of the Tavern Club from 1931 until his death. During the summer of 1933, he was contacted by Owen Wister, the club's president, about a retirement dinner being planned in his honor. Hale responded with the following letter, written left-handed:

> Intervale, N.H. Sept. 7, '33
>
> Dear Owen:
>
> I appreciate the wish of the Tavern Club to give me a dinner and am much affected, but at the risk of seeming ungracious I cannot accept and for several reasons.
>
> In the first place I shall in all probability not be in Boston this fall and winter for my neuritis, though mild[,] crippled my right hand and would prevent my writing. But I may be in Boston for a day on my way south—. A "testimonial dinner" would disturb—upset me greatly—i[t] would be in the nature of a wake—I would much prefer the joyous remembrance of past years and the knowledge that Tavern & St. Bt[2] think of me kindly.
>
> As you see I write with difficulty.
> With my affectionate regards
> I am yours faithfully
>
> Philip Hale[3]

When he did officially retire, Hale considered it to be temporary; it was announced as such. Olin Downes, who knew Hale well, commented about this in a lengthy laudation in the November 19, 1933 edition of the *New York Times*:

PHILIP HALE'S WORK

Contribution of Distinguished Critic Who
For a Period Lays Down His Pen

By OLIN DOWNES

Mr. Philip Hale, the very distinguished music critic of The Boston Herald, has relinquished his task, at least for a season, to take a much-needed rest from his arduous and modest labors. His reader and colleagues of two continents will sorely miss his writings, however ably his department of The Herald may be represented.

Not only in Boston, where he is lonely and unrivaled, but in the world of English letters that concern music (Mr. Hale's singular versatility and brilliancy in other fields than music must go unmentioned here), he is a man whose international reputation as a critic and writer could only be conditioned by his reticence in all that concerned his personal interests.

He was once well called by the late James Huneker "the phenomenal Philip Hale." Nothing offers stronger justification of the adjective than Mr. Hale's sense of proportion and his almost abnormal conscience about everything pertaining to his labors....

...Readers owe him a debt that is unpayable. No one can replace him, could be substituted, that would fully recompense us for the cessation of his efforts. But the work of the generation that follows Mr. Hale can never go back of a certain level, thanks to his accomplishment and its great and lasting effect.[4]

Two weeks later, however, *Minneapolis Tribune* critic James Davies, who never met Hale, did not treat Hale's retirement as temporary:

Tribute Paid
Boston Critic,
Retiring at 79

Philip Hale, Praised for His
Lucid, Honest Writings
On Music

By James Davies

I have frequently referred in this column to Philip Hale, oldest and most scholarly of American critics, who for a great many years has contributed to the progress of music in this country, and has illuminated many a dark hour for those who like to dip into the mysteries of musical knowledge. He has done this through his contribution to the Boston Herald and especially through the splendid program [notes] he has written for the Boston Symphony orchestra concerts.

> Why he should retire at the early age of 79 is his own particular business. It cannot be that he was tired, as one of his commentators has suggested, for his public documents read as fresh and youthful as they have ever done....
> The critical profession is proud of Philip Hale, proud of his accomplishments and of his qualities as an independent thinker. He was no dry as dust explorer into intellectual regions, not he, rather he possessed a certain blithesomeness that was re-echoed in his writings, learned as they indubitably were. Knowledge to him did not mean obscurity of thought, but rather thought clear and logical, expressed clearly and logically, that anyone might read and understand....[5]

As it turned out, Hale's temporary retirement became permanent. So where did Hale's retirement leave the Boston music criticism industry? Koussevitzky biographer Moses Smith provided a sufficient, if not totally accurate, summation:

> Of the two least friendly Boston critics during Koussevitzky's first ten years in America, one, Stuart Mason of the Christian Science Monitor, had been dismissed early. The other, Penfield Roberts (P.R.) of the Boston Globe, had resigned in 1932. Then, in 1934, the two leading Boston reviewers passed from the active scene. In the spring of that year H.T.P. (Henry T. Parker) died. Soon afterward Philip Hale, advanced in years, gave up most of his duties on the Boston Herald, as well as the task of supplying notes to the Symphony Orchestra's program-books. In the latter capacity he was succeeded by John N. Burk; in the former by Theodor W[ard] Chanler...Meanwhile I became H.T.P.'s successor after having been music critic of the Boston Evening American for ten years.[6]

Burk, of course, was quite successful; he had actually been assisting Hale with program notes toward the end. Chanler was another matter; he was primarily a composer. As a critic he was far from impartial and was out to get Koussevitzky. The *Boston Herald* dismissed him in a matter of weeks.[7] A replacement was found quickly and the news was carried in the *San Francisco Chronicle*:

> Noted S. F. Pianist Chosen as Critic
>
> George B. McManus, pianist, formerly of San Francisco, has been chosen t o succeed Philip Hale as music critic of the Boston Herald. Hale, nearly 80 years old, has retired. He is one of the most scholarly of American writers on music. His distinguished work as program annotator for the Boston Symphony Orchestra will be taken up by John N. Burk. McManus formerly was a member of the faculty of the University of California.[8]

In the meantime, Hale's eyesight finally failed him. This, coupled with the inability to use his right hand, for all practical purposes made him an invalid. Irene summed this up, referring to "the last year of his life, when his eyes gave out, and he could not read."[9] She had now become the "keeper of the flame."

On November 30, 1934, Philip Hale died from a cerebral hemorrhage. Word of his death spread across the country and beyond. Irene received nearly 200 letters of condolence and attempted to answer each one personally.[10] Among those paying personal homage was the prolific English novelist Robert Smythe Hichens (1864–1950) who had previously inscribed a copy of his 1932 novel *Mortimer Brice* "to Mr. and Mrs. Philip Hale." Shortly after Hale's death, Hichens wrote

Susie's Career (American title: *The Pyramid*), in which Hale is portrayed by the fictional character Stephan Harland, "foremost of American musical critics." A note pasted into the inside cover of the copy given to Irene reads:

> To Mrs, Philip Hale
>
> With friendship, and with admiration for the memory of her celebrated husband, Philip Hale
>
> From
> Robert Hichens[11]

Tributes poured in from the music profession, many in print. The critic of the *Boston Times* wrote, "Philip the Great has gone from us and there is no expressing the loss to music criticism and to American cultural life."[12] In *The Musical Quarterly* Carl Engel, chief of the Music Division of Library of Congress, wrote compactly, "Hale was philosopher, aesthete, savant, stylist."[13] Walter R. Spalding wrote of Hale's impact in Phi Beta Kappa's *American Scholar*:

> A critic has two responsibilities: first to help the public to receive more readily the message of the composer; secondly to call attention to merits or blemishes in the performance of any composition... How soon the working of Providence may send us another critic his equal no one can tell. He has left, however, the highest standards and ideals of insight and workmanship which, it may be hoped, his successors will keep steadily before them.[14]

Two years after Hale's death, Olin Downes appeared as the featured speaker of the second annual meeting of the Friends of the Boston Symphony Orchestra. His "eulogy," using bits and pieces of his article on Hale's retirement, gives insight into the critic's personality and provides a final homage to the greatness of both man and deed:

> I can see him now, entering the concert hall, a derby hat cocked on one side, a bow tie of wild colors, a gleam, according to the mood, of humor, or anger, or mockery, in the eye, that saw everything, and looked at and through everybody. People thought his intolerance of what was second class cruel. More often than not, he was tortured with pity, and the number of secret things he did for fellow men, musicians, newspaper writers and artists, never has and never will be known. Those near him found out some of those things. Artists have told me others. He would fight at the drop of a hat for a composition or a person he believed to be the victim of injustice, and whether he fought or praised he dipped his pen in heart's blood. How he could laugh! How that laughter could turn the perplexities and burdens of existence into something that set the devil of hopelessness and sorrow at naught. And how truly could Philip Hale find the word of comfort for the dark hour, and be, in the moment of bitterest trial, the unfailing and invincible friend!
>
> If I thought that memories of this kind would have any melancholy connection—for death where Hale is concerned is still very fresh and unforgotten to those of us who were personally near the man—I would not have had the courage to come here and speak of him to you. But that is not the case. Everything that Hale was and is whispers courage, and the clasp of a strong hand, and the faith that sustains us. So long as music is heard and discussed, his name will not only

be remembered, but passed along through the years. He would have been great in whatever he undertook. He chose to serve music as few other writers ever have. He could have gone to other cities. It is honor equally to him and to Boston that he refused ever to leave this place. When all is said and done, all that was great in his thought and in his achievement is packed into the program notes he wrote in conjunction with the ministrations of this Orchestra. The orchestra will go on to great honors but nothing will dim or cause Hale's achievement to perish. He will companion its fame.[15]

1 Philip Hale's childhood home, "The Gables," Round Hill, Northampton, MA. Author's private collection.

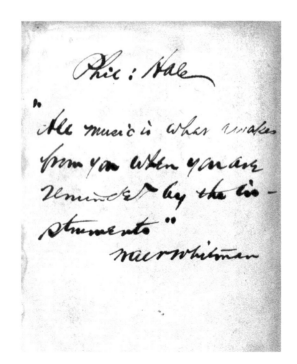

2 Walt Whitman's inscription from *Leaves of Grass* in the cover of *Quarante Mélodies Choises de F. Schubert*, given by him to Philip Hale. Mortimer Rare Book Room, Smith College, Northampton, MA.

3 Philip Hale, n.d. [probably 1890s]. Mortimer Rare Book Room, Smith College, Northampton, MA.

4 "Tanglewild," Philip Hale's summer home at Osterville, MA. Mortimer Rare Book Room, Smith College, Northampton, MA.

5 Philip Hale, Bachrach Studios, 1914. Boston Symphony Orchestra Archives, Boston, MA.

PART II

SELECTED WRITINGS OF PHILIP HALE

OVERVIEW

Philip Hale's genius for writing transcended the boundaries of the pre-established formats by which he was confined. Thoroughness of research, clarity of thought, honesty, and integrity exuded from his pen. The writings included here have been chosen largely on the basis of representation. Hale's commentaries about composers' works already printed in John Nagley Burk's *Philip Hale's Boston Symphony Program Notes* are somewhat less likely to appear here. Most of the concert reviews (and extracts drawn from them) chosen for Appendix III easily fall into one of the subcategories listed below; however, some could have been placed into two or more categories as there is overlap in the content.

APPENDIX I: FROM THE PROGRAM BOOKLETS

AmyB each(1917)	183
Beethoven: *Piano Concerto No. 1 in C* (1932)	186
Commentators on Beethoven's Seventh Symphony (1925, with *Boston Home Journal* extract, 1889)	187
Edward MacDowell (1897)	188
Modeste Moussorgsky: *Pictures at an Exhibition* (1925)	189
"OperaticE xtravagance"(1901)	190

APPENDIX II: ESSAYS FROM NEWSPAPERS

"The Hunting Expedition of Antonin Dvořák" (1894)	193
"Women in the List of Symphony Makers" (1896)	196
"The Attitude of American Critics toward Music" (1903)	198
"Music" (1926) and "'Paradise Lost' by Du Bois and the "Criticism of Music" (1904)	206
"Has the American Composer Been Neglected in Boston?" (1906)	207

APPENDIX III: FROM CONCERT REVIEWS

A. Composersa ndT heirW orks	**213**
Bartok: *Piano Concerto* [No. 1] (1928)	213
Beethoven: *Fidelio Overture* (1894)	214

Beethoven: *Ah! Perfido* (1925)	214
Beethoven: *Leonore Overture No. 1* (1900)	214
Beethoven: *Symphony No. 5 in C minor* (1889)	214
Beethoven: *Symphony No. 6 in F, "Pastorale"* (1921)	215
Beethoven: *Symphony No. 7 in A* (1889)	216
Beethoven: *Symphony No. 9 in D minor* (1899)	216
Berlioz: *Overture to Benvenutto Cellini* (1923)	217
Berlioz: *Harold in Italy* (1903)	217
Berlioz: *Overture to The Hugenots* (1918)	218
Brahms *Festival* (1930)	218
Brahms: *Double Concerto* (1917)	218
Brahms: *Symphonies Nos. 1–4* (1931, 1930, 1932. 1920)	218–220
Bruckner: *Symphony No. 4 in E flat, "Romantic"* (1899)	220
Copland: *Piano Concerto* (1927)	221
Dvorak: *Symphony No. 7 in D minor* (1894)	222
Hindemith: *Konzertmusik for Brass and Strings* (1931)	222
Holst: *The Planets* (1923)	223
Kalinnikoff: *Symphony No. 1 in G minor* (1921)	225
Loeffler: *Hora Mystica* (1917)	225
Mahler: *Symphony No. 5 in C-sharp minor* (1906)	227
Mozart: *Clarinet Concerto* (1918)	230
Mozart: *Piano Concerto No. 21 in C* (1927)	231
Mozart: *Piano Concerto No. 23 in A* (1930)	231
Mozart: *Serenade No. 10 in B flat* (1932)	231
Mozart: *Serenade No. 11 in E flat* (1903)	232
Mozart: *Symphony No. 35 in D, "Haffner"* (1926)	232
Mozart: *Symphony No. 36 in C, "Linz"* (1899)	232
Prokofieff: *Piano Concerto No. 3* (1926)	232
Prokofieff: *Symphony No. 4* (1930)	233
Prokofieff: *Violin Concerto* (1925)	234
Ravel: *La Valse* (1922)	234
Rubinstein: *Piano Concerto No. 4 in D minor*: see Carreño entry, also the Introduction	234
Saint-Saëns *Carnival of the Animals* (1922)	235
Saint-Saëns: *Piano Concerto No. 5 in F* (1920)	235
Schumann: *Symphony No. 4 in D minor* (1900)	236
Strauss, R.: *Suite in B flat* (1912)	236
Stravinsky: *Pulcinella* (1922, 1932)	237
Vaughan Williams: *Fantasia on a Theme by Thomas Tallis* (1922, 1932)	237

B. Conductors — 238

Beecham (1928)	238
Fiedler (1908)	239
Holst (1932)	240
Paur (1895)	242
Rabaud (1919)	243

Sousa (1892, 1906) — 244
Richard Strauss (1904) — 246
Virtuoso Conductors and Muck (1906) — 246
Walter (1923) — 248
Weingartner (1906, 1912) — 248

C. Soloists — 250

Teresa Carreño (1897) — 250
Josef Lhevine (1908) — 251
Nellie Melba (1903) — 252
Maud Powell (1907) — 252
Arthur Rubinstein (1921) — 253
Lionel Tertis (1923) — 253

Appendix IV: Sundry Topics in Newspapers

"Walt Whitman" (1892) — 255
"Talk of the Day" (1899) — 256
"The Harry Jewett Players" (1918) — 258
"As the World Wags" (1923) — 259

Appendix I

Essays in the Boston Symphony Orchestra Program Booklets

This following is just a small sampling of Hale's program essays. He wrote notes for 792 Boston Symphony Orchestra booklets from 1901 to 1933. With an average of four works appearing on each pair of programs, this meant over 3,000 works. Of course, many of these were repeated over the thirty-two-year span. Every effort is made to reproduce these notes just as Hale wrote them. Asterisks (*) were used by Hale for endnotes. Notes added by the author use bracketed asterisks [*].

Amy Beach

March 2, 1917, pp. 1016–1024:

Mrs. Henry Harris Aubrey Beach (born Amy Marcy Cheney) comes of old New England Colonial Stock. She showed musical talent at the age of four and soon began to write little pieces, which were musically correct. Nature gave her an unusually accurate ear. When she was six years old she began taking pianoforte lessons of her mother. Two years later she studied in turn with Johann Ernst Perabo, Junius Welch Hill, and Carl Baermann. She took harmony lessons from Mr. Hill in 1881–1882, but in counterpoint, fugue, and instrumentation she is wholly self-taught. The Treatises of Berlioz and Gevaert were read by her; she made translations from the text; and she studied analytically for many years symphonic works played at concerts of the Boston Symphony Orchestra, thus advised by Wilhelm Gericke.

Her first appearance in public as a pianist was in the Boston Music Hall on October 24, 1883, when she played Moschele's Concerto in D minor with orchestra.

During the ensuing winter she gave several recitals. She has played at concerts of the Boston Symphony Orchestra in Boston these concerts:

1885, March 28, Chopin Concerto in F minor (as Miss Cheney).
1886, February 20, Mozart, Concerto in D minor (as Mrs. Beach).
1888, April 21, Beethoven, Concerto in C minor (cadenzas by Mrs. Beach).
1895, February 16, Saint-Saëns, Concerto in G minor, No. 2.
1900, April 7, Beach, Concerto in C-sharp minor. First performance (MS).

On April 29, 1885, she played here at a Theodore Thomas concert Mendelssohn's Concerto in D minor, No. 2.

With the exception of a few songs, all her compositions were published since her marriage in 1885. Her larger compositions are as follows:

Symphony in E minor, "Gaelic," Op. 32. First played at a concert of the Boston

Symphony Orchestra on October 31, 1896, Mrs. Beach pianist; Emil Paur, conductor; repeated February 12, 1898.

Mass in E flat Major, Op. 5 for soprano, voices, orchestra, and organ. Produced by the Handel and Haydn Society in Boston February 7, 1892, Carl Zerrahn, conductor; B. J. Lang, organist. Solo singers: Mrs. Jennie Patrick Walker, Mrs. Carl Alves, Italo Campanini, Emil Fischer. At this concert Mrs. Beach played the pianoforte in Beethoven's Choral Fantasia.

Festival Jubilee for chorus and orchestra, Op. 18, composed for the dedication of the Woman's Building of the Columbia Exposition in Chicago, 1893; an aria, "Eilende Wolken," Op. 18 (scene from Schiller's "Maria Stuart"; produced for the first time at a concert of the New York Symphony Orchestra conducted by Walter Damrosch in December, 1982, and with Mrs. Carl Alwes as contralto soloist; "The Minstrel and the King," for male chorus and orchestra, Op. 16; "The Rose of Avontotown," "The Sea-Fairies," and "The Chambered Nautilus," all for women's voices and orchestra.

Sonata for violin and pianoforte, Op. 34, Kneisel Quartet, January 4, 1897.

Quintet for pianoforte and strings, Op. 67. Performed in Boston for the first time at her own concert, December 16, 1914, with the Hoffman Quartet. Kneisel Quartet concert, November (Mrs. Beach, pianist).

Romanza for violin and pianoforte (1893).

"Iverniana": Suite for two pianofortes, played from manuscript in Boston by Mrs. Beach and Carl Faelten, February 10, 1910.

Mrs. Beach has written many pianoforte pieces and many songs.

Concerto in C-sharp Minor for Pianoforte, Op. 45 .... Mrs. H. H. A. Beach
    (born at Henniker, New Hampshire September 5, 1867; now living)

This concerto was played for the first time, and from manuscript, at a concert of the Boston Symphony Orchestra on April 7, 1900; Mrs. Beach, pianist, Mr. Gericke, conductor. It was composed in 1899, partly in Boston, where Mrs. Beach was then living, and partly at her cottage near Centreville, Cape Cod.

The orchestral part of the concerto is scored for two flutes, two oboes, two clarinets, bass clarinet, two bassoons, four horn, two trumpets, three trombones, bass tuba, a set of three kettledrums, triangle, and strings. The score is dedicated to Mme. Teresa Carreño.

Mrs. Beach wrote the following description of the concerto for the Programme Book of the Chicago orchestra when she played with it in Chicago February 4, 5, 1916: "The concerto contains four movements, of which the opening *Allegro* is much longer than the others.["] This is built broadly upon the symphonic form, the orchestra and the piano sharing in about an equal degree in the development of the two contrasting themes. The second movement is a "Perpetuum mobile" for the solo instrument, with the melodic and harmonic structure supplied almost entirely by the orchestra. A short slow movement leads without break into the finale which is interrupted before the close by a recurrence of the *Largo*.

We quote form William Foster Apthorp's analysis of the concerto published in the Programme Book of the Boston Symphony Orchestra, April 6, 7, 1900: –

"The first movement of this concerto, Allegro Moderato in C-sharp minor, 4-4' time, opens with a short orchestral-prelude.... It merely announces the first theme and develops it to a certain extent. The pianoforte soon enters with a free cadenza on figures from this theme in the further development of which (and of its inversion, *motu contrario*), the orchestra soon joins it. At a slight slackening of the tempo, poco píu tranquillo, the development returns to the orchestra, while the pianoforte hits a new counter-theme against it. After what promises to be a modulation to the relative E major, but really ends with a return to the tonic C-sharp minor, the orchestra announces the first subsidiary...; and the pianoforte almost immediately takes part in the development of this theme, but soon leaves it to the orchestra again, while it accompanies the development with running bravura passages and arpeggios. As this passage dies away...the orchestra comes in with one more allusion to the first theme,["] leading over to the entrance of the second. This more cantabile melody enters in the pianoforte alone in A major, the orchestra taking up the development after a while (with the melody in a solo violin), in C-sharp major, against elaborate embroidery in the solo instrument. A concluding passage, for both pianoforte and orchestra, in which elements from the first theme, counter-theme, and subsidiary are to be detected, closes the first part of the movement, which merges into the free fantasia. The elaborate working-out of the free fantasia continues for some time; the beginning of the third part is not clearly indicated, the recapitulation not being distinctly recognizable until a second return of the second theme, fortissimo, in D-flat major (enharmonic of the tonic C-sharp major). The very extended development of this theme now leads to an unaccompanied cadenza for the pianoforte, which, in its turn, leads to a short and brilliant coda, principally on the first theme.

"The second movement,["] Scherzo (*Perpetuum mobile*): Vivace, in A major, 2–4 time, consists of the alternate development of two not very sharply contrasting themes, which development is given entirely to the orchestra. After some brief preluding by the orchestra alone, the first theme in announced in the tonic by the violas and violoncellos and then developed at length; the second theme enters considerably later, in the flute, in G major. The development of both themes is exceedingly elaborate. While this development is going on in the orchestra, the pianoforte keeps up a persistent accompaniment of counter-figures in sixteenth notes (the *perpetuum mobile*); this accompaniment never flags nor changes its rhythm for a moment.

"The third movement, Largo in F-sharp minor, 3–4 time, begins with some free orchestral preluding on its own theme. The pianoforte then enters with the theme, and the development is continuous to the end of the movement, being at times confided to the solo instrument, at others to the orchestra, against accompanying figures in the pianoforte. This movement is immediately enchained with the next."

"The fourth movement," "Allegro con scioltezza* in C-sharp minor, 6–8 time, opens immediately with its brilliant first theme in the pianoforte alone. After a while the orchestra steps in with accompanying chords. A brief *tutti* leads over to the entrance of the second theme in the relative E major; the development of this theme is partly in the pianoforte, accompanied by the orchestra, partly *vice versa*. An unaccompanied cadenza leads over to the recapitulation, the first theme returning regularly in the tonic, in the orchestra, against brilliant embroidery in the solo instrument. Just where the second theme ought to enter, there comes an episode in G-sharp minor, 9–8 time, on a more passionate cantilena, after which the second theme, followed by a brief coda, poco píu mosso, closes the movement.

In the fall of 1913 Mrs. Beach played her concerto in various German cities—Leipsic, Hamburg, Berlin.

*Allegro withf reedom.

Ludwig van Beethoven

Monday Evening, February 15, 1932, pp. 16–20:

Piano Concerto No. 1 in C, Op. 15

Though Hale wrote notes for practically all of the Boston Symphony Orchestra concerts from the 1901–1902 season through 1932–1933, he generally did not review the Monday evening concerts. This program note is particularly interesting because Hale, rather than discussing the work directly, not only lets Beethoven to do that for him (to a degree), but also allows a substantial amount of space for the composer's striking remarks about music critics:

> Although this concerto is listed as No. 1, it was composed after No. 2 (B-flat major). A still earlier concerto [WoO4], which was long unknown, manuscript written in a boy's handwriting, "Un Concert pour le Clavecin ou Fortepiano composé par Louis van Beethoven, agé de douze ans," was edited by Guido Adler and is published in the collected works of Beethoven. The manuscript contains the solo part complete, with the orchestral preludes and interludes in transcription for pianoforte. There are indications that it was scored for small orchestra—strings, flutes, and horns only. Another early concerto was one in D major [K. Anh. 7]. The first movement was performed in Vienna April 7, 1889. It was edited by Adler and is also in the edition of Beethoven's complete works. It was probably composed in the period 1788–93, "perhaps before rather than after 1790." Adler suggested that Beethoven attached little value to it and laid it permanently aside.
>
> Beethoven played the concerto in C major at his concert in the Konviktsaal, Prague, in 1798. He also played the Adagio and Rondo in A major from Op. 2, and improvised on a theme given him, "Ah tu fosti il primo oggetto" from Mozart's "Clemenza di Tito." This theme was given him by Countess Schick. Johann Wenzel Tomaschek* heard him and wrote in his diary: "Beethoven's magnificent playing and particularly the daring flights in his improvisation stirred me strangely in the depths of my soul; indeed I found myself so profoundly bowed down that I did not touch my pianoforte for several days." At his second concert in Prague, Beethoven played his concerto in B-flat major.
>
> Beethoven played the concerto in C major for the first time in Vienna on April 2, 1800. The concerto is dedicated to the Countess Odescalchi,** née Keglevich. It was published by Mollo at Vienna in 1801. There are three cadenzas for the first movement of the concerto.
>
> On April 22, 1801, Beethoven wrote to Breitkopf and Härtel: "One of my first concertos and therefore not one of the best of my compositions is to be published by Hofmeister, and that Mollo is to publish a concerto which indeed was written later,*** but nevertheless does not rank among the best of my works in this form. This is only a hint for your musical journal in the matter of criticism of these works, although if one might hear them (well played, that is) one would best be able to judge them. Musical policy requires that one should keep possession for a space of the best concertos. You should remind to Messrs. your critics great care and wisdom especially in the case of products of younger authors; many a one may by frightened off who otherwise might, probably, accomplish more; so far as I am concerned I am far from thinking that I am so perfect as not to be the subject of blame, yet the howls of your critics against me were at first so humiliating that after comparing myself with others I could not get angry, but remained perfectly quiet, and concluded they did not understand their business; it was easier

to remain quiet since I saw the praise lavished on people who have no significance *in loco* in the eyes of the better sort and who disappeared from sight here no matter how good they may otherwise have been—but *pax vobiscum*—peace for me and them—I would not have mentioned a syllable about the matter had not you yourself done so."

*Tomaschek, excellent organist and composer, renowned as a teacher (1774–1850).
**Anna Louisa Barbara was the daughter of Karl Count Keglevies de Busin and Barbara Countess Zichy. She married Prince Inno Lenz d'Era Odescalchi in 1801 (or 1800). Beethoven also dedicated to her the Sonata, Op. 7, the Variations "La stressa, la setessissima." He took part in musical soirées at the Odescalchi palace.
***The Concerto in C major, Op. 15.

January 31, 1925, pp. 31–32:

Symphony No. 7 in A, Op. 92

Mark what commentators have found in the Seventh Symphony:

One finds a new pastorale symphony, another a new "Eroica." Alberti is sure that it is a description of the joy of the German delivered from the French yoke. Dr. Iken of Brennan saw in it political revolution. Nohl shakes his head and swears it is a knightly festival. Marx is inclined to think that the music describes a Southern race, brave and warlike, such as the ancient Moors of Spain. An old edition of the Symphony gave this program: "Arrival of the Villagers; Nuptial Benediction; The Bride's Procession, The Wedding Feast." Did not Schumann discover in the second movement the marriage ceremony of a village couple? D'Ortigue found that the Andante pictured a procession in an old cathedral or in the catacombs; while Dürenberg, a more cheerful person, prefers to call it the love-drama of a sumptuous odalisque. The Finale has many meanings: a battle of giants or warriors of the North returning to their country after the fight; a feast of Bacchus or an orgy of the villagers after a wedding. Oulibichev goes so far as to say that Beethoven portrayed in this Finale a drunken revel to express the disgust excited in him by such popular recreations. Even Wagner writes hysterically about this Symphony as "the apotheosis of the dance," and he reminds a friend of the "Strömkarl" of Sweden, who knows eleven variations, and mortals should dance to only ten of them; the eleventh belongs to the Night spirit and his crew, and, if anyone plays it, tables and benches, cans and cups, the grandmother, the blind and lame, yea, the children in the cradle, fall to dancing. "The last movement of the Seventh Symphony," says Wagner, "is this eleventh variation."

In these days, the first question asked about absolute music is, "What does it mean?" The symphonic poem is free and unbridled in its choice of subject and purpose. The composer may attempt to reproduce in tones the impression made on him by scenery, picture, book, man, statue. He is "playing the plate" like the aesthete pianist in *Punch*.

Why should anything be read into the music of this Seventh Symphony? It may be that Abbé Stadler was right in saying that the theme of the trio in the Scherzo is an old pilgrim hymn of Lower Austria, but the statement is of only antiquarian interest.

To them that wish to read the noblest and most poetic appreciation of the symphony, the essay of Berlioz will bring unfailing delight. The Seventh Symphony needs no analysis; it escapes the commentator. As the landscape is in the eye of the beholder, so the symphony is in the ear of the hearer.

***
*

The symphony is scored for two flutes, two oboes, two clarinets, two bassoons, two horns, two trumpets, kettledrums, strings.
    I. The first movement opens with an Introduction, poco sostenuto, A major, 4–4. The main body is Allegretto, A minor, 2–4[*].
    II. Allegretto, A minor, 2–4.
    III. Presto, F major, 3–4.*
    IV. The Finale, Allegro con brio, 2–4, is a wild rondo on two themes. Here, according to M. Prod'homme and others, as Beethoven achieved in the Scherzo, the highest and fullest expression of exuberant joy,—"unbuttoned joy," as the composer himself would have said, – so in the Finale the joy becomes orgiastic. The furious bacchantic first theme is repeated after the exposition, and there is a sort of coda to it, "as a chorus might follow upon the stanzas of a song."

[* This is undoubtedly a misprint. The body is in A major, marked Vivace, in 6/8.]
* Alexander Siloti, the Russian pianist and conductor, contributed an article to the Signale of September 17, 1913, in which he argued that the whole Scherzo should be considered as being in 6–4 instead of 3–4.

Edward MacDowell

This special invited essay appeared in the December 4, 1897 Boston Symphony Orchestra program book. Hale was not program annotator at this time. Six years earlier, after writing notes for only three programs, Hale was removed from that position at the insistence of Arthur Nikisch and was replaced by William Foster Apthorp. It would be another three and a half years before Hale was reinstated:

EDWARD A. MACDOWELL
By Philip Hale

    I believe that Mr. MacDowell is one of the greatest of composers now living.
    This belief is based on his works for orchestra, his piano pieces, and his songs.
    I know of no composer now living who displays in more marked degree the combination of these qualities: pure, spontaneous, original melody; intimate knowledge of usual and unusual harmonic effects; musical, and not merely pedantic, employment of counterpoint; mastery of instrumental color; poetic inspiration and noble imagination; persuasive, lovable, authoritative individuality.
    His force is never intolerant or brutal; his sentiment is not cloying or effeminate; his singularly refined taste and his faculty of self examination keep him from abuse of power, the wish to startle or perplex, the craving to be recognized.
    It may be said—and it has been said by some—that Mr. MacDowell has never written a symphony. "Do you still give him such extravagant praise?" A good answer to this fetishistic, absurd proposition would be: "Mr. Friedrich Gernsheim has written four symphonies, and Mr. Heinrich von Herzogenberg has written at least two."
    Do you remember the words of Poe? "If by 'sustained effort,' any little gentleman has accomplished an epic, let us frankly commend him for the effort—if this indeed be a thing commendable—but let us forebear praising the epic on the effort's account. It is to be hoped that common-sense, in the time to come, will

prefer deciding upon a work of Art, rather than by the impression it makes—by the effect it produces—than by the time that it took to impress the effect, or by the amount of 'sustained effort' which had been found necessary in effecting the impression. The fact is that perseverance is one thing, and genius quite enough; nor can all the Quarterlies in Christendom confound them."

Thus to me such a piano piece as Mr. MacDowell's "The Eagle" outweighs a dozen symphonies written by Slaves of the Lamp. On this whizzing ball creep all sorts and conditions of man; and there are hearers who say honestly "I see nothing in that little thing" just as they see nothing in the poem itself. These good people prefer the complete works of Mrs. Lydia Huntley Sigourney to a fragment of Sappho.

But Mr. MacDowell is not a man of fragments. Two noble sonatas—though the Tragica is the nobler—two suites for orchestra, symphonic poems, two concertos for piano with orchestra can hardly be called fragments.

I have heard men say, "Yes, he is a composer of charming thoughts, but he has no respect for form." What do they mean by "form"? The charge is preposterous. Form to them means cut-and-dried, conservatory-crowned dullness. It means an obsequious attempt to follow with heavy feet in the footsteps of departed worthies. Form is not a Procrustean bed for all ages. Form in its essence is eternal; its outward appearance varies, changes, is transformed. Even, in the most fantastic of Mr. MacDowell's expressions of musical thought, there is an established plan, coherency of structure, logical result from a strong premise.

He chooses the symphonic poem rather than the symphony. He finds it more in accordance with the spirit of his age. How many symphonies in the strict sense have been written since the death of Beethoven that bid fair to be immortal?

In Mr. MacDowell we might look for the influences of Scotch blood, early French training, the supervision of Raff. He owes much to these influences; they have contributed gladly to the better expression of his own rare individuality. But he is not a copyist, he is not an echo. His own voice is unmistakable.

The character of the man has shaped his music. He is fond of sport, an admirer of physical prowess, not disdainful of the technic of the prize-fighter or the courage of the fireman; a man of blameless life, yet profoundly sympathetic, knowing the infirmities of others; singularly shy concerning his own work, indefatigable in the encouragement of others; a wise and helpful teacher. A virtuoso of the piano as well as the orchestra, a brilliant conductor, he now teaches others. He is not yet forty years old. He already has an international reputation. And I believe that he is only at the beginning of his career.

[*Unfortunately, Hale's prediction was not realized. MacDowell, already burdened with responsibilities at Columbia University, composed very little from this time forward. The composer's final orchestra work, *Suite No. 2*, Op. 48, "Indian," had been composed during the previous year. Tragically, MacDowell would soon suffer from a brain tumor; it cut short his life at the age of forty-seven.]

Modeste Moussorgsky

January 31, 1925, pp. 22–23:

Pictures at an Exhibition (Pianoforte Pieces Arranged for Orchestra by Maurice Ravel)

> Ravel has an intimate acquaintance with Russian Music. It is said that his memory is remarkable; that he can play at request passages from the whole musical literature

of Russia, even from the operas of Serov. Praising Moussorgsky's "Tableaux d'une Exposition" one day when he was talking with Mr. Koussevitzky, the latter asked him if he would not orchestrate them for his use. He gladly acceded to the request and the Suite in this form was performed at Mr. Koussevtzky's concert in Paris on May 3, 1923. The Suite was performed again in Paris at a Koussevitzky concert on May 8, 1924.

Ravel's was not the first nor the last orchestration of the pianoforte pieces. Eight of the pieces, orchestrated by Touschmalov, were performed at Leningrad on December 12, 1891. (This suite was played at Chicago by the Chicago Symphony Orchestra on March 19, 20, 1920). Sir Henry Wood afterwards tried his hand at orchestrations for his concerts in London. Leonidas Leonardi, a pianist and composer in Paris, orchestrated the Suite, which was performed at a concert of Russian music at the Salle Gaveau, by the Lamoureux Orchestra led by Leonardi as late as June 15, 1924. Concerning this orchestration, and for other information, we are now indebted to Dr. Zederbaum.

"Ravel scoring the Suite by Moussorgsky did not wish to modernize it much, therefore he tried, as much as possible, to keep the size of the orchestra in Rimsky-Korsakov's 'Boris Godunov', and added some more instruments only in a few movements of the Suite. All instruments are employed in threes; there are some more percussion instruments than those used by Rimsky-Korsakov; he uses two harps, kettledrums, bass drum, snare drum, celesta, xylophone, glockenspiel, rattle, bells. Only in one movement, 'Il Vecchio Castello' ('The Old Castle'), is the xylophone employed."

"The rights of all of Moussorgsky's compositions are held by the publishers Bessel, and these rights are still defended in Paris. Mr. Koussevitzky, therefore, had to ask permission from the firm for Ravel's orchestration. The Bessels granted permission under the condition that Mr. Koussevitzky should not rent or give the score to any other conductor even at a Koussevitzky concert; for they said this orchestration could not be of advantage to them. After the great success of Ravel's orchestration, they ordered one by Leonardi, whose idea of the art is very remote. The Parisian press found Leonardi's work, performed only once and under his direction, a rather 'temerarious attempt', (the expression used by Gustave Samazeuilh and Paul Le Flem) after Ravel's masterpiece."

[*There is much additional information in this essay, but only about the piano original, not as it pertains to the orchestral performance heard on this concert.]

OPERATIC EXTRAVAGANCE

April 5, 1901:

This Entr'acte was written during the spring before Hale was reinstated as program annotator. It may well have served as a re-audition essay:

ENTR'ACTE.
OPERATICE XTRAVAGANCE
By Philip Hale

The first operas were confined to the palace theatres. It was at Florence through the labors of Monteverdi that the first opera-house for the general public was established. In 1637 two Venetians, one a theorbo player, and one a composer, opened at their own risk an opera-house in Venice. The theatre was called San Cassiano. The price of admission was a sum equivalent to forty cents. Other theatres were soon established in Venice by private individuals or stock companies. Wealthy families and German princes sat in boxes. The citizens went two or three times a year with their families. The population of Venice at this time was about 140,00. The seasons of opera were in winter up to the end of the carnival, at the Feast of the Assumption for a fortnight, and in the fall. These opera houses were built with great care; the bill-boards and the hours of performance were regulated by a council, and the safety of the theatre was carefully considered. The hall was lighted by a huge lamp which disappeared when the curtain rose. Two rows of lamps were on the sides of the stage. If a spectator wished to follow the libretto, a wax taper was brought to him. The singers at first shared in the profits. They afterwards received modest salaries, which in the eighteenth century grew to be considerable. Thus in 1719 Lotti and his wife received 10,000 thalers at Dresden. When an opera succeeded, the composer might receive as much as 100 ducats. The librettist was content with the honor, although his dedications were often rewarded by those whom he flattered. The librettos were sold in quantities, and often outlived the music. If an opera was successful, the libretto was generally given to another composer for treatment.

The question of salaries paid opera singers has always been of interest to many. Statistics in this instance are sometimes to be viewed with suspicion, for neither singer nor manager is invariably truthful in statement. In the early days of opera in England, Mrs. Tofts, who went mad, was paid considerably over $3,000 for one season in 1708. About the middle of the eighteenth century, and at the same theatre, Farinelli earned at least $30,000 a year. Caffarelli st the King's Theatre received $9,000 for a season of three months. A famous soprano, Aguiari, whose phenomenal range elicited the wonder of the boy Mozart, was in 1775 paid $500 a night for two songs. In 1806 Catalani sang in London for $25,000 for the season, and her total profits in 1807, with all concerts included, amounted to nearly $100,000. For one festival she received $10,000. Malibran was engaged in London for nineteen nights at $750 a night, payable in advance. In 1833 at Drury Lane she received 80,000 francs for forty performances, with two benefits, which produced not less than 50,000 francs. Later she drew $12,000 for twenty-four performances, and at La Scala she received nearly $95,000 for eighty-five or ninety performances. The tenor Mario was offered $3,000 a month for his first appearance. Sontag received $30,000 for a season of six months at Her Majesty's Theatre in 1849. Rubini, who left behind him over $700,000, an enormous fortune for a singer in those days (he died in 1854), began his career at five francs a night, but later was paid $11,500 for one concert in St. Petersburg. On the other hand, a French singer in a concert at the Society Islands agreed to sing for a third of the receipts. Her share consisted of three pigs, twenty-three turkeys, forty-four chickens, five thousand cocoanuts, and bananas, lemons, and oranges. When Calvé was first engaged at the Monnaie, Brussels (1881–82), she received only 700 francs a month, and the highest salary paid there at the time was to the tenor Vergnet, who received 8,000 francs a month. The total sum paid monthly to the singers, and they were of excellent repute, was 41,000 francs. The next season Calvé's salary was raised to 1,200 francs a month. The large sums paid Sembrich, Calvé, Melba, Jean de Reszke during late years are known to all.

The opera has always been an expensive entertainment, either on account of the gorgeousness of scenery and costume, or on account of the exorbitant demand of the singers. Thus, the expense of the *Ballet de la Reine*, performed at the Palais du Petit Bourbon, Oct. 15, 1581, which was in reality an opera, amounted to $720,000—3,600,000 francs with the purchasing power of that day. This gorgeous scenery was inherited from the performance of Mysteries. In the first Mysteries there was no scenery, but little by little the stage scenery became most complicated.

There were all sorts of stage tricks and devices—eclipses, earthquakes, an imitation of the Deluge, water turned into wine, animals, giants. And wind-lasses, capstans, counterpoises were in general use to deceive the eye. Some who returned from the Crusades brought back incredible stage inventions. The actor who took the part of the Saviour made himself invisible. A saint who had been decapitated made his exit with his head in his hand.

In the earlier days, as now, the splendor of the stage was an important prop of opera. The prince of Rome, as of other towns, was pleased to ruin his fortune in a wild attempt to restore "the simplicity of the Greeks." The Royal Theatre of the Barberini family saw the introduction of ingenious machinery in 1637. Furies, and chariots drawn by dragons, flew through the air; hurricanes swept over plains and towns. And after opera found its way from the palace to the opera house, there was at first a brave attempt to maintain the magnificence of the show. The scenery in Bontempi's *Il Paride* at Dresden in 1662, cost $300,000. Some operas were only shows in five acts, with processions of nations, animals, marvelous costumes, exotic objects. In one of these operas the city of Persepolis was fired by a mine. In *Berenice* at Bologna in 1680, lions, elephants, horses, crowds, stables which held a hundred horses, hunting the boar, the stag, and the bear, were all upon the stage. John Evelyn went to the opera in Venice, and he marveled at the flying through the air, and at the general performance; "one of the most magnificent and expensive diversions the wit of man can invent." We find Addison sneering as Nicolini sailing in an open boat on a pasteboard sea, painted dragons spitting wildfire, enchanted chariots drawn by Flemish mares, real cascades in artificial landscapes, song birds filling Armida's bower, Rinaldo meeting a lion. Even the scenery and the costumes of an opera performed in the open air at Vienna, according to Lady Mary Wortley Montagu's description, cost $150,000.

We hear much to-day about the arrogance and the Fatuousness of celebrated singers, but these singers are men and women of shrinking modesty in comparison with some of their illustrious predecessors. Some of the male sopranos were the friend and counselors of monarchs. They were mixed up in political intrigue. The women stirred up strife in Courts. The rivalry of two prima donnas divided households. At London in 1725, the women in the fashionable world, during the opera season, adopted the brown silk dress embroidered with silver, which Baroni wore as the heroine in *Rodelinda*; "a national uniform of beauty and youth." The prima donna shared honors with the male soprano. She claimed the privilege of the escort of a page when she made her entrance. He held the train and followed her every movement. The tenor was obliged to be either a noble father, a traitor, or a tyrant, for the lover's part was given to the male soprano. His person was sacred. Others might slay and be slain; he was inviolable. Although the piece might wreak with blood, the male soprano was never allowed to be murdered. These sopranos were spoiled children. One must always enter on horseback, another sulked unless he made his entrance by descending a mountain, another refused to sing unless his hat-plumes were five and a half feet high. The sopranos would often stay upon the stage, sucking oranges or drinking wine, while their colleagues sang. Grétry said that during the seven or eight years he lived in Rome he never saw serious opera succeed: "If the theatre was crowded it was to hear a certain singer; when he left the stage the people in the boxes played cards or ate ices, and those in the pit yawned."

The conventions are mighty in opera. Even to-day the Italian prima donna, in all save the ultra-realistic operas, must wear a ball gown, and she still carries a handkerchief, which she will not drop even in a burst of passion.

Appendix II

Essays from Newspapers

Boston Journal, January 1, 1894:

ABOUT MUSIC

The Hunting Expedition of Antonin Dvorak

How He Went A-Gunning After Genuine American Music.

What Certain People Think of His Musical Game Bag

Inasmuch as Mr. Dvorak's symphony "From the New World" is considered by some as "an historical event," let us look at its origin.

According to the New York Herald, it was Mrs. Thurber's "fixed plan to persuade the composer to attempt a bold exploration into the musical material of America and lay the foundations for a national school of composition.

For this exploration and for incidental services as Director of the National Conservatory, Mrs. Thurber agreed to pay Mr. Dvorak $15,000 a year.

And what did Mr. Dvorak do?

*
**

According to the New York Herald, the said Mr. Dvorak began to study native music after his arrival in New York. Unfortunately, for the future historian, we are not told how he studied it, or whether he disguised himself in his exploration so that the music would not become suspicious, frightened, and then escape. It would be a pleasure to read of his wanderings in the jungles of the Bowery and in the deserts of Central Park. It would be interesting to know precisely his first thought on seeing the Harlem goat, an animal now rare. The composer is a modest man, and he has not even hinted at his perilous trips on the elevated railway or the Belt line.

But what a book he could write! For, according to the New York Herald, "there is no more impressionable man than Dvorak. His moods vary with the hours. He is sensitive as a child. His imagination will take fire immediately. He absorbs color, form, sentiment, everything from his surroundings."

At the end of his first year in America the intrepid explorer determined to visit Spillville, Ia., not for the purpose of tracing or shooting national music. He wished to take a vacation in this Bohemian village. Besides, he had made up his mind; he had bagged his game. Just before his departure he gave his conclusions to the New York Herald. These conclusions were as follows:

"I am now satisfied, "he said, "that the future music of this country must be founded upon what are called the Negro melodies. This can be the foundation of a serious and original school of composition to be developed in the United States. When I first came I was impressed with this idea, and it has developed into a settled conviction. These beautiful and varied themes are the product of the soil. They are American. They are the folk songs of America and your composers must turn to them. All of the great musicians have borrowed from the songs of the common people. Beethoven's most charming scherzo is based upon what might now be considered a skillfully handled Negro melody. I have myself gone to the simple, half forgotten tunes of the Bohemian peasants for hints in my serious work. Only in this way can a musician express the true sentiment of a people. He gets into touch with the common humanity of a country. In the Negro melodies of America I discover all that is needed for a great and noble school of music. They are pathetic, tender, passionate, melancholy, solemn, religious, bold, merry, gay, gracious, or what you will. It is music that suits itself to any mood or any purpose. There is nothing in the whole range of composition that cannot find a thematic source here."

*
**

Now, strange to relate, the American composer did not cut out at once this Dvorakian paragraph and paste it in his hat. As a rule, he was inclined to contradict the eminent Bohemian. There, was pother for a time. The views of celebrated Europeans who knew little of nothing about America, were cabled over at considerable expense and read at length by the idle of cultivated taste.

Then Mr. Dvorak went to work on his op. 95. He took the precaution of announcing, and it was in the New York Herald, that he would write a symphony based upon American Negro and Indian melodies "to prove that his position was sound and sincere."

Mr. Krehbiel states that this symphony, the fifth, was written in New York last spring, but revised and probably completed in its orchestration in the course of the composer's summer vacation, which he spent in Spillville, Ia.

The symphony was first played at the second public rehearsal and second concert of the Philharmonic Society, New York, Dec. 15 and 16 under the direction of Mr. Seidl.

*
**

It is of interest to note that the title on the manuscript of this American Symphony is in Bohemian.

This American Symphony is conducted in Boston by a German, who speaks little or no English.

And how many men in the orchestra that plays here this American Symphony were born in this country?

*
**

It will be observed that the folk songs of America are, according to Mr. Dvorak, peculiar to either the Negro or the Indian. The American, as an American, has no national music, no folk-song.

Why should not this symphony be called the "Negro-Indian Symphony," if it must have a special name?

*
**

Appendix II

Mr. Krehbiel is now inclined to believe that at last we really have a great national piece of music. In an interesting article, published lately in the New York Tribune, he reviewed the symphony from the standpoint of nationality, and, although he finds many things in the symphony, he finds also large quantities of Americanism.

But hold. How does Mr. Krehbiel deal with the fact that the American, in the modern sense of the word, is without folk-song? Hear him:

"He (Dvorak) recognized, too, what his critics forgot, that that music is entitled to be characteristic of a people which gives the greatest pleasure to the largest fraction of a people."

By this process of reasoning either Irish or German folk-song might be called properly the characteristic music of the city of New York.

*
**

Mr. Krehbiel finds an American tune in a phrase of four measures announced by the horn in the first allegro. It is "American," because it has a rhythmical construction "characteristic of the music which has a popular charm in this country;" and this rhythmical construction is what? Why, the Scot's snap, "a device common in Scottish music," and "it is found in Hungarian music, too." Therefore, it is American.

The phrase, this American phrase, "is built on the pentatonic, or five-note, scale, which omits the fourth and seventh tones of our ordinary diatonic series." Now, this scale, according to Mr. Krehbiel, is Scotch, Irish, Chinese, "for the old music of these peoples and many others is marked by this peculiarity." Therefore, it is American.

Then the subsidiary melody "gives a somewhat Oriental tinge to the movement." Therefore, it is American.

Let us quote again from Mr. Krehbiel:

"Here is the melody which will cling most pertinaciously to the memory of those who hear the symphony, and which they will most quickly recognize as containing the spirit of the music the people, as a whole, like best; it is Irish, it is Scotch, it is American."

The next specimen of Americanism discovered by Mr. Krehbiel is in the larghetto where, to use his language, "we are stopped from seeking forms that are naïve and thrown wholly upon a study of the spirit. It is Dr. Dvorak's proclamation of the mood which he found in the story of Hiawatha's wooing, as set forth in Longfellow's poem." Hiawatha was an Indian. Therefore, the symphony is American.

*
**

In the finale Mr. Krehbiel finds a paraphrase of "Yankee Doodle." Here at last by association is something American. But the tune is of English origin.

*
**

Some, with Mr. Krebiel, regard this symphony as an "American" work. Others, with that brilliant and accomplished writer, Mr. James G. Huneker, think that this symphony is delightful and not "American."

But let Mr. Huneker speak for himself concerning the symphony:

"The themes are simple and understandable, their exposition enjoyable, and the luster and brilliancy of the instrumentation, the many delightful rhythms, all conspire toward making the symphony a popular work. And it has that unmistakable ring of the folk song which will endear it to all nationalities. Yet the American symphony, like the American novel, has yet to be written. And when it is, it will have been composed by an American. This is said with all due deference to Dr. Dvorak.... Its (the symphony's) extremely Celtic character was patent to numerous people, and the general opinion seemed to be that Dvorak had not been long in discovering what a paramount factor the Irish were in the political life of this country. Said one: 'Why not call it the "Tammany Hall" Symphony? That is, Indian and Irish, and are not Indian and Irish American?'"

*
**

The discussion of other topics suggested by this word "American" in connection with music must be deferred for the present. A review of the symphony as performed last evening in Music Hall will be found in another column of this Journal.

[*See Chapter 2 for more about Hale and Krehbiel on this symphony.]

Boston Journal, November 4, 1896:

WITHM USICIANS

Women in the List of
Symphony Makers

Thoughts Suggested by the
Work of Mrs. Beach

Endeavor Counts for Little in
Judging Results

I spoke Sunday of symphonies written by women. From 1675 to 1892 there were at least 153 works for the stage by female composers. Mrs. De Laguerre's "Céphale et Procris," produced at the Paris Opéra March 15, 1694, had no more success than Augusta Holmés "La Montagne Notre," produced at the Paris Opéra Feb. 8, 1895. And since 1892 operas and operettas by women have been performed, and in certain instances conducted by the composers.

But symphonies by women are more easily counted.

First should stand the name of Jeanne Louise Farrene (1804–1875), a musician of indisputable talent and unusual fertility, who was praised by Schumann, as well as Joachim, for her chamber music, and Joachim gladly played first violin in her Nonetto in Paris in 1849. Mrs. Farrene wrote three symphonies. No. 1, in C minor, was played in Brussels Feb. 23, 1845, and in Paris April 27 of the same year, not April 17 as stated by Fétis. No. 2, in D major, was played in Paris May 3, 1846. No. 3, in G minor, was produced at a concert of the Paris Conservatory April 22, 1849. Fétis, the pedagogue, spoke of her as "the only woman in musical Europe, who, without scholastic pedantry, shows veritable knowledge combined with grace and taste."

Alice May Meadows White, born Smith (1839–1884), wrote two symphonies. No. 1, in C minor, was played in London in 1863. No. 2, in G major, was in manuscript at her death. I do not know if it was ever played.

A symphony in G major by Miss H. Edith Green was produced in London April 30, 1895. A gushing reviewer wrote of it "Titania in the 'Midsummer Night's Dream' called for 'Music! Such as charmeth sheep.' Had she been present at the performance of this symphony, Queen Titania would, apparently, have been amply satisfied."

I am told that Miss E[thyl]. M. Smyth, whose Mass in D was produced in London in 1893, under royal patronage, has written a symphony of unusual merit. I am unable to find any record of performance.

Otto Gumprecht mentions performances of the symphonies of Emilie Meyer, "which were written in the style of Haydn."

Then there is Aline Hundt, a pianist and pupil of Liszt. She conducted a performance of her symphony in G minor at Berlin in the spring of 1871. She died a year or two afterward, regretted deeply by musicians.

Two French women now living and of marked musical talent are the Viscontess de Grandvál and Augusta Holmés. The former, born in 1830, has written operas, operettas, masses, a Stabat Mater (sung in Paris in 1870 and in New York in 1893), an oratorio, chamber music, songs, etc. Her "Esquisses Symphoniques" was performed in Paris in 1874, and she has written a concert overture. I find no record of a symphony by this woman, who is respected highly by her male colleagues in France.

Augusta Holmés, born of Irish parents in Paris, became a French citizeness by law in 1879. Her mother was related to MacGregors and O'Briens. She has composed works of extraordinary length, and breadth and, possibly, thickness. An Andante pastorale, "fragment of a symphony," was played in Paris June 14, 1887, but was the symphony ever finished? There is her symphonic poem "Irlande"; there is a Suite symphonique; but did she finish her symphony? Miss Holmés is the woman to whom Wagner said at Triebschen: "I do not wish to be toward alert and creative spirits as in the manchineel tree, which by its shade, chokes birds. Take my advice: be of no school, especially not of mine.

*
**

Mrs. Beach is praised by some concert-goers on account of her "endeavor." She deserved louder praise than this.

What Edgar Allen Poe said of a certain kind of poetical achievement may be well applied to a musical composition. "If, by 'sustained effort,' any little gentleman has accomplished an epic, let us frankly commend him for the effort—if this indeed be a thing commendable—but let us forebear praising the epic on the effort's account. It is to be hoped that common sense, in the time to come, will prefer deciding upon a work of Art, rather by the impression it makes—by the effect it produces—than by the time it took to impress the effect, or by the mount of sustained effort which had been found necessary in effecting the impression. The fact is that perseverance is one thing and genius quite another; nor can all the Quarterites in Christendom confound them."

*
**

Four days have gone by since Mrs. Beach's symphony was played in Music Hall. Much of it is fresh in the memory. Of how many new works can you say the same thing after one hearing? I admit that the slow movement is too long, that the composer seems reluctant to reach the final cadence, that there is more elaboration than spontaneity in the movement. I go so far as to say that she might revise it with advantage. But how much there is to admire in the other movements!

I do not know what Mrs. Brach had in mind when she was writing the first movement. She was concerned chiefly, no doubt, with writing music. And yet the treatment of themes, which in themselves are of inconsiderable value, stimulated the imagination of the hearer. There was thought of

"Old unhappy, far-off things
And battles long ago."

A definite mood was created. The imagination of the hearer was quickened by the imagination of the composer. And in the symphony Mrs. Beach displays generously a musical imagination that I have not recognized in preceding works by her.

The scherzo is thoroughly admirable, a delight to the amateur and the musician. And in the last movement there are passages which proclaim loudly a breadth of conception, a skill in carrying out a grand design, a mastery of climax that are not always found in modern symphonies. Themes that arrest the attention are treated in heroic spirit. The climax is sure, irresistible.

I have already spoken of the skill shown by Mrs. Beach in the orchestration. It is not necessary now to enlarge upon this subject. I admit that occasionally she is boisterous, but the boisterousness is healthy, not merely vulgar. The only trace of woman that I find in this symphony is this same boisterousness.

Saint-Saëns once wrote of Augusta Holmés, "Women are singular when they concern themselves seriously with art: they seem first of all preoccupied with the wish to make you forget they are women, by showing an exuberant virility. They do not stop to think that it is this very preoccupation which betrays the woman. Like unto children, women know no obstacles; their will breaks everything. Miss Holmés is indeed a woman: she is extremist to the knife."

Mrs. Beach has more artistic control. She is not an "extremist." She is a musician of genuine talent who by the imagination, technical skill and sense of orchestration displayed in this symphony has brought honor to herself and the city which is her dwelling place.

Boston Herald, July 5, 1903:

THE ATTITUDE OF AMERICAN CRITICS TOWARD MUSIC

A review from the Earliest Days of Opera in This Country to the Present Time; the Work of Fry, Dwight, Woolf, Krehbiel and Others

There was talk the other day in Boston concerning the coming of Richard Strauss as the preacher of his own musical faith. Some wondered whether there would be general curiosity to see him, and they stated as a fact that many concert-goers of this city do not know of Tschaikowsky's visit to New York, so little interest was there in the presence of a great composer. And one said: "What do you suppose the attitude of the critics will be toward Strauss?" To which another answered: "The customary attitude of the critic the world over; one of suspicion and defiance toward the man and the composer.

The critics of New York in the first half of the 19th century were concerned chiefly with operatic matters. Before 1825 the only musical stage performances in New York were English operettas, which corresponded to the French vaudevilles. In 1825 the Garcia company, with Maria Garcia, who was afterward world famous as Malibrun, produced at the Park theatre Rossini's "Barber," and thus was there occasion for the first article written in this country concerning an operatic performance worthy of attention. The article was published in the Evening Post. A few abstracts will show the character.

"An assemblage of ladies so fashionable, so numerous, and so elegantly dressed was probably never before witnessed in our theatre. * * * In what language shall we speak of an entertainment so novel in this country, but which has so long ranked as the most elegant and refined among the amusements of the higher classes of the Old World? All have obtained a general idea of the opera from report. But report can give but a faint idea of it. Until it is seen, it will never be believed that a play can be conducted in recitative, or singing, and yet be nearly as natural as the ordinary drama. We were last night surprised, delighted, enchanted; and such were the feelings of all who witnessed the performance.* * *The daughter, Signorina Garcia, seems to us as a being of new creation, a cunning pattern of excellent nature; equally surprising us by the melody and tones of her voice, and by the propriety and grace of her acting."

This notice of an operatic performance might pass in some cities today. The critic was lost in wonder, love and praise. Neither audience, nor singers, nor manager could take exception.

Another critic was soon afterward a little more analytical in the consideration of Maria, although he began his review with this fine burst: "How can our feeble pen portray the loveliness of this admirable creature's face and figure, and give to our distant readers any conception of the wildering wonders of her almost unequalled voice! Compass, sweetness, taste, truth, flexibility, rapidity, and force do not make up half the sum of her vocal powers; and her voice is only one of the rare qualities with which nature has endowed her. She possesses in as high a degree as any actress we remember to have seen that exquisite perception of propriety in action, that delicate appreciation and graceful execution of the duties of her part, which constitute requisites so indispensable in the practice of her difficult profession." "The executions of the duties of her part"—this is vague; but the critic also wrote: "Her shake is good; her appoggiaturas beautiful; and her roulades whenever introduced, are thrown off with rapidity and ease." Here is seen an attempt, at least, to be exact, though something in our heart tells us that the writer would have been confused if he had been asked for a definition of "appoggiatura."

The attitude of the critic in those early years in New York was one of hearty welcome toward visitors and new work. His musical knowledge and experience were inconsiderable. A Mr. Berkeley, an Englishman who accompanied Mrs. Austin a few years later, as manager and press agent—he "managed all her affairs with an ardent devotion far beyond that of a n ordinary man of business"—wrote with understanding, and he undoubtedly educated the musical taste of the public.

Richard Grant White asserts in his entertaining articles on "Opera in New York" that in these early years the taste of the audience was far more trustworthy than the knowledge of the critics. This may be sadly believed, for as late as 1838 we find in the New York Mirror and in a criticism of a performance of "Amilie" the following singular statements: "the adagio in E, four sharps, major, is perfectly thrilling. The words 'Thou are gone,' with the response of the wind instruments, cannot be too highly appreciated, and a brilliant polonaise forms a happy termination.* * * The moment Mr. Seguin opened his mouth, the corresponding feature of his audience assumed the same appearance; one universal gape seemed to infect all: Such was the astonishment produced by his magnificent organ.* * * There is no straining after double F's, or S's (sic) or D's. They come round and full and harmonious." Those were glorious days. Even Plancon himself never sound a full and harmonious "S" in the Metropolitan.

Little by little critics became more sane and discriminative. Thus, in the forties, we find the limitations and faults, as well as the merits of singers, carefully discussed. In the early fifties, Richard Grant White was writing the musical criticisms for the Courier and Enquirer; George William Curtis was the musical critic of the Tribune. The former had some practical knowledge of music, and many of his articles are worthy of consideration today, for they are something more than occasional and ephemeral. So pure was White's taste, so shrewd his observation, so keen his judgment, so persuasive his enthusiasm, so irresistible his gusto that his criticisms may, like the dramatic reviews of William Hazlitt, be pondered with profit by those who lazily think that music in America is an art of only recent standing.

Until his death, White was deeply interested in operatic singers and in all stage people. (Did he not write a glowing eulogy of Pauline Markham, in which he said that she had the lost arms of Venus of Milo?) He insisted that Adelina Patti, by reason of her physical nature and her mental nature, could not be a great prima donna; Clara Louise Kellogg's Marguerite was purely poetic and ideal; Nilsson was a very gifted and highly finished vocalist of the second rank; Campanini, with a worn voice which was never rich or sympathetic, was a fine dramatic singer' Lucca was a coarse peasant woman, "whose inherent rudeness of fibre was softened and enriched by a warmly emotional nature and by humor—it would have been impossible to have had more local color and less of poetic feeling and of sentiment in Lucca's presentation of Goethe's heroine"; Gerstar was simply a vocalist of wonderful capacity and skill "as awkward as a clothes-horse." He found the music of "Carmen" not of a high order: "it has a character of its own—a rhythm and a swing which, although undeniably vulgar, are captivating, for a time at least, to the general ear."

When Mr. W. F. Apthorp wrote many years ago for the Atlantic Monthly reviews of musical performances in Boston, it was said that no American magazine had before that time paid attention to the art. But there was such a department in the United States Magazine and Democratic Review of 1847, and the writer showed vigor as well as intelligence and taste. This vigor was often intensely personal. We quote from the April number of that year:

"In his vocalization, Beneventano usually contrives to introduce all the vowels of the alphabet in the space of a couple of bars, and when he starts one of the meaningless roulades, with which he is fond of interluding his music for the purpose of displaying the flexibility of his voice, we may be generally sure of his going through most of the bodily contortions of an "india rubber posture man" in a circus ring. In the midst of the famous quartet (sic) of 'Loria' he breaks the dramatic interest of the scene by striding to the front of the stage, with his arms extended, when, clapping both hands upon his breast, after the fashion of a goose foot, and with his body imminent about the footlights, as if about diving head first into the astonished kettledrums, he shouts forth sounds like 'ay-hay heel meo sa-han-gway-hay lo-lo tradeetahah-hah-hah-ha,' etc. which is his version of 'ella e il mio sangue l'ho tradita.'"

"The verdict of an Italian audience upon the merits of a composer is worth less than that of any other audience in the world, if perhaps we except the Chinese and the Choctaws."

Verdi's "I Lombardi" was the great novelty of the season and over a page was devoted to the work. "He has given us no fresh melody, no new harmony, even to condemn; though he has made many feeble and some pleasing imitations of the French and German manner.* * * In 'Nabucco' he has written a canon upon a modern Italian melody, producing very mush the effect of putting the Apollo Belvidere into the green velvet and scarlet ribbons of a theatrical bandit. He introduces death scenes by a solo, with brilliant florituri for the violin, and accompanies a prayer by a jigging moment on the flute. In "I Lombardi" the dine of brass prevents what music there is to be heard, until the hearer is as used to it as a resident at Niagara to the roar of the falls. We are at a loss to conceive what is the meaning of that eternal brass band on the stage. But there it is, and indoors and out of doors, in season and out of season we have Lombards in helmets and spectacles, and Turks in turbans and spectacles, blowing ophecleides, trombones and E flat clarinets, as if each man considered himself the impersonation of Fame, and that he was sounding his own praises to the listening world."

We see that in 1847 when the Italians ruled the stage in New York as well as in London, a music critic protested against a tenor's rush to the footlights in his vicious maltreatment of the text; and waged war against disturbing incongruities and unmeaning noise in opera.

Probably the first influential critic in this country who was a professional musician was William H. Fry (1813–1864), for whose picture, reproduced from a portrait by Healey, we are indebted to the J. B. Millet Company. Fry composed the operas "Leonora" and "Notre Dame de Paris," which were produced, and programme-symphonies, as "Santa Claus," "Childe Harold," "A Day in the Country." For some years he was critic of the New York Tribune. He had studied and thought; he was born, as those who knew him say, with the creative musical faculty and with fine perceptions in musical rhetoric; but his musical compositions were so influenced by models dear to him that they seemed mere imitations. His mind was not prepared for changes in melodic form, for novel harmonic or orchestral treatment; and so when Gounod's "Faust" was first produced in New York, he declared in an exceedingly long review that the opera did not contain one melody. His attitude was not one of suspicion or defiance. His mind was so charged with Italian thought that he could find no melody unless it were cast in the conventional mode and bore the familiar appearance. And it must be remembered that "Faust" was condemned in Paris and London for melodic poverty.

The popular interest for many years was confined to operatic matters. The attitude of American critics, as well as of the American public, was chiefly one of curiosity; their desire was to [be] entertained, moved, thrilled by personal beauty and artistic song. The critics, for the most part, engaged freely in personal gossip, in descriptions of face and figure, in sentimental rhapsodies over the delivery of an ear-tickling or spirit-stirring aria. A graceful writer, like N. P. Willis, would corroborate the musical opinions of the "fashionable["] readers of the Mirror. The opera was the plaything of fashion, as it was in the 17th century in Italy, as it was in the days when Faustina and Cuzzoni stirred up strife in London, as it was when the French court was divided between Gluck and Piccini, as it is today, whether the season be devoted to works of the French and Italians or of Wagner.

The best reviews in the leading newspapers were more or less polished articles, which were concerned chiefly with the personality of the singers. Sometimes the article was enlivened by a dash of malice; yet it is doubtful whether any of his predecessors rivaled a description to be found in one of White's pages of reminiscences: "She (Miss Paton) was a 'fine woman,' but not handsome—her mouth being so large that, when she opened it, it became cavernous, with stalactite teeth. But her eyes were bright, and her face when she was acting, pleased her audiences. She had been married to Lord William Lenox, a squint-eyed scapegrace, who treated her so brutally that she obtained a divorce from him, and eagerly accepted as her second husband Joseph Wood, a tall, handsome pugilist, whose fine but uncultivated tenor voice took him out of the prize ring, and who won her heart by giving her noble husband a thrashing."

The Germans brought with them to the United States their love for music. They established singing societies; they formed the rank and file of orchestras; they supplied leaders for these orchestras; they made the people acquainted with chamber music. They naturally preferred the music of their own country, and he that is ready to accuse them of narrowness, of Chauvinism, should remember that for years there was practically no purely orchestral music worth serious consideration other than German music, with the exception of the works of Hector Berlioz, who was made known, both in New York and Boston, at a comparatively early period in the history of concerts in America. In the forties, fifties and sixties French composers worked for operatic renown, and only during the last 20 years have the young French striven for reputation in the concert hall. There was then only one Russian, Glinka, and he was a name. And in what other country were orchestral works produced? There was Gade, and he was practically a German of the Leipsic brand.

These Germans, indefatigable, not to be discouraged, exerted and still exert a mighty influence. Their chief spokesman in this country was the late John S. Dwight, who for at least 25 years, was the foremost critic in the United States. His practical knowledge of music was slight; but he had a marked faculty of appreciation, a taste that had been carefully trained in sister arts, a talent for listening; and he was clear, persuasive, apparently fair, and at times eloquent in the expression of his opinions. He considered aesthetic rather than technical values. Well versed in German literature, acquainted with the theories, speculations, dreams of German philosophers, he was half German, half Greek in his ideas concerning ideal beauty.

While he fought valiantly the cause of the German masters, he was touched by the melancholy sweetness of Bellini and gladdened by the gayety of Rossini's and Donizetti's comedies. He had his foibles, prejudices, limitations. He could not endure that which seemed to him bizarre, unpleasant, morbid. He once told us that the finale of Berlioz's "Fantastic" symphony was bad music, on account of the subject it illustrated. "Every great work of art," he said, "should have a serene or noble close." Raff's "Lenore" symphony was to him a graveyard horror. Liszt's "Mephisto" waltz was the apotheosis of vileness. Ultra-romanticism disturbed and confused him. He could find no exhibition of talent in Offenbach's delightful operettas, perhaps because his favorite gods and goddesses were held up to ridicule by the librettists. He could not, or would not, find strength or beauty in the music-dramas of Wagner. And what would he say today about composers who believe in the beauty of ugly and common things, and set themselves deliberately and resolutely to interpret the ugliness through the medium of music? His occupation was gone years before he died. From 1850 to 1876 he was the very man for the period, although his worship of the great classic masters was not far removed from fetishism. His incessant appeal to the consideration of the best in art brought about this result: His readers were thoroughly informed about the great works that marked in turn this development; by his personal as well as literary influence, he had much to do with the establishment of sound rules and canons that regulated the musical thought of the community in which he moved; and by the courageous expression of opinion in his Journal of Music he stimulated healthy curiosity and gave encouragement beyond his own parish, at a time when such help was sorely needed.

Mr. Dwight, in his later years of activity, became more and more opposed to new forms of musical expression. His immediate followers became clannish, at times intolerant. Had not music died with Mendelssohn? Was Schumann a safe man? Little mutual admiration societies spent their time in the adoration of the old and the approved. Mediocrity in performance was applauded when it was displayed on the side of orthodoxy. Musical righteousness in Boston was not without a decided taint of snobbishness. The late Benjamin E. Woolf did much to change and better this condition in the city of his adoption, and many of his articles, circulated wisely, proved a corrective in the musical circles outside the commonwealth.

Mr. Woolf had been trained as a musician from his youth up, and he thus triumphed easily over Mr. Dwight in the discussion of technical matters. He was a man of wide and curious reading, he was intimately acquainted with the stage and all that belonged thereto, and he was master of controversial language. He wrote without parade of learning, yet no one but a learned man could have written so simply and with such convincing force. He made his points clearly, logically. His conclusions were inevitable. Furthermore, he was witty, humorous, ironical, and, when the occasion demanded, splendidly savage. Snobbishness is not to be put down by polite argument; bumptious pretence is not to be exposed effectually by genteel generalizations. There was work for some one to do, and Mr. Woolf did it. The musical life of this city is today more tolerable, more liberal by reason of his critical writings. A man of deeply rooted beliefs and prejudices, he realized that forms of art are not inflexible, nor did he insist that an Italian, a Russian, a Frenchman should use the language of a German in the expression of musical thought. He did more than fight against local abuses; he welcomed strange composers. He fought at first against Wagner; but he learned before he died to find much that was grand and beautiful in the music-dramas; and his keenest shafts were shot against the ignorant and the fashionable who chose Wagner as their idol of an hour, not against the composer himself. He was one of the first to appreciate the greatness of Tschaikowsky; he was by no means inclined to reject the claims of Richard Strauss; he was by nature an admirer of the clearness and the elegance of musical expression so long the characteristics of French composers, yet he was enthusiastic over the romanticism of Berlioz. He judged visiting virtuosos by their performance, not by the report that preceded them, not by the behavior of the audience, not by the earnest words of the passionate press agent. Mr. Woolf was at times misunderstood by those who believed that honey-daubing is synonymous with criticism and by those who did not know the constitutionally kindly, sympathetic, generous nature of the man. It is not paradoxical to say that his work, destructive as it seemed to the superficial reader, supplemented that of Mr. Dwight. He, too, was the man for his period.

Mr. Woolf was never weary of combating the opinion still entertained by some today—fortunately they are fewer in number—that music is distinctively a German institution; that the Germans are the musical people and that musical knowledge will dies with them. The influence of the Germans in this country had much to do with the establishment of this belief, and for many years Americans studied in Germany without thought of possible advantage elsewhere. These students returned more German than the Germans; when they wrote, they wrote in the German manner. Today Paris and Brussels are recognized as towns that present rare musical advantages to students. Today the French, the Russian, the Scandinavian, the Italian composers are classed more justly, and Cesar Franck, d'Indy, Gabriel Faure, Debussy, Rimsky-Korsakov, Sinding, Puccini are something more than doubtful names in a catalogue. Yet there are so-called music lovers even now in Boston who are under the impression that all the music that is good is made in Germany, where it was invented. Now neither the symphony nr the sonata nor the concerto, nor any form of chamber music, nor the symphonic poem nor the opera nor the oratorio nor the cantata was invented by a German. And, with the exception of the hotly-discussed Richard Strauss, what composer of marked merit is now at work in Germany?

We have said that for years Italian opera was the one form of music which truly interested the critics and the public of New York. Attention was paid the concerts given by the Philharmonic Society and other orchestras, by chamber clubs and by virtuosos, but the opera was the thing. The enormous growth of the German population in that city gradually worked a change. Concerts of the first class began to be considered of importance. As many became interested in them the concerts had a news value, and the standard of criticism was raised. German-Americans who revolted against Italian domination and were stirred by the legends of Wagner and his sonorous and never-ceasing orchestra, finally succeeded in bringing Wagner's operas before the public. They were helped in their cause by certain critics, at first by Mr, Otto Florscheim and other German-born New Yorkers, then by Messrs. Finck, Krehbiel, Henderson, Huneker, Kobbe and others. The pioneers were Mr. Florscheim and his friends and Mr. Finck. Wagner became a fashionable man; conductors and critics made money by explaining his music dramas in lectures before performances, and soon there was a disease, at the time infectious and easily recognizable, known as Wagneritis. Wagner has now his appointed place, in a row with Verdi, Mozart, Bizet, Gounod and other makers of operas; Wagneritis is now confined to a few isolated cases, but the efforts then made by these critics of New York still influence music and musicians to a certain degree. There was a time— and not long ago—when modern French and Russian and Italian composers were looked at skew-eyed; they were accused of imitating or reproached for not imitating Wagner. Critics who had written columns of mad praise over the story of "Die Walkure" or "Tristan" were shocked at Massenet's "Manon" or the horrors of the neo-Italians, and called hysterically for an ounce of civet. Richard Strauss was accused of writing "charnel house" music, and our townsman, Mr. Loeffler, was charged with "morbidness" because he had chosen a tragedy by Maeterlinck and poems by Rollinat and Verlaine as subjects for orchestral treatment. It is natural that opinions pronounced by influential journals of New York should carry weight throughout the country.

The most prominent critics of New York who are now writing about music are Messrs. H. T. Finck, W.J. Henderson and H. E. Krehbiel. Mr. Huneker, catholic, enthusiastic and brilliant in appreciation, is now interested in the drama, but his musical influence is still felt. Mr. Richard Aldrich, fair-minded, cool, accurate, well-equipped, is now so widely known.

Appendix II

Mr. Krehbiel, who may be called the dean of New York critics, has German blood in his veins, as had Mr. Finck. Mr. Huneker is of Hungarian and Irish parentage, and he has been a professional musician; he has earned money by teaching the piano, which he studied in this country and at Paris. Mr. Krehbiel was at first strongly conservative. Converted to the cause of Wagner, he was a zealous preacher of the gospel of that composer, and for some years he was a staunch partisan. He was a German of the Germans and for the Germans. His motto seemed to be "No French, Russians, Italians need apply." His influence, through sermons from a daily pulpit, through admirable books, was and is indisputable, not only in New York, but throughout the country. He has grown tolerant. He now strives to recognize musical worth wherever it is to be found. He is still an idealist, a German idealist, with a reverence for the pure and beautiful in music as these qualities are understood by him. Impressionism in music does not make a strong appeal to him, and a composer like Debussy, who writes literary or intellectual music in which, to quote Landormy, "the art of combining sounds is subordinated to the intention of expressing a thing or sentiment," is not so near to him as he that writes a symphony or a sonata in conventional form. Mr. Krehbiel's historical knowledges and his charm in imparting it, his admiration for the ideal, his dislike for that which is merely eccentric or flambouyant—these characteristics have been potent factors in his educational influence, although some of his warm friends and admirers may find him reluctant to accept new doctrines which will, in the course of years, be traditions, or to grasp the full meaning of new and subtle expressions of emotion.

Mr. Henderson, a man of varied, liberal education, of musical training, of true poetic fancy, of biting wit, has a more pronounced individuality as a critic than any of his colleagues, with the exception of Mr. Huneker. If Mr. Krehbiel reminds one at times of Mr. Dwight, Mr. Henderson recalls the memory of Mr. Woolf. He, too, is impatient with airy, bustling mediocrity, with snobbish and unintelligent admiration. The singers and pianists and violinists and conductors whom he discusses are not to him persons of flesh and blood; they are as the checker men on the board with which he plays his game, that he may win for truth and righteousness as they are known to him. He writes with the authority born of knowledge; with the warmth of artistic appreciation; with the severity of a just man moved to indignation.

Mr. Finck is frankly an honest partisan who glories in his partisanship. Baudelaire wrote that the critic should be a partisan, and he elaborated his statement. Mr. Finck has his idols; Wagner, Chopin, Grieg, Johann Strauss, Tschaikowsky, MacDowell, Jean de Reszke, Paderewski, Nordica—there are others—and he sings their praise in and out of season. He is ready to welcome a composer or a singer of any nationality, provided the stranger has some unusual or original characteristic. He is the sworn foe of routine. Conventional forms are to him as the abomination of desolation. His honesty is unquestioned; he is as brave as Ney; he declares his likes and dislikes; his theories and beliefs with the bluntness of a child. He is a singular and fascinating mixture of catholicity and intolerance. His earnestness and sincerity and his devotion to art command respect and wield an influence, even when his deliberate opinion would seem wanton extravagance, coming from another.

A critic of whatever nationality he may be must be influenced largely by the conditions of his education, by his mental equipment, by his inherited and acquired disposition, and somewhat by his prevailing physical condition. It is not likely that a German, reared musically at Leipsic, should feel toward Tschaikowsky as a Russian would feel, or toward Saint-Saëns as a Frenchman would be disposed. An Italian, with the best intention, would fail to appreciate the melodic thought of Brahms. No two persons in an audience are reminded of precisely the same things when they hear a musical composition. "The landscape is in the eye of the beholder," and this saying may be applied to music. Why, then, should exact uniformity of opinion be expected from any half-dozen critics? The majority will undoubtedly agree as to fixed and established matters, such as the character of a composer's workmanship, the purity or impurity of a singer's intonation, but concerning questions of aesthetics there will always be dispute. And the intelligent reader of conflicting opinions will take note of the personal equation; he will not jump at once to the conclusion that one writer is wise and honest, the other foolish or a knave.

The American critic should be the most receptive of all. There is no American school of composition with binding or prejudicial traditions. He should welcome all comers, listen patiently to them, and neither blame them because they present new and strange views for consideration, nor praise them for following prudently in well beaten and dusty roads.

Boston Herald, December 18, 1926:

This excerpt is included as a prelude to the next article. Hale spoke of music itself many times; in this instance, it is in respect to his expectations of the conductor:

> As we have said before, music is not music until it is performed, until it sounds. It is the task of the conductor to make it sound so that it stirs or moves the hearer. There should not be too rigid a respect for the letter, for the mint and cummin. Indications of tempo should be as signposts, pointing the general direction, but allowing the traveler to loiter or hasten on the way, so that he finds new beauty in a landscape, or gathers flowers here and there, or passes quickly over muddy or rocky stretches.

The following about the pratfalls in writing a review follows a long review of Arthur William Symons's book, *Plays, Acting, and Music*:

The Sunday Herald, February 7, 1904:

'Paradise Lost' by Du Bois and the "Criticism of Music"

Review of an Interesting Volume by Arthur Symons;
the Handel and Haydn in Symphony Hall Tonight;
Debussy's "Nocturnes"; Many Recitals and Concerts, Personals, etc.

...A musical review should breathe the enthusiasm of belief, the joy of appreciation and the equal joy of rejection. For this reason there is much to be said in favor of the criticism written immediately after a performance for a morning newspaper. The music is surging in the writer's head; he is under the spell; or he is fully conscious of the composer's vain attempt to put him in another world, to enwrap him in a hitherto unknown atmosphere. He has no time for wary or commercial reflection. The article is within him, and it must out. As Hazlitt put it: "The stimulus of writing is like the stimulus of intoxication, with which we can hardly sympathize in our sober moments, when we are no longer under the inspiration of the demon, or when the virtue is gone out of us. While we are engaged in any work, we are thinking of the subject, and cannot stop to admire ourselves; and when it is done, we look at it with comparative indifference. I will venture to say that no one but a pedant ever read his own works regularly through. They are not his—they are become mere words, wastepaper, and have nothing of the glow, the creative enthusiasm, the vehemence, and natural spirit with which he wrote them,["*] add to the freshness of the enthusiasm, the silence and the concentration of the night, the knowledge that the city at large is donning its nightcap, the feeling of responsibility for the public declaration at daybreak—if there is any individuality in a man, will it not out?

The criticism is for a day, and it should perish with the day. Is there any more melancholic reading than volumes of collected criticisms written originally for newspapers? Look over the many volumes, and you wonder at the blunt perceptions, the lack of prophetic vision, the willingness to accept the ephemeral as everlasting, the inability to distinguish between orthodox commonplace and new and glorious flights of imagination. You wrong the writers, for you are not of their time and generation. Things now clear were then vague. They wrote under conditions unknown to you. The beautiful in one generation may be ugliness in the next. Their milieu was not the same as yours. You are still more unfair and you are unphilosophical if you twit them with inconsistencies in the course of 20 years. Should not a man be able to change his opinions as well as his skin every seven years?

Yet often in these same volumes are shrewd observations on man in general, and when there is so pronounced an individuality as that of Berlioz we read from beginning to end with delight, although many of the titles of works discussed are as the names in a hillside cemetery visited aimlessly although the interpreters are not so near to us as the mummy of an Egyptian princess who has escaped the greed of mixers of colors and still sleeps peacefully in a well ordered museum.

We fear that Mr. [Arthur] Symons, writing about music, will stop as Mr. Hazlitt said, to admire himself, for such has been his inclination as poet and essayist. The moment the critic stops to consider himself or the public, he is lost. He must be unconscious of self. He must not wonder whether this one will disapprove or that one say "Amen." With each thought of the neighborhood or the morrow, his individuality shrinks. When a man is concerned chiefly with the matter of style, he has little to say. The style is formed by the thought. Whether the thought be subtle or straightforward, ingenuous or affected, the words shape themselves to it.

*From William Hazlitt, English writer (1778–1830), "The Dinner."

The Boston Herald, January 14, 1906:

HAS THE AMERICAN COMPOSER BEEN NEGLECTED IN BOSTON?

AN ALLEGED "EMBARGO" ON AMERICAN MUSIC

Reply to a Complaint from a Concert-Goer

The Herald has received the following letter from a concert-goer in the western part of the commonwealth:

"I am keenly impressed with what Mr. Lawrence Gilman lately called the embargo on American music. This seems to me such a pity and so unworthy a great and good band like the Boston Symphony orchestra. If so-called classical music alone formed the backbone of Mr. Gericke's programme, one might keep silent. But he does a deal of exploiting of modern European mediocrities. Witness, for example, that thin and colorless and inane symphony by Amherst Webber, which he produced. And the saddest part of the affair is the content of you Boston folks in the manifest policy of exclusion of everything American save our shekels. Only lately I wrote Mr. Gericke and asked him if it would not be possible to favor us with an American composition on his next visit to Springfield. His reply: "The unwritten law with us is never to play in any of the cities we visit any selections which have not been rehearsed and played the same season in Boston." That, so far as I can learn, is the regular and uniform reply to requests for American compositions. Boston has had no American compositions, therefore 'the road' can have none.

"I am not asking for weak and trivial music simply because it is American and it seems to me so unfair to treat requests for native composition in this light. To borrow your significant phrase, I have no desire to cover mediocrity with a cloak of patriotism. But the embargo of Mr. Gericke and his confreres, as Mr. Lawrence Gilman has so well pointed out, affects American composers of acknowledged ability not less than the younger group of men who are doing serious and individual work. Worst of all, this practice of exclusion stifles composition of a higher order. I wrote to a well-known orchestral conductor some years ago and called his attention to the omission of American compositions from his programme. He replied: 'You Americans are incapable of doing serious orchestral work. They do well with coon songs and ragtime, and they ought to remain content in that field.'

"The silence of our own press on this matter is painful. That America has some very fair and a little really good orchestral music must be well known to every music newspaper man. But as Mr. Gilman asks: 'Who ever hears an American orchestral score?' MacDowell, Parker, Gleason, Paine, Kelley, Loomis, Chadwick, Templeton, Strong, and Shelley are less well known, I feel certain, to you of Boston than Dargomyschski, Mussorgsky, Ippolitoff-Ivanoff, Gretchaninoff and Rachmaninoff of Russia, or Diwangira, Dharm-Raja, Tasichozong and Angdaphorang of Bhutan.

"I wish the Herald man might see his way clear now and then to say a good word for the better sort of American music. Keep on damning the poor, but discriminate the better from the poorer."

AC OMMONW ALL

Our correspondent is not the only one who honestly believes that there is an "embargo" on American music. There are others who burst into a passionate flood of tears at the noon meal or toss feverishly on luxurious beds at the thought of the American composer, shabbily clad, subsisting chiefly on free lunches, despised, ground under the iron heel of arrogant and imported conductors, hissed at by a reptile press.

There are American composers who are sure that there is a sworn conspiracy to crush them. Mr. Zenas T. Field cannot understand why Mr. Gericke will not produce his tone poem, "Lucy of Hockanum Ferry," and Mr. Bela Graves knows that there sinister and malignant influences against him, otherwise Mr. Walter Damrosch would look favorably on his great orchestral fantasia, "The Springfield Arsenal."

Mr. Field is sure that if he had been born at Cracow and his surname were Fielieski, his remarkable compositions would command universal recognition and Mr. Graves said only a day or two ago that his fantasia was as good as "any of the symphonic poems by old man Strauss."

American is a great country: everything in it is great; therefore the music of its native composers must be great. The imported conductors, pianists, fiddlers and the rest of them are naturally supercilious, envious, sceptical. They will not give the American a chance to show what he can do. Audiences are hypnotized, or they have dull ears, or they have decreed that American music is not in fashion. The newspapers are undoubtedly paid to keep silence; they are paid enormous sums in roubles, marks, or francs at the current rate of exchange.

HEROIC ATTEMPTS

There are some heroic attempts on the part of some of three composers and their friends to awaken the American people from its lethargy. A publisher has taken it upon himself to discover and encourage certain composers. It is true that the majority of these composers write vague, chaotic, even ungrammatical music that, when they would be their most impressive, they are wonderfully dull; that when they would be most original, they are either writers of balderdash or imitators.

And now a society has been formed in New York for the glorification of American composers. The Herald quoted last Sunday excerpts from the preliminary announcement of the "New Music Society of America." The most significant of these excerpts reads as follows: "The society believes that present conditions in the American music world, so far as they govern native compositions, are hostile to the normal development of a vigorous creative art, and that until the situation is bettered and American works obtain a just representation in our concert rooms, there is need of the activities of such an organization as the New Music Society of America."

Who will produce the neglected and despised compositions by American composers? An orchestra of Americans led by an American all exulting in their birthright and bubbling over with patriotism? Oh. No! The Russian Symphony Society, led by a Russian, Mr. Modest Altschuler, is the chosen interpreter of the true American musical spirit, and he is a Russian, not a sturdy New Englander. By the way, where is there a first-class orchestra composed of Americans and with the English language spoken at rehearsals? And will Mr. Altschuler wear the star spangled banner instead of a dress coat at these concerts?

Our American composers must at present rely on the services of musicians of foreign birth or descent, on the zeal and intelligence of foreign, imported conductors. For if it be said that Mr. Van der Stucken was born in Texas, the answer is that he is not of American stock; he was sent to Antwerp when he was eight years old; he studied and exercised his profession in Europe, and not until 1884, when he was 25 years old, did he return to this country. Yet he may fairly be reckoned by his work of late years among American composers.

FACTS IN THE CASE

Our correspondent makes specific charges. Let us examine them.

Has the Boston Symphony Orchestra put an "embargo" on music by American composers?

The first concert of this orchestra was on Oct. 22, 1881. The last concert was on Jan. 6, 1906. The following works by American composers have been played at Symphony concerts in Boston. The number of performances of any one work is indicated in paretheses.

Beach, Mrs. H.H.A.—Gaelic Symphony (2); Piano Concerto

Bird, Arthur—Two Episodes

Brockway, Howard—Sylvan Suite

Buck, Dudley—Song, "Sunset"

Chadwick, G. W.—Overture "Thalia;" Scherzo in F major; Symphony No. 2 (2); "Melpomene" Overture (5); Pastoral Prelude; Symphony No. 3; Overture "Adonala;" Overture "Euterpe."

Converse, F. S.—First movement of Symphony No. 1; "Festival of Pan;" Endymion's Narrative; two orchestral poems, "Night" and "Day"

Foote, Arthur—Overture "In the Fountains" (2); Suite for Strings, No. 2; Symphonic Prologue, "Francesca da Rimini" (2); "The Skeleton in Armor;" Suite in D minor (two movements repeated at another concert)

Goldmark, Rubin—Overture to "Hiawatha" (2)

Hadley, H. K.—Symphony No. 2, "The Four Seasons"

Huss, H. H.—Rhapsody for Piano and Orchestra; Piano Concerto in E major (2)

Johns, Clayton—"Berceuse" and "Scherzo" for strings

Lang, Margaret R.—Dramatic Overture; Concert Aria, "Armida," with orchestra

MacDowell, Edward—Piano Concerto No. 2 (3); Symphonic Poem, "Lancelot and Elaine" (2); Suite in A minor, No. 1 (2); Piano Concerto No. 1; Symphonic poems "Hamlet" and "Ophelia;" Suite No. 2, "Indian" (3)

Paine, J. K.—Prelude to "Oedipus" (3); Symphonic Poem, "The Tempest" (2); Symphony No. 3 (2); "An Island Fantasy" (2); Columbus, March and Hymn; Prelude to "The Birds" of Aristophanes

Parker, H. W.—"Cahal Mor" for baritone and orchestra; A Northern Ballad; Concerto for Organ and Orchestra

Weil, Oscar—Song, "Spring Song"

Weld, Arthur—Suite, "Italia"

Whiting, Arthur—Piano Concerto; Suite for Strings and Four Horns; Fantasia for Piano and Orchestra (2)

Furthermore, Mr. Charles Martin Loeffler and Mr. Gustav Strube may well be reckoned as American composers in consequence of long residency and musical activity in this country.

Loeffler, C. M.—"Les Veillees de l'Ukraine;" Cello Concerto (2); Divertimento for Violin and Orchestra (2); "Le Mort de Tintagiles" (3); Two poems "Avant que tu no t'en afiles" and "Villanelle du Diable" (3)

Strube, Gustav—Overture, "The Maid of Orleans;" Symphony in D minor; Violin Concerto No. 1; Rhapsody; Fantastic Overture; "Longing" for viola and orchestra; Violin Concerto No. 2

And these works by composers living at the time and musically active in the United States have been played here at concerts of the Boston Symphony orchestra:

Floerscheim, Otto—"Consolation;" "Elevation;" Scherzo; Prelude and Fugue

Kaun, Hugo—"Minnehaha"

Korbay, Francois—Nuptiale
Maas, Louis—Piano Concerto
Singer, Otto—Fantasia
Van der Strucken—Prologue to "William Ratcliff;" Prologue, "Pax Triomphans.'

GENTLEQUERIES

Now, does "X" seriously insist that there has been an "embargo" put on American music by the conductors of the Boston Symphony orchestra? We have known Mr. Henschel, Mr. Gericke, Mr. Nikisch and Mr. Paur, both musically and personally. No one of them was prejudiced for a moment against American music because it was American. Each one of them brought out in turn compositions by Americans when the music seemed good to him and worthy of performance at a Symphony concert; for to them music was either good or bad irrespective of the nationality of the composer.

We hold no brief for Mr. Gericke, Mr. Kneisel, Mr. Hess, Mr. Adamowski or Mr. Longy. Is it likely that any one of them would refuse to put on the programme of a society led by him an interesting work simply because an American wrote it?

Programme making is a difficult art, and there are excellent conductors who never master it. A large audience is seldom satisfied. Some think that there has been no music composed worthy of performance since Mendelssohn and Schumann, with the exception of a few works by Brahms. Others protest against symphonies by Haydn and Mozart, and they would fain hear music only by Berlioz, the later Beethoven, Franck, Tschaikowsky and the living ultra-moderns.

No conductor can hope to suit his programme to the taste of all in the audience. There are certain classic works that should be heard; there are compositions of romanticists who are now among the classics, for death has awarded them this degree; then there are the new works of contemporaries. All these composers are entitled to a hearing, but without any regard to their nationality. The question is not "Is this composer a Swede, a Russian, an American?" It is this: "Is this music interesting and worthy of performance?"

Mr. Gericke is obliged to arrange 24 programmes for the concerts in Boston. It is customary to play an overture at each concert. We happen to know that he is constantly searching for new overtures. Would he not gladly play one by an American composer if it were worthy a place on a Symphony programme?

"X" may name certain overtures by American composers and mourn because Mr. Gericke has not produced them. But are these works worthy of performance except at a popular concert, or at a concert of some teachers' convention? It is not given to many Americans to write an overture that can be put by the side of Mr. Chadwick's "Melpomene" or Prof. Paine's "Oedipus," When such an overture is composed "X" may rest assured that Mr. Gericke will produce it.

Our correspondent is singularly unfortunate in his choice of Russian composers whose names he thinks are to Boston music lovers as household words. Theodore Thomas in 1869 produced here a Cossack fantasia or caprice by Dargomyschski, and we believe he repeated the performance a year or two later. But the name of this composer and of the others mentioned are merely names known to the great majority of our music lovers only through music lexicons and journals, though a part song by Gretchaninoff has been sung here by the Choral Art Society, and an orchestral piece by Mussorgsky has been performed at a subscription concert of the Boston Orchestral Club, an amateur society. It is not worthwhile to insist on this point.

The Herald believes in American music, if the music is good. It does not believe that the protective system will be of any benefit to the American composer. The American painter does not paint any better because there is a protective duty on imported pictures, nor is the American public educated by this protective tariff. The Herald believes in the great republic of music, a country that has no geographical boundaries. It does not believe in coddling a composer who has not learned the technique of his art and is without fancy or imagination, simply because he is an American.

The inferior composers in France, Germany, Italy—wherever they may be—are sure that there is a conspiracy against them; that conductors and other interpreters, publishers, critics, are leagued against them. Their works are not performed; they are unappreciated; their genius is openly denied.

The composer of true talent in any country is not materially assisted by the establishment of prize competitions or by the organization of societies for the purpose of boosting the good, bad, indifferent into the public view. Music that has genuine beauty or strength, music that is charged with emotion will surely make its way. Mr. Richard Aldrich of the New York Times, in his review of the performance of Mr. Loeffler's "Death of Tintagiles," at a concert of the New York Symphony orchestra last Sunday night, wrote: "It is agreeable to note that no society or organization of any sort is needed to insure its production."

A reader may say: "But the Herald published the statement of the MacDowell club of New York." The Herald published the announcement as it published that of the New Music Society of America. It published these announcements as a matter of musical news; it published them without editorial comment. It may here be said, however, that the MacDowell Club of New York was not founded first of all for spreading the knowledge of Mr. MacDowell's works. The compositions of "gifted composers with kindred aims and ideals whose works are not as yet widely known" are to be performed at the club meetings; there is to be discussion of "the generic principles and vital motives of the correlated arts." Mr. MacDowell did not believe in "American concerts." He was bitterly opposed to such wool-wrapping and Chauvinism. He believed that the American, the German, the Frenchman, the Bulgarian, should musically all stand on the same level and be judged by composers solely by the music they had written, that an American's name should be on a program of a Symphony concert, not because he was born in Boston, East Haddam, Terre Haute, or Putney, but because his overture or symphonic poem is worthy of a performance in company with the works of other composers of talent. He sympathized with Theodore Thomas, who neither refused nor accepted a work because it was by an American.

"X" has read the Herald to little purpose if he now feels it is his duty to address to it a Macedonian cry. The Herald has always welcomed the appearance of any American musical composition that showed skill in construction, or fancy or imagination or an emotional appeal in its contents. It believes in the better works of the ultra-modern school in any country. It knows that forms of beauty are shifting, but that beauty is eternal. It does not believe that art has parochial boundaries. It does not believe that an "undying devotion to the American flag" should rule appreciation or condemnation in the examination of works of art.

Appendix III

Concert Reviews and Extracts in Newspapers

A. Composers and Their Works
Bartok

Piano Concerto No. 1
Boston Herald, February 18, 1928:

Mr. Bartok's Concerto, produced at the Frankfort Music Festival in July, 1927, was played by him with the Cincinnati orchestra visiting New York, a few days ago. The performance yesterday was the first in Boston.

For over 20 years Mr. Bartok has been devoting himself to the study of Hungarian folk music. His own compositions, of late years at least, show the results of this study. Nor are Rumanian folk tunes and even Arabian outside of his attention. It would hardly be right to say that he is a local composer; he is decidedly a radical one, and for this reason it is doubtful whether his music will make a universal appeal. Smetana was intensely Bohemian, and in a cycle of symphonic poems glorified his country. As he was of an emotional nature, writing from his heart, and with no mean skill, not exclusively from his head, his music passed beyond the national boundaries and was welcomed.

It is a question whether Mr. Bartok will in the end gain or lose by following the path he has chosen. A musician of indisputable talent and technical equipment, he does not sacrifice to tonal sensuousness, but pursues his sternly logical methods. Mere tonal beauty apparently does not interest him. If he is emotional by nature, he seems to shrink from a display of feeling, either in themes, the treatment of them, or in his peculiar orchestration.

The concerto heard yesterday will not for some years to come, if then, be popular outside of Slav countries. If it were immediately popular, he would probably think little of the work and say to himself, "Why did I do this thing?" As a skillfully constructed work built out of what to our public would seem scanty, if not impossible material, the concerto deserves respect, even admiration. It cannot justly be classed with what are known as ultra-modern, flagrantly dissonant compositions; nor is it wildly irregular in form. In a large measure it accepts structural traditions, though here and there it is rhapsodic. His repeated use of a three-note motive tossed to various sections of the orchestra, is inexorable; his answering of a phrase for the piano by snorts from brass instruments, or from taps of drums is peculiar, at times disturbing. (Seldom is a side-drum so busied in a symphonic work of any kind.) Mr. Bartok shows his mastery of technic especially in the second movement where four melodies, each for a wood-wind instrument, all four in different keys, are contrapuntally treated; this page is undoubtedly the one at present that will attract the favorable attention of a miscellaneous audience. The concerto in certain respects, unusual as it is, unusual as it is, was well worth hearing, worthy of study.

Beethoven

Ah! Perfido, Op. 65
Boston Herald, February 7, 1925:

...Mme. Matzenauer sang the dramatic recitative, "Ah! Perfido," and the lyric measures of the two arias with incomparable beauty of tone, surpassing vocal skill and deep contagious emotion....The greater part of "Ah! Perfido" is uninspired and boresome. We have read that Beethoven himself did not care for this scene with aria and thought it unsuitable for the concert hall. Mr. Hadley's orchestral accompaniment was sympathetic and supporting.

Fidelio Overture, Op. 72
Boston Journal, December 22, 1894:

...In the overture to "Fidelio," there was a lack of precision, and the horn theme in the main allegro was wobbly. Then, too, the overture—for Beethoven—is pretty poor stuff. In comparison with the great Lenore [sic] overtures it sinks into insignificance. [This overture closed the concert.]

Overture to Leonore No. 1, Op. 138
Boston Journal, March 4, 1900:

The first overture to "Leonore" (listed without number on the program) is interesting chiefly because it is so different from the third. Yet there are passages in it that only Beethoven could have written, passages that are of elemental simplicity, tenderness and depth of thought.

Symphony No. 5 in C minor, Op. 67
Boston Home Journal, after November 9, 1889:

How should the first five measures of Beethoven's Fifth Symphony be played? Perhaps there is no passage in instrumental music about which conductors so essentially differ. Colonne of Paris who gives a singularly virile "reading" of this first movement, declaims the first phrases with the eighth notes heavily and deliberately detached; while his "holds" are as long sustained as the "holds" of Mr. Nikisch. With Wagner they hear Beethoven's voice crying "Hold my *fermate* for a long time, so as to inspire awe. I do not write them merely for a joke, or as though I wanted time to ponder on what comes after." (And our orchestra held the long sustained tones without wavering; no easy task.) Mr. Nikisch's performance of the symphony has brought out much adverse criticism; it certainly was remarkable, at times curious and almost perplexing; it was radically different from others which have been heard and applauded. Was it therefore wrong? Were all the others right? Now it is easy to say the conception of Mr. Nikisch was bombastic and "un-Beethovenish," and to call down upon his head all the curves uttered by Dr. Slop when he could not untie the knot. But this fifth symphony abounds in daring violations of rules: there are passages of great difficulty which were once thought impossible and were omitted; there are mysterious and overwhelming things hinted at darkly which are followed suddenly by grotesque ideas. It is a Gothic cathedral where grinning gargoyles squat by the side of the statue of the Virgin.

There were passages which under Mr. Nikisch's direction assumed new and unpleasing forms. Perhaps a second hearing would confirm this opinion; perhaps it would remove it. In hearing a work which has been so often given, a musician must necessarily have preconceived ideas of its proper performance; if the performance agrees with them he is apt to praise the conductor. But his ideas may be erroneous. Are there any formulas for directing the fifth symphony? Is there any carefully prepared receipt which no conductor should be without?

The great audience, which had given hearty signs of approval after each number of the symphonies, at the end of the concert broke out in wild and long continued applause. And the orchestra deserved this tribute; for although there was at times a noticeable lack of precision and unity, the individual and ensemble playing as a whole was remarkably good. In this connection it may be proper to remark that the orchestra, while it has gained in fire and swing and all the details necessary for necessary for producing great effects, has apparently lost a little of that exquisite and delicate finish which characterized the concerts of Mr. Gericke. This is spoken of the orchestra as a whole, and not of the individual members, for nothing could have excelled the work of the double-basses, bassoons, and in fact all the individual playing heard last Saturday. To combine the qualities of finish and power may appear an impossible task; yet the superb orchestra of Mr. Lamoureux comes very near to this perfection. Better than unrelieved polish and such careful attention to detail that the effect of the whole is lost, is a performance full of virility, manly beauty and dramatic intensity, even though exaggeration may enter and annoy.

Symphony No. 6 in F, "Pastorale," Op. 68
Boston Journal, January 18, 1898:

I did not hear the first two movements of the Pastoral Symphony, and I hope I shall never be obliged to hear them. To me, the whole symphony is one of the stupidest works ever penned by a great man.

Boston Herald, March 26, 1921:

There was a remarkable fine performance of the Symphony; the most beautiful, the most appealing we have ever heard. As a rule, this symphony is anticipated with dread: Many conductors take it too seriously, laboriously, lead it with a heavy hand; they are often unfortunate in their choice of tempi, and so the hearer is bored, not yawning, visibly out of respect to Beethoven or fearing lest a neighbor may frown on him, regarding him coldly, counting him disrespectful, irreverent, no doubt a dissolute person. But yesterday the Symphony was indeed pastoral, light hearted, something more than a fearsome length, relieved only by the little ornithological passage in which nightingale, quail, and cuckoo are neatly imitated; at least, it is fair to suppose this: we have never heard the nightingale sing. Jean Cocteau, in his amusing little book, full of aphorisms, designed to make the bourgeois sit up, says that the nightingale sings badly. So we must not be unduly prejudiced by praise of the bird coming from Milton, Matthew Arnold and other poetical enthusiasts. Yesterday there was a thunderstorm, a tempest to use the good country term that has come down from Shakespeare and those before him. How admirably Mr. Monteux interpreted this action of the Symphony, which is often a laughable little shower hardly warranting a spread umbrella or a flight to shelter. How charming the first two movements as played yesterday by the superb orchestra! To borrow the Host's characterization of Master Fenton, the Symphony yesterday smelt April and May.

Symphony No. 7 in A, Op. 92
Boston Home Journal, October 26, 1889:

What an amount of nonsense has been written about the Seventh Symphony. Victims of hysteria have claimed that it portrayed everything in heaven above, in the earth beneath, in the water beneath the earth. One man claims that it "paints" a low carousal; another sees it in a procession in the catacombs; while one honest German declares it to be an odalisque's dream of love!

As if music could express anything but musical ideas. As if two people were affected in precisely the same way by a composition. Walt Whitman comes nearer the truth when he says, "All music is what awakens from you when you are reminded by the instruments,....it is not the oboe, nor the beating drums, nor the score of the baritone singer singing his sweet romanza,...it is nearer and farther than they."

Is there not pleasure enough in "pure musical beauty, inherent in sounds and their combinations?" Is it necessary for complete enjoyment to say of music, "It means this, it means that?"

[*See also Appendix I.]

Symphony No. 9 in D minor, "Choral," Op. 125
Boston Journal, after April 29, 1899:

Do you really find the 9th symphony as great a work of art as the symphony in C minor? I mean, from beginning to end. The Adagio is indisputably a miracle of wondrous song. But do you think a condensed scherzo would be more to the purpose? And were you not reminded once or twice in the finale of the music that is so dear to the Chinese? Do you really think that the tune which tells of "Freude, Freude, schoener Goetterfunken, Tochter aus Elysium" is a good tune? There are many vocal passages in this finale that would no doubt be wonderful if only they could be performed just as the defiant Beethoven heard them with his deaf ears. But I am not prepared to admit that music which cannot be performed is therefore the greatest.

Mr. Gericke gave a thoughtful and careful reading of the symphony. The first movement was not as clear as on former occasions, and the andante in the adagio movement might have been taken slower with advantage. Indeed, the whole performance was a little formal and precise. But on the whole the performance of this difficult work was far above the average.

Musical Record, June 1, 1899:

We heard lately in Boston the Ninth Symphony of Beethoven. The performance was technically most admirable. But is not worship paid this Symphony mere fetishism?

Is not the famous Scherzo insufferably long-winded? The Finale is to me for the most part dull and ugly. I admit the grandeur of the passage 'und der Cherub steht vor Gott' and the effect of "Seid unschlungen Millionen!" But oh, the pages of stupid and hopelessly vulgar music! The unspeakable cheapness of the chief tune, 'Freude, freude!' Do you believe way down in the bottom of your heart that if this music had been written by Mr. John L. Tarbox, now living in Sandown, N. H., any conductor here or in Europe could be persuaded to put it in rehearsal?

Berlioz

Overture to Benvenuto Cellini
Boston Herald, January 20, 1923:

Mr. Monteux led a remarkably brilliant performance of the overture: a performance that in itself was enough to make the concert noteworthy. The overture is Berlioz at his best; and, at his best he is among the immortals.

Harold in Italy
Boston Herald, December 6, 1903:

Harold in Italy was originally slated for a projected Berlioz centenary concert that had to be modified. It remained the only Berlioz work on the program:

Perhaps "Harold in Italy" was originally chosen for the Berlioz anniversary as a mean of introducing Mr. Ferir, the new viola player. He displayed a rich and beautiful tone and he played with taste. The work itself is curiously characteristic for Berlioz, but it is inferior in imaginative force and intensity of musical grip to either the "Romeo and Juliet" or the "Symphonie Fantastique." Yet, it is a marvelous composition when we remember the year that gave it birth. "Harold in Italy" is 69 years old. Wagner in 1834 was writing his opera "Das Liebesverbot," at Magdeburg; Verdi had not written his first opera. Schumann at the age of 34 was founding his musical journal; Tschaikowsky was not born; Brahms was a year old. For its time, Berlioz's symphony was a marvel of orchestra imagination and imagination, as Jacob Boehme says, is the first emanation of the divinity.

This is a gross and material age and it is hard for us to realize the sincerity of the old-fashioned romanticists. It is hard for us to understand the once enormous popularity of "Childe Harold." Who reads the poem today? Yet it entered into the thought of Europe; certain phrases, lines are a part of the English language wherever it is spoken; and, without reference to the descriptive forces shown by the poet, it may be said without fear of contradiction that "Childe Harold" contains the noblest apostrophe to liberty to be found in the whole range of English literature. It would be as impossible today to compose the symphony as it would be to write the poem.

Gone are those days of revolt against tyranny in thought as well as in government, the revolt that idolized the disorderly, turned pirates, cutthroats, as well as all defiers of conventionality into heroes, the revolt which might have been amusing had it not been so bitterly honest. Berlioz, delighted in the horrors of romanticism as he would have found supreme joy in the splendid extravagance and madness of Marlowe, Tourneur and other raging Elizabethans, in the tragic intensity of John Webster's Italian villains and lawless women had he been able to read the plays. And he thought romantically of romantic subjects. It is as though he wrote "Harold in Italy," in a long cloak and a bandit's hat, with a dagger dipped in red ink. The melancholy wanderer over the mountains, the muttering pilgrims, the mountaineer with his serenade, the orgy of brigands—these were as real to him as the strollers and scenes on the boulevard. And this music should be played in the wild, fantastic spirit, otherwise it is impossible. This is no symphony for the lecturer and the analyst and the learned professor in front of the blackboard.

Regarded as a symphony with themes and development and sections and codas, it is impossible. When the music is bizarre or ugly the interpretation should bring out these qualities; they should not be softened for genteel ears. Let the composer fume and rave or wax sentimental and melancholy; let him be fantastical. Otherwise we are reminded of the fact that there once lived a man with wild ideas and a singular faculty for instrumentation; for we all are inclined to forget that the truly great, the men who have done might deeds, have been suspected of madness by the eminently respectable and by those at the time successful and envied.

Overture to Les Francs-Juges
Boston Herald, January 19, 1918:

> Is it wise to perform an inferior work of a composer long after he died? Is the performance fair to the audience or to the reputation dead musician? Possibly there are some that still believe in the plenary inspiration of a composer, poet, essayist; some that find the inferior music of a great composer preferable to the best work of a man ranked in the second class.

Brahms

Double Concerto in A minor, Op. 102
Boston Herald, February 24, 1917:

> The double concerto of Brahms cannot justly be ranked among his more important works. His warmest friends and admirers shook their heads when they heard it. Even Hanslick, whose articles about him were often as the rhapsodies of passionate press agents, had much to say by way of apology for not liking the concerto. He found that it was a mistake for Brahms to choose the two instruments, that the work was not a concerto after all, but a symphonic composition with embroidery for two solo instruments, that the thematic material was not happily invented and the development was laborious, that the chief theme of the Finale was insignificant, etc., etc. In other words Hanslick was probably bored stiff when Joachim and Hausmann played the concerto in Vienna. Age has not blunted the boring force, which surpasses that of the celebrated teredo, or ship worm. There are pleasing measures in the Andante, which is by far the spontaneous and musical movement. What possessed Messrs. Witek and Warnke to spend their time in preparation and performance? Had they registered an oath in heaven that before they were overtaken by the Lean Fellow with his scythe they would play together this concerto?

[*See also Chapter 2.]

Symphony No. 1 in C minor, Op. 68
Boston Herald, April 4, 1931:

> Dr. Koussevitzky gave an unusually eloquent interpretation of the symphony; surpassing even former performances conducted by this admirer of Brahms. Who has

been singularly fortunate in revealing the poetic and dramatic side of a composer whose music led by other conductors, otherwise worthy men, has often seemed only pedantic, dry, oppressively respectful. Even at the risk of being called a blasphemer, one wishes that Brahms had lived up to the magnificent introduction to the Finale of the symphony. After the exposition of the chief theme of the Allegro, Johannes is seen as one condemned to hard labor.

Symphony No. 2 in D, Op. 73
Boston Herald, March 26, 1930:

But how can recent biographers find the symphony in D major a work of epic grandeur? It has hitherto been regarded as agreeable in the Mendelssohn manner, tuneful, with a piquant Scherzo, and a reassuring Finale, music that is free from storm, stress, and passion; music that almost as a quotation pays a graceful compliment to Mendelssohn in flowing measures, as there is a tribute to Wagner in the first movement of the Third Symphony, a glimpse of Venus and her voluptuous train, refreshing after the crashing, defiant opening measures.

There is also a wide-spread tendency in performing the orchestral music of Brahms to make it more dramatic than the contents suggest. This comes from the wish to avoid the academic, respectful, perfunctory, one might say obsequious readings that in times past led many to find the symphonies too sober, if not dull. If jog-trot interpreters thought to reveal "the spirit of Brahms"—meaningless phrase to apply to any composer, but one that sounds well and impresses some—contemporary interpreters are often tempted to treat Brahms as if he were possessed with a demon; as if he were a daring innovation, with fire, not celestial ichor in his veins. Or in order to make the music more intense, there is undue importance given to episodes so that there is no continuous musical flow. The latter course appeals to the great majority. The music is, then, exciting; the dynamic contrasts hold the attention; the composer in the minds of the hearers is glorified; they might exclaim: "Is this Brahms? Who would have thought the old man to have so much blood in him?"

After all, whatever the purist may say, it is better to be pleasurably excited at a concert than to be lulled to sleep. In all probability the magnificent performance by the orchestra and the roaring applause of the audience would have delighted Johannes, for he was mortal, and all mortals like appreciation.

Symphony No. 3 in F, Op. 90
Boston Herald, December 31, 1932:

We doubt if a Boston audience has ever heard as magnificent performance of Brahms' Third Symphony as that given yesterday by the conductor [Serge Koussevitzky] and the orchestra. The symphony itself is to us the most genial of the four. If one points to the first movement and the introduction to the finale of the first symphony, there is the intensely dramatic first movement of the third for an answer. The two middle movements of the same symphony are full of beauty. And in this symphony as in certain other works of Brahms—notably in the finale of the second piano concerto—there is the refreshing Hungarian influence that enlivens—not to say atones for acid pages; pages not so dry and labored in this symphony as elsewhere in Brahms' music. It would seem as if Brahms found beauty as well as dash remembering Hungary and its gypsies. While there is a melancholy flavor to the third movement, the music has a peculiar grace and fascination. It is wholly free from the granite pessimism which at times Brahms into a dismal Jemmy in doleful dumps.

Symphony No. 4 in E minor, Op. 98
Boston Herald, November 18, 1920:

What a pity it is that Brahms in his fourth symphony did not stop after the second movement! The triangle and the piccolo do not relieve the clumsy dreariness of the Scherzo; the Finale, with the exceptions of a few Variations, as the solemn passage for trombones, is a sad falling off from the first Allegro. Mr. Monteux gave an admirable reading of the work, bringing out clearly the innumerable details—and more than once Brahms is found treading water—sparring for wind...

Bruckner

Symphony No. 4 in E flat, "Romantic"
Boston Journal, February 11, 1899:

The program of the 15th symphony concert last night in Music Hall, Mr. Gericke conductor, was as follows:

Overture, "Leonore No. 3" .... Beethoven
Piano Concerto No. 2 .... Brahms
Symphony No. 4, E flat major .... Bruckner
  (First time in Boston)

[Hans] Von Bülow was for a time talking and writing incessantly about "the three B's"—Bach, Beethoven, Brahms—possibly hoping that some would say, "You forget yourself: there are four."

The program last night was devoted to three B's—and, by the way, the program was too long.

Is Bruckner one of the great B's? I have no opinion on this subject, for I heard his music last night for the first time.

I had been warned against it. I had been told by some that his symphonies were drearier than the dreariest pages of Brahms. Others had whispered in my ear that he was a genius—at remembering Wagner. Then, too, there was the saying of some German musician who heard one of Bruckner's symphonies: "The wild dream of an orchestra-player who had been unduly excited by twenty rehearsals of 'Tristan'."

There was this consolation: The symphony was at the end of the concert: if it became unendurable, the door was close at hand.

This consolation was taken away. Mr. Gericke, with Yankee shrewdness, changed the order; and lo, the symphony came first.

The disappointment was great. I mean by this that I enjoyed the first three movements of the symphony hugely. The influence of Wagner was not disturbing. For a moment there was the suggestion of Siegfried in the forest; and there were a few other hints at "The Ring" and "Tristan"; but Bruckner had plenty to say on his own account, and he said it in his own way.

Here is music that gives a new sensation, and by means that are often artfully artless. Themes that are apparently insignificant are extremely effective in development. The harmonic structure and the orchestration are of constant interest. And there is so much that is fresh and clean! The style, in the first three movements, at least, which had been described as so complex and cumbrous, is often as straightforward as the English of Defoe.

After the first movement, it was easy to breathe freely. A man that could write such beautiful music would surely not go to pieces in the next five minutes or develop suddenly into a fearsome bore. The andante is even more beautiful than the preceding movement. Mr. Apthorp refers to it in the program book as a sort of romanza. I heard it rather as a dirge, a burial fantasia, but without the vulgar pomp of hearse and horses draped in black, without the thought of thread-bare crape and tears. It is more like the apostrophe to Death in Whitman's sonorous nocturne, "When lilacs last in the door-yard bloomed." Now the idea of death may have been farthest from Bruckner's mind when he composed this music, which to one hearer may have suggested a summer night, to another the chorus of the spheres. But the music is more than decorative; it is exceedingly suggestive, whatever mood you choose.

The scherzo is also a rare delight, with its invitation to the hunt, with the trio that tells of village dance and simple joy. Bruckner's peasants are of the soil. They are not Watteau, smirking figures, or operetta characters with ribboned hats and rakes.

The finale staggered me. I could not discover what the man was driving at. There are imposing passages, preludes to great events, that are postponed; then it seems as though Bruckner suddenly said to himself, "This will never do; I must try another tack." There are halting, as though in deliberation or doubt. There are harassing, vexing, changes of thought. In one or two instances apparently downright triviality follows the almost sublime. This is the only movement that disappointed. It disappointed, not from the lack of skill, but from seeming absence of cohesion and logical development. There is counterpoint galore, but the train of thought is as though it were subject to constant interruption from an outsider.

Copland

Piano Concerto
Boston Herald, January 29, 1927:

One should be sorry for Mr. Copland. His "Music for the Theatre," played here late in 1925, was much more to his credit than his Symphony for organ and orchestra heard earlier in that year. One hoped to note continued progress in the invention of thematic material; in firmness of control, so that one could say he was the experimental state and writing with surety, no longer relying on what he thought would attract attention by novelty and audacity.

If this concerto shows the present state of Mr. Copland's musical mind, he is on the wrong track. One is not easily annoyed in these days by a free use of dissonances, by daring juxtapositions of tonalities, if they are effective; if they serve in establishing a mood, contemplative, fiery, somber; if there is a revelation of strength, however barbaric, of beauty, however strange and fantastical. In this concerto we found little to attract, little to admire, much to repel.

Jazz is not the monster it has been called; it has already had its uses; it has stimulated symphonic composers to greater rhythmic energy and freedom. It all depends on the use made of this form of music. There must also be originality in the "tune" and in the treatment when it is allowed to influence a work of importance. Mr. Copland is not yet an adept in this field.

The Concerto also shows a shocking lack of taste, of proportion. The first measures are proof enough. After thunderous, blaring measures in which one brass instrument vies with another in arrogant announcement—announcements without logical connection, though the composer says this introduction proclaims the principal thematic material—there are gentle, purposeless measures for the piano, which is struck by fingers apparently directed at random, as a child amuses itself by making noises when it is restless in the room.

We do not doubt Mr. Copland's honesty of purpose; it is the purpose, the musical scheme that is to be deplored. Yesterday some in the audience laughed, as if the concerto were a huge joke on Mr. Koussevitzky, who, as Mr. Copland says, suggested to him the composition of it.

The question comes up legitimately; Does Mr. Copland hear music in this way? Is his musical speech natural or acquired? His next composition may satisfactorily answer these questions.

Let us not forget that the leading English reviewers characterized Schumann's Symphony in B flat [No. 1, Op. 38] when they first heard it as belonging to the "Broken Crockery School." Our objection to Mr. Copland's broken crockery is that it is not of first quality.

Dvořák

Symphony No. 7 in D minor, Op. 70
Boston Herald, November 17, 1923:

The Dvorak of this symphony [No. 7, in Hale's time listed as No. 2] is a greater man than the Dvorak of the more familiar one, entitled, "From the New World." When he wrote the one in D minor, he was still the Bohemian musician, gifted with an uncommon sense of color and rhythm. He remembered the folk songs of his country and the dances for which he had played in his early years. English flattery and over-praise had not turned his head; he liked his own music, but he did not take himself too seriously. He was not afraid to let himself go in a symphony; he did not stand in the awe of professors and critics. When he came to write "From the New World," he was musically sophisticated; musically, we say, for as a man he was simple and naïve til the end.

It is easy to find here and there a weak spot in the construction of the earlier symphony, especially in the development of the music materials where even blowing colors do not hide the halting workmanship. It is easy to say there are a few "reminiscences"; one might go so far as to say that some of the melodies are almost vulgar, saved only by the refreshing simplicity of the inventor; but when all this is said, the symphony remains after nearly forty years, fresh, vigorous, often beautiful in color, often stirring rhythmically and by reason of the contents and the manner in which they are clothed. Mr. Monteux caught the spirit of the composer, rejoiced with him in his stormy glee, and sympathized with him in the moments of sentiment. The orchestra played gloriously and what a magnificent orchestra it is today—thanks to Mr. Monteux and the men themselves.

Hindemith

Konzertmusik for Strings and Brass
Boston Herald, April 4, 1931:

There have been many "explanations" of Hindemith: why he is what he is. Some apologize for him by saying that he has journeyed much as a viola virtuoso and a member of a string quartet, observing the rhythm of railway trains, he, as a composer, is interested chiefly in rhythmic combinations and inventions. The conservatives have, justly or unjustly, classed him with contemporaneous composers who, though they have talent, are nevertheless to be avoid; the conservatives have put Hindemith on the list of those who never would be missed; but he has the fertility of a rabbit: one work breathlessly follows another. But he is a composer not to be carelessly put aside.

He often disappoints those who would give him more than respect for his technical requirements. Take the composition for the 50th anniversary of the Boston Symphony Orchestra, performed yesterday for the first time. Hindemith likes to experiment with groups of instruments. In this Konzertmusik the brass choir, in the first section punctuates what the strings have to say in a dry manner with growls and snorts. The opening of a long cantilena for strings, at first alone, gives the hope of melodic beauty. But the music of Hindemith is not sensuous. Did the muses endow him with a melodic gift? We doubt it. Nor can one justly characterize his musical nature as emotional. Writing for a festival occasion, one would have anticipated sonorous pomp, stately declamation or at least tumultuous rejoicing; but this music was not even laboriously ugly. There can be ugliness that at the same time may be impressive; but the "Konzertmusik" is for the most part worse than ugly—it is dull, nor does the display of technical ingenuity save it.

Holst

The Planets, Op. 32
Boston Herald, Saturday, January 27, 1923

The 13th concert of the Boston Symphony orchestra, Mr. Monteux, conductor, took place yesterday afternoon in Symphony Hall. The program included "The Planets" a set of seven tone-poems by Gustav Holst, and MacDowell's "Indian" Suite.

Some, reading the announcement of this concert, may have thought that the composer of "the Planets" purposed to give his hearers a fair idea of the music of the spheres[*]. This music, by the way, has never been heard by mortal man, except by Pythagoras. We do not hear it, he said, because we are accustomed to it from our birth and cannot distinguish any sound wave by the silence opposed to it. According to the great philosopher, so cruelly mocked by Lusian, Saturn sounds the lowest tone; the moon the highest. Those who wish to inquire curiously into this celestial music should read the treatise by the learned Professor Piper, "Von der Harmonie der Sphaeren," published in 1849.

Holst, an Englishman of Swedish descent, born in 1874, and now reckoned as a leader in the more advanced body of British musicians, was not so ambitious. He contented himself by composing in 1915 and 1916 seven tone-poems which should illustrate musically the astrological significance of Mars, the Bringer of War; Venus, the Bringer of Peace; Mercury, the Winged Messenger; Jupiter, the Bringer of Jollity; Saturn, the Bringer of Old Age; Uranus, the Magician and Neptune, the Mystic.

The composer has said that these tone-poems are without a program; they have no connection with the deities bearing the same names; the subtitles are a sufficient guide.

It will astonish some to find Venus described as the Bringer of Peace. The common opinion is that she has stirred up foreign and domestic strife, invaded households; a goddess smiling on battle, murder, and sudden death. A famous but unquotable line of Horace tells how she brought on the Trojan War. In astrology Uranus is a transformer, hence a magician, while Neptune represents the state of union with the infinite, the seeking after the ideal. We fear that those now consulting the astrologers are more concerned with fortunate days for doing business or marrying than the sublime attributes of the planets.

Holst has certainly written uncommon music. He has fancy, if not imagination, and the two are not always easily distinguished in spite of Coleridge's long-winded definitions. He has learned thoroughly harmonic and orchestration technique, and, as his invention is fertile and he has a pronounced sense of color, this cycle contains in turn ravishing, impressive, surprising pages. Take "Mars" for example. There is the suggestion of iron and brass; defiant inexorable militarism. And here the tremendous effect is gained by comparatively simple means. In "Venus," charming as much of the music is, Holst is more sophisticated, more audacious in his harmonic scheme. "Mercury" is, appropriately, a nimble Scherzo, lightly scored, for the most part. The "jollity" in Jupiter is inspired by ale rather than wine; it is heavy-footed and the tunes are not free from vulgarity. The composer's imagination is at its height in "Saturn" and in "Neptune." The former is music that should not accompany old age as Walt Whitman knew it: "Old Age superbly rising! Ineffable grace of dying days." Here is sullen, complaining, dismal old age, but how graphic the expression! "Neptune," on the contrary, is, indeed, mystic, beautifully so, not vaguely, not gropingly.

There are drawbacks to the full enjoyment of this cycle. There is the besetting sin of many modern English composers – prolixity. Endless repetitions of unimportant themes or fragments of themes fret the nerves, no matter how ingeniously they are tossed from one group of instruments to another or proclaimed by the full orchestra. Mr. Carpenter of Chicago puts his trust in the xylophone; Mr. Holst puts his in the celesta, which is worked overtime. Mr. Holst once told a friend that he loved to write a tune. Unfortunately, some of his tunes, such as those in "Jupiter" are common. Strange to say in this cycle there are few, if any, truly sensuous strains. "Mercury" in myth was the god of thieves as well as the heavenly messenger. Mr. Holst did not take advantage of this fact in his "Mercury," but when the bassoons began their business early in "Uranus" we thought for a moment that Mr. Monteux was interpolating "The Sorcerer's Apprentice" by one Paul Dukas.

"The Planets" is in many ways a remarkable work, one that should be heard again, and soon. The performance was brilliant.

Mr. Monteux gave a sympathetic reading of MacDowell's Suite. The noble and affecting "Dirge" is truly the orchestral masterpiece of the lamented composer.

[*Editor's note: Hale here is making an allusion to the Protestant church hymn,"This Is My Father's World," written in 1901 by Rev. Maltbie Davenport Babcock (1858–1901) and published in his *Thoughts for Everyday Living* (New York: Charles Scribner's Sons, 1901). Its opening lines are as follows:

This is my Father's World, and to my listening ears
All nature sings and round me rings the music of the spheres.]

Ode to Death
Boston Herald, February 11, 1928:

...That an "Ode to Death" immediately followed the symphony [Conrad Beck's *Symphony No. 3*, for strings] was peculiarly fitting....

Gustav Holst was a brave man when he set out to add music to the famous excerpt from Walt Whitman's "When Lilac's Last in Dooryard Bloom'd" or "President

Lincoln's Burial Hymn," a title perhaps more familiar. There are poems that mock the efforts of composers; yet [Granville] Bantock presumed to write music for the choruses in "Atalanta in Calydon" and neither Shelley nor Keats has escaped the ambitious endeavors of British composers. No one will deny that there are poetic and impressive passages in Holst's music—as when he came to "the huge and thoughtful night." The music for the lines beginning "Dark Mother always gliding near" is poetically imagined; there are impressive climaxes of a quiet nature: there is a largeness to "The night in silence," but on the whole, in spite of certain pianissimos emphasizing Whitman's thought, the Ode is of uneven merit. One turns to Whitman's rapt song and finds it the more imaginative, the more musical.

Kalinnikoff

Symphony No. 1 in G minor
Boston Herald, April 2, 1921:

Kalinnikoff's symphony, which was produced at Kieff in 1897, should have been heard in Boston long before yesterday. Why did the conductors neglect it? Is it too melodious? Is it too "light"? The audience found it most agreeable music, unmistakably Slav in spirit, yet not aggressively nationalistic. Here and there the influence of Tschaikowsky is felt, but there is no servile imitation. On the contrary, Kalinnikoff has much to say for himself. He was very poor in his early years. When he was 27 years old his future was bright: his ability as a composer was recognized; he had an honorable position at Moscow in the Italian Opera House. The next year he was "ordered South." During his remaining years—he died within two days of being 35—he composed in the Crimea and waited for the end.

It is customary to say when a composer is thus fated that his works show a melancholy akin to despair. This has been said of many in various walks of life. The fact remains that some do not thus betray physical weakness and mental perturbation. Beethoven in a most dismal mood wrote a singularly cheerful symphony. Brahms was sometimes musically in doleful dumps when he was enjoying his restaurant life in Vienna, gay in his rude manner with his many friends.

Now in Kalinnikoff's Symphony certain themes and phrases of their development are tinged with melancholy. But it is not a personal lamentation, never a wail, never a shriek, as is the case with many pages of Tschaikowsky; there is no suggestion of sullen, morose despair as in the pages of Brahms. There is the melancholy that so often characterizes the Russian folk song, though the words of the song may be anything but somber. Kalinnikoff's themes are often simple, but they make a direct appeal through their honesty of sentiment and expression. He had a great sense of grace and beauty. He could be ingenious in harmonic and orchestral treatment without seeming merely a haphazard experimenter. Contriving unusual effects for the Andante, and the Trio of the Scherzo, he knew well what he was about. The symphony, finely played, was welcomed yesterday with more than ordinaryw armth.

Loeffler

Hora Mystica
Boston Herald, March 3, 1917:

It was first played at a concert of the Litchfield County Choral Union at Norfolk, Ct., June 6, 1916, when Mr. Loeffler conducted the Philharmonic Orchestra of

New York. He has given the argument of his composition. Put in a few words it is this: The mood is one of religious meditation and adoration of nature. A Pilgrim goes his way through an enchanting country. He hears shepherds piping to their flocks; he hears church-bells tolling curiously in a far-off village. At last he comes to the cathedral of a Benedictine Monastery. He gazes on its beauty and its gargoyles. In the church the office of compline—the last service of the day, the Hora Mystica as it is known to Benedictine monks—is tendered unto God. Peace enters the soul of the pilgrim. The symphony is woven around the recitation of "Te autem in nobis es Domine," the chant "In manus tuus, Domine," and the antiphon, "Salve Regina." The chief theme of the symphony is inspired by the response, "Deo gratias."

When Debussy's Nocturnes were performed here for the first time under Mr. Lang's direction, they were played twice in the same concert. It might have benefitted the composer and the audience if the program yesterday had consisted of "Hora Mystica" played twice with an intermission between the performances.

Walter Savage Landlor, speaking of "Imaginary Conversations," said with superb confidence in his future: "I shall dine late; but the dining room will be well lighted, the guests few and select." This proud speech is sometimes quoted by a reviewer, who knowing that a new book, an ultra-modern picture, or a musical composition is caviare to the general, looks forward to confirmation of his superior judgment by the avenger Time. He may be found intimating that his own seat is already secure, reserved for him as guest of honor at the right hand of the gracious and patient host.

The speech of Landlor might be fairly applied to the composer of "Hora Mystica," but who of us will be among the guests? Mr. Loeffler is a musician of so marked and subtle technic, of so pure and lofty purpose, of so fastidious taste; furthermore he is so intelligently musical, that the boldest reviewer may hesitate in recording even impressions of this uncommonly complex work, especially when he is not filled with the spirit in which it was written, when his acquaintance with the music necessarily be superficial. He recognizes gladly and admirably the supreme workmanship; he feels the spirituality of the composer; but he is in the dark concerning the exact train of thought as it is expressed in the music.

It was not to be expected of so rare a composer as Mr. Loeffler that in the section describing the pilgrim's journey through a landscape, now smiling and lovely. Now mysterious, with the wayfarer reminded of humanity only by shepherds' pipes and distant bells, he should write program-music in a conventional and obvious manner. But this section seems to be first of all a study in overtones resulting at times in harmonic expression that unnecessarily throws off beauty without compensating effects. The landscape is for the most part a cerebral projection not seen by painter or strolling lover of nature. In preceding compositions Mr. Loeffler has shown himself to be a master of exquisite coloring; in "Hora Mystica" the music, especially in the first section, is monochromatic. Nor do we understand the meaning of the anguish expressed by wailing or angry phrases, unless it be that Nature does not give rest to the soul of the pilgrim until he stands before the cathedral.

The Adagio section is warmer and more human. The use of the plain song for the male voices has the desired solemnity and mysticism. It might be said, however, that certain accompanying harmonies in the "Salve Regina," while they may suggest the sighing, mourning, and weeping of supplicants in this vale of tears by their realism, disturb the prevailing serenity of the prayer to the Blessed virgin. As performed yesterday, those harmonies at times obscured the chanting of the singers.

A remarkable work, this "Hora Mystica" suffered from its position after the long concerto of Mrs. Beach. We also think it a doubtful experiment to write an orchestral work of this importance and uncommon nature in one movement, when the ears of the most receptive hearers would be taxed if the music were in a more conventionalm anner.

Mahler

Symphony No. 5 in C sharp Minor
Boston Herald, February 3, 1906:

This is one of the longest of Hale's concert reviews; it is included here in its entirety:

MAHLER'SF IFTH SYMPHONY GIVEN

First Performance Here of His
Collossal [sic] Work at the 14th
Symphony Concert Last Evening

A COMPOSITION OF LENGTH AND STRENGTH

Mr. Bauer's Delightful Performance of Schumann's
Piano Concerto "The Pipe
of Desire" at Popular Prices

The programme of the 14th Symphony concert, Mr. Gericke conductor, given last night in Symphony Hall, was as follows:

Overture to Goethe's "Egmont"	Beethoven
Concerto in A minor for piano	Schumann
Symphony in C sharp minor, No. 5	Mahler

This concert was one of unusual interest. Mr. Gericke conducted the great overture without attempting to find in it effects that the composer did not imagine or contrive; he let the music speak for itself; he did not interrupt the flow of the main movement by changing deliberately the tempo at the appearance of the heavy chords, which are by some supposed to typify the Duke of Alva, or Spanish oppression in the Netherlands. There have been German post-Wagner conductors who were sad offenders in this instance, Franz Wueller, for instance. Mr. Gericke did not sentimentalize by means of impertinent slackening the pace and so-called "interpretation" of measures without special significance, and thus was his reading the more effective.

Mr. Harold Bauer gave a very musical and charming performance of Schumann's concerto. There was an exquisite sense of proportion; there was both poetic expression and suggestion, and in the last movement, which is rhythmically often a stumbling block to many, he played with an apparent simplicity that would have deceived anyone not acquainted with the peculiar difficulties. The concerto displayed Mr. Bauer at his best, and all in all his performance is to be ranked with his memorable one of Cesar Franck's quintet with the Kneisels a few seasons ago.

Mahler's first symphony was produced in 1894, if not in 1891. Each symphony excited in turn hot discussion. The composer was hailed by some a genius: by others he was mocked as a madman. Now the term "madman," as applied to one who has departed from the conventions or invented something new in art, has lost any peculiar significance of reproach. Disraeli frankly admitted that he was on the side of the angels; the student of musical history can well afford to run the risk of espousing the cause of the madmen. Mahler has his band of wide-eyed partisans, his pamphleteers, who no doubt have done him harm. His foes have served him. His five symphonies have been played in German cities; they have been frantically applauded and fiercely hissed; his first symphony has been played even in London (1903), but no one of his important have been heard in Boston before last week. The first performance in this country of any symphony by Mahler was that of the fourth, in New York, in 1904. The fifth was performed at Cincinnati March 25, 1905. These performances and those of last week in Boston have been the only ones in America.

Conductors have had a reasonable excuse for not producing the second and the third, which demand an extraordinarily large orchestra. The second, also, calls for solo voices and mixed chorus; the third for a solo contralto, female chorus, and boy choir. The two symphonies are very long—the second consumes an hour and 49 minutes. Furthermore, the technical difficulties are great.

Thanks to Mr. Gericke for Producing Mahler's Work

Mr. Gericke therefore deserves hearty thanks for producing one of Mahler's symphonies, producing it with the infinite care in preparation that is characteristic of the man. The production of a work of such huge dimensions, a work peculiar in structure and in its musical speech, does not contribute necessarily to the immediate popularity of a conductor. There are concertgoers who do not to hear new music unless it makes a direct appeal to them in ways that are obvious, familiar, approved. They do not wish to exert themselves mentally at a concert.

Like Polonius, they are for a jig or a tale of bawdry, or they sleep. Or, fortified with scraps of pedantic information, they turn deaf ears to that which is new, as did the Mastersingers hearing Walther's free rhapsodic song. Vexed, bored, sometimes dimly conscious that there is something in the music which is strangely beautiful or great, and that in the course of time they, too, may understand and enjoy it. Their vanity is piqued at the moment, and they either leave the hall unwilling to confirm their suspicions or they remain in sullen silence to sho courage as well as disapproval.

The conductor and the orchestra have rehearsed with utmost patience and with anxious care. Extra rehearsals have been called. The hearer jauntily pronounces a snap judgment: "The symphony does not mean anything. I couldn't make anything out of it. Why does Mr. Gericke put such stuff on the programme?" But is this fair to composer, conductor, orchestra? We all remember how Cesar Franck's great symphony was at first regarded here as the abomination of desolation; how Richard Strauss' "Don Juan," when it was first played here, was ranked as a slap in the face from a lunatic or charlatan; yet last season both symphony and symphony poem were repeated "by request," listened to with grateful attention and applauded tumultuously.

There is no programme for Mahler's 5th symphony, and the composer abhors analytical notes. He wished the audience to hear his music, not to read about it while it is playing. This music needs no programme. It is eloquent in itself.

It has been said that life in Vienna influenced its moods; the the opening dead march was suggested by the military funerals in Vienna; that the scherzo, a Laendler, is characteristically local in spirit; but Mahler's mighty dead march, with its episode of shrieking and heaven-defying grief is universal music and the dance was an expression of joy or of religious feeling centuries before Austria was a marquisate, centuries before the Sultan Soliman laid siege to take the Kaiserstadt with his army of 200,000 men. Fortunately for Mahler, the characteristics of his symphony are not merely local.

The movements that will make a direct appeal to the average audience are the dead march, the second movement, or rather the section of it that contains the second theme announced by the cellos and the fourth movement, an exceedingly poetic adagietto with themes of rare beauty, especially beautiful in these days when too many themes are purely of cerebral invention. The portions of the Scherzo which are frankly in slow waltz time will please those who do not at one hearing appreciate the significance of the ideas that are tributary to the main waltz themes, or the surprising technical skill displayed in the treatment of the motives. The Rondo Finale is not as a whole so impressively sonorous as the other movements, although the use of the choral[e] which has already appeared in the second movement is most effective.

No Two Persons Hear Music in One and the Same Way

Music which reaches the heart as well as the nerves and the brain is of all music the most difficult to describe so that a reader who did not hear it can understand in some degree why the emotion of the composer made its irresistible way. Purple phrases and resounding rhetoric may be a sanitary relief to the writer, but they do not convince the reader who had not the opportunity of being moved. It should also be remembered that no two persons, intelligent and sensitive though they may be, hear music in one and the same way. Each is "reminded by the instruments," but that which is awakened in the breast of each is seldom, if ever, the same.

Mahler has been reproached for his poverty of thematic invention. The reproach, as far as this symphony is concerned, is unjust. The simplicity of some of the themes is the simplicity that marks genius. The rich beauty of some of them is enhanced by the spontaneity. The dramatic stab of other themes is equally spontaneous. Nor is there any suspicion of insincerity in the treatment of these themes. Whether the mood be one of grim resignation, wild despair, naïve joy in mere existence, contemplation of beauty in nature or in woman, or whooping exultation, it is never feigned never forced. The hearer knows that Mahler himself had these mighty or whirring or calm and solemn thoughts and expressed them in his own grandiose or passionate or excited manner. The personality as well as the individuality of this music is overpowering.

The reminiscence-hunter has driven the hunter after forbidden intervals and progressions out of the field, and he will find the happiness peculiar to his kind in detecting here a few measures that suggest thoughts in Beethoven's Ninth, and here a cry that sounds for a moment as though it had been wrenched from Berlioz, and there the Kundry theme from "Parsifal," but in a long work of such amazing originality in conception and execution, such reminders serve a purpose: they entertain those who are unable to find anything else in the symphony that deserves their approbation.

Orchestral technique in this period, when expression is reckoned as of more importance than thought, runs in the streets, as Goethe said of talent. There are a few passages in the symphony that are scored thickly, harshly; yet they make their way, and the instrumentation as a whole is strikingly sonorous, while there are many instances of remarkably individual orchestral expression. The finale on the whole is orchestrally perhaps the least interesting; yet the music itself is potent; it recalls that music heard by De Quincy in an opium dream, the music that suggested to him the "undulations of fast gathering tumults...multitudinous movements, infinite cavalcades, tread of innumerable armies." It is music of a mighty preparation; nor does the choral[e] at the end disappoint the expectation.

Music That Is Human Even When Most Fantastical

This music of Mahler has blood in it. It is human even when it is most fantastical. Its extravagance in expression is titanic, but never incredible. It contains an elemental quality that is often confounded by the super-refined with coarseness; the display of native strength that alarms all the feeble folk and all the genteel; this quality is found in nearly all the great in art, from Aeschylus to Thomas Hardy, from Bach to Tschaikowsky. It is never to be confounded with downright vulgarity which is always inartistic, while this peculiar coarseness is heroic, whether it be found in Victor Hugo or Verdi; in Henry Fielding or in Wagner. You find it in Shakespeare, Cervantes, Rabelais. You find it in Beethoven and in Michael Angelo.

This symphony has blood and tears, frantic joy and wild despair; it also has the saving quality of humor, as in the scherzo. Mahler has expressed his thoughts in a heightened musical speech of richest harmonic, contrapuntal and orchestral vocabulary. After two hearings, it is an amazing work, full, as is nature, of inequalities, no doubt, but it is the symphony of no ordinary man and no ordinary musician. Long as it is, it rivets the attention from the beginning to the end, and last night the great majority of the audience listened gladly to a new and compelling voice.

The performance was one of extraordinary brilliance, one of which both Mr. Gericke and the orchestra may well be proud. The orchestra was one of virtuosos controlled by the intelligence and the will of a leader who had made the symphony his own. To particularize is always invidious, yet it may be allowed for once to praise especially the manner in which the first trumpeter performed his arduous and formidable task.

Such a symphony should not be heard once and then put away for a season. It should be heard at two or three concerts in succession and then impressions might be turned to firm convictions.

Mozart

Clarinet Concerto in A, K. 622
Boston Herald, March 30, 1918:

The 19th concert of the Boston Symphony orchestra took place yesterday afternoon in Symphony Hall. The program was as follows: Cherubini, Overture to "Les Abencerages;" Mozart, Clarinet Concerto (first time at these concerts); Rameau, Ballet Suite; Schumann, Symphony in B-flat Major No. 1. Mr. Schmidt conducted.

Mr. Sand, the first clarinet of the orchestra, is the second to play a solo at these concerts. Mr. Strasser played Weber's Concertino in E-flat early in 1884. The oboe, flute, and horn have been heard as solo instruments, but the wind choir, as a rule, has not been largely represented in this manner. Years ago the bassoon in many European orchestras insisted on the privilege. Many of us have the trombone play "with great depression" Stigelli's "Tear" or some other sentimental ditty.

Mozart wrote this concerto two months and a few days before his death. He wrote it for a famous clarinetist, Anton Stadler, who, outside of his ability as a virtuoso, was not a desirable or restful companion. He was a toss-pot, a loose-liver, and he had a trick of borrowing money and not repaying it. Mozart, who was very poor, was fascinated by him, enjoying his animal spirits, his jests that set the tavern table in a roar. He lent him money. He wrote for Stadler this concerto and the clarinet quintet.

The concerto is an amiable bit of music. Mozart wrote it in a day. No doubt he could have easily written one each day of the week, so that Stadler could have had one for daily use, as some men possess a case of seven razors. The music has all the Mozartean flavor. It is suave, graceful, spontaneous, with the slight tinge of melancholy in certain pages that one finds ever in joyous scenes of "Le Nozze di Figaro" and "The Magic Flute;" an inconsequential piece on the whole. Sand played the concerto expressively. His tone was agreeable; his mechanism was fluent and polished. The audience was greatly pleased.

The other compositions do not call for comment. Cherubini's overture and the charming music of Rameau were played last season. Schumann's Symphony is perhaps too familiar.

Piano Concerto No. 21 in C, K. 467
Boston Herald, January 15, 1927:

Mozart's Concerto was no doubt unfamiliar to the great majority of the audience. No wonder that those who first heard it in Vienna, when Mozart was the pianist, were loud in praise for here is pure music; music without alloy for virtuoso display; music that is golden; of wondrous charm. And it is a true concerto in which orchestra and piano unite and form a perfect ensemble.

It is not given to every pianist, not even the most celebrated, to catch the spirit of Mozart and his period, to be his sympathetic interpreter. Many who would shine brilliantly as performers of Liszt, Brahms, Tchaikovsky, would come to grief, attempting to ravish the ear by "condescending" to play Mozart's concertos, rondos, or sonatas. Each note must be a thing of beauty; passages, as he himself said, must flow like oil; there is nothing for vain glorious, arrogant assertion; there must be constant worship at the shrine. A pianist may thunder through a modern concerto and excite admiration by his strength, endurance, yet fail even technically when he plays Mozart.

Piano Concerto No. 23 in A, K. 488
Boston Herald, December 13, 1930:

Mr. [Bruce] Simonds played accurately and glibly Mozart's notes; he played with undeviating tonal monotony. For this performance without nuances in tempo or color, he was warmly applauded.

Serenade No. 10 in B flat, K. 361(370a)
Boston Herald, December 7, 1932:

Five of the seven movements in Mozart's Serenade were played. The performance was the first at these concerts; it was probably the first in Boston. The Serenade in

E flat major was played in 1895. The Longy Club played two or three serenades, but passed by the one in B flat.

The divertimenti and serenades, by Mozart are too little known, yet there are some who find them among Mozart's finest works. Let no one think that the Serenade in B flat was chosen only to display the skill and musicianship of a section of the orchestra. The performance was indeed remarkable, for quality of tone, beauty of phrasing and for technical proficiency; but the music itself is delightful; varied, now beautiful, now gay. Variations for wind instruments—or in fact for any instruments—are often the abomination of desolation. The invention shown by Mozart in this serenade—variations in which beauty is never forgotten—is surprising. They are not exercises in variation form. It seems as if Mozart for the time being could not express his musical ideas in any other manner; there is nothing cut and dried about them, no suggestion of the conservatory's prize pupil, a pedagogue anxious to point out flaws. The audience warmly appreciated the music and the excellent performance.

Serenade No. 11 in E flat, K. 375
Boston Herald, December 1, 1903:

> ...If the average hearer is a bit less discerning, or less imaginative than the enthusiastic Jahn [*faithful admirer of Mozart's works], nevertheless the work holds plenty of matter to interest him.

Symphony No. 35 in D, "Haffner," K. 385
Boston Herald, April 25, 1926:

> ...The concert began with a delightful interpretation of Mozart's unpretentious, but fresh and pleasing, symphony—fresh now that it is nearly 150 years old.

Symphony No. 36 in C, "Linz," K. 425
Boston Journal, March 17, 1899:

> An unfamiliar symphony by Mozart is in nine cases out of ten a weariness to the flesh, and it is mistaken reverence to exhume it, with the intention of galvanizing it. Better one strong modern work than a wilderness of symphonies of ancient pattern and conventional manufacture. The one chosen last night has interesting passages, especially in the finale. The middle movements are dull, and Mozart himself, if he were living, would be the first to yawn at them.

Prokofieff

Piano Concerto No. 3
Boston Herald, January 30, 1926:

> Apparently there are two Prokofieffs: one the composer of the splendidly barbaric "Scythian" suite, which was heard here in 1924; the other the composer of the Third Piano Concerto, a work in comparatively more academic form, but without a trace of academic rigidity and dullness. The music is refreshingly individual. One does not find in it the influence of any school nor of any composer, past or present.

Thematically, harmonically, it is Mr. Prokofieff's own, as is his employment of orchestral instruments. While the music has not the engaging and engrossing wildness of the "Scythian" suite, it is music of the East rather than the West. Here and there one finds the melodic and rhythmic repetition dear to Oriental rejoicing in the consequent hypnosis. When this repetition gains little by little in intensity, the effect is exciting and at the last overpowering, so that the coolest hearer is seized with rhythmic fever and, like the inhabitants of ancient Abdera, is haunted by a simple melody. The theme of the second movement—we believe it to be original with Mr. Prokofieff, for no contrary statement has been made—is of exotic beauty, while the postlude of a few measures, ingeniously varied after each one of the set variations will long haunt the memory, the more so by its simplicity. These variations are ingenious, free from pattern works. The fourth, marked Andante meditativo, is unaffectedly poetic. Throughout the concerto theme there is no effort to stun or dazzle the hearer. It is if Mr. Prokofieff had composed it for his own pleasure, without thought of possible audiences, indifferent to words of praise or blame.

It is often said disparagingly of a musician playing his own composition for the piano: "He plays like a composer." This sneer cannot be directed against Mr. Prokofieff, any more than it is true of Mr. Rachmaninoff. Mr. Prokofieff in the most modest manner in the world played like a virtuoso who was not first thinking of technic, not trying to impress hearers by technical proficiency, conscious, but not too self-conscious of his own ability. He played as if he were a member of the orchestra, displaying sufficient fluency, a command of nuances and of sentiment, emotion, and brilliance. He was recalled several times.

Symphony No. 4
Boston Herald, November 15, 1930:

The "Classical" symphony was western in thought and expression. This fourth symphony is oriental as was to be expected after one knew that Prokofieff had used some of his ballet material. Hearing the music, one recognized a spirit that was not western in any way: not in thematic invention, not in harmonic progressions; decidedly not in the orchestration. For his "Classical" symphony, the composer was quoted as saying that he had written after manner of Mozart. In the fourth symphony he went back to the earlier Profofieff. Nor is there in the later work the melodic inspiration that is desired. There are tunes that promise beauty; they are soon tortured. There are also patterns that are ingeniously used, for it would be foolish to question the technical skill of the composer, but one can not live on patterns.

One can easily think that this or that section, especially in the Scherzoso, was planned for dancers; that in the other movements there are pages for those on the stage telling the story in pantomime. A glance at the ballet score might easily show the folly of fancied identifications. The symphony as it stands is absolute music, and as music pure and simple it cannot be ranked with the best of Prokofieff's works. There is no objection to his being the wild man, as in the "Scythian Suite," and "They Are Seven," but in this symphony there is not the barbaric outpourings that have a beauty of their own and impress one by strength. In former works the orchestration when clangorous was effective; more than a mere shock to the nervous system. In the symphony the orchestration in fortissimo is often only blatant; and when objective or subtle beauty is sought by the blending of instrumental timbres there is, as a rule, a disappointing experiment.

Violin Concerto
Boston Herald, April 25, 1925:

> [Schubert] believers probably looked with dread on the production of Prokofieff's violin concerto. "Prokofieff": Any man with a name like that must be a terrible, a dangerous fellow, given to nerve-rasping dissonances, moanings, shrieks, squeals, squeaks and grunts. But, lo, this concerto turned out to be a delightful work, as delightful as it is unusual and individual. Violin concertos in orthodox form are too often boresome. Even those by Beethoven and Brahms are distressingly long-winded, with pages or irritating repetition and yawn-compelling padding. The majority of these concertos should be put in a duck-press before serving. Lalo's Symphonie Espagnole is an exception, as Hans von Bülow remarked long ago when he freed his mind about Max Bruch and thus annoyed many respectable persons who were "fond of music."
>
> Prokofieff's concerto is not too deliberately unusual. It is free and unconfined, but not laboriously so; not from any want of technical skill in composition. It abounds in ideas, in turn beautiful and joyously humorous. The treatment of these ideas for solo violin and orchestra is as refreshing as it is original. The "accompaniment" is more than an "accompaniment" in the common meaning of the word; it is symphonic: mastery in itself. There are charming effects of color, surprising but not extravagant; the unexpected is the real fascination. The effects in the whole work are gained with such audacious simplicity! Mr. Burgin played superbly and Mr. Koussevitzky reveled in the brilliance of the orchestral performance.

Ravel

La Valse
Boston Herald, January 14, 1922:

> Ravel's "Waltz"—not "a waltz," but "the waltz," first performed at a Lamoureux concert late in 1920, had been played in San Francisco and in St. Louis before it was produced in Boston. Ravel says that the tempo is "the movement of the Viennese waltz." Mr. Casella, with whom Ravel played a four-handed arrangement for piano in Vienna, says that the work is a triptych: 1. The birth of the waltz, from chaotic measures to form and development; 2. The waltz; 3. The apotheosis of the waltz. Ravel has written a little "argument," a fanciful description of a court hall about 1855. One commentator sees an "ironical" treatment of the dance; another finds "implied anguish" in the "apotheosis," somewhat threatening in the bacchanale; he hears a voice crying: "We dance on a volcano." Well, years ago Marcel saw all things in a minuet, Senac de Melhan likened life to one and Count Moroni saw in that dance the portrayal of the 18th century. Hearing Ravel's—"Waltz," we do not find irony, prophecy or symbolism; we hear certain agreeable measures that remind one of Johann Strauss, the father, who composed the haunting and pathetic "Sophie" waltz; the son, whose waltzes are world famous; for the better measures of Ravel's are purely Straussian, but not of the first order. Has Ravel shot his bolt? Is he now only writing in the manner of Ravel? In the language of New England, has he "run emptins"?

Rubinstein

Piano Concerto No. 4 in D minor, Op. 70
[*See C: Teresa Carreño, also the Introduction.]

Saint-Saëns

Carnival of the Animals
Boston Herald, November 4, 1922:

Saint-Saëns, a man of wit and irony, wrote his "Carnival of the Animals: A Grand Zoological Fantasy" as a joke for a Mardi-Gras concert of Lebouc, a violoncellist. That was in 1886. Played in a semi-private fashion several times, the Suite was not published as a whole til this year, for permission was granted to Saint-Saëns in his will. "The Swan," however, was published in 1887 and has been made familiar in concert halls and by the dance of Anna Pavlowa.

For once the Symphony audience laughed not at a composer, but with a composer. Deliberately funny music is as a rule about as humorous as a railway accident. Many a "Humoreske" is funereal. Saint-Saëns was too clever to fall into a trap. Here is music that is amusing, witty, and without the assistance of words. The lion roars, the barnyard is vocal, tortoises move to the can-can of Offenbach's "Orpheus" played at a slow pace; pianists are among the animals, practicing their exercises. In "Fossils" Saint-Saëns does not spare himself; the unwieldy elephant "to make them mirth us'd all his might and wreath'd his little proboscis"; kangaroos leap and donkeys bray. By the side of this musical jesting are the charming Aquarium, the "Aviary" (with the flute brilliantly played by Mr. Laurent) and "The Swan."

The performance was characterized by what Mr. Hazlitt would have called gusto. Mr. Kunze played the double bass in "The Elephant" as seriously as if the music were by Johannes Brahms; the pianists, Messrs. De Voto and Stevens, having no easy task, were wholly adequate, and Mr. Bedetti played the Swan's song with adorable simplicity, beauty of tone and feeling.

Does someone say: "But such music is beneath the dignity of a Symphony concert?" Go to pish; likewise piffle. We take our music too seriously. Does one always wish it to be "educational"? Trying to solve problems, to put philosophical theories into music to be psychical? There are many rooms in the great temple of the muse. One of the chambers is a banqueting hall. There is room for Offenbach, for Johann Strauss, for the Sullivan of the operettas.

It is a pleasure to find Saint-Saëns unbuttoned and in a jocose mood. Let us remember the saying in the "Deipnosophists" of Athenaeus: "Music softens moroseness of temper, for it dissipates sadness, and produces affability and a sort of gentlemanlike joy."

The joy of Saint-Saëns in "The Animals' Carnival" is gentlemanlike. And his joy yesterday was contagious.

Piano Concerto No. 5 in F
Boston Herald, April 2, 1920:

We became acquainted with Saint-Saën's concerto 16 years ago, when Mr. Ferruccio—we are tempted to write "Ferocious"—Busoni introduced it, and it made little impression at the time. Yesterday it was played by Mr. Ganz and the orchestra, the concerto was engrossing. The thematic material of the first movement no longer seemed almost childish; it reminded one of Mozart's adorable simplicity. Nor is it necessary to say that this material is finely employed. The rhapsodical orientalism, with the use of a Nubian boat song, is fascinating; it does not for a moment degenerate into anything merely bizarre. Saint-Saëns here catches the spirit of the East, but he is not mastered by it; he does not lose his shrewdly observing, coolly reflecting western head. Then comes the rushing finale, which, however, does not throw aside in the excitement the traditional French elegance that characterizes the work of Saint-Saëns. Mr. Ganz played as Saint-Saëns played when he was in his highest estate; but with more warmth in the lyric passages. In the bravura and more furious passages he, too, kept his head, ever mindful of clarity and elegance. All in all, a most elegant performance.

Schumann

Piano Concerto in A Minor, Op. 54:

[*See the entry for Mahler: *Symphony No. 5 in C-sharp Minor*.]

Symphony No. 4 in D minor, Op. 120
Boston Journal, March 4, 1900:

W[eingartner] regards the D minor symphony of Schumann as inferior to the First and Second of the same composer. I fail to see why. It is true that Schumann's symphonies might as well have been written for a piano and four hands as for an orchestra as he understood it; but surely this symphony of peculiarly romantic flavor does not fall behind its companions and the rhythmic treatment of the trio in the scherzo adds wondrously to the gentle regret and vague longing of musical thought.

Sibelius

Violin Concerto

[*See C. Soloists: Maud Powell]

Strauss, R ichard

Suite in B flat, Op. 4
Boston Herald, December 18, 1912:

The Longy Club gave the first concert of its season last night in Jordan Hall. The program was as follows: Mozart, Quintet in E flat major (K. 452), for oboe, clarinet, horn, bassoon, and piano; Reinecke, "Undine," op. 167, sonata for flute and piano: R. Strauss: Suite in B flat major, for two flutes, two oboes, two clarinets, four horns, two bassoons and double bassoon.

The Suite of Strauss was performed here for the first time. It was composed when Strauss was about twenty years old and known as a reverer of the classics. He had already composed a Serenade for wind instruments—the Serenade in E Flat and in one movement, op. 7, which was published in 1881. It was produced at Dresden, Nov. 27, 1882 and Bülow brought it out in Meiningen in 1883 and played it on a concert tour, describing Strauss as a young Munich composer, classical school, and adding that the music displayed the brilliant virtuosity of the wind instrument players of his orchestra.

Bülow was so pleased with the Serenade op. 7 that he asked Strauss to write another work for 13 players, and mapped out a plan for him but Strauss had already sketched the first movements and could follow Bülow's suggestions only in the Gavotte and Finale with Fugue. The work was completed in Munich. Strauss' father,

Franz, a celebrated horn player, begged Bülow, whon was coming to Munich with the Meiningen orchestra, to rehearse the new work. Bülow agreed to the plan, but insisted that Strauss should conduct. There was no rehearsal. The first performance, then, of this suite was by players of the Meiningen orchestra in the Odeon, Munich, Nov. 11, 1884, and Strauss for the first time held a baton. The father went into the artist's room to thank Bülow, who was smoking cigarettes, nervous, and in a fiendish temper. As the son relates, "He fell like a raging lion on my father and screamed out: 'I have not forgotten all that you have done against me here in this cursed Munich. What I did today, I did because your son has talent, not for you'."

The suite was not published until the fall of 1911. In some way, Mr. Barrere, flute player in New York, obtained a manuscript score and produced the suite at a concert of the Barrere Ensemble in that city on Feb. 6, 1911.

There are these movements: Prelude, Romance, Gavotte, Introduction and Fugue. The instruments are used with the appreciation of their respective capabilities and limitations, and there are effective combinations and contrasts of timbres. The stately Prelude has no so much individuality as the Romance, which is thematically beautiful and rich in color. The Gavotte is interesting, especially in the section beginning with the drone-bass. The Introduction is impressively sombre, but the Fugue is disappointing. The exposition, as heard last night, seemed clumsy, and it was surely not euphonious, nor was the counterpoint at the beginning much better than ordinary student's work. There was great mastery shown in the final pages.

Stravinsky

Pulcinella
Boston Herald, December 21, 1922:

Stravinsky used music by Pergolesi for the ballet "Pulcinella." When he is content with a simple treatment of music by the Italian who died too young, the suite is agreeable, but not very significant. When he Stravinskyizes the airs with curious and unexpected harmonies, the effect to the theatre may emphasize the pantomimic action, but in a concert hall the result excites only surprise if not consternation. The finale, for example, doubtless accentuates some amusing episode on the stage, but yesterday it seemed only a deliberate and far-fetched excitement to laughter. The suite was played for the first time in this country. We prefer Stravinsky working his will without foreign aid, as we prefer Pergolesi's melodies when they are not tinkered.

Boston Herald, March 12, 1933:

The suite "Pulcinella" has not been played here since 1922. There are amusing sections, some ingeniously orchestrated, but for full appreciation there is a need of the stage dances.

VaughanWilliams

Fantasia on a Theme by Thomas Tallis
Boston Herald, November 24, 1922:

The fantasia of [Vaughan] Williams was produced here last fall. It displays at great advantage the incomparable band of strings; more than that, by its strains of solemn beauty it induces the deep fit of devotion and profound contemplation of the First Composer, in which the whimsical Sir Thomas Browne indulged even when he heard only vulgar and tavern music. But Vaughan Williams, as his colleagues in the ultra-modern English school, sins in one respect: he knows not the value of brevity.

Boston Herald, December 7, 1932:

The Fantasia by Vaughan Williams was first heard under Mr. Monteux's direction in 1922. Yesterday the composer was present to acknowledge shyly the spontaneous applause that compelled him to come on the platform two or three times. This applause was more than a welcome to distinguished English composer who has given pleasure to the Symphony audience by his "London" symphony—there have been three performances of it—by one of his Norfolk rhapsodies, by this Fantasia; and moved other audiences in the city by his "On Wenlock Edge." It is to be hoped that at no distant day we may hear other symphonic compositions by him and his important choral works.

The Fantasia may awaken spiritual thoughts that are not suggested by texts even when they are taken from Holy Writ, as there are slow movements in Handel's concertos that soar above the pathetic pages in his oratorios; as there are preludes by Bach for the Well-tempered Clavichord that breathe prayer. This Fantasia was first heard in Gloucester Cathedral; it was written for a Gloucester festival. Played in a concert hall, as it was performed yesterday, it suggested a cathedral service, with choirs solemnly chanting, now antiphonally, now with full voices. Impressive music, truly ecclesiastical; music for a cathedral, not for a Clapham chapel, not for a New England meeting house; music that purges the hearer of worldly thoughts, and sobers the understanding.

B. Conductors
SirT homasB eecham

Boston Herald, January 21, 1928:

Sir Thomas Beecham, Bart., conducted, as a guest, the 13th concert of the Boston Symphony orchestra yesterday afternoon in Symphony Hall.

The idle looker-on, the man of eyes, not ears, might call Sir Thomas a violent wooer of the Muse but the goddess does not shrink back startled from his gesture and advances. She knows that there is tenderness in true virility. Rejoicing in his strength, she yields herself gladly to his honeyed speech, his irresistible caresses.

Sir Thomas conducts like Safonov when he was in this country, without a baton. He conducts from memory. Not as one beating the air in spectacular fashion and trusting a well drilled orchestra to see him through. In this instance every gesture has significance. Hand scan be informing; they can also be eloquent.

The program arranged for the concert was an unusual one. Some reading the order for the performance might wonder at Mozart's Symphony [No. 34](the one in C major without the minuet, K. 338) coming immediately after the excerpt from "The Trojans," ending the first part, and coming before Strauss' "Heldenleben," in the concert this symphony was admirably placed. The "great machine" of Strauss should not have been preceded by any work of sumptuous orchestration, much less by music of storm and stress.

The concert began with a suite arranged by Sir Thomas from three of Handel's operas: the magnificent opening of the overture to "Teseo," a charming musette from "Il Pastor Fido," and an energetic, bustling bouree from "Rodrigo." Sit Thomas has made several suites from Handel's forgotten operas, which are a vast storehouse of arias and instrumental numbers. Has any composer equaled for strength with tenderness the great Handel? In the performance yesterday the strength was not unduly exerted; the simple, appealing tenderness was not sentimentalized. Here it may be remembered that Sir Thomas does not give way to sentimentalism. This was also shown in the beautiful interpretation, a flowing continuous song, of Mozart's andante; and note the manner in which the lyrical measures in "The Royal Hunt and Tempest" from Berlioz' "Trojans" were sung with classic simplicity and warmth.

The Suite from Handel's operas was performed here for the first time; so was the Intermezzo, "The Walk to the Paradise" from Delius' opera "A Village Romeo and Juliet." The musical idiom of this composer has baffled many of us; seeming to some the expression of a singular aloofness; music of one almost detached from humanity; music indifferent to the effects of glowing color; now pale and drab; not without a touch of acerbity; music of a thinker free from passion. This Intermezzo reveals another Delius. Seldom does one hear for the first time music that is so enchanting, music so charged with poetic emotion. One is confident that admiration and enjoyment would grow with repeated hearings; that a first impression would only be confirmed and enlarged. It is true that to Sir Thomas the performance of this Intermezzo was a labor of love, for he, always a staunch friend to Delius, brought out this opera in London and revived it only seven years ago. Admirable as was the performance yesterday, the music itself was there, calling only for a skillful and sympathetic interpreter.

From his conducting of music by Handel, Delius, Berlioz, and Mozart, and the results he obtained, it was plain that Sir Thomas is not a "specialist," but a man acquainted with schools ancient and modern, realizing that old music of the finest quality is modern, yes, contemporaneous with us while much modern music, even music of recent years, is hopelessly old-fashioned. The reading of Mozart's symphony was delightful, so frank, so well-proportioned, without the taint of exaggeration or perverted reading in the vain search after modernization.

MaxFi edler

Boston Herald, October 10, 1908:

The first public rehearsal of the 28th season of the Boston Symphony orchestra took place yesterday afternoon at Symphony Hall. Mr. Max Fiedler, the new conductor, led for the first time in this city. The programme was as follows:

Overture. "Leonora," No. 3 .... Beethoven
Symphony No. 1 in C minor .... Brahms
Love scene from "Feursnot" R. .... Strauss
Overture to "Tannhaeuser" .... Wagner

It has often been said that the first concert given by an orchestra with a new leader serves chiefly as a means of introducing the conductor to his audience. The public rehearsal yesterday seemed more than this, for the enjoyment of the audience was evident. Seldom, if ever, has there been more spontaneous or more hearty applause at any public rehearsal in the history of this orchestra. Mr. Hess, returning after a year's absence to take his place as concertmaster, was warmly greeted, and when Mr. Fiedler came on the stage for the first time before an audience in this city his welcome was as one given to a familiar, long-established favorite.

Nor did the audience seem critically disposed during the concert. It was not disposed to be impatient when there was occasionally sluggishness and irregularity of attack or when or when horns were overblown or uncertain in solo passages. The applause, except that after the third movement of the Symphony, was unusually warm, at times enthusiastic, and Mr. Fiedler was recalled more than once.

We all have a right to infer from what Mr. Fiedler has said that he is especially drawn to the music of Beethoven, Brahms, Richard Strauss, Wagner and Tschaikowsky. A conductor chooses naturally for his first program music with which he is in fullest sympathy, music that appeals to him, compositions that have already served him as battle horses to ride to victory.

Four of Mr. Fiedler's favorites were represented. It was his intention at first to conduct Strauss' "Death and Transfiguration," but a performance of this impressive work would have made the programme too long, so the "Love Scene" from "Feuersnot," that strange opera founded on a grotesque or, as some might say, porcine legend, was substituted, a scene that in the concert room excites surprise and makes no deep, no lasting impression. Nor is it too much to say that this music in concert shows Strauss at his finest.

Mr. Fiedler's programme pleased the audience, for the three important pieces were well known. The hearers were not obliged to question themselves as to the intrinsic worth of the music. They were not forced to hear a musical speech that was strange to them, perplexing, disquieting. In thus choosing familiar compositions Mr. Fiedler was eminently wise.

It is not necessary to speak in detail of Mr. Fiedler's interpretation of the compositions. The orchestra has been only a week under his direction. No matter how honestly the players may already respect him, no matter how eagerly they may anticipate his wishes, it would be too much to expect at present the close relationship that insures performances of flawless mechanism and highly poetic interpretation.

Yet it may be said that Mr. Fiedler revealed certain qualities that will undoubtedly make him popular. He conducts with a gusto that is unmistakable. He is not afraid of stormy crescendos and clashing climaxes. He is eminently virile. Whether he be a master of finesse; whether he be endowed with an exquisite sense of proportion; whether he delights in delicate nuances as well as in primitive and strongly opposed colors; these are questions not now to be answered jauntily.

There were admirable features yesterday in his reading of the overture to "Leonora" and in the first two movements of the symphony. Certainly his interpretation throughout was sturdy and its stirring effect on the audience was indisputable. His manner of conducting is more exuberant in the matter of gestures than that of his two last predecessors, but he did not indulge himself in mere calisthenics, nor was there any suspicion of a desire on his part to affect the audience through the eyes. His sincerity and his absorption in the appointed task are unquestionable.

GustavH olst

Boston Herald, January 23, 1932:

Gustav Holst of London was the guest conductor of the Boston Symphony orchestra yesterday afternoon. The program comprised four of his compositions: St. Paul's Suite for strings (first time at these concerts); Prelude and Scherzo:

"Hammersmith" (first time in Boston); Ballet from the opera "The Perfect Fool" (first time in Boston) and "The Planets," a suite of seven movements. When "The Planets" was first performed under Mr. Monteux there was no female chorus for "Neptune the Mystic." Yesterday there was a chorus. Which having been trained by Mr. [Arthur] Fiedler, sang unseen. The beauty of the ending was thereby enhanced.

To devote an orchestral concert of nearly two hours' length to any composer, whether he be Bach or Brahms, Beethoven or Honegger, is a doubtful venture. Mr. Holst stood the test well, yet if two or three of the "Planets" had been omitted, the others would have gained in effect. Certainly "Venus," "Mercury," "Uranus" and "Neptune" could not have been spared. "Mars" might be shortened; the warlike mood fortissimo leads one to wish at least an armistice. The jollity in Jupiter is distinctly English in character; like all jollity, one could wish that brought by Jupiter, to be less prolonged.

The suite for strings is a pleasing work that one would gladly hear again. The interest is unflagging; the thematic material is fresh; the treatment of it is scholarly without for a moment being pedantic i.e. dull. When there is counterpoint, it is not for the purpose of showing what a fine fellow the composer is. If the jig and if the finale with its use of old tunes "Dargason" and "Green Sleeves" are unmistakably English, the Intermezzo is exotic, suggestive of the Orient, melodically and in the prevailing mood. This suite was brilliantly played. It was written for the orchestra at St. Paul's School for Girls. For practice or for performance? If for performance, these girls must be singularly accomplished in the use of stringed instruments.

"Hammersmith," which gives Mr. Holst a high position in the rank of contemporaneous composers, was played for the first time last November, at a concert in London. The 'Planets' as a whole were first heard in 1919–1920. In the years between the composer has gained in depth of thought, conciseness and power of expression, control of imagination. The imperturbable prelude is, as he has said publicly, a background: the river, heedless of the cockneys swarming in the district: the river, knowing that it will flow long after the invaders are no more: as the river which will then be as unconcerned as it was when the Romans were by its banks. Now other composers have felt the spell of a river. Wagner, Smetana, Griffes, Vaughan Williams among them, but Mr. Holst's river is his own, as is his music. There is more in 'Hammersmith' than mere contrast between calm, serenity, peaceful indifferences and the rough merriment of an unthinking crowd, "Arry" and "Arriet'" enjoying life after their manner. This is not program music in the anecdotal or pictorial sense. There are two moods, eloquent in tonal expression. The searcher after symbolism in all art might say: "Nature heedless of mortals' joys or sorrows." (Mr. Holst had already written his "Egdon Heath" after Thomas Hardy.) But Mr. Holst, a thinker even outside of music; and this cannot be said of every composer: a man fascinated by the poetry and philosophy of India, when he girds up his loins to write music is first of all a musician. In "Hammersmith" there is no waste of notes, no undue elaboration of musical ideas; no districting elegancies; no incongruous ornamentation.

The ballet music for the dancing spirits of the earth, water and fire is grateful to the ear, with fine effects in orchestration, rhythmically exciting—yet one would fain hear it in the theatre and see the elements, obedient to the Wizard's incantation.

The composer of "Hammersmith," the ballet music, the suite for strings, "Venus," "Saturn," "Neptune" and pages of "Mercury" is modern in the best sense, as masters of the past are modern, not as the contemporaries who are futile experimenters: who, barren of truly musical ideas, without poetry in their soul, put their faith in rhythm, repetitions of insignificant phrases, eccentric harmonic schemes and instrumentation. Mr. Holst still has confidence in normal scale. To him, dissonances have their rhetorical use and are of value, too good to be prodigally lavished on that which is itself insignificant.

Warmly greeted, he was warmly applauded throughout the concert. Dignified, modest, he conducted quietly and none the less effectively. He knew what he wanted and was able to share this knowledge with the sympathetic players.

EmilP aur

The Musical Courier, August 4, 1895:

There are stories afloat concerning the possibility of a new conductor for the Boston Symphony Orchestra. Some gossipers go as far to say that Mr. Higginson visited Europe in the summer in search of a successor to Mr. Paur. So, too, there are stories about the nature of Mr. Paur's Contract.

According to some, who say they know, the present contract is an extraordinary one. By it Mr. Paur was engaged for five years at a yearly salary of $10,000. At the expiration of the term he is to have the option of renewal. If, like "Barkis," he is still willing, and the management is unwilling, Mr. Paur is to receive $10,000 as a salve to irritated self-esteem. If the management wishes to break the contract before the expiration of five years, Mr. Paur is to receive the whole of his salary for the remain term besides the $10,000 to put a man securely in Mr. Paur's place.

This story seems to me incredible. I do not know Mr. Paur, so I have never had the pleasure of conversing with him on this and kindred subjects. It seems impossible, however, that such a shrewd business man as Mr. Higginson—no matter how enamored with music he may be—would ever have signed such a jug-handled and preposterous contract.

The name of the new conductor has been mentioned. One day it is Weingartner, another day it is Richter, or it is Gericke, who is no longer connected with the Viennese Society. But Weingartner has just signed a contract; Richter has said repeatedly that he will not come, and I hope he will stick to his resolution; and why in the world should Gericke wish to return to a town where the climate distressed him sorely. Of one thing you may be sure, no names have been mentioned, save those of Germans. There has been no thought of France, or Italy, or Russia, or Scandinavia, or Belgium, or Holland, or Spain, or even the United States as a possible country of the desired conductor.

The news of Mr. Paur's withdrawal, spontaneous or enforced, would be received with equanimity by the orchestra, nearly all the local composers and the majority of the Symphony audience. I am sure about the equanimity of orchestra and composers; and although the audience in bulk is kindly disposed toward the present conductor and respects certain estimable qualities of the man, yet we must take into account the constant desire to become acquainted with something or somebody new. The methods of Mr. Paur are known to all. His good points, his weaknesses, are now familiar. I do not believe that if he even appeared on a Saturday night in a Tuxedo coat there would be a noticeable stir or commotion in the audience. He has already worn his hair long and short and in a medium way. In fact I do not see how he can attract attention at this late day unless it should occur to him to introduce orchestral works of freshness and worth.

Next October will in all likelihood see Mr. Paur at the old stand, drawing Beethoven and Brahms from the wood for the benefit of old customers. The same old tunes will give the same enjoyment; there will be exhibitions of the same well-bred and moderate rapture, and there will be the same questions, "Why was Miss Blank invited to sing?" and "Why did they let Mr. Boarnerges play?"

Sometimes Mr. Paur reminds one of a well fed family horse, warranted sound and kind, who draws safely his load through the musical streets or meadows and looks steadily ahead, thoughtful of duty done and consequent oats and hay. You have seen such horses with carry-alls hitched to them, with asparagus boughs in their harness to keep off the flies as they stand in front of the store, on Sunday, in the horse-shed near the steepled meeting-house. Don't think for a moment that I insinuate the presence of flies on Mr. Paur. Perish the thought!

After all, I am not sure that such a good, patient nag—I believe the irreverent use of the word "plug"—is not to be preferred to your high stepping, prancing, foaming thoroughbred, who takes the bit in his teeth and respects not the traveled road, fears not stumps or fences, and smashes buggy and human collarbones for his own glory. He may snort and paw the air, and his neck may be clothed with thunder instead of asparagus boughs, and he may say among the trumpets "Ha, Ha!" but I think it's safer to drive behind old Dobbin, and work the whip gently so that flies will not settle and annoy. And, above all, spare him the gadfly of criticism! Let the band play the three familiar overtures by Weber, the three familiar symphonies of Mozart, and the overture to La Dame Blanche as a novelty; let Miss Blank or Mrs. Ampersand sing for the twenty-fifth time at these concerts any familiar aria; let Mr. Boanerges give his impassioned performance of the concerto in D minor by Rubinstein, or Mr. Trocken his scholarly interpretation of the Emperor concerto; and so let us all jog along together, comfortably and safely.

Besides, you must remember that, as one of my colleagues strenuously insists, these symphony concerts are educational. If they did not educate they would have no reason for existing. And in sound education, let the brilliant, the dazzling, the magnetic, the hypnotic, the meteoric, the Vesuvian conductors stand off, far distant.

HenriR abaud

Boston Herald, February 8, 1919:

The 17th concert of the Boston Symphony Orchestra, Mr. Rabaud conducting, took place yesterday afternoon. The program was as follows: Beethoven, Overture to "Coriolanus," Tschaikowsky, Variations on a Rococo Theme for violoncello and orchestra, Joseph Malkin (violoncellist); Debussy, Three Nocturnes; Mendelssohn: Symphony in A major, "Italian."

Mr. Rabaud gave a remarkable interpretation of Beethoven's overture. We do not recall a performance here or elsewhere that could be compared to it. It was dramatic, but not theatrical. Mr. Kikisch took liberties with the music in the hope of making it more impressive, but he sentimentalized the second and lyrical theme and dragged the final measures beyond endurance. Mr. Rabaud's interpretation was in the Plutarchian spirit. Someone said—was it A. W. Thayer?—of this overture, that he could not understand it—until he read Collin's tragedy: that he could not reconcile the music with Shakespeare's text. Pray, what would the gentleman have had? It is immaterial whether Beethoven had Collin or Shakespeare in mind. The name "Coriolanus" was enough, even if he knew it only from some schoolboy history of Rome: for in this music we hear the proud voice, we see the haughty, inexorable bearing of the soldier-patrician. Nor does it matter whether the lyrical theme, as some believe, is the entreating voice of wife or mother. Possibly if one should read Collin's play he would wonder that Beethoven should have thought of writing an overture for it. There it is: one of Beethoven's greatest workers. From his own disdain of the mob, from his own contempt for what the public thought of his music, he recognized in Coriolanus a kindred spirit. Mr. Rabaud comprehended the overture: its aristocratic sternness, austerity. Not for a moment did he allow a perfunctory interpretation because Beethoven died, shaking his fist at a thunderstorm, nearly 100 years ago, and now sits enthronged among the immortals in the temple of art. Some conductors are careless of his reputation.

It appears that Debussy before his death made an important revision of his Nocturnes. This revision was heard yesterday for the first time in Boston. Whether it was due to the changes or due to Mr. Rabaud's imaginative interpretation, this is certain: The Nocturnes were more beautiful and haunting than ever before....

John Philip Sousa

Boston Journal, November 19, 1892 [*the very year that Sousa left the United States Marine Band to form his own]:

The New Marine Band, under the direction of John P. Sousa, gave a concert last evening in Music Hall. The band was assisted by Miss Marcella Lindh, soprano; Antonio Galassi, baritone, and Mr. Liberati, cornet. There was a large audience and the enthusiasm was great. Each number of the programme stood for two numbers that were played: dances, marches, and arrangements of popular tunes were given to the heart's desire of the most insatiate encore fiend. The band is composed of excellent material, and it would be invidious to particularize. The men have been drilled carefully, and the precision is worthy of high praise. There is also an observance of dynamic marks, of gradiations of tone that is unusual of bands of this character. The concert reflected credit on the leader and the men. Mr. Sousa does not always ride in the whirlwind and direct the storm; he has a lively appreciation of the value of contrasts, and certain numbers, as the arrangement of the dirge from "Peer Gynt" suite were played with delicacy and feeling. Miss Lindh sang the scene and aria from "Lucia," and displayed therein more than ordinary agility. Mr. Raffaolo played his concerto on the euphonium, and Mr. Liberati far away from the true pitch in his cornet solo. This band, which is well worth hearing, will give a concert in Music Hall next Sunday evening.

Boston Herald, January 11, 1906:

SOUSA GREETED
AT HIS CONCERTS

———

"March king" Produces Two
New Numbers, "The Diplo-
mat," March and a Suite
"The King's Court"

———

AUDIENCES PLEASED
WITH OLD MARCHES

———

Appendix III

This Music Strikes Eye as Well
as the Ear, and Famous
Conductor's Calisthenics
Are Popular As Ever.

Mr. John Philip Sousa and his band gave concerts in Symphony Hall yesterday afternoon and evening. Miss Elizabeth Schiller, soprano, sang at both concerts, and Miss Jeanette Powers, violinist, played at both. Mr. Leo Zimmerman played a trombone solo in the afternoon and Mr. Herbert L. Clarke a cornet solo last night. The audience in the afternoon was of good size, and at night there were very few vacant seats in the hall.

There are some who tend to think poorly of such bands. They admit the technic of Sousa's, the rhythm, the accent and all that, but they admit these things as if they were of little consequence, and they insist that a brass band should be heard only in the streets at a fireman's muster, in a stand by the beach, in processions. They secretly enjoy this sort of music anywhere, but by admitting their pleasure they fear they would betray poor taste.

Let such feeble and timorous souls read the noble apothegm of Mr. G. K. Chesterton and take courage: "A brass band is purely spiritual and seeks only to quicken the internal life."

For the hearer of such music thinks better of himself. For the time he, too, is courageous; he too could drink delight of battle with his peers. His back is straightened, his chest is thrown out, Rheumatism quits his sculptural legs, and eczema is only a word in advertisements. He renews his youth at the sound of the cornet.

Great is Sousa! His greatness now is international. Kings and Queens, potentates of all grades and statesmen of all parties have wondered at his lines and curves and sweeps and dashes and gentle repressions and coaxing ways and side-stepping and prancing and imperious commands and launching of thunderbolts. They have asked for private conversations. They have gladly accepted homage in march form and dared in some instances to hope for personal dedications. Serene, he marches on his triumphant way, confident in his mission of bringing all nations to march in peace together. Hence the new march composed for his coming tour around the world, "The Diplomat." And who, pray, is the diplomat thus honored? Was he snatched from some editorial chair to amaze a foreign ruler by his shrewdness and eloquence? Was he chosen for his wealth or the fact that he once studied French in school? O, no. The true diplomat is Mr. Sousa. His band speaks the international language; it appeals to all nations, it makes for the glory of America.

Then there is Mr. Sousa's new suite, "At the King's Court." Mark how easy and familiar intercourse with Dukes, belted earls, and noble dames has taught this stalwart patriot nice verbal distinctions and brought full acquaintance with the forms that are so envied by our untitled aristocracy. The suite is in three movements: Her ladyship, the countess; her grace, the duchess; Her Majesty, the Queen. And these grades in the aristocracy are cunningly differentiated in the music. Her Ladyship is not disinclined to a dancing romp, but she is a high stepper and now and then her foot is shot skyward. Her grace prefers the languorous waltz, the old-fashioned melting, swimming waltz with a suspicion of a glide and no thought of a two step. Flourish of trumpets without. Roll of drums. Her majesty enters as though drawn in on casters. Cheers of the populace. Indescribable enthusiasm.

After all, it is not the overture to "Oberon," it is not the Welsh Rhapsody of Mr. Edward German, whose real name is Jones; it is not the "Ride of the Valkyries" that draws the crowd to Sousa's concerts. The Welsh Rhapsody, from its pervading melancholy, might have been inspired by immoderate indulgence of rabbits in that land did we not know the Welsh to be dismal in their folk-songs, especially when they are jovial. No, the men and women who crowd the halls wish to hear Mr. Sousa's marches and see him conduct them. The music strikes the eye as well as the ear. The more marches the better. Welcome, too, are such pieces as "The Mouse and the Clock" and the symphonic fantasia on "Everybody Works but Father." Such music brings joy to the complaining millions of men; it stiffens the backbone; it stills the collywobbles; it warms the cockles of the heart; it brushes cobwebs from the brain. Great, then, is Sousa, diplomat and benefactor. May his calisthenics never grow less.

Strauss, Richard

[*See Chapter 4]

Virtuoso Conductors and Karl Muck

Boston Herald, October 13, 1906:

Dr. Karl Muck made his first appearance in America as a conductor yesterday afternoon in Symphony Hall at the first public rehearsal of the Boston Symphony Orchestra this season, the 28th of this organization. The review of the concert this evening will be published in The Herald tomorrow. The feature of the public rehearsal was the personality of Dr. Muck.

This is the period of the virtuoso conductor. He is the rival of the prima donna with her dazzling bravura or dramatic intensity of the applauded and fatuous tenor with his eagerly awaited and robust high C. He journeys from city to city in a conqueror's car, and there is hardly a reviewer who dares to remind him that he, too, is mortal. He rides his war horses, Beethoven, Berlioz, Wagner, Strauss, Tschaikowsky to victory. "What does he find in the Eroica symphony?" "How does his reading differ from that of the famous Herr Bullfinger?" "He is the only interpreter of the Fantastic and the Pathetic symphonies." The curiosity is concerning the conductor, not the composer.

The peculiarities, the mannerisms of the conductor when he is in action are noted minutely and passionately discussed. "Did you see that he did not turn the leaves of the score?" "How he glared at the orchestra when he made that tremendousc limax!"

Virtuosity of the Rope-Dancer

Something of the artistry of the rope-dancer enters into the composition of the acclaimed virtuoso conductor. He is never wholly unconscious of the audience. He bears in mind the fact that there are ladies in the gallery as on the floor. Perhaps his charm is in a delicate [movement of the] left hand which he...due force. Or his face has passion paleness, the paleness of a Vanderdecken once more allowed to land in search of the faithful bride. He is thus interesting, sympathetic. Or he is leonine and he shakes a formidable mane. Or he is demonstratively 'spectacular.' His gestures are semaphoric; he is all x's and y's. He coaxes the strings; he tootles with the flute; he faces the brass in stormy passages, goads trumpets, horns, and trombones to fury, and in the orgasm of sound reels and totters and mops his glowing forehead. From the moment of raising the baton he courts, anticipates applause.

And there is the conductor who disdains the stick. He thrills his audience by the operations of his hands. With his fingers he plucks a pizzicato from the strings, a cadenza from the oboe, a gurgle from the reluctant, agonized bassoon.

Dr. Muck of a Different Breed

Dr. Muck is, fortunately for us, not of this virtuoso family. He is a musician-virtuoso. When he came upon the stage he was welcomed warmly. Many on the floor stood up; some to show in an uncertain way their respect for his office and to pay homage to his reputation; some no doubt that they might obtain a clearer view of the man. He acknowledged the tribute modestly, as he did the recalls after the performance of Beethoven's Fifth Symphony and at the end of the concert. He was simple and modest throughout. He was neither anxious to show his pleasure at the reception nor stiff in dignified acceptance.

He nothing common did, or mean,
Upon that memorable scene.

A celebrated English general once said, "Give me a man with plenty of nose." A conductor should have a good back. For the time has gone by when a conductor of a symphony concert faced the audience. Bilse of Berlin was probably the last to show thus his face and decorations. There have been memorable backs, and perhaps the most distinguished was that of Theodore Thomas. A back should neither be obsequious nor arrogant. It should not suggest nervousness or rigidity. Dr. Muck has a good back.

No Play-Actor with Baton

He is not a play-actor with his stick. He does not give a pantomimic display of musical emotions. He is conscious of the fact that he has an orchestra to serve as his medium, nor does he endeavor to play tunes on the baton. His attitude is authoritative, but not military; it is friendly and not that of a task master. His action has a sobriety that is not indifferent or dull. His use of the left hand is discreet and in gesture he is temperate. In a word, he has no mannerisms that might cause remark. He conducts like a thoughtful musician who, after he has shared with the players his convictions and beliefs about the interpretation of a composition, is willing that they should express the composer's thoughts with an occasional reminder, but without annoying interference.

Such interpreters are re-creators. Through them the hearer recognizes the intention of the composer. They do not stand behind, hinder, obstruct. The highest praise of a conductor is that the chief thought of the hearer is concerning the music. Only when the concert is overdoes he realize the all-important part so modestly assumed and maintained by the conductor.

It is a pleasure to welcome this sincere and accomplished artist, who now makes Boston his dwelling-place. His influence in the making toward musical righteousness will be all the more potent because it is not flamboyant; because his personality is not too personal.

The deeply interested audience was quick to appreciate this.

Bruno Walter

Boston Herald, March 31, 1923:

The 20th concert of the Boston Symphony Orchestra took place yesterday afternoon in Symphony Hall. Bruno Walter conducted as a guest. He arranged this program: Weber, Overture to "Euryanthe"; Mozart: Symphony, D major (K. 385); Beethoven, Piano Concerto, G major, No. 4; Strauss, "Till Eulenspiegel's Merry Pranks." The pianist was Arthur Schnabel.

When Arthur Schnabel rehearsed for the first time the Boston Symphony Orchestra, he marveled at the perfection of the instrument which had been fashioned by Mr. Gericke, and he exclaimed: "All I have to do is poetize."

Mr. Walter, coming to Boston, found the orchestra that had been created and moulded by Mr. Monteux into a plastic, euphonious, superb instrument, ready for him to play upon.

It was evident, before he arrived, from his programs arranged for New York, Detroit, and Minneapolis, that he is not anxious to make a sensation by riding foaming battle horses. He has not announced himself in trumpet tones as a "specialist." He has not declared Beethoven or Wagner, or Brahms, or Strauss, or Mahler to be the only god, nor pointed to himself as the prophet of this or that deity. He has an enviable reputation in Europe as an interpreter, not a perverter, of Mozart. Perhaps it is characteristic of the man that he chose for Boston a symphony of Mozart that is less familiar than the immortal three; that, looking at the works of Richard Strauss, ne chose an early tone poem, not a later one of thunderous speech. Add a familiar overture by Weber, and for a concerto that is lacking in pyrotechnical display.

There is little to be said concerning the program. And, fortunately, there is little to be said in discussion of Mr. Walter's interpretation of the various pieces, for his conducting was conspicuous for its sanity. He did not attempt to bring out "hidden voices" in order to make unexpected effects; he did not take surprising liberties with rhythm or with melodic figures.. Nor did he fume and rage in fortissimo passages. He was thinking more about the music than about himself or what sort of an impression he was making. The memorable feature of the afternoon was the exquisite fine performance of Mozart's beautiful symphony. The performance of "Till Eulenspiegel" revealed a lyrically and dramatically romantic Till, not the irreverent, cynical, Puckish, obscene jester.

Mr. Walter's personality is pleasing. He evidently enjoyed the music, also the orchestra. There were extravagant semaphoric gestures; no bodily appeals to the audience; no suggestion of "Now I'll show you how this thing should go." The performance of the orchestra was brilliant throughout, but this orchestra has contracted the habit of being brilliant.

Mr. Schnabel, who played here for the first time, is evidently a well-equipped and musical pianist....

Felix Weingartner

Boston Herald, January 6, 1906:

Mr. Felix Weingartner will make his first appearance in Boston as a conductor next Wednesday evening with the New York Symphony Orchestra in Symphony Hall.

The opportunity of observing his methods and studying his musical character should not be neglected by anyone that pretends to interest in music.

It would be impertinent to him to speak at length of his reputation as a conductor. He is known in the chief European cities and in New York as one of the greatest orchestral interpreters now living. For many years he has been an enthusiastic admirer of Hector Berlioz, and it is only natural that the Fantastic Symphony—a cyclical work of the wildest imagination—should be on the programme of Wednesday night.

There are many pen-portraits of Mr. Weingartner. Perhaps the most picturesque is that by Edouard Schure of Paris, the well-known writer and Wagnerian: "As soon as he takes the stand, we feel the presence of a master. His personality is both gentle and strong, serious and full of inspiration. His body is thin, his face, with dominating forehead, has the leanness of a Botticelli. His sober gestures are of an incisive precision, and it would be hard and it would be hard to paint the flowing grace of this left hand, which now orders a pianissimo with an elemental gesture, now seems to float on the dying wave of melody and now shoots a magnetic current to the brass to awaken its sonorousness. "Tis the eye, rather than the hand, that guides the violins. In great moments the eye flashes and it is always on his loved strings, which murmur as the singing soul of humanity in the grand orchestra of nature. Always characteristic, never exaggerated; the movements in Weingartner are graphic signs which paint the identification of his sensitiveness with all the instrumental timbres and all the orchestral voices....there is a still more curious phenomenon: The musician is suddenly transformed each time he conducts a work; at the very moment his baton raps the call for attention, he is the incarnation of the composer whom he is about to interpret."

Boston Herald, February 13, 1912 [*following Weingartner's opening performance of Wagner's *Tristan und Isolde* at The Boston Opera House]:

...The great feature of the performance was Mr. Weingartner's interpretation of the score. Mr. Mahler had an unusually fine sense of proportion; he respected the singers; he had a firm command of the tonal gradations; but on the whole his reading was irreproachably academic. Mr. Toscanini's interpretation is still gratefully remembered. It was characterized by qualities that made Mr. Mahler's conspicuous, but led by the Italian the music has a sensuous glow, a poetically romantic spirit.

It should be remembered the Mr. Mahler and Mr. Toscanini led an orchestra that had been carefully and patiently drilled by each one in turn. Mr. Weingartner has had but few rehearsals. Mr. Conti had prepared the orchestra for his coming, but Mr. Weingartner had only a short time to poeticize these willing men.

His reading of the score will not be soon forgotten. There was fineness in the working out of detail, but there was a continuous flow of musical thought, with its bursts and lulls of passion. The orchestra sang a marvelous song. And this song was heard with the musical dialogue and monologue on the stage, not above them...each voice in the orchestra and on the stage was allotted its allotted say, to borrow the formula in "the Thousand Nights and a Night."

There was a control that was not tyrannical. And all these results were brought about with apparent ease and simplicity without spectacular gestures and there was never the thought of a conductor standing between the composer and the audience. The composer spoke through him, and it was though composer and interpreter were one.

The Boston Herald, February 18, 1912 [*after the second performance of the above]:

Mr. Weingartner again gave a most illuminative reading of the score. The music of Wagner was never so eloquent. Here was a noteworthy instance of a conductor dominating a performance, not in the spirit of self-glorification, but as the loving interpreter of a master.

C. Soloists

Selected soloists have been included here when their work dominates Hale's review of a particular concert. Reviews of dozens of others are scattered throughout the text and appendices.

TeresaC arreño

Boston Journal, February 21, 1897:

SYMPHONY NIGHT

Reappearance of Mrs. Teresa Carreño, The Celebrated Pianist—Superb Performance of Rubinstein's Concerto in D Minor.

The program of the sixteenth Symphony concert given in Music Hall last night, Emil Paur conductor, was as follows:

Academic Festival Overture	Brahms
Concerto for Pianoforte, No. 4, in D minor	Rubinstein
Symphony No. 1 in C major	Beethoven
Hungarian Rhapsody, No. 6, "The Carnival in Pesht"	Liszt

The chief interest was in the reappearance of Mrs. Carreño, who, since her début here in 1863, has, like Ulysses, seen many cities and men. I tell in another column of the Journal this morning of her first appearance here as an infant phenomenon, and her first concert tour in Europe.

The reports that have crossed the Atlantic may no longer be reckoned extravagant. Mrs. Carreño is a great pianist. She has gained immeasurably in breadth, dignity and deep musical intelligence. She was always a passionate creature, and she was at times daemoniacal in her performance; but in earlier years she often seemed to miss the composer's real purpose; she did not always think beyond the printed page.

However unpleasant her association with d'Albert may have been—and it seem incredible that such a stately, superbly sensuous woman should have thrown her handkerchief to the gnome-like d'Albert—she undoubtedly learned much from him of the higher art of piano playing. She might well have taught him passion; he, on the other hand, knew a dignity and a serenity in performance that she did well to study.

Her choice of the concerto last night was wise; for this work of Rubinstein is not only one of his greatest achievements—in that the high level is steadily maintained—but it is one of the greatest of concertos. There is little or nothing that you would have changed. The themes are expressive, often beautiful; the development is generally masterly the orchestration is effective without extravagance—notice, for instance, the skillful use of the solo trumpet, the manner in which the solo horn and solo clarinet are employed, and the concerto as a whole has an invigorating and noble atmosphere. In this work an accomplished pianist can move, thrill, suggest, startle.

Too much cannot be said of Mrs. Carreño's performance. It was heroic, with haunting episodes of tenderness. From the standpoint of him who merely watches technique with a powerful field glass it was amazing in its perfection; to him who is not dazzled by more technical display it was soul-satisfying. The woman was a part of the concerto, the concerto was her voice. There was then an apparition of glorified sex, splendid in beauty, caressing in appeal, irresistible in passion, still more dangerous in languor. There was a realization of the woman in the Oriental rhapsody: "She that looketh forth as the morning, fair as the moon, clear as the sun, and terrible as an army with banners."

No wonder that the spontaneity, the strength, the grandeur of the performance excited most hearty and long continued applause.

*
**

The dry Overture of Brahms was dryly read, and it was played in perfunctory yet none too precise fashion. The symphony—would that Mr. Paur had omitted the first and third movements—was played delightfully, with marked finish. So too the accompaniment to the concerto was played con amore.

*
**

It seems hardly possible that the Rhapsody by Liszt was heard in Boston last night for the first time. The program-book is not always to be trusted in these matters, and this music of Liszt is so inherently vulgar and bombastic that it must have appealed to some wandering, visiting conductor. Neither the body of this music nor its orchestral dress is worthy of serious attention.

JosefL hevinne

Boston Herald, December 19, 1908:

Josef Lhevinne Plays Superbly a Dry
Concerto by Rubinstein

Rubinstein's fifth concerto was played for the first time at a [Boston] Symphony concert. Mme. Schiller introduced the work in 1876 at one of Theodore Thomas' concerts in Music Hall. Either the great difficulties of a purely technical nature or the dryness of the music itself discouraged other pianists. Mr. d'Albert used to play the concerto occasionally, but he, like the Hebrew prophet who displeased Voltaire on account of his name, was capable of doing anything. Josef Lhevinne, who played here at a Symphony concert for the first time, is passionately fond of this fifth concerto. It is his favorite battle horse. With it he won the Rubinstein prize. He chose it when he played in this country for the first time. He goes about with it as though it were his mission in life to persuade all hearers that it is a thing of grandeur and beauty. There is something pathetic in this devotion.

It matters not who plays the fifth concerto; the work is long and it seems longer in performance. As a whole it is dull and futile music. Here and there is a page that has a faint melodic charm; here and there are pages that excite curiosity for a moment. Much of the concerto is only wearisome. It bristles with difficulties, but this is no longer a recommendation. Rubinstein could probably have written a still more difficult concerto.

Mr. Lhevinne is a virtuoso of the first rank. His uncommon mechanical proficiency is indisputable. He has both power, which last night he did not abuse, and delicacy. He is master of many nuances, and the quality of tone is always charming or distinguished. Since he last played here in recitals he has gained in aesthetic breadth and dignity. Last night he was more than an admirable virtuoso in the restricted meaning of the word. He played that which is for the most part inherently unmusical most musically. By the clearness of his interpretation he showed the deformity of the concerto, so that by the excellence of the performance the concerto was "most intolerable and not to be endured." Furthermore, he accomplished this: the hearer was fascinated by the superb character of the performance and often clean forgot the music. He was conscious only of Mr. Lhevinne displaying with the utmost ease beautiful or impressive arrangements of tones.

Nellie Melba

Australian soprano Nellie Melba, born Helen Porter Mitchell (1861–1931), was scheduled to appear three weeks earlier with the Boston Symphony Orchestra, but had to cancel due to illness:
Boston Herald, December 26, 1903:

Mme. Melba sang Handel's "Sweet Bird" for the third time at these concerts. The flute obbligato was played by Mr. Andre Maquarre. The air itself belongs to a class that is made tolerable only by the consummate art of a great virtuoso in perfect condition. The bravura passages must, like the cataract in Tennyson's song, leap in glory. Mme. Melba's upper tones in this air were not so clear and of such exquisite quality as on former occasions, nor was her coloratura so spontaneous. No doubt her late indisposition had something to do with this. The fact remains that the middle and lower registers of her voice were last night the most effective.

In the old story used by the poets Ford and Crashaw, it was the bird with warbling throat that failed to imitate the lute and at last dropped and "brake her heart." No such fate befell Mme. Melba, although Mr. Maquarre set her a brave example for vocal emulation, but the voice in this air was not the incomparable organ that moved and thrilled by power of golden beauty in the late performance of "The Damnation of Faust," when Mme. Melba's performance was memorable, unforgettable. In the familiar scene of Ophelia's Madness (from Ambroise Thomas' *Hamlet*) she sang with greater brilliance and with more confident bravura. Here there was no thought of technical difficulties and anxious labor. The applause and the recalls were richly merited.

Maud Powell

Boston Herald, April 21, 1907:

Thirty years ago Mr. Thomas Hardy declared that the haggard Egdon Heath appealed to "a subtler and scarcer instinct, to a more recently learned emotion, than that which responds to the sort of beauty called 'charming'. He questioned whether the exclusive reign of orthodox beauty was not approaching its last quarter. 'The new Vale of Tempe may be a gaunt waste in Thule' human souls may find themselves in closer and closer harmony with external things wearing a somberness distasteful to our race when it was young."

The violin concerto of Sibelius and in fact the symphonies of this composer recall this saying of Hardy. The somberness of the Finn is not an affection; it is not worn as a costume for a masquerade; it is constitutional; it is the color of his natural speech. It is not the expression of a peevish pessimist; it is broad and deep and elemental. There is something titanic about it. It is as though the composer were still under the spell of old northern mythology. There is the thought of the rhapsodic bard; there is the suggestion of the Saga. Look at the face of this composer. Mark the firmness, the determination, the grimness of the expression. Would you expect genteel phrases, sugared, sensuousness, irresistible appeals to palpitating ladies from such a man?

The first movement is as a Bardic improvisation. It is in a sense emotional. Yet its emotional effect on an audience will be slight until the audience is accustomed to this strange language. The second movement is one of grand and constant beauty. The long melody is as the large utterance of an early goddess. It is shot through with emotion of the noblest kind. This mood is established at once and is not changed or lessened. There is no reminder of composer or interpreter.

The music is not laboriously invented. It did not come to Sibelius by accident as he was looking for a theme. The finale is not a perfunctorily brilliant ending written because no concerto should be without a finale. It has marked character, a character consistent with what has gone before. In the aggressive lightness of the opening measures there is the playfulness of a cave man, rude exultation at the sight of more friendly nature after long hibernation.

No mere virtuoso greedy for popular favor would choose this concerto for personal display. Mme. Powell has never been in the habit of setting applause-traps. I know of no violinist now before the public who is better entitled to respect and admiration. In whatever she has undertaken in the course of her long and honorable career, she has been true to herself and to art in its highest form. No merchant ever trafficked in her heart. To speak of her mechanism at this late day would be an impertinence, for her abilities have long been recognized by two continents.

The greater the task to which she devotes herself, the more quickly do her skill, her brains, her soul respond. It is enough to say that her performance of this exceedingly difficult concerto was worthy, both in mechanism and in aesthetic and emotional quality, of the high ideal which she has had steadily before her.

The concerto is not a concerto in the ordinary meaning of the term; it is rather a symphonic poem with a violin obbligato.

The task appointed for conductor and orchestra is also one of extreme difficulty, yet the ensemble performance was of such a nature that the composer was glorified and the occasion made memorable.

ArthurR ubinstein

Boston Herald, April 2, 1921:

Mr. Rubinstein, who played here for the first time with the orchestra, gave an excellent performance of the [*Beethoven Fourth Piano] Concerto. The Andante is one of Beethoven's supreme conceptions. Its very simplicity is a stumbling block to many, the simplicity of Beethoven when he was greatest. Mr. Rubinstein's technical ability, conspicuous as it is, was not ostentatiously displayed; it served gladly the composer.

Lionel Tertis

Boston Herald, December 15, 1923:

The newspapers of Boston made the statement in the spring of 1908 that Mr. Tertis would arrive here in the fall to be leader of the viola section of the Boston Symphony Orchestra and the viola of the Hess-Schroeder String quartet. The pleasurable anticipation was not fulfilled. Mr. Tertis did not come. Mr. Ferir, the admirable viola player, came in his place.

For many years Mr. Tertis has devoted his art to the viola. In an interesting article contributed to the Daily Telegraph of London last February and reprinted in the symphony program book of this week he tells of the early and long-continued prejudice against the viola as a solo instrument and how he struggled to remove this prejudice from the minds of composers and other musicians. Cecil Forsythe, who has also labored in this vineyard, recognizes the prejudice in his "Orchestration." Speaking of the viola being somewhat affected by the disease commonly known as "sleep," he says: "Perhaps its constitution inured for centuries to sleepy passages, has by now become immune to the microbe of sleeping sickness," and he refers to the "bad old days" when viola players in an orchestra were selected "merely because they were too wicked or too senile to play the violin."

York Bowen, as a composer and pianist, has long been associated with Mr. Tertis. Besides the concerto played yesterday, Mr. Bowen has written a sonata and smaller pieces for the viola. The concerto was played in London by Mr. Tertis as far back as 1908. It is evidently a composition for a virtuoso, for display. It might be said to sound the height and the depth of the instrument, as far as the compass is concerned. The value of the purely musical contents is slight, but one can easily see how the concerto gains popular favor when played by an accomplished artist. Perhaps the most pleasing portion is the Andante with its sentimental theme, but an audience would also be impressed by the orchestration that has a glitter, that abounds in surprises, of which are not to the advantage of the solo instrument. The concerto chiefly served this purpose: the exhibition of Mr. Tertis' remarkable technical proficiency and his musical phrasing. With all due deference to the opinion of Mr. Tertis, it is doubtful whether the viola is an instrument for a concerto in conventional form. There were many times in the performance when the hearer forgot there is such an instrument as the viola and thought he was listening to a huge violin played with great skill. Mr. Monteux and the orchestra accompanied in a masterly, a brilliant manner. Fortunate, indeed, is the artist who has as sympathetic, experienced and helpful a conductor as Mr. Monteux.

Appendix IV

Columns on Sundry Topics

Walt Whitman

Boston Journal Monday, April 4, 1892:

The Thoughts of Walt Whitman
ConcerningM usic

Walt Whitman was passionately fond of music. The allusions in his writings to opera, song and orchestra are many and they are often singular. First of all, he commands the respect of musicians for his definition of music. It is found in the first edition, that thin quarto of 1855, now rare:
All music is what awakens from you when you are reminded by the instruments.
It is not the violins and the cornets, it is not the oboe nor the beating drums—nor the notes of the baritone singer singing his sweet romanza, nor those of the men's chorus, nor those of the women's chorus,
It is nearer and farther than they.

*
**

In "Good-bye, my Fancy," he speaks of the deep and lasting effect made upon him by Alboni, the famous contralto, and by Bettini, the tenor, years ago in New York. He also mentions the drunken song of Peter Richings as Caliban; the "nontechnical singing performances" of the Hutchinson Band, three brothers and the sister, the red-cheeked New England carnation, sweet Abby; sometimes primitive and balladic—sometimes anti-slavery, anti-calamel and comic. Then he speaks of Templeton, Russell, Dempster, Jenny lind, Mrs. Wood, Mrs. Seguin, Mrs. Austin, Grisi, La Grange, Steffanone, Bosio, Trufti, Parodi, Vestvali, Bertucca, Gazzaniga, Laborde; and "the opera men," Bettini, Badiali, Marini, Mario, Amodio, Beneventano, Briguoli. "I was fed and bred under the Italian dispensation, and absorbed it, and doubtless show it." But he also says, "The experts and musicians of my present friends claim that the new Wagner and his pieces belong far more truly to me, and I to them." His love for Italian opera is clearly shown in "Proud Music of the Storm," where he gives thumb-nail sketches of six favorite operas. Here, for example, is "Ernani" in a nutshell:
I see where Ernani, walking the bridal garden,
Amid the scent of night roses, radiant, holding his bride by the hand.
Hears the infernal call, the death-pledge of the horn.

*
**

It would be interesting to trace his musical thoughts and fancies from the book of '55 to that of '91. His comparisons are often subtle and suggestive, although they are couched in singular, sometimes grotesque, language. I quote from the quarto:

I hear the violoncello or man's heart's complaint.

Here are two more instances:

A tenor large and fresh as the creation fills me. The orbic flex of his mouth is pouring and filling me full.

The next is still more extraordinary:

The orchestra whirls me wider than Uranus flies.
It wrenches unnamable ardors from my breast,
It throbs me to gulps of the farthest down horror,
It sails me, I dab with bare feet, they are licked by indolent waves,
I am exposed,, cut by bitter and poisoned hail.
Steeped among honeyed morphine, my windpipe squeezed in the fakes of death,
Let up again to feel the puzzle of puzzles.
And that we call Being.

*
**

Whitman, too, longed for a national school of music. In "Democratic Vistas" he utters this prophecy:

A few years, and there will be an appropriate native grand opera, the lusty and wide-lipped offspring of Italian methods. Yet it will be no mere imitation, nor follow precedents, any more than Nature follows precedents. Vast oval halls will be constructed, on acoustic principles, in cities, where companies will perform lyrical pieces, born to the people of These States; and the people will make a perfect music a part of their lives. Every phase, every trade will have its songs, beautifying those trades. Men on the land will have theirs, and men on the water theirs. Who now is ready to begin that work for America, of composing music fit for us—songs, choruses, symphonies, operas, oratorios fully identified with the body and soul of The States? Music complete in all its appointments, but in some fresh, courageous, melodious, undeniable styles—as all that is ever to satisfy us must be. The composers to learn such music are to learn everything that can possibly [be] learned in the schools and traditions of their art, and then calmly dismiss all traditions from them.

Talk of the Day

Boston Journal, June 3, 1899

We passed where flag and flower
Signaled a jocund throng;
And, kindling, laughed at life and care,
Although we knew no laugh lay there.

We walked where shy birds stood
Watching us, wonder dumb;
Their friendship met our mood;
We cried: "We'll often come;
We'll come morn, noon, eve, everywhere!"
—We doubted we should come again.

———

There is a dispute concerning the true function of the napkin—the common table napkin. Some deep thinkers, to true Diabolonian spirit, are wrecking the happiness of many luxurious homes by thundering against the extravagant use of this article of household furniture, against the acceptation of it as a shield and a buckler. The napkin, they argue, should not take the place of bib, even when the soup is thickest and most splattery, even when the beard is like unto lush vegetation, or the moustache is as a weeping willow by a lake.

The question is one chiefly of soup. Thus "Old Reliable," a correspondent of the N. Y. Sun, abhorring the tucked in napkin, insists that there no danger of "splattering" if you half fill your spoon and take it on the side, "providing, of course, you keep your moustache properly trained."

But this is timid eating. We prefer to see a man grab his spoon boldly, as though it were a nettle. Let him not be too finicky about the quantity that rests in the bowl of the weapon; let him plunge bowl with contents into the wide-stretched mouth. No splattering will attend such heroism.

And let us consult the oracles.

*
**

In England, in the 16th century, even wiping the spoon was thought to be a dandyism. Thus we find Sir John Harrington writing, "All amorous young youths...especially if they be so cleanly that they will not eat pottage (no, not alone), but that they will wipe their spoon between every spoonful, for fear that their upper lip should infect the nether...I heard of one the last day in a town a hundred miles from London that had engrossed all the fine fashions into his hands, of the curling, perfuming, wiping the spoon, etc."

England, you may say, was a rude country in that century, and Aldermen today at London banquets tuck napkins into the collar. Let us turn to a politer nation.

The use of spoons in France was not general even in the 14th century. The wife of Louis le Hutin, owned only 42, and yet her collection of plate was very large. Charles V, who had 480 plates of gold and silver, had only 66 spoons. In 1680 Montaign states with surprise that among the Swiss there was a spoon for each one at table. Under Louis XIV, each guest possibly had a spoon, but he took his turn at the one and common soup-tureen. Thus when Jean d'Aspermont, Sleur de Vandy, dined one day with de Grand pré, a soup with only two little pieces of bread floating in it was put before the guests. Vandy tried to spear one, but, missing his aim, he called to his valet, "Pull off my boots." "Why?" asked his neighbor. "Because," said Vandy coldly, "I propose to swim in that soup so as to get a piece of bread." This was considered at the time a pleasing exhibition of wit. Later, Nicolas de Bonnefons in a book of etiquette tells us that each guest should have his own soup-plate and not be obliged to dip a spoon into the general dish. Antoine de Courtin in 1695 recommends this innovation: "It is also necessary," he adds, "to dry your spoon when, having used it for soup, you wish to help yourself with it from another plate, for there are people so fastidious that they do not wish to eat anything that has been touched by a spoon coming directly from a mouth." Madame de Saint-Germain toward the end of the reign of Louis XIV, wishing to show a neighbor a courtesy, put a spoon fresh from her mouth into a sauce, to give her a portion. We read this advice in a Civilité published in 1749: "Put your napkin decently, so that it covers you up to your neck, and having wiped your spoon with the end of your napkin, wait until someone has taken soup from the tureen or his own dish. If the soup is in a toureen, put your spoon there in turn, but do not hurry in so doing." Jean Baptiste de La Salle, founder of the Brothers of Christian Schools, wrote in 1713 "Les règles de la bienséance et la civilité chrétienne." He insists on spreading the napkin so that it will cover the feeder up to his neck. "It is not decent to wipe the face with the napkin; it is still worse to rub your teeth with it, and it would be an intolerably offence to wipe your nose with it. It is also indecent to use it for cleaning plates or platters. A napkin is for cleansing mouth, lips, and fingers when they are greasy, for cleaning the knife before cutting bread, and for cleaning the spoon and the fork after you have used them...When you take soup with a spoon, you should not fill the spoon, lest something fall on your dress or the table-cloth; and when you take the spoon out of the dish, draw it lightly over the edge, to remove the drops that may cling to the spoon." And then he devotes two pages to the manner in which soup should be eaten. Thus, you should not put your empty soup-plate on the floor; you should not hold the plate firmly in your left hand as though someone were trying to get it away from you; you should not make windy noises, or suck the soup in two gulps, or open the mouth too wide, or bend over till your head is nearly in the plate, or use the tongue externally, or cool the soup by blowing, as a New England spinster cools a dish of tea. On the other hand, a writer in "La Gastronome Francais" (1828) says, "It is not de bon ton to stretch your napkin and pass one corner of it through a button hole of your coat." And we were about to quote from "Apician Morsels," but the following paragraph prevented:

Whenever it happens that you have the misfortune of being placed by the side of a little girl, or, what is still worse, between two little boys, the best means to be employed to get rid of them is to make them tipsy as soon as possible, that papa or mama may send them to bed.

*
**

Thus do authorities differ. Let us hear the conclusion of the whole matter. Whatever your hirsute ornamentation may be, have your soup served in a little bowl, and drink it as quietly as good men and women have done before you. Montaigne tells us that he almost never used a spoon or fork. We recommend, however, the assistance of a fork in spearing stray pieces of vegetables, or cabbage. You will find handsome bowls admirably adapted for table use in Japanese shops. And private letters tell us that several of the howling swells of New York, howling enough to gain the respectful attention of Dervishes, now take soup in no other way.

THE HARRY JEWETT PLAYERS

Boston Herald, January 6, 1918:

The Harry Jewett Players began their repertory season at the Copley Theatre with a performance of "Fanny's First Play," that oven hardened theatergoers pronounced as excellent. Mr. Jewett manfully withstood the temptation of making up the critics in the prologue so that they should resemble in face and arrangement of hair the young and old lions of the Boston newspapers.

The second play was "General John Regan," by Canon J. O. Hannay, known as George A. Birmingham. Its dramatic quality is slight. The worth of the play is in its vivid characterization of Irish villagers of great and less local importance and in the racy dialogue. We have not seen the printed play. Did Mr. Joy, who took the part of the hustling American, introduce slang of this country? The motive of the drama is of universal application. If the villagers, the high officials and the British Masoum had never heard of Gen. Regan that was no reason why the "liberator of Bolivia" should not have a statue in his honor. As one of the villagers remarks: There are many statues erected to men whom nobody knew or knows. Tom Corwin said to his son, calling his attention to a statue "My son, statues are erected to solemn scenes." Corwin knew that he had suffered politically from his wit, as did "Sunset" Cox and later Thomas B. Reed. It is true that the committee for the Regan monument bought a statue of a graveyard sculptor that had been ordered for another man than the general; but did not some years ago a statue stand in the Public Garden of Boston in honor of a soldier in our civil war; a statue that came from a stone cutter's yard and did not bear the slightest resemblance to the soldier commemorated? The performance at the Copley Theatre was excellent. Certain parts stood out because they were inherently the fattest. Mr. Permain's Golligher, the flamingly patriotic editor, was admirably conceived and carried out. No one will soon forget his conviction that he had heard the tune of "Rule Britannia" before, or his behavior when he mistook "The Wearing of the Green" for that British anthem. Capital too, for its lightness and plausibility was the impersonation of the astonishingly resourceful Dr. O'Grady by Mr. Wingfield. Mr. Matthew's Doyle was appropriately and unctuously commercial. Mr. Gordon was the bored and officially ignorant gentleman from Dublin, to the life. Miss Sawyer was pretty even in her dirty and tattered garments. The other women of the company had little to do. Miss Roach, an attractive Mrs. Gregg, should carry herself better. In a standing position she was unnecessarily stiff and awkward. Why did not Miss Newcombe, as Mrs. De Courey, present the illuminated address in the scene of the unveiling? Was her absence from the stage Wednesday night in accordance with the dramatist's intention? She was a dashing figure in the first act when she entered with her well-behaved dog.

As the World Wags

Boston Herald, November 11, 1923:

We have received so many letters about the text and authorship of the old song, "Sally Come Up" that through the courtesy of Oliver Ditson Company, The Herald publishes all the verses on the dramatic page of this issue. It appears that the song was sung by David Reed of Buckley's Serenaders.

David Reed was born in New York in 1830; he died there in 1906. As Mr. Edw. Leroy Rice says in his "Monarchs of Minstrelry": "He it was, with Dan Bryant, who did so much to popularize 'Shoo Fly'...and 'Sally Come Up' will always be identified with his memory. But as a bone player, Dave Reed is probably best remembered; his imitation of drums, horses running and the like were wonderful; the art practically died with him." About 1844 he was with a small travelling company. In 1856, dave Reed's minstrels performed on the Mississippi steamboat "James Raymond." He was with Bryant's Minstrels, also Kelly and Leon's, and later he, his wife and four children were in vaudeville as the Reed family, known also as the Reed Birds. He retired in 1903.

Mr. Rice says nothing about Reed's association with Buckley's Serenaders nor does he mention the fact that in 1881, Reed, with Dan Emmett, Archie Hughes, Sam Sanford, Frank Moran and Cool Burgess was engaged for M. B. Leavitt's "Gigantean Minstrels." "They made," says Mr. Leavitt in his "Fifty Years in Theatrical Management," "a quick change from a modern first part to the ancient first part while the entire company sat in a semi-circle across the stage, and used the same musical instruments employed in minstrelsy, viz., the jawbone, accordion, triangle, banjo, violin, bones, and tambourine."

(from a restaurant's bill of fare)
Special: Spanish Omelet with Egg 40

ADD "COMMERCIAL CANDOR"
(Maywood, Ill. Herald)

FOR SALE—ONE OLD BROKEN DOWN acorn range, burns wood, sometimes hard to bake in, rusted, one leg gone, cheap. 1011 South Third Avenue.

THROUGH THE MAGNIFYING GLASS
(New York dispatch to the Chicago Tribune)

***inside the Metropolitan Opera House, where 4300 were seated in the famous Golden Horseshoe.

WILDCATS AND GLASS

As the World Wags:

Two serious questions have been raised by your correspondents, fundamental questions. Both may be answered by the Empirical Method:

The wildness of the wildcat is not only revealed, but explained in recent news items setting forth the consternation in Athol caused by the appearance there of wildcats. A visit to Athol would supply the need data.

Likewise to the method of identifying Sandwich glass. Natives who have tried many devices declare that the best test is to take any given piece suspected of being the genuine, pulverize with a hammer into pieces the size of either half a split pea (which is coarse powder), spread thick between two slices of gluten bread or stale cake and eat with a relish.

If there are no ill effects you may be sure it was genuine Sandwich glass.

CAPE COD

POETIC LICENSE

As the World Wags:
"Flaccus" of the New York World, recently quoted in your column, says:

"If the lovely Miss Godiva
Rode through Coventry today
It is doubtful if a dozen
Men would turn to look her way.
And the traffic, thanks to Ziegfeld,
Now would scarcely block the street,

APPENDIX IV

For the well-known female figure
Isnolon gera nyt reat."

Miss or Mrs., however, would have made no difference to Peeping Tom of odious memory.

Dorchester. BAIZE.

Apropos of the recent performance of "The Merchant of Venice," a correspondent informs us that in Mt. Vernon St., near Joy, the Portia law school is close to the West End Young Men's Hebrew Association.

We have not the time to verify this statement.

A KITCHEN NEED

We are indebted to the Vita-Sulphur Company for this communication:

"This thought often occurred to the writer: The type and standard of our educational system is certainly wonderful. It is claimed that our foresight and intellectual powers are marvelous. For protection of the public we license everything in the world, from the incipient lapdog to the professional man. We license the coal hustler in the furnace regions and call him 'engineer'; we license the undertaker, auto drivers, marriages. We license everything. A license is required for everything a man can conceive. But for the one sane thing is license is really needed, the chef and the cook, it seems we do not use the sense we were born with."

FOR MEDICAL USE

Here is a report of a town agency for sale of alcoholic medicine—instituted under thea ctof M ay22 ,1 852:

Paid: E. Preston & Co.

For 1 Bbl. N. E. Rum, 37 galls. At 28c	10 36
For one eighth cask. A. Seinett Cog. Brandy, at $1.05, 20 1/2 galls	33 32
For 10 Galls. 86 per c. Alcohol, at 52.—Keg 87	6 07
For 10 Galls. (pine apple) Holland Gin, at 95.—Keg 37	10 37
For 2 Galls. St. Cx. Rum, at 1. Demj. 50	2 40
For 2 Galls. Steny Wine, at 95. Demj 50	2 40
For 2 Galls. Port Wine, at 1.50. Demj 50	3 50
For 2 Galls. Brown Sherry Wine, at 1.38, Demj	3 26
	$72 28
Stary and Surrill, for carting same	1 00
D. M. Swift, for 4 months service as Agent for the Town for the Sale of Alcoholic Medicines.	26 67
Whole expense	99 95

The report ended as follows: "The auditors hope they may be pardoned. If they just hint, very delicately, that should the Town Officers at any time feel unwell, they might be allowed to obtain their remedies from the Town's stock of medicine...."

Notes

Introduction

1. E. R. Warren, untitled and unpublished eulogy in Tavern Club Records, Carton 3, "Philip Hale—folder A," Massachusetts Historical Society: SH13D3M.
2. Olin Downes, "Philip Hale—His Genius as a Critic" in *Friends of the Boston Symphony Orchestra Second Annual Meeting* (Boston: Boston Symphony Orchestra, 1936), pp. 14–15.
3. *Boston Journal*, December 6, 1894.
4. *Boston Herald*, November 28, 1909.
5. Georg Solti, *Memoirs* (New York: Alfred P. Knopf, 1997), pp. 105 and 147.
6. Philip Hale quoted in Nicolas Slonimsky (ed.), *The Concise Baker's Biographical Dictionary of Music*, 8th ed. (New York: Schirmer Books, 1994), p. 384.
7. E. R. Warren, *loc. cit.*
8. Mark N. Grant, *Maestros of the Pen: A History of Classical Music Criticism in America* (Boston: Northeastern University Press, 1998), p. 77.
9. John N. Burk (ed.), *Philip Hale's Boston Symphony Programme Notes: Historical, Critical, and Descriptive Comment on Music and Composers*, 2nd ed. (New York: Garden City Publishing, 1939).

1   1854–1889

1. Different sources list the year of her death as 1872 and 1882. What is probably the most reliable of these, Robert Safford Hale's *Geneology of Descendants of Thomas Hale* (Albany: Weed, Parsons, and Co., 1889), lists the date of her death as December 10, 1872 on p. 386. William Bainbridge Hale remarried on July 7, 1886 to Mrs. Victoria Philips Morris in Grassdale, Louisa County,Virginia.
2. Jacob G. Ullery and Hiram Huse (eds.), *Men of Vermont: An Illustrated Biographical History of Vermonters and Sons of Vermont* (Brattleboro, VT: Transcript Publishing Co., 1894), p. 172.
3. Edward Hale (1858–1918) became an ordained Unitarian minister, eventually becoming an assistant professor of Homiletics at Harvard University (1888–1906) and minister of First Church, Chestnut Hill (Newton), MA, 1897–1918.
4. "Elm Street Historic District: Round Hill Road Expansion Preliminary Report," Elm Street Historic District Commission, Northampton, MA, December 14, 2011, p. 7.
5. John S. Bowman (ed.), "Musical and Theatrical Life in a New England Village in the Sixties: A Paper Delivered on June 14, 1923 before The Massachusetts Historical Society by Philip Hale," Northampton, MA (Massachusetts Historical Society), 2010, p. 10. Though the speech is by Hale, Bowman's extensive editorial comments occupy roughly four times as many pages.
6. Probably the British poet Algernon Charles Swinburne (1837–1909).
7. Photocopy of personal correspondence, Philip Hale to Walt Whitman, Sep[tember] 9, 1871, at Smith College, William Allen Neilson Library, Mortimer Rare Book Room: Philip Hale Papers, II: Correspondence: Folder 3.

8. Philip Hale, "Walt Whitman," in *The Yale Literary Magazine*, XL, No. 2 (November, 1874), pp. 98, 101.
9. Edward Dowden, "The Poetry of Democracy: Walt Whitman," in *Westminster Review*, XL (July 1871), pp. 16–32. The *Westminster Review* was a British quarterly published from 1824 to 1914.
10. Walt Whitman, *Democratic Vistas*, a critical sociopolitical essay self-published as a 45-page pamphlet in 1871.
11. A poem grouping in Whitman's *Leaves of Grass*.
12. Photocopy of personal correspondence, Philip Hale to Walt Whitman, Oct[ober] 7th, 1875, at Smith College, Mortimer Rare Book Room: Philip Hale Papers, II: Correspondence: Folder 4.
13. Whitman's 1876 companion volume to *Leaves of Grass*.
14. Personal correspondence, Walt Whitman to Philip Hale, July 11 [1876?]. 1876 is the probable year, for that is when *Two Rivulets* was published. Smith College Mortimer Rare Book Room: Philip Hale Papers, II: Correspondence: Folder 9.
15. *Quarante Mélodies Choises de F. Schubert*, Alfonse LeDuc, Paris, France (n.d.) Piano Seul (Piano Solo).
16. The entire passage, found in *Leaves of Grass*, p. 61, is as follows:
    All music is what awakens from you when you are reminded by the instruments,
    It is not the violins and the cornets . . . it is not the oboe nor the beating drums—
       nor the notes of the baritone singer singing his sweet romanza . . . nor those
       of the men's chorus, nor those of the women's chorus,
    It is nearer and farther than they.
17. George Rogers Howell and Jonathan Tenney (eds.), *Bi-centennial History of Albany and Schenectady Counties, New York* (New York: Munsell & Co., 1886), Vol. 4, pp. 743–745.
18. *The New York Times*, January 17, 1883.
19. The *Albany Evening Times* was published daily except Sunday, while the *Albany Weekly Times* was published each Thursday.
20. *The Albany Weekly Times*, September 26, 1878.
21. July 9, 1884, according to *The National Cyclopaedia of American Biography*, p. 462.
22. "Contemporary American Composers," AOLib.com, 2009–2011.
23. Théodore Salomé, *Dix Pièces pour Orgue*, Vol. III, Op. 48 (Mainz, Germany: Schott, 1894).
24. Howell and Tenney (eds), *Bi-centennial History of Albany and Schenectady Counties, New York* , p. 745.
25. Ibid.
26. Albany would not have a permanent professional orchestra until 1930, when the Albany Symphony Orchestra (originally the People's Symphony Orchestra) was founded.
27. *Albany Evening Union*, November 22, 1888.
28. *The Musical Courier*, No. 468 (January 30, 1889), p. 88.
29. *Albany Times*, January 31, 1889.
30. Leonard Burkat and Pamela Fox, "Boston 5: Opera and Musical Theatre" in *Grove Music Online*.
31. *Albany Evening Union*, February 8, 1889.
32. *Albany Evening Union*, April 2, 1889.

2   1889–1900

1. The United States Marine Band was founded in 1798. The Old Stoughton Musical Society also predates it (1786).
2. American Antiquarian Society AAS BDSDS1853. Today, in addition to the chorus, the Handel and Haydn Society features a period instrument orchestra, though the ensemble remained strictly a choral entity until 1900.
3. John Ogasapian, *Music of the Colonial and Revolutionary Era* (Westport, CT: The Greenwood Group, 2004), p. 137.

Notes

4. Ora Frishberg Saloman, *Beethoven's Symphonies and J. S. Dwight: The Birth of American Music Criticism* (Boston: Northeastern University Press, 1995), p. 21.
5. John Sullivan Dwight, "The History of Music in Boston" in Justin Windsor (ed.), *The Memorial History of Boston Including Suffolk County, 1630–1880* (Boston: Ticknor & Co., 1881), p. 416.
6. Joseph Horowitz, *Classical Music in America: A History of Its Rise and Fall* (New York: Norton, 2005), p. 29.
7. *Boston Globe*, April 22, 1917.
8. Dwight, "The History of Music in Boston," p. 423.
9. *Boston Herald*, April 22, 1917.
10. Louis Charles Elson, *The History of American Music* (New York: Macmillan, 1904), p. 57.
11. *Boston Herald*, April 22, 1917.
12. Joseph Horowitz, *Classical Music in America: A History of Its Rise and Fall*, provides a detailed chapter on what he calls "Boston and the Cult of Beethoven."
13. Dwight, "The History of Music in Boston," p. 463.
14. Personal correspondence, Henry Lee Higginson to members of the Boston Symphony Orchestra, April 27, 1914, quoted in Bliss Perry, *The Life and Letters of Henry Lee Higginson* (Boston: The Atlantic Monthly Press, 1921), pp. 291–293.
15. Joseph Horowitz, *Moral Fire: Musical Portraits from America's Fin de Siècle* (Berkeley: University of California Press, 2012), p. 34.
16. Higginson mentioned "Mr. Zerrahn is worn out" in Mark Antony DeWolfe Howe, *The Boston Symphony Orchestra: An Historical Sketch*. (Boston and New York: Houghton-Mifflin, 1914), p. 46. It is possible that Zerrahn was Higginson's first choice, although any documentation related to this is unknown to the author.
17. Howe, *The Boston Symphony Orchestra*, p. 35.
18. Ibid., p. 250. By the fall of 1889, when Hale started to review Boston Symphony Orchestra concerts, the numbers had increased to 84.
19. *Boston Journal*, April 18, 1896.
20. Dwight, "The History of Music in Boston," p. 422n.
21. H. Earle Johnson, "*The Folio* of White, Smith and Company" in *American Music*, II, No. 1 (Spring, 1984), p. 88.
22. *Boston Home Journal*, September 14, 1889.
23. Some of the building still stands, having been incorporated into the Orpheum Theatre.
24. Howe, *The Boston Symphony Orchestra*, p. 158.
25. Moses Smith, *Koussevitzky* (New York: Allen, Towne, & Heath, 1947), p. 132.
26. *Boston Home Journal*, October 12, 1889.
27. Olin Downes, "Philip Hale—His Genius as a Critic," in "Friends of the Boston Symphony Orchestra, 2nd Annual Meeting" (Boston: Boston Symphony Orchestra, 1936), p. 12.
28. *Art Journal [Boston Home Journal]*, October 19, 1889.
29. *Boston Home Journal*, October 26, 1889.
30. *Boston Home Journal*, November 9, 1889.
31. Ibid.
32. This review of Beethoven's fifth is included in Part II.
33. *Boston Home Journal*, November 9, 1889
34. *Boston Home Journal*, December 29, 1889.
35. *Boston Home Journal*, February 21, 1890.
36. *The Musical Courier*, March 5, 1890.
37. *Boston Home Journal*, April 18, 1890. This symphony was listed incorrectly as Symphony No. 2 in C minor (probably the typesetter's error) at the top of the column. The C minor was, of course, Brahms' First Symphony.
38. This caste system is apparent even today, especially in education. Massachusetts' privately schooled politicians have not properly funded its state-run universities, where the less affluent generally attend.
39. *Constitution and By-laws of the St. Botolph Club in Boston with a List of the Officers and Members of the Club*, printed by Order of the Executive Committee. February 1898, p. 32

40. In separate writings, John Ogusapian and Joseph Horowitz label Philip Hale a snob. While there is a certain justification for this is in regard to Hale's social status, it must be remembered that he was a product of the time, place, and circumstances in which he lived. In terms of Hale's writings, opinion of whether or not he was a snob depends upon the eye of the beholder, but in terms of his generosity toward others he clearly was not one. See Olin Downes's commentary in the Introduction.
41. Personal correspondence, Philip Hale to Charles Martin Loeffler, February 25, 1908. Boston Public Library MS2468(8).
42. Personal correspondence, Philip Hale to Charles Martin Loeffler, January 5, 1908. Boston Public Library MS2468(7).
43. *Boston Post*, October 11, 1890.
44. Ibid.
45. *Boston Post*, November 23, 1890.
46. Other works included Saint-Saëns's symphonic poem *The Youth of Hercules*, Xaver Scharwenka's *Piano Concerto No. 1 in B flat minor*, Op. 32, and Richard Wagner's "Waldweben," from *Siegfried*.
47. *Boston Post*, February 6, 1891.
48. "VergeblichesS tändchen."
49. "Voi che sapeta" and "Non so píu cosa son" from *The Marriage of Figaro*.
50. *Boston Post*, February 16, 1891.
51. *Boston Post*, February 22, 1891.
52. *Boston Musical Herald*, Vol. XIII, No. 1 (November, 1891), p. 1.
53. *Boston Symphony Orchestra Programme Booklet*, December 4 and 5, 1891, p. 264.
54. *Boston Musical Herald*, Vol. XIII, No. 2 (December 1891), pp. 19–20.
55. Frank L. Mott, *A History of American Magazines*, 1865–1885 (Boston: Harvard University Press, 1938; 4th printing: London: Oxford University Press, 1970), p. 197n.
56. *The Beacon*, December 19, 1891.
57. *Boston Journal*, December 26, 1891.
58. Ibid.
59. *Boston Times*, January 2, 1892.
60. *Boston Transcript*, December 10, 1894.
61. *Boston Journal*, January 9, 1892.
62. *Boston Transcript*, January 9, 1892.
63. William F. Apthorp, "Some Thoughts on Music Criticism," p. 297, in Apthorp, *Musicians and Music Lovers and Other Essays* (New York: Charles Scribner's Sons, 1894), quoted in Robert B. Nelson, "The Commentaries and Criticisms of William Foster Apthorp," unpublished PhD dissertation, University of Florida, 1991, pp. 233–234.
64. *Boston Journal*, January 6, 1893.
65. *Boston Journal*, December 29, 1894.
66. *Boston Journal*, October 17, 1897.
67. *Boston Journal*, February 26, 1898.
68. *Boston Journal*, February 2, 1899.
69. *Boston Journal*, January 26, 1895.
70. *Boston Journal*, March 14, 1897.
71. *Boston Journal*, January 26, 1900.
72. Personal correspondence, Philip Hale to Charles Martin Loeffler, August 2, 1908. Boston Public Library MS2468(9).
73. Personal correspondence, Henry Lee Higginson to Oscar W. Donner, esq., April 25, 1893. "Microfilmed Papers of Henry Lee Higginson concerning the Boston Symphony Orchestra and other Musical Matters from the Baker Memorial Library, Harvard Business School," Boston Symphony Orchestra Archives, 2000.
74. *New York Herald*, May 21, 1893.
75. Personal correspondence, Philip Hale to Charles Martin Loeffler, March 29, 1906. Boston Public Library MS2468(6).

76. The last chronologically, it was originally billed as "No. 5." The first four had not been published and the renumbering of the symphonies would not be resolved until after the middle of the twentieth century.
77. The second movement of Chadwick's *Symphony No. 2 in B flat*, Op. 32.
78. *Boston Journal*, January 1, 1894.
79. *Boston Journal*, January 26, 1895.
80. *Boston Herald*, December 12, 1929.
81. *Boston Journal*, October 29, 1892.
82. *The Musical Record*, No. 428 (September 1897), p. 11.
83. *Boston Journal*, January 7, 1895.
84. *Boston Journal*, February 4, 1899.
85. *Boston Journal*, December 19, 1896.
86. *Boston Journal*, January 25, 1896.
87. Edward MacDowell quoted by Robert S. Clark in record jacket notes for *MacDowell: Suite for Large Orchestra; Suite No. 2 "Indian,"* Eastman-Rochester Orchestra, Howard Hanson, conductor. Mercury Golden Imports SRI 75026.
88. This is a rare "Entr'acte" article for the program booklet that Hale was invited to write while Apthorp was still programme essayist.
89. *Boston Journal*, December 4, 1897. Ironically, the *Indian Suite* was the last major orchestral work that MacDowell would compose. The strain from his administrative position at Columbia University, coupled with a street accident, led to dementia and premature death in 1908 at the age of 47.
90. *Musical Record*, No. 432 (January 1, 1898), p. 13
91. The 1896 presidential election.
92. *Boston Journal*, October 31, 1896.
93. Hale's follow-up article in the November 4, 1896 *Boston Journal* on women composers, including another detailed look at this symphony, is located in the Appendix.
94. *Boston Journal*, April 8, 1893.
95. *Library of Congress Performing Arts Encyclopedia*.: "Margaret R. Lang," athttp://lcweb2.loc.gov/diglib/ihas/loc.natlib.ihas.200153251
96. Ellen Knight, *Charles Martin Loeffler: A Life Apart in American Music* (Urbana and Chicago: University of Illinois Press, 1993).
97. *Boston Journal*, January 7, 1895.
98. *New York Times*, October 14, 1893.
99. *Petite Symphony* (1888), scored for flute, two oboes, two clarinets, two bassoons, and two horns.
100. *Boston Journal*, November 18, 1893.
101. *Boston Journal*, April 8, 1894.
102. *Boston Journal*, January 1, 1895.
103. Howe, *The Boston Symphony Orchestra*, pp. 178–179.
104. Ibid.,p p.1 80–181.
105. *The Musical Record*, No. 428 (September 1897).
106. *The National Cyclopaedia of American Biography* (New York: James T. White & Co., 1910), pp. 462 and 464.

3   1900–1903

1. Richard Poate Stebbins, *The Making of Symphony Hall Boston* (Boston: Boston Symphony Orchestra, 2000), p. 13.s
2. Renamed Massachusetts Avenue.
3. Stebbins, *The Making of Symphony Hall Boston*, p. 19.
4. Robert Kirzinger, Kim Noltemy-Ugorji, Caroline Smedvig, Mark Volpe, and Bridget P. Carr (eds.) *Symphony Hall: The First 100 Years*. (Boston: The Boston Symphony Orchestra, Inc., 2000) p. 34.

5. *Boston Journal*, May 21, 1899.
6. Kirzinger (ed.) et al., *Symphony Hall*, p. 42.
7. Personal correspondence Charles A. Ellis to Henry Higginson, August 24, 1900, quoted in Stebbins, *The Making of Symphony Hall Boston*, pp. 184–185.
8. *Boston Globe,* September 22, 1900.
9. *Boston Journal*, October 16, 1900.
10. *Boston Journal*, November 5, 1900.
11. Ibid.
12. Ibid.
13. *Boston Journal*, May 4, 1901.
14. *Boston Journal*, November 24, 1901.
15. David Whitwell, *The Longy Club: A Professional Wind Ensemble in Boston* (1900–1917) (Northridge, CA: WINDS, 1988), p. 8.
16. *Boston Journal*, December 19, 1900.
17. This is incorrect. The date should be 1917.
18. *Boston Herald*, April 26, 1925.
19. William C. Loring, Jr., "Arthur Bird, American," in *The Musical Quarterly*, Vol. 29, No. 1 (January, 1943), p. 85.
20. *Boston Journal*, April 1, 1902.
21. *Boston Journal*, March 6, 1903.
22. *Boston Journal*, May 7, 1901.
23. *Boston Journal*, October 19, 1901.
24. Ibid.
25. *The Musical Courier*, October 28, 1901.
26. Warren Storey Smith, "Four Distinguished American Music Critics—A Centennial Note," in *Musical America* (February 15, 1954), p. 134.
27. Mark Antony De Wolfe Howe, *The Boston Symphony Orchestra: An Historical Sketch* (Boston: The Atlantic Monthly Press, 1914), pp. 138–139. This may have been the source of Hale's well-known comment "She consumed valuable time."
28. Robert B. Nelson, "The Commentaries and Criticisms of William Foster Apthorp" (University of Florida unpublished PhD dissertation, 1991), pp. 192, 164.
29. Smith, "Four Distinguished American Music Critics," p. 6.
30. James Gibbons Huneker, *Steeplejack*, Vol. II (New York: Charles Scribner's Sons, 1920), p. 190.
31. Personal correspondence, Philip Hale to Richard Aldrich, January 5, 1903. Houghton Library, Harvard University: Richard Aldrich papers, HOU b MS Am2592.
32. Personal correspondence, Philip Hale to Richard Aldrich, February 24, 1908, Houghton Library, Harvard University: Richard Aldrich papers, HOU bMS Am2592.
33. Undated personal correspondence, Philip Hale to Richard Aldrich, Houghton Library, Harvard University: Richard Aldrich papers, HOU bMS Am2592.
34. Personal correspondence, Philip Hale to Richard Aldrich, February 26, 1908, Houghton Library, Harvard University: Richard Aldrich papers, HOU bMS Am2592.

4   1903–1917

1. *Musical Courier*, December 28, 1904.
2. *Boston Herald*, April 14, 1904.
3. *Boston Herald*, December 14, 1908.
4. *Boston Herald*, November 26, 1905.
5. This is included in Part II, Appendix II.
6. *Musical Courier*, n.d. November, 1903.
7. *Boston Herald*, October 17, 1903.
8. *Musical Courier*, October 21, 1903.
9. *Musical Courier*, n.d. after October 27, 1903.
10. *Boston Herald*, December 6, 1903.

11. *Boston Herald*, April 3, 1904.
12. *Boston Herald*, April 20, 1904.
13. Personal correspondence, Henry Lee Higginson to Wilhelm Gericke, December 28, 1918, "Microfilmed Papers of Henry Lee Higginson concerning the Boston Symphony Orchestra and other Musical Matters from the Baker Memorial Library, Harvard Business School," Boston Symphony Orchestra Archives, 2000.
14. Personal correspondence, Philip Hale to Wilhelm Gericke, April 21, 1904, Harvard University Houghton Library, bMS Mus 132 (103).
15. *Boston Herald*, October 22, 1904. The vast majority of modern audiences have been introduced to the work by one of the segments of the Walt Disney animated movie *Fantasia* (1940) in which Mickey Mouse serves as the apprentice. The Disney animators followed Goethe's storyline, although about 30 percent of Dukas' music is cut.
16. Ibid.
17. Philip Hale, *Modern French Songs*, 2 vols. (Boston: Oliver Ditson Co., 1904).
18. *Boston Herald*, December 3, 1905.
19. This article is included in Part II, Appendix II.
20. Mark Anthony DeWolfe Howe, *The Boston Symphony Orchestra: An Historical Sketch* (Boston and NewYork: Houghton-Mifflin, 1914), p. 211.
21. *Boston Herald*, December 18, 1904.
22. *Boston Herald*, March 26, 1905.
23. *The Musical Courier*, December 28, 1904.
24. *Boston Herald*, February 7, 1904.
25. Personal correspondence, Philip Hale to Wilhelm Gericke, February 11, 1905, Harvard University Houghton Library, bMS Mus 132 (104).
26. Personal correspondence, Philip Hale to Wilhelm Gericke, May 18, 1905, Harvard University Houghton Library, bMS Mus 132 (105).
27. Personal correspondence, Henry Lee Higginson to Wilhelm Gericke, May 1, 1898. Correspondence between Wilhelm Gericke and Henry Lee Higginson, 1885–1918, from the Boston Symphony Orchestra archives and the George F. Baker Library, School of Business Administration, Harvard University.
28. Personal correspondence, Henry Lee Higginson to Wilhelm Gericke, January 22, 1906. Correspondence between Wilhelm Gericke and Henry Lee Higginson, 1885–1918, from the Boston Symphony Orchestra archives and the George F. Baker Library, School of Business Administration, Harvard University.
29. Personal correspondence, Philip Hale to Charles Martin Loeffler, April 26, 1906. Boston Public Library MS2468(5).
30. Edmund A. Bowles, "Karl Muck and His Compatriots: German Conductors in America during World War I (and How They Coped)," in *American Music*, XXV, No. 4 (Winter, 2007), p. 411.
31. *Boston Herald*, September 23, 1906.
32. Personal correspondence, Philip Hale to Wilhelm Gericke, December 9, 1906. Harvard University Houghton Library, bMS Mus 132 (107).
33. James Gibbons Huneker, *Steeplejack*, Vol. II (New York: Charles Scribner's Sons, 1920), pp.3 6–37.
34. Lawrence Gilman, *Strauss' "Salome:" A Guide to the Opera with Musical Illustrations* (New York: John Lane Co., 1907). Gilman in turn provided the introduction to John N. Burk (ed.), *Philip Hale's Boston Symphony Programme Notes: Historical, Critical, and Descriptive Comment on Music and Composers*, 2nd printing (New York: Garden City Publishing Co., Inc.,1 939).
35. French Novelist Remy de Gourmont (1858–1915).
36. Maud MacCarthy (1882–1967), Irish violinist who became an expert in the music of India.
37. Approximate translation from the German: "To me, I couldn't care less."
38. The 1899 novel of French writer Anatole France (pseudonym for Jacques Anatole Thibault (1844–1924).
39. Osterville is one of seven villages located within the Town of Barnstable on Cape Cod, Massachusetts. The Hales had a summer home there, "Tanglewild" (not to be confused

with the Tanglewood Music Center in Lenox, Massachusetts, the Boston Symphony Orchestra's summer home since the late 1930s).

40. Personal correspondence, Philip Hale to Charles Martin Loeffler, August 21, 1907. Boston Public Library MS2468(6).
41. Though the focus of Hale's career (and consequently this book) remained centered on music, his dramatic reviews display a similarity of approach. Occasionally, when the Boston Symphony had a week off, his Sunday "Dramatic and Musical Review" page would focus on the theater. His 1918 review of the Harry Jewett Company, which headed such a page, is included in Part II, Appendix IV.
42. *Boston Herald*, September 20, 1908.
43. *Boston Herald*, November 8, 1910.
44. *Boston Herald*, October 16, 1912.
45. John R. Tedesco, "A History of Opera in Boston," unpublished MM dissertation (University of Massachusetts, 2010), pp. 100–101.
46. Ibid., pp. 105–106.
47. Boston Symphony Orchestra Program Booklet, October 29–30, 1909.
48. Gustav Klemm, "Gustav Strube: The Man and Musician," *The Musical Quarterly*, XXVIII, No. 3 (July, 1942), p. 293.
49. *Boston Herald*, December 17, 1910.
50. Appearing in the same issue as this review (*Boston Herald*, Sunday, February 27, 1910) was Hale's extensive article "The Ancestral History of the Popular Piano Family."
51. *Boston Herald*, February 27, 1910.
52. *Boston Herald*, November 11, 1911.
53. Ibid.
54. Ibid.
55. *Boston Herald*, November 11, 1912.
56. *Boston Herald*, February 15, 1911.
57. *Signale für die Musickalische Welt* (1843–1941) was a musical journal founded by the publisher Bartholf Senff in Leipzig.
58. *New York Times*, June 12, 1911.
59. Personal correspondence, Philip Hale to Henry L. Higginson, February 6, 1911. "Microfilmed Papers of Henry Lee Higginson concerning the Boston Symphony Orchestra and other Musical Matters from the Baker Memorial Library, Harvard Business School," Boston Symphony Orchestra Archives, 2000.
60. "Thursday Evening Club List of Members," in Thursday Evening Club Records, Carton 3, Massachusetts Historical Society.
61. "The Thursday Evening Club," p. 7, unpublished manuscript address given by Reginald Fitz on October 24, 1946, in Thursday Evening Club Records, Carton 3, Massachusetts Historical Society.
62. Personal correspondence, Philip Hale to Harold E. Ernst, November 25, 1919, Thursday Evening Club Records, Carton 1, Massachusetts Historical Society. Hale gave the following speeches: February 15, 1917: "Boston Newspapers," March 7, 1918: "Theatrical Conditions in Music," and two others of unknown topics on February 19, 1925 and November 15, 1928.
63. The Tavern Club also had 33 nonresident members and 8 honorary members in 1894.
64. "Tavern Club Valentine" in Tavern Club Records—Carton 3 3 SH13D3M, Folder: Hale, Philip—A (1917–1933), Massachusetts Historical Society.
65. *The Rules of the Tavern Club of Boston, with a List of the Officers & Members* (Cambridge, MA: University Press, 1894), p. 25.
66. *Boston Herald*, October 3, 1912.
67. *Boston Herald*, October 1, 1912.
68. *Boston Herald*, October 12, 2012.
69. *Boston Herald*, October 3, 1912.
70. *Boston Globe*, December 19, 1914.
71. This quote has also been attributed to Mark Twain.

72. *Boston Herald*, December 19, 1914.
73. Personal correspondence, Philip Hale to Clara Kathleen Rogers, September 22, 1912, Harvard University Houghton Library bMS Thr 470(712).
74. Personal correspondence, Henry Lee Higginson to Philip Hale, January 12, 1915, "Microfilmed Papers of Henry Lee Higginson concerning the Boston Symphony Orchestra and other Musical Matters from the Baker Memorial Library, Harvard Business School," Boston Symphony Orchestra Archives, 2000.
75. Chalmers Clifton (1889–1966) became conductor of Boston's Cecilia Society that same year. He pieced together a successful guest-conducting career, as conductor of the New York's American Orchestral Society (1922–1932), and founder of the Federal Music Project of New York City in 1936. He also appeared as a guest conductor for the Boston Symphony Orchestra in January 1932.
76. Personal correspondence, Philip Hale to Henry Lee Higginson, January 13, 1915, "Microfilmed Papers of Henry Lee Higginson concerning the Boston Symphony Orchestra and other Musical Matters from the Baker Memorial Library, Harvard Business School," Boston Symphony Orchestra Archives, 2000.
77. Personal correspondence, Henry Higginson to Philip Hale, May 14, 1917, *loc. cit.*
78. Personal correspondence, Henry Higginson to Philip Hale, March 11, 1918, *loc. cit.* Higginson also requested opinions about these men from George W. Chadwick, Joseph Adamowski, Charles Martin Loeffler, and Clayton Jones.
79. *The Panama-Pacific International Exposition Official View Book*, 3rd ed. (San Francisco: Robert A. Reid, 1915), p. 20.
80. Boston Symphony Orchestra concert programs, Season 34, May 14 to May 26, 1915, Panama-Pacific International Exposition, San Francisco, California (Volume 1915: Panama-Pacific), Boston Symphony Archives.
81. *Boston Herald*, May 7, 1916.
82. *Boston Herald*, October 28, 1916.
83. Brian Bell, liner notes for *The First Recordings of the Boston Symphony Orchestra*, BSO Classics 171002 (1995).

5 1917–1933

1. *Providence Journal*, November 8, 1917. Kreisler had been an officer in the Austrian army but was discharged in 1914, long before US involvement in the war.
2. *Providence Journal*, October 30, 1917.
3. *Providence Journal*, October 31, 1917.
4. Boston Symphony Orchestra program (October 30, 1917) in *Boston Symphony Orchestra Concert Programs, Season 37, 1917–1918, Trip (Volume 1917–1918, Trip)*, Boston Symphony OrchestraA rchives.
5. *Providence Journal*, November 1, 1917.
6. *New York Times*, November 3, 1917. The "Damrosch" referred to would have been Walter Damrosch, conductor of the New York Symphony.
7. Boston Symphony Orchestra program, November 5, 1917, in *Boston Symphony Orchestra Concert Programs, Season 37, 1917–1918, Trip (Volume 1917–1918, Trip)*, Boston Symphony Orchestra Archives. Ironically at this time the United States had no official national anthem. *The Star Spangled Banner* would finally become the national anthem in 1931.
8. *Boston Symphony Orchestra Concert Programs, Season 37, 1917–1918, Trip (Volume 1917–1918, Trip)*, Boston Symphony Orchestra Archives. An examination of the 1916–1917 Trip programs, nearly all performed before the United States entered the war, reveals only four all-German programs, one being an all-Wagner program performed at the Arcadia in Detroit on January 1, 1917.
9. *Providence Journal*, January 15, 1918.
10. Brian Bell, liner notes, *The First Recordings of the Boston Symphony Orchestra*, BSO Classics 171002(1995).

11. Ibid.
12. *Boston Herald*, January 22, 1918.
13. Personal correspondence, Philip Hale to Richard Aldrich, March 17, 1918, Harvard University Houghton Library HOU b MS Am2592 (24), Richard Aldrich papers, 1842–1956. Oswald Garrison Villard (1872–1949), who inherited the *Saturday Evening Post* from his father, was an outspoken pacifist. He ended up selling the newspaper later that year.
14. Ibid.
15. *Boston Herald*, March 26, 1918.
16. *New York Times*, March 26, 1918.
17. *Boston Herald*, March 27, 1918.
18. "Orchestra Feels Dr. Muck's Absence," *Boston Advertiser*, March 30, 1918.
19. In personal correspondence dated April 29, 1918 to Abbott Holker, Secretary, Tavern Club 4/29/1918, Higginson asks Holker to request Muck's resignation, "that Muck hadn't used the club since the start of the war, that Muck probably meant to stay here for the rest of his life, but now would try to get out of the country as soon as possible." Tavern Club Records—Carton 3 3 SH13D3M, Folder: Higginson, Henry L. Massachusetts Historical Society.
20. Personal correspondence, Henry L. Higginson to Philip Hale, October 29, 1918 in "Boston Microfilmed Papers of Henry Lee Higginson concerning the Boston Symphony Orchestra and other Musical Matters from the Baker Memorial Library," Boston Symphony Orchestra Archives, 2000.
21. Personal correspondence, Philip Hale to Henry L. Higginson, November 3, 1918, *loc. cit.*
22. Business correspondence, Henry L. Higginson to United States Attorney General Thomas Watt Gregory, March 13, 1918, in Harvard Business School, *loc. cit.*
23. On this concert Rosamond Young sang three songs with orchestra: Wagner's "Schmerzen," Franck's "La Procession," and Grieg's "Zur Johannisnacht," in *Boston Symphony Archives: Boston Symphony Orchestra Concert Programs, Trip Series, Season 37 (1917–1918)*, Concert 1: Mechanics Hall, Worcester. No program note about her professional or personal life appears. Her first name is spelled "Rosamund" (perhaps Muck's spelling) on the program, yet "Rosamond" on the advertisement for the ill-fated January 15, 1918 Providence concert that appeared in the October 30, 1917 program booklet.
24. Edmund A. Bowles, "Karl Muck and His Compatriots: German Conductors in America during World War I (and How They Coped)," *American Music* XXV, No. 4, p. 434.
25. "Love and Intrigue Mingle in the Story of Karl Muck [,] Departed Orchestra Leader," *The Washington Times*, December 17, 1919. In order to protect her identity, Rosamond Young's name was changed. The following was printed within the article: "This girl, who is known in Washington society circles, and whose name cannot be given because of her loyalty to her country, is known in the publication of the Muck letters as Miss Adele Marvin."
26. The Mann Act, also known as the White-Slave Traffic Act, had been in effect only since June 25, 1910.
27. Bowles, "Karl Muck and His Compatriots," p. 434.
28. Following Anita's death, there may have been more concerning Rosamond Young and Muck. The author has been unable to personally substantiate this, although information from two reliable sources does. According to Brian Bell, Rosamond, upon hearing of Anita's death, went to Germany to be with Muck in 1922 and according to Joseph Horowitz on p. 69n of *Moral Fire* (Berkeley: University of California Press, 2012), a September 30, 1924 clipping from a San Francisco newspaper announced their engagement.
29. Bowles, "Karl Muck and His Compatriots," pp. 425–426.
30. BSO Classics 171002.
31. Personal correspondence, Philip Hale to Richard Aldrich, January 4, 1920, Harvard University Houghton Library HOU b MS Am2592 (24), Richard Aldrich papers, 1842–1956.

32. "Dr. Muck Bitter at Sailing," *New York Times*, August 22, 1919.
33. Personal correspondence, Henry L. Higginson to Wilhelm Gericke, December 28, 1918 in "Boston Microfilmed Papers of Henry Lee Higginson concerning the Boston Symphony Orchestra and other Musical Matters from the Baker Memorial Library," Boston Symphony Orchestra Archives, 2000.
34. Personal correspondence, Philip Hale to Henry L. Higginson, November 3, 1918 in "Boston Microfilmed Papers of Henry Lee Higginson concerning the Boston Symphony Orchestra and other Musical Matters from the Baker Memorial Library," Boston Symphony Orchestra Archives, 2000.
35. Bliss Perry, *The Life and Letters of Henry Higginson* (Boston: Atlantic Monthly Press, 1921), p. 554.
36. *Boston Herald*, November 23, 1918.
37. *Boston Herald*, January 1, 1921.
38. *Boston Herald*, November 1, 1919.
39. Personal correspondence, Philip Hale to Richard Aldrich, January 4, 1920, *loc. cit.*
40. *Boston Herald*, January 24, 1920.
41. Business correspondence, R. C. Ringwall to Frederick P. Cabot, February 6, 1920 in TRUS 49: Frederick R. Cabot Subject Files, Box 4, S-W, Boston Symphony Orchestra Archives.
42. Business correspondence, Boston Symphony Orchestra Members Association to Frederick P. Cabot, February 27, 1920 in TRUS 49: Frederick R. Cabot Subject Files, Box 4, S-W, Boston Symphony Orchestra Archives.
43. Personal correspondence, Frederick P. Cabot to Fredric Fradkin, January 13, 1919 in TRUS 49: Frederick R. Cabot Subject Files, Box 4, S-W, Boston Symphony Orchestra Archives.
44. Business correspondence, Frederick P. Cabot to Jerome H. Remich, March 3, 1920 in TRUS 49: Frederick R. Cabot Subject Files, Box 4, S-W, Boston Symphony Orchestra Archives.
45. Business correspondence, Frederick P. Cabot to Alexander H. Rensselaer, President, Philadelphia Orchestra Association, March 3, 1920 in TRUS 49: Frederick R. Cabot Subject Files, Box 4, S-W, Boston Symphony Orchestra Archives.
46. *Boston Herald*, March 6, 1920.
47. Business correspondence, Frederick P. Cabot to Fredric Fradkin, March 5, 1920 in TRUS 49: Frederick R. Cabot Subject Files, Box 4, S-W, Boston Symphony Orchestra Archives.
48. *Boston Herald*, March 6, 1920.
49. *Boston Herald*, March 7, 1920.
50. *Boston Transcript*, March 10, 1920.
51. "To the Supporters of the Boston Symphony Orchestra," a published pamphlet from the Trustees of the Boston Symphony Orchestra, March 10, 1920 (Boston: Boston Symphony Orchestra, printer unknown).
52. Ibid.
53. Business correspondence, Boston Symphony Orchestra members to Frederick P. Cabot, November 25, 1925 in TRUS 49: Frederick R. Cabot Subject Files, Box 4, S-W, Boston Symphony Orchestra Archives.
54. *Boston Herald*, March 13, 1920.
55. *Boston Herald*, April 2, 1920.
56. *Boston Herald*, April 19, 1920. *The Tower of Babel* choruses performed were "Ham" and "Japheth."
57. *Boston Herald*, March 26, 1921.
58. Richard Burgin, *Memoralia*, Part 1. English version, ed. Diana Lewis Burgin. www.dianaburgin.com,2 011.
59. *Boston Herald*, January 15, 1921.
60. *Boston Herald*, March 5, 1921.
61. *Boston Herald*, January 14, 1922.

62. Louis Leonard Tucker, *The Massachusetts Historical Society; A Bicentennial History, 1791–1991* (Boston: Northeastern University Press, 1995), p. 498.
63. Personal correspondence, Eleanor Melville Metcalf to Philip Hale, October 22, 1921 in Smith College, Mortimer Rare Book Room, William Allen Neilson Library, Philip Hale Collection, Folder 5.
64. Personal correspondence, Philip Hale to Richard Aldrich, April 29, 1923, Harvard University Houghton Library HOU b MS Am2592 (24), Richard Aldrich papers, 1842–1956.
65. Personal correspondence, Philip Hale to Richard Aldrich, November 11, 1923, *loc. cit.*
66. Business correspondence, Philip Hale to Fervis Greenslet, November 25, 1923, Harvard University Houghton Library HOU bMS Am 1925.
67. *Boston Herald*, Saturday, November 11, 1923. Roland Hayes made the Boston area his home, living with his family in Brookline. The Roland Hayes School of Music (named for him), a part of Madison Park High School, is one of only four public high schools in Boston that offers instrumental music.
68. Richard Burgin, *Memoralia*, Part 2. English version, ed. Diana Lewis Burgin. www.dianaburgin.com,2 011.
69. Moses Smith, *Koussevitzky* (New York: Allen, Rowne, & Heath, Inc., 1947), pp. 180–181.
70. *Boston Post*, October 20, 1924.
71. Ibid.
72. Burgin, *Memoralia*, Part 2.
73. *Boston Herald*, October 11, 1924.
74. *Boston Herald*, January 24, 1925.
75. *Boston Herald*, February 21, 1925.
76. *Boston Post*, February 21, 1925. From the article itself, it is evident that Smith did not mean for the phrase "Woman Organist Soloist" to have the same negative connotation as the previous two.
77. *Boston Herald*, January 29, 1927. This review is quoted in its entirety in the Appendices.
78. *Boston Herald*, January 30, 1926.
79. *Boston Herald*, December 11, 1926.
80. Smith, *Koussevitzky*, pp. 162–163. Hale's quote is from the *Boston Herald*, December 13, 1924.
81. *Boston Herald*, April 25, 1925.
82. Ibid.
83. Serge Koussevitzky, "American Composers," in *Life*, XVI, No. 17 (April 24, 1944), p. 56.
84. Koussevitzky's record twenty-five-year tenure was eventually broken by Seiji Ozawa, who served as music director for twenty-nine years. The jet-setting Ozawa, however, did not convey the feeling of vested interest to either the orchestra or the public that Koussevitzky had.
85. *Boston Herald*, January 15, 1926.
86. Brian Bell, liner notes, *The First Recordings of the Boston Symphony Orchestra*, BSO Classics 171002(1995).
87. Ibid.
88. *Boston Herald*, December 21, 1929.
89. Smith, *Koussevitzky*, p. 210.
90. E. R. Warren, untitled and unpublished eulogy in Tavern Club Records, Carton 3, "Philip Hale—folder A," Massachusetts Historical Society: SH13D3M.
91. Smith, *Koussevitzky*, p. 214.
92. At this point in time, The Sunday editions of the *Boston Herald* still had a wide column titled "The Theatre by Philip Hale." While Hale was active as a drama critic for both the amateur and professional levels, for obvious reasons he was never quite as comfortable reviewing theatre as he was with music. The Sunday editions also carried his column, "Concerts."
93. Personal correspondence, Philip Hale to James Lincoln Huntington, n.d., in Massachusetts Historical Society Tavern Club Records—Carton 3, 3 SH13D3M, Folder: Hale, Philip—A (1917–1933).

94. *Boston Herald*, October 5, 1930.
95. *Boston Herald*, October 11, 1930.
96. http://www.bso.org/brands/bso/about-us/historyarchives/archival-collection/bso-commissions.aspx.
97. Arthur Fiedler (no relation to Max Fiedler) had just begun his long tenure as conductor of the Boston Pops.
98. English author Sir Thomas Browne (1605–1689).
99. *Boston Herald*, December 20, 1930.
100. Ibid.
101. Howard Pollack, *Aaron Copland: The Life and Work of an Uncommon Man* (New York: Henry Holt & Co., 1999), pp. 147–148.
102. That is, if this were indeed one of the commissioned works. It is listed by Smith, *Koussevitzky*, pp. 217–218, though it is not listed on the Boston Symphony Orchestra website: http://www.bso.org/brands/bso/about-us/historyarchives/archival-collection/bso-commissions.aspx.
103. Personal correspondence, Philip Hale to Frances Sharf Fink, April 27, 1930, in Harvard University Houghton Library [bMS Am 1954 (8), Frances Sharf Fink letters, 1929–1930.
104. Personal correspondence, Philip Hale to Richard Aldrich, April 17, 1932, in Harvard University Houghton Library HOU b MS Am2592 (24), Richard Aldrich papers, 1842–1956.
105. Personal Correspondence, Philip Hales to James [Lincoln Huntington], August 28, 1931 in Massachusetts Historical Society: Tavern Club Records, Carton 3, 3 SH13D3M. Hale was an ex-officio member of the Executive Committee at this time and about ready to begin his second stint as vice president.
106. Personal Correspondence, Mark Antony DeWolfe Howe to Philip Hale, October 6, 1931, in Harvard University Houghton Library bMS Am 1826 (261), Mark Antony DeWolfe Howe papers.
107. Personal correspondence, Philip Hale to Richard Aldrich, July 21, 1932, in Harvard University Houghton Library HOU b MS Am2592 (24), Richard Aldrich papers, 1842–1956.
108. *Boston Herald*, March 28, 1931.
109. *Boston Herald*, December 19, 1931.
110. Haydn's original instrumentation was two oboes, two horns, and strings. In his often-used arrangement, Belgian composer François-Auguste Gervaert (1828–1908) expanded the instrumentation to include pairs of flutes, clarinets, and bassoons as well. There were also other adaptations.
111. *Boston Herald*, April 2, 1932.
112. *Boston Herald*, March 25, 1933.
113. Actually, there were a number of concertos now in the core repertoire that Hale did not hear. For example, Beethoven's *Piano Concerto No. 1 in C*, Op. 15 was performed once, on a Monday concert in 1932. Hale wrote program notes for it, but did not review the concert. Beethoven's *Piano Concerto No. 2 in B flat*, Op. 19 wasn't even performed by the Boston Symphony Orchestra until 1946, and not at Symphony Hall until 1953.
114. Gustav Holst also conducted the Boston Symphony Orchestra in Haydn's *Symphony No. 99 in E flat* in January, 1932, but the concert was in Providence, not at Symphony Hall.
115. *Boston Herald*, April 1, 1933.

6 Aftermath and Conclusion: 1933–1936

1. Abbott Lawrence Lowell quoted by Carl Engel in "Philip Hale," *The Musical Quarterly*, XXII, No. 1 (January, 1936), pp. 114–115.
2. St. Botolph Club.

3. Personal Correspondence, Philip Hale to Owen Wister, September 7, 1933, Massachusetts Historical Society Tavern Club Records—Carton 3 3 SH13D3M, Folder: Hale, Philip—A (1917–1933).
4. *New York Times*, November 19, 1933.
5. *Minneapolis Tribune*, December 3, 1933.
6. Moses Smith, *Koussevitzky* (New York: Allen, Towne & Heath, 1947), pp. 243–244.
7. Ibid.,p .2 47.
8. *San Francisco Chronicle*, December 3, 1933.
9. Irene Hale, miscellaneous notes, Smith College, William Allen Neilson Memorial Library, Mortimer Rare Book Room, Folder 12.
10. Massachusetts Historical Society Tavern Club Records—Carton 3 3 SH13D3M, Folder: Hale, Philip—B (1934–1936).
11. Robert Hichens, *Susie's Career: A Novel by Robert Hichens* (London: Cassell and Co., Ltd., 1935), Irene Hale's personal copy, Smith College, William Allen Neilson Memorial Library, Mortimer Rare Book Room.
12. E. R. Warren, untitled and unpublished eulogy in Tavern Club Records, Carton 3, "Philip Hale—folder A," Massachusetts Historical Society: SH13D3M.
13. Engel, "Philip Hale," pp. 114–115.
14. Walter R. Spalding, "Philip Hale" in *American Scholar*, Vol. 4, No. 2 (1935), p. 242, carbon copy at Smith College, William Allen Neilson Memorial Library, Mortimer Rare Book Room.
15. Olin Downes, "Philip Hale—His Genius as a Critic" in "Friends of the Boston Symphony Orchestra Second Annual Meeting" (Boston: Boston Symphony Orchestra, 1936), pp. 15–16.

Bibliography

Books

Burgin, Diana Lewis. *Richard Burgin: A Life in Verse.* Columbus, OH: Slavica Publishers, 1989. 2nd ed. www.dianaburgin.com, 2007.
Burgin, Richard. *Memoralia.* St. Petersburg, Russia: Inapress, 2011, Rusian version ed. Diana Lewis Burgin. English version, ed. Diana Lewis Burgin. www.dianaburgin.com, 2011.
Burk, John N. (ed.). *Philip Hale's Boston Symphony Programme Notes: Historical, Critical, and Descriptive Comment on Music and Composers,* 2nd printing. New York: Garden City Publishing Co., 1939.
Eaton, Quaintence. *The Boston Opera Company.* New York: Appleton-Century, 1965.
Elson, Louis Charles. *The History of American Music.* New York: Macmillan, 1904.
Faucett, Bill F. *George Whitefield Chadwick: The Life and Music of the Pride of New England.* Boston: Northeastern University Press, 2012.
Federal Writers' Project of the Works Progress Administration for the State of Massachusetts. *The WPA Guide to Massachusetts.* New York: Pantheon Books, 1983. Reprint, originally published as *Massachusetts: A Guide to Its Places and People.* Boston: Houghton Mifflin, 1937.
Gienow-Hecht, Jessica C. E. *Sound Diplomacy: Music and Emotions in Trans-Atlantic Relations, 1850–1920.* Chicago: University of Chicago Press, 2009.
Gilman, Lawrence. *Strauss' Salomé: A Guide to the Opera with Musical Illustrations.* New York: John Lane Co., 1907.
Grant, Mark N. *Maestros of the Pen: A History of Classical Music Criticism in America.* Boston: Northeastern University Press, 1998.
Hale, Robert Safford. *Geneology of Descendants of Thomas Hale of Watton, England and of Newbury, Massachusetts.* Albany, NY: Weed, Parsons, & Co., 1889.
Hichens, Robert. *Susie's Career: A Novel by Robert Hichens.* London: Cassell and Co., Ltd., 1935.
Horowitz, Joseph. *Classical Music in America: A History of Its Rise and Fall.* New York: Norton, 2005.
———. *Moral Fire: Musical Portraits from America's Fin de Siècle.* Berkeley: University of California Press, 2012.
Howe, Mark Anthony DeWolfe. *The Boston Symphony Orchestra: An Historical Sketch.* Boston and New York: Houghton-Mifflin, 1914.
———. *The Boston Symphony Orchestra, 1881–1931.* Boston and New York: Houghton-Mifflin, 1931.
Howell, George Rogers and Tenney, Jonathan (eds). *Bi-centennial History of Albany and Schenectady Counties, New York.* New York: W. W. Munsell & Co., 1886.
Huneker, James Gibbons. *Steeplejack,* Vol. II. New York: Charles Scribner's Sons, 1920.
Johnson H. Earle. *Symphony Hall, Boston.* Boston: Little, Brown, & Co., 1950.
Robert Kirzinger, Kim Noltemy-Ugorji, Caroline Smedwig, Mark Volpe, and Bridget P. Carr (eds.). *Symphony Hall: The First 100 Years.* Boston: The Boston Symphony Orchestra, 2000.
Knight, Ellen E. *Charles Martin Loeffler: A Life Apart in American Music.* Urbana and Chicago: University of Illinois Press, 1993.

McCormick, Charles Howard. *Hopeless Cases: The Hunt for the Red Scare Terrorist Bombers.* Lanham, MD: University Press of America, 2005.

Miller, Edwin Havilland (ed.). *The Collected Writings of Walt Whitman, Vol. III: 1876–1885.* New York: New York University Press, 1964.

Mott, Frank L. *A History of American Magazines, 1865–1885.* Boston: Harvard University Press, 1938. 4th printing. London: Oxford University Press, 1970.

The National Cyclopaedia of American Biography. New York: James T. White & Co., 1910.

Ogasapian, John. *Music of the Colonial and Revolutionary Era.* Westport, CT: The Greenwood Group, 2004.

Ogasapian, John and Orr, N. Lee. *Music of the Gilded Age.* Westport, CT: Greenwood Publishing Group, 2007.

Perry, Bliss. *The Life and Letters of Henry Lee Higginson.* Boston: The Atlantic Monthly Press, 1921.

Pisani, Michael. *Imagining Native America in Music.* New Haven: Yale University Press, 2005.

Pollack, Howard. *Aaron Copland: The Life and Work of an Uncommon Man.* New York: Henry Holt & Co., 1999.

Saloman, Ora Frishberg. *Beethoven's Symphonies and J. S. Dwight: The Birth of American Music Criticism.* Boston: Northeastern University Press, 1995.

———. *Listening Well: On Beethoven, Berlioz and Other Music Criticism in Paris, Boston, and New York, 1764–1890.* New York: Peter Lang, 2009.

Schabas, Ezra. *Theodore Thomas: America's Conductor and Builder of Orchestras, 1835–1905.* Urbana and Chicago: University of Illinois Press, 1989.

Slonimsky, Nicolas (ed.). *Lexicon of Musical Invective: Critical Assaults on Composers Since Beethoven's Time*, 2nd ed. Seattle: University of Washington Press, 1965.

———. (ed.). *The Concise Baker's Biographical Dictionary of Music*, 8th ed. New York: Schirmer Books, 1994.

Smith, Moses. *Koussevitzky.* New York: Allen, Towne, and Heath, 1947.

Solti, Georg. *Memoirs.* New York: Alfred P. Knopf, 1997.

Stebbins, Richard Poate. *The Making of Symphony Hall, Boston: A History with Documents.* Boston: Boston Symphony Orchestra, 2000.

Tawa, Nicholas E. *From Psalm to Symphony: A History of Music in New England.* Boston: Northeastern University Press, 2001.

Tucker, Louis Leonard. *The Massachusetts Historical Society: A Bicentennial History, 1791–1991.* Boston: Northeastern University Press, 1995.

Ullery, Jacob G. and Huse, Hiram (eds). *Men of Vermont: An Illustrated Biographical History of Vermonters and Sons of Vermont.* Brattleboro, VT: Transcript Publishing Co., 1894.

Wagner, Mary H. *Gustav Mahler and the New York Philharmonic Tour America.* Lenham, MD: The Scarecrow Press, 2006.

Whitman, Walt. *Democratic Vistas.* Walt Whitman, 1871.

———. *Leaves of Grass. 1855.* New York: Library of American Poets/Collectors Reprints, 1992.

Whitwell, David. *The Longy Club: A Professional Wind Ensemble in Boston (1900–1917).* Northridge (Los Angeles), CA: WINDS (Wind Instrument New Dawn Society), 1988.

Articles

Aldrich, Richard. "Henry Edward Krehbiel." *Music & Letters*, IV, No. 3 (1923), pp. 266-268.

Beckerman, Michael. "Henry Krehbiel, Antonín Dvorak, and the Symphony 'From the New World.'" *Notes*, XLIX, No. 2 (December, 1992), pp. 447-473.

Bowles, Edmund A. "Karl Muck and His Compatriots: German Conductors in America during World War I (And How They Coped)." *American Music*, XXV, No. 4 (Winter, 2007), pp. 405-440.

Burkat, Leonard and Fox, Pamela. "Boston 5: Opera and Musical Theatre" in *Grove Music Online*. http://www.grovemusic.com.
Davies, James. "Tribute paid to Boston Critic, Retiring at 79." *Minneapolis Tribune*, December 3, 1933.
Downes, Olin. "Philip Hale's Work: Contribution of Distinguished Critic Who for a Period Lays Down his Pen." *New York Times*, November 19, 1933.
Dwight, John Sullivan. "The History of Music in Boston," in Windsor, Justin (ed.), *The Memorial History of Boston Including Suffolk County, 1630–1880*. Boston: Ticknor & Co., 1881, p. 416.
Engel, Carl. "Philip Hale." *The Musical Quarterly*, XXII, No. 1 (January, 1936), pp. 114–116.
Hale, Philip. "Musical and Theatrical Life in a New England Village in the Sixties." *Massachusetts Historical Society Proceedings 56* (paper presented June 14, 1923), pp. 335–343.
———. "Walt Whitman." *The Yale Literary Magazine*, XL, No. 2 (November, 1874), pp. 96–104.
———. "Review of the 5th Symphony Concert." *The Musical Record* (Boston), No. 428 (September, 1897), p. 11.
Horowitz, Joseph. "Moral Fire: Convocation Speech to the Graduating Class of 2012." *Sonorities: The News Magazine of the University of Illinois School of Music* (Winter, 2013), pp. 20–21.
Johnson, H. Earle. "*The Folio* of White, Smith and Company." *American Music*, II, No. 1 (Spring, 1984), pp. 88–104.
Kenny, Ellen. "Some Letters to Emil Paur." *Notes*, VIII, No. 4 (September, 1951), pp. 631–649.
Klemm, Gustav. "Gustav Strube: The Man and Musician." *The Musical Quarterly*, XXVIII, No. 3 (July, 1942), p. 293.
Koussevitzky, Serge. "American Composers." *Life*, XVI, No. 17 (April 24, 1944), pp. 55–56, 58, and 60–62.
Loring, William C. Jr., "Arthur Bird, American." *The Musical Quarterly*, 29, No. 1, January, 1943, pp. 78–91.
"Love and Intrigue Mingle in the Story of Karl Muck, Deported Orchestra Leader." *Washington Times*, December 17, 1919, p. 12.
Mitchell, Jon Ceander. "Critical Glimpses: Philip Hale's Correspondence to Charles Martin Loeffler, 1905–1908." *Journal of the College Orchestra Directors Association*, III (2010), pp. 30–39.
———. "Hale and Wind: Philip Hale's Commentaries on Wind Ensemble Works programmed by the Boston Symphony Orchestra, 1890 to 1932." *Kongressbericht Echternach, Luxembourg, 2008*. Tutzing, Germany: Haus Hans Schneider, 2010, pp. 263–282.
Schwartz, Lloyd. "So Long, Seiji." *Boston Phoenix*, April 25–May 2, 2002.
Smith, Warren Storey. "Four Distinguished Music Critics—A Centennial Note." *Musical America*, February 15, 1954, pp. 6, 130, and 134.
Spalding, Walter R. "Philip Hale," in *American Scholar*, 4, No. 2 (1935), pp. 241–242.

Unpublished Documents

Boyd, Jean Ann. "Philip Hale: American Music Critic, Boston, 1889–1933." Unpublished PhD dissertation, University of Texas at Austin, 1985.
Mahinka, Janice L. "Philip Hale: A Crucial Link in the History of American Music Criticism." Unpublished MA dissertation, Graduate School of Arts and Sciences, Boston University, 2009.
Markow, Robert. "The Music Criticism of Philip Hale: The Boston Symphony Orchestra Concerts 1889–1933." Unpublished MA dissertation, McGill University, 1981.
Nelson, Robert B. "The Commentaries and Criticisms of William Foster Apthorp." Unpublished PhD dissertation, University of Florida, 1991.

Richmond, David L. "Debussy in Boston's Imagination: The Performance of Sensuality (1902–1907)." Unpublished AB Honors dissertation, Department of Music, Harvard College, 2006.

Stebbins, Richard Poate. "Inventory of the Microfilmed Papers of Henry Lee Higginson concerning the Boston Symphony Orchestra and other Musical Matters from the Baker Memorial Library, Harvard Business School." Compiled for the Boston Symphony Orchestra Archives, 2000.

Tedesco, John R. "A History of Opera in Boston." Unpublished MM thesis, University of Massachusetts Amherst, 2010.

Turk, Gayle Kathryn. "The Case of Dr. Karl Muck: Anti-German Hysteria and Enemy Alien Internment during World War I." Unpublished AB Honors Dissertation (History), Harvard University, 1994.

Collections

Boston Public Library Philip Hale Collection MS 2468: Correspondence from Philip Hale to Charles Martin Loeffler, 1905–1908.

Boston Public Library Print Department: Postcard Collection.

Boston Symphony Orchestra Archives: Boston Symphony Orchestra Press Clippings Microfilm Collection.

Boston Symphony Orchestra Archives: Boston Symphony Orchestra Program Books Bound Collection.

Boston Symphony Orchestra Archives: Boston Symphony Orchestra Scrapbooks Microfilm Collection.

Boston Symphony Orchestra Archives: HENRY. www.bso.org.

Boston Symphony Orchestra Archives: "Microfilmed Papers of Henry Lee Higginson concerning the Boston Symphony Orchestra and other Musical Matters from the Baker Memorial Library, Harvard Business School," 2000.

Boston Symphony Orchestra Archives: TRUS 49: Frederick P. Cabot Subject Files, Box 4, S-W.

Boston Symphony Orchestra Archives: Works Performance History Catalog.

Frances Sharf Fink Letters from Various Correspondents, 1924–1963 (MS Am 1954). Houghton Library, Harvard University.

Massachusetts Historical Society: St. Botolph Club Records. Carton 4: SH 18 CL: B: Officers' Correspondence and Carton 6: Member Lists.

Massachusetts Historical Society: Tavern Club Records. Carton 3: SH 13 D3M.

Massachusetts Historical Society: Thursday Evening Club Records, 1846–1999: Cartons 1: SH 15 EVA and 3: SH 15 EXC.

Mortimer Rare Book Room, William Allen Neilson Library, Smith College, Northampton, MA: Philip Hale Papers.

Richard Aldrich Papers (MS Am 2592). Houghton Library, Harvard University.

Rogers Memorial Collection (MS Thr 470). Houghton Library, Harvard University.

Wilhelm Gericke Papers (MS Mus 132–132.1). Houghton Library, Harvard University.

Other

Boston Music Herald, XIII, Nos. 1–12 (November, 1891–October, 1892).

Boston Symphony Orchestra CD: *The First Recordings of the Boston Symphony Orchestra*. BSO Classics 171002.

Bowman, John S. (ed.). "Musical and Theatrical Life in a New England Village in the Sixties: A Paper Delivered on June 14, 1923 before The Massachusetts Historical Society by Philip Hale." Northampton, MA (Massachusetts Historical Society), 2010.

Clark, Robert S. Record Jacket Notes for *MacDowell: Suite for Large Orchestra; Suite No. 2 "Indian,"* Eastman-Rochester Orchestra, Howard Hanson, conductor. Mercury Golden Imports SRI 75026 (n.d.).

"Elm Street Historic District: Round Hill Road Expansion Preliminary Report." Northampton, Massachusetts, December 14, 2011.

"Friends of the Boston Symphony Orchestra Second Annual Meeting." Boston: Boston Symphony Orchestra, 1936.

Handel & Haydn Society Concert Program, February 20, 1853. American Antiquarian Society BDSDS.1853.

http://www.bso.org/brands/bso/about-us/historyarchives/archival-collection/bso commissions.aspx.

http://www.dvoraknyc.org/Dvorak_in_America.html. Dvorak American Heritage Association.

http://www.ripm.org/journal_info.php5?ABB=MUW. Randi Trzesinski, "The Musical World, Boston 1901–1904."

Library of Congress Performing Arts Encyclopedia. http://lcweb2.loc.gov/diglib/ihas/loc.natlib.ihas.200153251

The Panama-Pacific International Exposition Official View Book, 3rd ed. San Francisco: Robert A. Reid, 1915. Forty-eight page pamphlet with no page numbers.

The Rules of the Tavern Club of Boston, with a List of the Officers & Members. Cambridge, MA: University Press, 1894. Also editions of 1904, 1912, 1918, 1922–1923, 1926–1927, 1930, 1932.

Trustees of the Boston Symphony orchestra, Frederick P. Cabot, President, "To the Supporters of the Boston Symphony Orchestra," published letter in pamphlet form dated March 10, 1920 (Boston: Boston Symphony Orchestra, printer unknown).

Index

Abel, Carl Friedrich, 132
Adamovsky, Josef, 112, 269
Albany, New York, 12, 15, 16, 17, 18, 22, 27, 43
Albany Express, 15
Albany Music Association, 12
Albany Philharmonic Society, 15
Albany Times, 1, 2, 13, 17, 264n29
Albany Union, 2, 15
Alboni, Marietta, 66
Alcantera, Mr., 79
Alcock, Merle, 128, 131, 133
Aldrich, Richard, 78–9, 128, 136, 141, 151–2
Aldrich, Mrs. Richard, 78
Alien Enemies Act, 123
American Federation of Musicians, 145
American Orchestral Society, 271n75
American Scholar, 174
Anderson, George Weston, 133
Ansermet, Ernst, 165
Apollo Club, Boston, 22, 78
Apollo Singing Society, Albany, 15
Apthorp, William Foster, 27, 43–6, 73, 77, 84, 163
  "Musicians and Music Lovers," 43
  "Some Thoughts on Music Criticism," 43–4
Arbós, E. Fernandez, 81, 96, 158
Arcadia, Detroit, 271
Arden, Edwin Hunter Pendleton, 16
Arlington Club, 78
Arnedo, 78
Arnold, Matthew, 152
Artaria Music Publishers, Vienna, 120
L'Association Artistique du Châtelet, Paris, 14
Association Hall, Boston, 70
Astarte (Ishtar), 43

Athenaeus, 84
Atlantic Monthly, 27
Atwood, Ethel, 26
Auber, Daniel, 84, 159
  La Muette de Portici, 159
  Massaniello, 84

Babylon, 169–70
Bach, Carl Philip Emmanuel
  Concerto in D, 160
Bach, Johann Christian, 132
  Orione, 132
Bach, Johann Sebastian, 12, 17, 29, 32, 36, 37, 67, 105–6, 130–2, 156, 165
  Cantata No. 20, 167
  Cantata No. 85, 167
  Concerto in D minor for Two Violins in D minor, 36
  Orchestral Suite No. 3 in D, 167
  St. Matthew Passion, 130, 131, 132
  Suite for Orchestra, 105–6
Baden, 116
Baernstein, Joseph S., 67
Bagahot, Walter, 107
Ballet Russes, Paris, 137, 141
Baltimore, 104, 127
Baltimore Symphony Orchestra, 104
Band of the, 22nd Regiment, 22
Band of the, 64th (British) Regiment, 22
Bargiel, Woldemar, 14
Barnum, P. T., 98
Bartok, Bela, 2, 3, 159
  Piano Concerto No. 1, 159
Bauer, Harold, 85–6
Baugham, E. T., 152
Baumgras, Mary Brainerd née Thomson, 14
Baumgras, Peter, 14

Bayreuth, 46, 99, 135
Beach, Amy, 3, 51, 54–5
  Symphony in E minor, "Gaelic," Op. 32, 54–5
Beacon, 41
Beecham, [Sir] Thomas, 2, 158
Beethoven, Ludwig van, 3, 21, 29–30, 31, 32, 48, 49, 59, 60, 66, 67, 68, 74, 76, 81, 82, 89, 90, 93, 94, 102, 104, 107, 108, 109–10, 114, 119, 120, 125, 135, 142, 146, 148, 159, 164, 167
  Christ on the Mount of Olives, Op. 85, 21
  Consecration of the House Overture, Op. 124, 82, 164
  Coriolanus Overture, Op. 62, 29
  Egmont Overture, Op. 84, 82, 125
  Grosse Fugue, Op. 134, 120
  Missa Solemnis, Op. 123, 66–7
  Overture to Leonore No. 2, Op. 72, 89
  Overture to Leonore No. 3, Op. 72, 105
  Piano Concerto No. 1 in C, Op. 15, 275n113
  Piano Concerto No. 2 in B flat, Op. 19, 275n113
  Piano Concerto No. 3 in C Minor, Op. 37, 5, 109–10
  Symphony No. 1 in C, Op. 21, 119
  Symphony No. 2 in D, Op. 36, 34, 119
  Symphony No. 3 in E flat, Op. 55, "Eroica," 32, 36, 37, 59, 60, 114, 115, 135
  Symphony No. 4 in B flat, Op. 60, 93, 145, 146
  Symphony No. 5 in C minor, Op. 67, 3, 23, 29–30, 33, 34, 66, 68, 108
  Symphony No. 7 in A, Op. 92, 32, 74, 76, 104
  Symphony No. 8 in F, Op. 93, 90, 91
  Symphony No. 9 in D minor, Op. 125, 23, 35, 81, 82, 90
  Violin Concerto, Op. 61, 49
Belcher, Supply, 21
Bell, Alexander Graham, 112
Bell, Brian, 271n83, 272n28, 274n86
Bellini, Vincenzo
  Norma, 66

Bendix, Max, 58
Berlin, 14, 16, 31, 44, 46, 54, 56, 69, 71, 73, 92, 97, 98, 99, 102, 11, 114, 134, 138
Berlin Philharmonic Orchestra, 97
Berlin Royal Opera House, 98, 102, 114
Berliner Börsen Courier, 71
Berlioz, Hector, 31, 44, 45, 88, 95, 105–6, 107, 114, 140, 142, 143, 153, 167
  Benvenuto Cellini, 44, 88
  The Damnation of Faust, 88
  Dance of the Sylphs, 88
  The Flight into Egypt, 153
  Harold in Italy (*Childe Harold*), 45, 140
  King Lear, 88
  "My Heart with Grief is Heavy," 88
  "The Repose of the Holy Family," 153
  Roman Carnival Overture, 114
  Romeo et Julliette, 45, 88
  Symphonie Fantastique, 88, 105–6, 142, 143
  Les Troyens, 88
  Waverly Overture, 95
Bernard, Anthony, 153
Bernard, Paul, 70
Bernsdorf, Eduard, 53
Bible, 11, 169
  Vulgate Verses, 165
Billings, William, 21
  "Chester," 21
Bird, Arthur, 31, 70, 71
Bizet, Georges, 44, 110, 159
  L'Arlesienne, 44, 110
  Carmen, 159
Bloch, Ernest, 141, 150, 166
  Psalm 114, 137, 141
Boettcher, Georg, 168
Boito, Arrigo
  Mefistofele, 103
Bonn, 73, 146
Borgault-Ducoudray, Louis-Albert, 17
Borodin, Alexander, 31, 142, 143
  On the Steppes of Central Asia, 142
Boston Academy of Music, 22
Boston Advertiser, 27, 39, 133
Boston Brahmins, 3, 35

Index

Boston Brigade Band, 22
Boston Conservatory, 23
Boston Courier, 27
Boston Daily Advertiser, 27
Boston Daily Traveler, 27
Boston Evening American, 173
Boston Evening Transcript, 27, 46
Boston Festival Orchestra, 64
Boston Flute Players Club, 26
Boston Globe, 65, 115, 173
Boston Grand Opera Company, 26, 173
Boston Herald, 2, 27, 36, 39, 83, 86, 102, 109, 114, 129, 144, 152, 163, 166, 171, 172, 173, 275n94, 95, 99, 108, 109, 111, 112, 115
Boston Home Journal, 2, 27, 28, 31, 34, 36, 40
Boston Ideal Opera Co. (a.k.a. The Bostonians), 17, 22
Boston Journal, 2, 36, 40, 41, 73, 78, 83
Boston Music Fund Society, 23
Boston Musical Association, 70
Boston Musical Herald, 2, 39, 40, 41
Boston Musicians' Protective Association, 144
Boston Opera Company, 1, 26, 103
Boston Opera House, 143
Boston Orchestral Club, 26
Boston Philharmonic Society, 23
Boston Pops, 72, 104, 131
Boston Post, 2, 36, 39, 76, 135, 151, 154, 158
 "The Taverner," 36
Boston Public Library, 64
Boston Saxophone Orchestra, 26
Boston Singers, The, 78
Boston Singers Club, 78
Boston Singers Society, 78
Boston Symphony Orchestra, 1–5, 16, 2, 24, 25, 28, 31, 35, 36, 39, 41, 43, 46, 47, 49, 52, 55, 56, 57, 61, 63, 64, 65, 71, 73, 76, 77, 81, 82, 83, 84, 86, 88, 89, 91, 92, 94, 96, 97, 98, 99, 102, 104, 109, 114, 115, 118, 119, 120, 121, 123–9, 131, 134–7, 139, 141–9, 153–5, 161–4, 168, 169, 171–4, 275n102, 113, 114
Boston Symphony Orchestra Members Association, 141

Boston Symphony Orchestra Pension Fund, 81, 82, 90, 91, 96, 147
Boston Symphony Orchestra Quartet, 100
Boston Times, 42, 174
Boston Transcript, 42, 76
Bostonians, The. *See* Boston Ideal Opera Co.
Boulanger, Nadia, 3, 157–8
Bowles, Edmund A., 269n30
Bowman, John S., 280
Boye-Jensen, Margaret, 65
Boyle, George, 151
 Piano Concerto in D minor, 151
Boyleston Club, 78
Boynton, Thomas Jefferson, 129
Braham, David, 38
Brahms, Johannes, 2, 4, 5, 32, 35, 38, 41, 48, 57, 58, 59, 69, 73–5, 84, 85, 90, 102, 107, 108, 135, 148, 162
 Academic Festival Overture, Op. 80, 41, 73–5, 88, 135
 Double Concerto in A minor, Op. 102, 58
 Hungarian Dances, Set I, 69
 Symphony No. 1 in C minor, Op. 68, 35
 Symphony No. 2 in D, Op. 73, 35, 84
 Tragic Overture, Op. 81, 59
 Variations on a Theme by Haydn, Op. 56b, 32
 "Vier cruste Gesange," 69
 Violin Concerto, Op. 77, 108
Breese, IL, 123
Brennan, William H., 148, 151
Breslau, 45, 73
Breton, Tomas, 78
 Dolores, 78, 79
Bristow, George, 51
Brookline, MA, 161
Brooklyn, 12, 131, 157
Brown, Allen A., 66, 97
Brown, F. Potter, 17
Browne, Sir Thomas, 165
Bruch, Max, 115, 116, 149, 164
 Achilleus, 164
 Arminius, 164
 Concerto No. 1 for Violin in G minor, 150
 The Cross of Fire, 115
 Odysseus, 164

Bruckner, Anton, 89–90, 92, 148, 159
  Symphony No. 9 in D minor, 89–90, 92
  Te Deum, 89
Bruneau, Alfred, 84–6
  Messidor, 84–5
  L'Ouragan, 85
  The Sleeping Beauty, 85
Brünn, 126
Brussels, 71, 97, 165
Buck, Dudley, 12
Buckle, Henry Thomas, 159
Budapest, 46, 47
Bülow, Hans von, 24, 59, 60, 85, 139
  Funerale, Op. 23, No. 4, 59
  Julius Caesar, Op. 10, 60
Bumcke, Gustav, 70
Bumstead Hall, Boston, 64
Burgin, Richard, 2, 81, 148, 154, 155
Burk, John Nagley, 5, 173, 263n9, 269n34
  Philip Hale's Boston Symphony Program Notes, 5, 263n9, 269n34
Busoni, Ferruccio, 3, 109–10, 120
  Turandot Suite, 109–10, 120
Bussine, Romain, 14
"By-and-By," 153
Byron, Lord, 149

Cabot, Frederick P., 112, 136, 141, 143, 144, 163
Calatazud, Aragon, 79
Calvocoressi, Michel-Dmitri, 153
Cambridge, MA, 21, 38, 71, 117, 118, 129
Camden, NJ, 11, 12, 121
Campanini, Italo, 15–16, 67
Campanini Opera Company, 15–16
Candidus (pen name of Samuel Adams), 67
Capen, C(harles) L(emuel), 27–8
Caplet, André, 70
Carreño, Teresa, 3, 4
Caruso, Enrico, 119
Cary, Annie Louise, 67, 164
Casella, Alfredo, 150, 158
Cassado, Gaspar, 168
Cassidy, Claudia, 4
Castellanoi, Mme., 79
Catlin, George, 53

Cecilia Society, Boston, 22, 43, 78, 100, 165, 169
Celler, 45
Cervantes, Miguel de, 92
  Don Quixote, 92
Chabrier, Emmanuel, 99, 141
  Bouree Fantastique, 141
  Gwendoline, 99
Chadwick, George Whitefield, 37–8, 49, 50, 51, 76, 119, 140
  Angel of Death, 140
  Symphonic Sketches, 119
  Symphony No. 2 in B flat, Op. 32, 37–8, 50, 51, 267n77
Chaminade Club, Providence, 125
Chanler, Theodor Ward, 173
Chattanooga, TN, 135
Cherubini, Luigi, 120, 167
  The Abercerrages, 120
  Requiem in C, 167
Chesterian, 150
Chicago, 4, 26, 39, 41, 46, 47, 53, 56, 68, 69, 85, 89, 93, 116, 159, 164
Chicago Lyric Opera, 4
Chicago Opera Association, 143
Chicago Opera Company, 103
Chicago Symphony Orchestra (a.k.a Theodore Thomas Orchestra), 4, 26, 56, 88, 120
Chicago Tribune, 4
Chickering Hall, Boston, 116
Chopin, Frédéric, 39, 54
  Piano Concerto No. 2 in F minor, Op. 21, 39, 54
Chopin Club, Providence, 125
Choral Art Society, Boston, 78
Christian Science Monitor, 166, 173
Christiania (Oslo), 148
Church Music Association, New York, 67
Cincinnati, 14, 48, 67, 93, 135
Cincinnati Conservatory of Music, 14
Cincinnati Gazette, 48
Cincinnati Symphony Orchestra, 135
Cleveland, 169
Cleveland, Bessie, 17
Cleveland Symphony Orchestra, 169
Clifton, Chalmers, 118, 158, 271n75
Colles, H. C., 152
Cologne (Köln), 31, 58

Colonne, Eduard, 14, 31
Comee, Frederick, 72, 74
Concert de la Loge Olympique, Paris, 139
Concert des Amateurs, Paris, 139
Conrad, A. Z., 124, 126
Conreid, Heinrich, 101
Constitution Hall, 165
Converse, Frederick, 51, 151
   Symphony in C minor, 151
Cooper, James Fennimore, 53
Copland, Aaron, 157–9, 166
   Music for the Theatre, 158
   Piano Concerto, 158
   Symphonic Ode, 166
   Symphony for Organ and Orchestra, 157–9
   Two Pieces for String Orchestra, 158
Corona, Mme., 79
Cossart, Leland A., 70
Couperin, François, 29
Coussemaker, Charles Edmund Henri de, 45
Cowen, Frederic, 45–6
   Harold, 46
   Pauline, 46
   Signa, 46
   Thorgrim, 46
Cranch, Emma, 67
Currier, T. P., 39
Cutter, Benjamin, 39
Czernowitz, 57

Daily Telegraph (London), 151
Damrosch, Walter, 124, 126, 141, 157, 271n6
Darmstadt, 126
Dartmouth College, 73, 162
Daudet, Alphonse
   Tartarin de Tarascon, 31
Davenport, Ambrose, 27
Davenport, Warren, 27, 39, 42, 43
Davies, James, 172
Davison, Archibald T., 147
De Quincy, Thomas, 169
De Vere, Elise, 15, 67
De Voto, Alfred, 131
de Wally, Paul, 70
Debussy, Claude, 30, 70, 104, 115, 116, 119, 143, 148–50
   La Mer, 148–50

   Nocturnes, 116
   Pelleas et Mellisande, 143
DeKoven, Reginald, 53, 63
Delano, Alina, 42
   "Opinions of Rubinstein" (trans.), 42
Denayer, Frédéric, 140
Denner, J. C., 132
Destinn, Emmy, 134
Detroit, 271n8
Detroit Symphony Orchestra, 141
Dewey, Judd, 129
Diaghilev, Serge, 137
Dickens, Charles
   Great Expectations, 160
Diderot, Denis, 156
Diémer, Louis, 70
d'Indy, Vincent, 30, 69, 70, 94, 95, 99
   Ishtar, 94
   Symphony No. 2 in B flat, 94
   Wallenstein's Camp, 69
Dohnányi, Ernö, 151
   Violin Concerto, 151
Dole, Nathan Haskell, 39
Donizetti, Gaetano, 107
   La Fille du Regiment, 66
Donner, Oscar W., 46, 47
Dowden, Edward, 264n9
Downes, Olin, 3, 30, 151, 163, 172, 174, 263n2, 276n15
   "Philip Hale—His Genius as a Critic," 263n2, 276n15
Downing, Andrew Jackson, 9
Dresden, 16, 31, 97, 100, 120
Dresden Court Opera, 100
Dresden Royal Orchestra, 97
DuBois, Théodore, 17
Dukas, Paul, 70, 93, 94, 269n15
   Polyeacte, 93
   The Sorcerer's Apprentice, 93, 94
Duncan, Isadora, 104
Duparc, Henri, 141
   "Invitation au Voyage," 141
Dvořák, Antonin, 43, 48, 49, 50, 51, 52, 53, 76, 89, 119, 153
   Carnival Overture, 52
   Concerto for Violoncello in B minor, 49, 52
   Czech Suite, Op. 39, 51
   "Gute Nacht," 89
   Serenade for Strings in E, Op. 22, 51

Dvořák, Antonin—*Continued*
   Serenade for Winds in D minor, Op.
     44, 51, 70
   Symphony No. 7 in D minor, Op. 70,
     153
   Symphony No. 8 in G, Op. 88, 47
   *Symphony No. 9 in E minor, "From the
     New World,"* Op. 95, 48–51, 53
   Violin Concerto, 49, 52
Dwight, John Sullivan, 24, 27, 30, 95,
   265n5, 8, 13, 20
   The History of Music in Boston,"
     265n5, 8, 13, 20
Dwight's Journal of Music, 27

Eastman-Rochester Orchestra, 267n87
Edison, Thomas Alva, 112
Egdon Heath, 116
Eisleven (Eisleben), 132
Ellis, Charles A., 65, 72, 74, 99, 124–6,
   130, 135
Elman, Misha, 108, 109
Elson, Louis Charles, 23, 28, 39, 77,
   265n10
   The History of American Music, 265n10
Enesco, George, 70
Engel, Carl, 174
Epstein, Julius, 26
Ernst, Harold E., 112, 270n62
Espionage Act of, 1917, 123
Esterhazy, Prince Nicolas, 168
Euterpe Chamber Music Society, 78
*The Euterpiad, or Musical
   Intelligencer,* 27
Evening Bulletin, 124
Exeter Academy, Exeter New
   Hampshire, 10

F. I. Ilsley & Co., Albany, 12
Fadette Ladies' Orchestra, Boston, 26
Faelten, Carl, 76
Faisst, Immanuel Gottlob Friedrich, 14
Falconi, Alfonso, 70
Fantasia (Disney film), 269n15
Farrar, Geraldine, 100
Faure, Gabriel, 70, 94, 95, 110, 139
   Pelleas et Melisande, 94, 95, 110
Fay, Elise, 101
Fay, Mr., 101
Federal Music Project of New York,
   271n75

Feliú y Codina, José, 79
Ferir, Émile, 86, 111
Fiedler, Arthur, 165, 169, 275n97
Fiedler, August Max, 2, 82, 102, 109,
   110, 111, 114, 275n97
Finck, Henry Theophilus, 39, 76, 77, 151
Fink, Frances Sharf, 166
First New England School, 21
First Religious Society (Unitarian)
   Church, Roxbury (Boston), 16,
   19, 27
Fitz, Reginald, 112
Flagg, Josiah, 22
The Folio, 27
Fontainebleau, 157
Foote, Arthur, 112
Forest, Armand, 70
Fort Oglethorpe, GA, 135
Foster, Muriel, 89
Fradkin, Frederic, 81, 141, 142
France, Anatole, 101, 269n38
   Pierre Nozièr, 101
Franck, César, 14, 30, 31, 67, 69, 94,
   99, 116, 141
   "La Procession," 272n23
   Psyche and Cupid, 94
   Redemption, 141
   Symphony in D minor, 99, 115
Frankfurt, 31
Franz, Robert, 132
Fried, Oskar, 70
Friends of the Boston Symphony
   Orchestra, 174, 263n2
Frijsh, Povia, 141
Fry, William Henry, 51

Gadski, Johanna, 107
Galassi, Antonio, 16, 67
Garcin, Jules, 31
Gardner, Isabella Stewart, 36, 103
Gaugengigl, Ignaz, 100
Gebhard, Heinrich, 70, 143, 145, 146
Gérardy, Paul, 75–6
Gericke, Miss, 97
Gericke, Mrs., 97
Gericke, Wilhelm, 2, 26, 28, 29, 31, 61,
   64, 67, 75, 76, 81, 84, 86, 87, 88,
   89, 90, 91, 92, 93, 95, 97, 98, 99,
   100, 128, 136, 141, 154, 155, 169
Germania Orchestra, 13, 23
Germania Serenade Band, 66

Index

Gershwin, George, 3, 159
   Second Rhapsody, 159
Gervaert, François-Auguste, 275n110
Gesang-Verein Eintracht Singing Society, 12
Gewandhaus, Leipzig, 58, 59, 64
Gieseking, Walter, 3
Gilibert, Charles, 70
Gilibert, Mme. Charles, 70
Gilman, Lawrence, 101, 152, 269n34
Gilmore, Patrick Sarsfield, 22
Gilmore's Band, 22
Glazounov, Alexander, 145, 158
   Symphony No. 6 in C minor, 145
Gleason, Frederick Grant, 39
Gluck, Christolph Willibald von, 58–9, 89, 164
   Iphigenia en Aulide, 58–9
   Orfeo ed Eurydice, 164
"Go Down Moses," 153
Godesciani, E., 79
Goethe, Johann Wolfgang von, 93, 269n15
Goldmark, Karl, 39, 45
   Rustic Wedding, 39
Goltermann, Georg, 32
   Concerto for Violoncello in A minor, 32
Goodrich, J. Wallace, 67, 78, 100
Goosens, Eugene, 158
Göttingen, 73
Gounod, Charles, 57–8, 59, 70, 81
   Feilicher Marsch (Marche Romaine), 58
   Petite Symphonie (Nonetto), 58, 70
   Romeo et Juliet, 81
   Symphony No. 2 in E flat, 58
Gourmont, Remy de, 101, *54n*
   Une nuit au Luxembourg, 101
Gouvy, Louis Théodore, 70
Gozzi, Carlo, 109–10
   Turandot, 109–10
Grainger, Percy, 3, 138
Grand National Peace Jubilee, 22
Grant, Mark N., 5, 263n8
   Maestros of the Pen: A History of Classical Music Criticism in America, 263n8
Grau, Maurice, 99
Graupner, Gottlieb, 22
Gravés, 78
Graz, 126

Greene, Plunkett, 109
Greenslet, Ferris, 153, 274n66
Grétry, André Ernest Modeste, 57
Grieg, Edvard, 70, 137, 138, 145, 146
   Piano Concerto in A Minor, 137, 138, 145, 146
   "Zur Johannisnacht," 272n23
Griffes, Charles Tomlinson, 151
   The White Peacock, 151
Grisez, Georges, 96
Guild, Courtenay, 154
Guilmant, Alexandre, 14, 17

Habeneck, François Antoine, 31
Hackebarth, Albert, 70
Hadley, Henry, 2, 158
Hahn, Reynaldo, 70
Hale, Edward, 9, 263n3
Hale, Harriet Amelia née Porter, 9
Hale, Irene née Baumgras, 14, 78, 152, 166, 173, 174
   Morceaux de Genre, Op. 15, 14
   Pensees Poetiques, Op. 16, 14
Hale, Philip
   "The Ancestral History of the Popular Piano Family," 270n50
   "As the World Wags," 5, 83
   "The Attitude of American Critics toward Music," 83
   "The Baffled Enthusiast," 77
   "Bohemianism in Literature," 112
   "Boston Newspapers," 112, 270n62
   "The Manner of Mozart's Death," 41
   Modern French Songs, 94, 269n17
   "Music and Musicians," 40, 64
   "Musical and Theatrical Life in a New England Village in the Sixties," 9, 263n5
   "Notes and Lines," 102
   "Opera in English and in Foreign Tongues, and the Relation of Language and Music," 83
   "Operatic Extravagance," 73
   "Talk of the Day," 5, 40
   "Theatrical Conditions in Music," 112, *55n*
   "Two Foes to Criticism," 40
   "Walt Whitman," 10, 263n7
   "Weekly Comment," 102
Hale, Philip Leslie, 113
Hale, Robert L., 12

Hale, Robert Safford, 263n1
  Geneology of Descendants of Thomas Hale, 263n1
Hale, Thomas, 9
Hale, William Bainbridge, 9, 263n1
Hall, Elise, 70
Halle, Lady, 3
Halli, Marguerite, 88
Hamburg, 102, 114, 135
Hamburg Philharmonic Orchestra, 135
Hammerstein, Oscar (Sr.), 100
Händel, Georg Friedrich, 21, 37, 41, 42, 67, 70, 146
  Concerto for Strings and Two Wind Orchestras in F, 41
  Concerto Grosso No. 5 in D, 146
  Messiah, 21, 65, 66
  "Sweet Bird," 89
Handel and Haydn Society, 21, 22, 23, 64, 67, 82, 147, 264n2
Hannover, Germany, 31
Hanslick, Eduard, 39, 52, 78, 90
  "Fünf Jahre Musik," 78
Hanson, Howard, 165, 267n87
  Symphony No. 2, "Romantic", 165
Hardy, Thomas, 116
Harmonia Society, Albany, 12
Harrigan, Edward, 38
Harry Jewett Company, 270n41
Harvard Glee Club, 22, 147
Harvard Musical Association, 22, 23, 24, 25, 27
Harvard University, 1, 22, 63, 68, 117, 141, 147, 162, 171
Harvey, Frederick, 67
Haupt, Carl August, 14
Hausmann, Robert, 58
Haydn, Franz Joseph, 12, 21, 22, 32, 33, 69, 90, 115, 116, 119, 136, 139, 141, 143, 149, 150, 164, 165, 168, 169
  The Creation, 12, 21
  The Seasons, 12
  Symphony in D, 119
  Symphony No. 1 in D, 167
  Symphony No. 9, 32
  Symphony No. 85 in E flat "La Reine," ("The Queen of France"), 139
  Symphony No. 88 in G, 33
  Symphony No. 94 in G "Surprise," 115, 167
  Symphony No. 97 in C, 90
  Symphony No. 99 in E flat, 169, 275n114
  Symphony No. 100 in G "Military," 149–50
  Symphony No. 102 in B flat, 164
  Symphony No. 104 in D "London," 167
  Violoncello Concerto [No. 2] in D, 167–8
Hayes, Roland, 3, 153, 274n67
Heidelberg, 73, 116, 126
Heilman, William Clifford, 118
Heinrich, William, 58
Heintz, Albert, 14
Hellmesberger, Joseph, 36
Helsingfors (Helsinki), 148
Henderson, W. J., 15, 39, 76
Henry III, 44
Henschel, Isidor Georg [later Sir George], 2, 25, 26, 67, 82, 98, 99, 149, 153, 162, 163, 164
  Concert Overture, 25
Herbert, Victor, 58, 127
Hermann, MO, 123
Hérold, Louis Joseph Ferdinand
  Zampa, 84
Hertz, Alfred, 101
Herwig, Leopold, 23
Herzogenberger, Heinrich, 70
Hess, Willy, 81, 94
Hichens, Robert Smythe, 173, 174
  Mortimer Brice, 173
  Susie's Career (The Pyramid), 174
Higginson, Maj. Henry Lee, 24–6, 28, 30, 36, 46, 47, 57, 61, 63–7, 70, 73–5, 81, 88, 91, 91, 95, 97, 98, 103, 104, 11, 112, 117, 118, 121, 124–6, 128–30, 133–7, 141, 144, 154, 163, 164, 265, 266, 268, 269, 270, 271, 272, 273
Higginson, Thomas Wentworth, 24
Hill, Edward Burlingame, 118, 165
  An Ode, 165
Hill, Thomas C., 118
Hiller, Adam, 29
Hindemith, Paul, 165
  Konzertmusik, 165
Hinkle, Florence, 115, 131, 132

Index

Hitler, Adolph, 135
Hochschule für Musik, Berlin, 14
Hodgkins, Doris, 154
Holker, Abbott, 272n19
Holmés, Augusta, 31, 55
Holmes, Jr. Oliver Wendall, 112
Holmes, Sr., Oliver Wendell, 35, 112
Holst, Gustav, 2, 5, 51, 151, 158, 275n114
   Beni Mora Suite, Op. 29, No. 1, 51
   The Planets, Op. 32, 5, 151
Holy Trinity Church, Brooklyn, 12
Holyrood, 150
Honegger, Arthur, 158, 165
   Symphony for Orchestra, 165
Hopkinson. Francis, 21
   "My Days Have Been So Wondrous Free," 21
Houghton Mifflin Co., 153
Howe, Marc Antony De Wolfe, 112, 167
Hudson, Henry, 21
   Beethoven's Oratorio of Engedi, or David in the Wilderness, 21
Hughes, Herbert, 151
Hugo, Victor, 86
Humperdinck, Engelbert, 119
   The Forced Marriage, 119
Hundt, Aline, 54
Huneker, James Gibbons, 48, 77, 101, 141, 172
Huntington, James Lincoln, 163, 167
Huré, Jean, 70
Huss, Henry H., 44, 60
   Piano Concerto in B flat, 44, 60

Ilsley, Ferdinand Ingersoll, 12
Infantry Hall, Providence, 123, 124–5

James, Henry, 112
Jarbeau, Vernona, 17
Jean-Aubry, M., 152
Jewish Advocate, 166
Joachim, Joseph, 58, 73, 93–4, 137
   Hungarian Concerto, 93–4
Joncières, Victorin de (Félix-Ludger Rossignol), 35
Jones, Clayton, 271
Jones, J. G., 23
Jordan, Eben Dyer, Jr., 103

Jordan Hall, 76, 82, 83, 100
Joseffy, Rafael, 34
Juon, Paul, 70

Kalinnikoff, Vasily, 151
   Symphony No. 1 in G minor, 151
Kassel (Cassell), 57
Kauffmann, Georg, 70
Kautz, John, 13
Keats, John, 138
   Hyperion, 138
Kendall, Ned, 22
Kennedy, John Fitzgerald, 112
Kileski-Bradbury, Mrs., 82
Klemm, Gustav, 270n48
Klughardt, August, 70
Kneisel, Franz, 36, 59, 67, 75, 81, 95
Kneisel String Quartet, 69, 81, 100, 120
Königsberg, 57, 98
Koussevitzky, Mme., 156
Koussevitzky, Serge, 2, 3, 98, 148, 154, 155, 156, 158, 159–62, 164–70, 173, 274n83
   Overture, 166
Koussevitzky Music Foundation, 161
Kovaček, 70
Krafft-Ebing, Richard Freiherr von, 101
Kraft, Anton, 168
Krasseit, Rudolf, 86, 92
Krehbiel, Henry, 15, 39, 43, 48, 50, 52, 53, 76, 100, 151
Kreisler, Fritz, 30, 73, 119, 123
Kreismann's Liedertafel, 66
Kriens, Martinus, 70
Kubelik, Rafael, 4
Kunwald, Ernst, 135

Lachmann, Hedwig, 100
Lacroix, 70
Lalo, Eduard, 74, 75
   Violincello Concerto, 74, 75
Laloy, M. Louis, 149
Lamoureux, Charles, 14, 34, 66
Lampe, Jens, 70
Lang, B(enjamin) J(ohnson), 23, 55, 67, 78, 95
Lang, Margaret Ruthven, 55–6
   Dramatic Overture, Op. 12, 55
   Witchis, Op. 10, 56
Laurent, Georges, 146

Laus, Abdon, 26
Lazzari, Sylvio, 70
Leclercq, Louis, 44
  "Les Origines de l'Opera," 44
Lee, Higginson, & Co., 24
Leeds Festival, 169
Leipzig (Leipsic, Leipsig), 31, 45, 57, 58, 59, 64, 98, 99, 126, 132, 143
Leipzig Stadt Theatre, 98
Leisring, Volckmar, 147
Leland Opera House, Albany, 13, 15, 16, 17
Lenin, Vladimir, 154, 155
Leningrad, 154, 155
Lenom, Désiré, 71
Lent, Mrs. Ernest, 3
Leutgeb, Joseph, 168
Library of Congress, 174
Listemann, Bernhard, 24, 94, 163
Liszt, Franz, 34, 54, 69, 74, 75, 82, 108, 118, 125
  Fest-Kläng, 74
  Mazeppa, 69, 114
  Piano Concerto No. 2 in A, 34
  Prometheus, 125
  Tasso, 108
Litke, Paul, 70
Loeffler, Charles Martin, 36, 46, 48, 56, 57, 70, 75, 81, 95, 97, 98, 101, 120, 143, 169, 266n41, 42, 72, 75, 267n96, 269n29, 270n40, 271n78
  Divertimento in A minor for Violin and Orchestra, 56
  Evocation, 169
  Hora Mystica, 120
  A Pagan Poem, 143
Loeillet, Jean-Baptiste, 70
London, 21, 22, 35, 46, 54, 97, 115, 116, 117, 120, 132, 140, 148, 150, 151, 152
London Times, 152
Long, Marguerite, 166
Longy, Georges, 1, 26, 69–71, 95, 133
Longy Club, 1, 26, 70–1
Looker-on, 2, 40
Lotti, Antonio, 147
Lowell, Abbott Lawrence, 171
Lowell Institute, 44
Lucian of Samosata, 93
Ludwig, August, 43

MacCarthy, Maud, 101, 269n36
MacDowell, Edward, 51–4, 119, 162, 267n87
  Piano Concerto No. 2 in D minor, Op. 23, 51
  Suite No. 2 "Indian," Op. 48, 52–3, 119, 267n87
MacDowell Club, Boston, 70
MacDowell Club, Providence, 125
Madison Park High School, Boston, 274n67
Madrid, 78, 79
Maeterlinck, Maurice, 79
  Pelleás 79
Magnard, Albéric, 70
Mahler, Gustav, 48, 97, 99, 105–6, 107, 108, 127, 151, 159
  Symphony No. 1 in D, 151
  Symphony No. 2 "Resurrection," 127–8
  Symphony No. 5 in C-sharp Minor, 97
Malherbe, Charles, 70
Malipiero, Gian Francesco, 142–3
  Pauses of Silence, 142–3
Manhattan (Metropolitan) Opera House, 100
Mannheim, 57, 98, 99
Maquarre, Andre, 70
Marshall, John P., 131
Mary of Cleves, 44
Mascagni, Pietro, 39
  L'Amico Fritz, 39
Mason, Lowell, 21, 22
Mason, Stuart, 173
Massachusetts Bay Colony, 163
Massachusetts Historical Society, 9, 151
Massenet, Jules, 69
Mastres, M., 79
Materna, Amalie, 67
Matzenauer, Margaret, 164
McCarthy, Maud. *See* MacCarthy, Maud
McCloskey, David Blair, 169
McCormack, John, 119
McKim, Charles Follen, 63, 64
McKim, Mead & White, 63
McManus, George B., 173
Mechanics Hall, Worcester, MA, 134
Mees, Arthur, 53
Méhul, Étienne, 57
  Uthal, 57

Melba, Nellie, 86, 88, 89
Melville, Herman, 151
Mendelssohn, Felix, 13, 30, 31, 32, 36, 69, 85, 89, 143, 145, 150
  Elijah, 13
  The Fair Melusina, 89
  The First Walpurgis Night, 150
  Hebrides Overture (a.k.a. *Fingal's Cave*), 32, 36
  A Midsummer Night's Dream, 143, 145–6
  St. Paul, 66
  "Songs without Words," 146, 150
  Symphony No. 3 in A minor, "Scottish," 150
Mendelssohn Choral Society, 22
Menges, Isolde, 149–50
Metcalf, Eleanor Melville, 151
The Metronome: A Monthly Review of Music, 27
Meyer-Helmund, Erik, 17
  Marguerita, 17
Meyn, Heinrich, 43
Miaskovsky, Nicolas, 159
Milan, 46, 78, 132
Milhaud, Darius, 150, 159, 160
  The Carnival of Aix, 159
Milton, MA, 134
Minerviad, 27
Minneapolis Tribune, 172
Mole, Charles, 70
Molique, G. Bernard, 59–60
  Concerto No. 5 for Violin in A minor, Op. 21, 59–60
Mollenhauer, Emil, 78
Monday Morning Club, Providence, 125
Monteux, Germaine, 154
Monteux, Pierre, 2, 3, 137–51, 153–6, 158
Monteverdi, Claudio, 38
Moore, George, 40
Moréas, Jean, 57
Morgan, W. S., 22
Morris, Victoria Phillips, 263n1
Moszkowski, Moritz, 14
Mouquet, Jules, 70
Moussorgsky, Modeste, 5, 141, 153
  "Hopak," 141
  Night on Bald Mountain, 153
  Pictures at an Exhibition, arr. Ravel, 5

Mozart, Wolfgang Amadeus, 3, 5, 29, 32, 33, 38, 41, 58, 69, 70, 82, 110, 115, 136, 153, 156, 160, 167, 168
  La Clemenza da Tito, 88
  Concerto for Clarinet and Orchestra in A, K. 622, 5, 132
  Cosi fan Tutti, 82, 153
  Don Giovanni, 29, 41
  "Dove Sono," 41
  "Un Hora Amorosa," 153
  Horn Concerto No. 3 in E flat, K. 447, 168
  The Magic Flute, 41, 66
  The Marriage of Figaro, 41
  Masonic Funeral Music, 41
  Requiem, K. 626, 167
  String Quintet in G minor, K. 516, 33
  Symphony No. 35 in D, K. 385 "Haffner," 32
  Symphony No. 36, "Linz," 160
  Symphony No. 38 in D, K. 504, "Prague," 95
  Symphony No. 39 in E flat, K. 543, 41
  Symphony No. 40 in G minor, K. 550, 33
  Symphony No. 41 in C, K. 551, "Jupiter," 3, 58
  "Voi che Sapete," 115
Mozart Society, Albany, 13
Muck, Anita, 130, 134, 135
Muck, Karl, 2, 6, 92, 98, 99, 100, 102, 109, 111, 114–21, 123–36, 141, 142, 151, 154, 161, 269n30, 272n18, 19, 23–5, 27–9, 273n32
Mueller, C. H., 23
Mugget, L. H., 74
Mulligan, Lt., 129–30
Munch, Charles, 140
Munich, 14, 16, 31, 90
Murphy, Lambert, 131, 133
Museum of Fine Arts, Boston, 113
Music Fund Orchestra, Boston, 23
Music Hall, Boston, 23, 28, 36, 44, 49, 51, 55, 58, 59, 63–6, 77, 94, 162–4
Musical America, 27, 76
Musical Courier, 2, 17, 35, 48, 62, 74, 77, 81, 86, 87
Musical Educational Society, Boston, 66
Musical Quarterly, 174

Musical Record, 2, 54, 61, 62, 77
Musical World, 2, 77, 78
Musikverein, Vienna, 64
Myers, Arthur, 131

Naples, 159
Narragansett Hotel, Providence, 125
National Conservatory of Music, New York, 47
National Cyclopaedia of American Biography, 62
Nazi Party, 2, 135, 147
Nelson, Robert B., 77
New England Conservatory, 27, 37, 39, 58, 82, 117
New Harmonia Singing Society, Albany, 15
New Music Review, 78
New York (City), 1, 2, 11, 12, 13, 15, 22, 35, 39, 43, 47, 48, 50, 52, 53, 62, 63, 67, 81, 83, 87, 96, 99, 100, 105, 111, 120, 124, 127, 128, 131, 132, 137, 140, 141, 151, 152, 153, 157
New York Herald, 47
New York Metropolitan Opera, 100, 137
New York Philharmonic Orchestra, 1, 48, 61, 105, 107, 158
New York Post, 151
New York (State), 16
New York Symphony Orchestra, 157, 184, 212, 248
New York Times, 39, 78, 133, 151, 152, 163, 172
New York Tribune, 39, 43, 48, 151
New York World, 12
Newbury, MA, 9
Newman, Ernest, 152
Nichols, Caroline B., 26
Nikisch, Amelie, 38, 43
Nikisch, Arthur, 2, 3, 28–39, 42, 43, 46, 47, 57, 61, 75, 87, 88, 98, 99, 112, 120, 136, 155, 161
Nordica, Lillian, 46, 64, 65, 103
Northampton, Massachusetts, 9, 10, 12, 76
Northeastern District, National Federation of Music Clubs, 125
Norton, Annie B., 67
Norwich, VT, 9

Nürnburg (Nuremburg), 132
Nye, Bill, 116

Ochs, Adolph Simon, 152
Orchestral Club, Boston, 26, 69, 70, 104
Orchestral Union, Boston, 23
Osgood, George, 78
Osterville, MA, 101, 117, 269n39
Ozawa, Seiji, 274n84

Pach, James, 67
Paderewski, Ignatz, 3, 71, 113, 119
Paganini, Nicolo, 45, 120
    Moto Perpetuo, 120
Paine, John Knowles, 51
Panama-Pacific International Exposition, 118, 271n80
Paris, 14, 16, 31, 32, 34, 45, 54, 60, 70, 71, 93, 95, 101, 120, 132, 139, 140, 148, 154, 157, 158, 159, 165
Paris Conservatoire, 31, 32, 45, 139
Paris Opera, 136, 140
Park Street Congregational Church, Boston, 124
Parker, H. T., 161, 173
Parker, Horatio, 51, 112
Parker, J. C. D., 23
Parker, John Rowe, 27
Pasdeloup, Jules, 14
Paul, St., 66
Paul Whiteman's Concert Orchestra, 1, 4
Paur, Emil, 3, 44, 47, 50, 54, 57–61, 75, 76, 87, 95, 98, 99
Peabody Conservatory, 104
Périhou, Albert, 70
Perkins, C. C., 23
Perry, Bliss, 112, 137
Perry Building, Albany, 13
Peterson, May, 128
Petrograd, 154–5
Petrograd (St, Petersburg, Russia) State Orchestra, 154
Philadelphia, 23, 72, 87, 132, 141, 159, 160, 166
Philadelphia Orchestra, 141, 159, 160
Philharmonic Society of Boston, 15, 23, 24
Philo-Harmonic Society, Boston, 22
Piatigorsky, Gregor, 167, 168
Pierian Sodality, 22

Pierne, Gabriel, 70
Pittsburgh, 123
Pittsburgh Symphony Orchestra, 61
Plotinus, 149
Poe, Edgar Allen, 86
Ponchielli, Amilcare, 103
   La Gioconda, 103
Popper, David, 32
   "Papillon," 32
Poupiliniere, Le, 132
Powell, Maud, 3, 101
Prague, 79, 95, 96, 99, 126
Pratt, William Fenno, 9
Press, Michael, 158
"Pro Bono," 74–6
Prokofieff (Prokofiev), Sergei, 48, 159, 165
   Piano Concerto No. 3, 159
   Piano Concerto No. 5, 159
   Symphony No. 4, 165
Providence, 123–7, 130, 134, 272n23, 275n114
Providence Journal, 123, 124
Providence Symphony Orchestra, 127
Putnam, Karl, 9
Pygmalion and Galatea, 17

Quef, Charles, 70
Quimby, Winfred S., 161

Rabaud, Henri, 2, 136–8, 139, 141, 151
   Marouf, 151
Rabinoff, Max, 103
Rachmaninoff, Sergei, 3, 89, 139, 140
   Piano Concerto No. 3 in D minor, 139
   "Von Jenseits," 89
Radcliffe Choral Society, 147
Radio-Victor Corporation of America, 161
Raif, Oscar, 14
Rameau, Jean-Philippe, 132
Rathom, John R., 123, 124, 126, 127
Ravel, Maurice, 5, 70, 151, 158, 162, 166
   Daphnis et Chloé, 162
   Piano Concerto for the Left Hand, 166
   Piano Concerto in G, 166
   La Valse, 151
RCA-Victor, 161
Read, Daniel, 22

Reger, Max, 70
Rehan (Crehan), Arthur, 16
Reiner, Fritz, 4
Reiter, Xavier, 108
Respighi, Ottorino, 158, 165
   Metamorphoseon modi XII, 165
Retté, Adolphe, 57
Rheinberger, Josef, 14, 17, 37
Rhene-Baton, René-Emmanuel, 140
Rhode Island Liberty Loan Committee, 124
Rhode Island State Federation of Music Clubs, 125
Rhode Island State Federation of Women's Clubs, 125
Richter, Hans, 57, 99
Riddle, George, 43
Rietz, Julius, 70
Rimbaud, Jean Nicolas Arthur, 57
Rimsky-Korsakov, Nicolai, 70
   Scheherazade, 149
Ringwall, Rudolf C., 141, 144
Roberts, Penfield, 173
Roeningen, 70
Rogers, Clara Kathleen Barnett, 117, 55n
Roland Hayes School of Music, Boston, 274n67
Rollinat, Maurice, 101
Rome, 13, 159
Rosenthal, Moriz, 100
Rossini, Gioachino, 107, 149, 150
   Barber of Seville, 66
   La Cenerentola, 66
Roth, Otto, 60
Roussel, Albert, 153, 165
   The Rose-Colored City, 153
   Symphony No. 3 in G minor, 165
Royal Institute for Church Music, Berlin, 14
Royal Opera House, Berlin, 98, 102, 104
Royal Stockholm Philharmonic Orchestra, 148
Rubini, Giovanni Battista, 29
Rubinstein, Anton, 3, 23, 41, 147
   "Opinions of Rubinstein" (trans. Delano), 42
   Piano Concerto No. 4 in D minor, Op. 70, 3
   Symphony No. 2 in C, Op. 42 "Ocean," 23, 41
   Tower of Babel, 147, 273n56

Rubinstein, Artur, 3
Rudolphsen, J. F., 67

Sabine, William Clement, 64
Sainte-Trinité, Paris, 14
Saint-Saëns, Camille, 14, 54, 55, 69, 119, 132, 137, 138, 151, 266n46
　Carnival of the Animals, 151
　Piano Concerto No. 2 in G minor, Op. 22, 54
　Symphony No. 3 in C minor, Op. 35 "Organ," 137–8
　The Youth of Hercules, 266n46
Salem, MA, 9
Salem Band, 22
Salomé, Théodore, 14, 17
　Dix Pièces pour Orgue, Vol. III, Op. 48, "Prière," 14
Salzburg, 126, 168
Samaroff, Olga [née Lucy Mary Agnes Hickenlooper], 4, 137, 138
San Francisco, 118, 173
San Francisco Chronicle, 173
Sanders Theatre, Cambridge, MA, 38, 68, 141
Sanromá, Jesus Maria, 3, 166
Sargent, John Singer, 112
Sargent, Sullivan, 82
Satie, Eric, 104
　Gymnopedies, 104
Saturday Evening Post, 128, 272n13
Scharwenka, Xaver, 3, 14
　Piano Concerto No. 1 in B flat Minor, Op. 32, 266n46
Scheel, Johann Friedrich Ludwig "Fritz," 87
Schenectady, New York, 12, 16
Schirmer, G., 78
Schmidt, Ernst, 131–3, 136
Schmidt, Henry, 23
Schmidt, Minister, 135
Schmitt, Florent, 70
Schnabel, Artur, 3
Schneévoight, Georg Lennart, 148
Schönberg (Schoenberg), Arnold, 2, 48, 115–16, 165
　Five Pieces for Orchestra, 115–16
Schreck, Gustav, 70
Schroeder, Alwin, 59, 75, 81

Schubert, Franz, 12, 29, 69, 119, 136–8, 149, 150, 161, 164
　"Current a Calamo," 138
　"Doppelgaenger," 138
　"The Dwarf," 138
　"Gruppe aus Tartarus," 138
　Overture in the Italian Style in C, 149
　Quarante Mélodies Choises de F. Schubert, 12, 264n15
　Rosamunde, 29, 68, 164
　Symphony No. 5 in B flat, 160
　Symphony No. 8 in B minor, "Unfinished," 43, 119, 137
Schubert Club, Albany, 15
Schubert Club, Providence, 125
Schuch, Ernst Gottfried, 31
Schulert, 38
Schumann, Clara, 14
Schumann, George, 68
　Symphonic Variations for Orchestra and Organ, 68
Schumann, Robert, 29, 30–2, 43, 54, 69, 99, 102
　Kreisleriana, Op. 16, 30
　Manfred, 43
　Symphony No. 4 in D minor, Op. 120, 29, 99
　"Traumerei," 32
Second New England School, 51, 54, 56, 119
Selmer, Alexandre, 70
Senff, Bartolf, 270n57
Severance, Elisabeth, 169
Severance, John Long, 169
Severance Hall, Cleveland, 169
Shakespeare, William, 43, 86, 146
　A Midsummer Night's Dream, 146
Sherwin, Amy, 67
Shostakovitch, Dmitri, 2
Sibelius, Jean, 101, 159–60
　Finlandia, 159–60
　Symphony No. 7, 159–60
　Violin Concerto, 101
Sigler, 79
Sigma Delta Chi, 1
Signale für die Musikalische Welt, 58, 79, 111
Simeon, St., 66
Simonetti, Mr., 79

Simpson, H. D., 37
Sinding, Christian, 96
  Episodes Chevalieresques, 96
Singing Schools, 21
Singing Society Caecilia, Albany, 12
Sitwell, Osbert, 169
Slonimsky, Nicolas, 5, 155
Smetana, Bedrich, 45, 146
  The Bartered Bride, 146
Smith, Moses, 28, 154, 160, 162, 173, 276n6
Smith, Sydney, 37
Smith, Warren Storey, 76–7, 158, 268n26, 29
Smith College, 9
Société de Musique de Chambre pour Instruments à Vent, Paris, 70
Société des Nouveaux-Concerts, Paris, 14
Société Nationale de Musique, Paris, 14
Sokolov, Nikolay Alexandrovich, 169
Solti, Georg, 4
  Memoirs, 4
Sousa, John Philip, 4, 52, 88, 119
  Dwellers of the Western World, 52
Spalding, Walter Raymond, 118, 174
Spanuth, August, 67, 111
Speyer, Louis-Marius, 143
Spohr, Ludwig, 69
Springfield Republican, 9
Squire, John Collings, 152
St. Albans, 100
St. Botolph Club, 35, 36, 46, 111
St. Gaudens, Augustus, 112
St. John's Episcopal Church, Albany, 13
St. John's Episcopal Church, Troy, NY, 15
St. Peter's (Lutheran) Cathedral, Berlin, 14
St. Petersburg, Russia, 154, 155
St. Thomas Cathedral (Thomaskirche), Leipzig, 132
Staats-Zeitung, Berlin, 67
"Starlight" company, 17
"Star-spangled Banner," 124–7, 129, 130, 133
Stebbin, H. L., 39
Stein, Gertrude May, 67

Steinberg, Maximillian, 160
Steinway Hall, New York, 67
Stoessel, Albert, 158
Stokowski, Leopold, 164
Strangways, Arthur Henry Fox, 152
Stransky, Josef, 106, 107, 108, 124
Strauss, David, 33
  "Old and New Faith," 33
Strauss, Richard, 2, 48, 68, 69, 70, 82, 87, 89–92, 99, 100, 105–6, 108–10, 116, 119, 120, 168
  Also Spracht Zarathustra, 99
  Burleske, 120
  Death and Transfiguration, 69
  Don Juan, 91–2
  Don Quixote, 91–2, 109–10, 168
  Feuersnoth, 91, 108
  "Mutterlaenderlei," 89
  Salome, 100
  Suite in B flat, Op. 4, 70
  Till Eulenspiegel, 105–6, 116
Stravinsky, Igor, 2, 48, 137, 139, 140, 151, 153, 156, 157, 160, 162, 165–6
  Apollon Musagète, 162
  Capriccio for Piano and Orchestra, 166
  Concerto for Piano and Wind Orchestra, 156–7
  Firebird Suite, 139, 156, 160
  Petrouchka, 140, 156, 160
  Pulcinella, 151, 153
  Le Rossignol 140
  Le Sacre du Printemps (*The Rite of Spring*), 137, 151
  Symphonie de Psaumes (*Symphony of Psalms*), 165–6
Strube, Gustav, 70, 104
  Concerto for Violoncello and Orchestra in E minor, 104
Stuttgart, 14
Suck, F., 23
Suffolk Band, 22
Sunday, Billy, 124
Sundelius, Mme., 70
Suppe, Franz von
  Poet and Peasant, 84
Sussmayer, Franz Xaver, 167
Svečenski, Louis, 81

Swinburne, Algernon Charles, 10, 149, 263n6
Symphony Hall, Boston, 5, 22, 63–8, 72, 82–4, 89, 91, 103–5, 108, 109, 114–16, 123–6, 128, 131, 132, 137, 139, 140, 142, 144, 145, 149, 151, 153, 158, 161, 163, 168, 267n1, 3, 268n7, 275n113

Taffanel, Paul, 70
Tammany Hall, 74
Taneleff, Serge, 69
  Symphony No. 1 in C, 69
Tanglewild, 269n39
Tanglewood, 161, 269n39
Tarbell, Edmund, 112
Tavern Club, 3, 36, 92, 111, 112, 113, 128, 133, 163, 167, 171, 263n1, 270n63, 64, 272n19, 274n90, 93, 275n105, 276n3, 10, 12
  The Rules of the Tavern Club of Boston, with a List of the Officers & Members, 113
Tchaikovsky [also spelled Tschaikowsky], Piotr, 2, 24, 39, 44–6, 48, 49, 57–9, 69, 82, 84–6, 88, 99, 159
  1812 Overture, 49
  Capriccio Italien, 159
  Hamlet, 58
  Piano Concerto No. 1 in B flat minor, Op. 32, 44, 84–6
  Romeo and Juliet, 39, 58, 99
  Sleeping Beauty (La Belle au Bois Dormant), 69
  Suite No. 1, 127
  Symphony No. 4 in F minor, Op. 36, 125, 127
  Symphony No. 6 in B minor, Op. 74 "Pathetique," 44
  Violin Concerto, 46, 49
  Voyode, 88
Tedesco, John R., 270n45
Tennyson, Alfred Lloyd, 90
Tertis, Lionel, 3
Thacher, George Hornell, Jr., 15
Thayer, Alexander Wheelock, 48
  Life of Beethoven, 48
Theatre Château d'Eau, Paris, 14

Theatre du Châtelet, Paris, 14
Theodorowicz, Julius, 81
Thomas, Ambroise, 18, 89
  Hamlet, 89
Thomas, Theodore, 23, 26, 31, 32, 56, 67, 68, 88, 93, 94, 120
Thuille, Ludwig, 69
  Romantic Overture, 69
Thurber, Jeanette Meyers, 47
Thursday Evening Club, 111, 270n260-2
Toscanini, Arturo, 137, 164
Townsend, Stephen, 128, 131–2
Tracy, James M., 42
Trotsky, Leon, 155
Troy, New York, 12, 15, 16
Tsing-Tao Orchestra, 135
Tucker, H., 78
Twain, Mark (Samuel Clemens), 3, 270n71
Tweddle Hall, Albany, 13

Union Musical Association, Albany, 12
United States Marine Band, 264n1
University of California, 173
Urban, Heinrich, 14

Van der Stucken, Frank, 93
Van Yorx, Theodore, 82
Vaughan Williams, Ralph, 151
  Fantasia on a Theme by Thomas Tallis, 151
Vera, 79
Verdi, Giuseppi, 81, 167
  Ernani, 84
  La Traviata, 81
Verlaine, Paul-Marie, 3, 57
Vevay, 46
Victor Talking Machine Company, 121, 127, 136, 161
Vienna, 24, 26, 31, 47, 57, 64, 89, 95, 98, 99, 100, 105, 106, 129, 168
Vienna Court Opera, 98
Vienna Philharmonic Orchestra, 99, 100, 105
Villard, Oswald Garrison, 128, 272n13
Visconti, 79

Index

Walter, Bruno, 2
Wagner, Richard, 2, 23, 29, 31, 35, 41, 43, 46, 48, 51, 59, 69, 70, 73, 90, 91, 93, 99, 101, 106–9, 114–17, 119, 125, 127, 142, 143, 147, 266n46, 271n8, 272n23
  Die Meistersinger, 114, 164
  A Faust Overture, 29, 115
  The Flying Dutchman, 69, 142
  Gotterdammerung, 31
  Lohengrin, 91, 127
  Parsifal, 41, 42, 85, 147
  Ring Cycle, 93
  "Schmerzen," 272n23
  Siegfried, 266n46
  Tannhäuser, 93, 125
  Three Poems, 125
  Tristan und Isolde, 31, 91, 101, 107
Walton, William, 169
  Belshazzar's Feast, 169
Ward, Artemis, 3
Warnke, Heinrich, 104, 111
Warren, E. R., 5, 276n12
Warren, John Collins, 112
Warren Club, 112
Washington, D.C., 133, 135, 165, 272n
Washington Times, 134, 272n25
Weaver, Raymond, 151
Webb, George James, 22, 66
Weber, Carl Maria von, 33, 68, 70, 74, 84, 108, 164
  Euryanthe, 68, 84, 108
  Jubilee Overture, 68, 164
  Oberon, 37, 66
Weber, Wilhelm, 67
WEEI, 161
Weingartner, Felix, 3, 45, 70, 103, 106, 142
  Genesius, 45
Weiss, Felix, 135
Weld, William, 112
Wendler, George, 146
Wendling, Carl, 81
Werrenrath, Reinald, 131
West, Mr., 125
Westminster Review, 11
Wetzler, Hermann, 87
Whasby, Dr., 169
White, Smith & Co., 27
Whiteman, Paul, 1, 4

Whitman, Walt, 10, 11, 12, 149, 263n7, 264n8–14
  After All, Not to Create Only, 12
  "Burial Hymn of Lincoln," 10
  "Calamus," 11
  "Democratic Vistas," 11, 264n10
  Leaves of Grass, 10–12, 264n11, 13
  "Sea Shore Memories No. 1," 10
  "Two Rivulets," 12, 264n14
Whitney, M[yron]. W., 67
Whitney, Jr., Myron, 82
Whittingham and Atherton, 40
Wilde, Oscar, 100, 101
Wilhelm, Kaiser (Emperor William), 99, 121, 126, 134, 134
Williams, Evan, 67
Williams College, 73
Wilson, George Henry, 39, 41, 77
Winant, Emily, 67
Winch, W. G., 78
Winternitz, Felix, 94
Wister, Owen, 67, 171
Witek, Anton, 81, 134
Witek, Mrs. Anton, 134
Witherspoon, Herbert, 131
Wittgenstein, Paul, 166
Wolf-Ferrari, Ermanno, 70
Woltmann, Pauline, 82
Wood, Henry, 115
Woolett, Henry, 70
Woolf, Benjamin Edward, 42
Worcester, MA, 123, 134
World Peace Jubilee, 22
World's Fair (World's Columbian Exposition), Chicago, 46, 47, 56
The World's Work, 123
Würzburg, 126
Wyman, Mr., 153

Y Sayes, Theodore, 97
Yale College [University], 1, 10, 12, 48
Yale Glee Club, 10
Yale Literary Magazine, 10
Yale Record, 10
Young, Rosamond (Rosamund), 134, 272n23, 25, 28

Zerrahn, Carl, 23, 25, 265n16
Zola, Émile, 30, 85
Zürich, 126